VB.NET

Hacks & Pranks

Alexander Klimov

alist

A-LIST, LLC
295 East Swedesford Rd.
PMB #285
Wayne, PA 19087
702-977-5377 (FAX)
mail@alistpublishing.com
http://www.alistpublishing.com

This book is printed on acid-free paper.

All brand names and product names mentioned in this book are trademarks or service marks of their respective companies. Any omission or misuse (of any kind) of service marks or trademarks should not be regarded as intent to infringe on the property of others. The publisher recognizes and respects all marks used by companies, manufacturers, and developers as a means to distinguish their products.

Alexander Klimov. *VB.NET Hacks & Pranks*
ISBN: 1-931769-44-3

Printed in the United States of America
05 7 6 5 4 3 2 First Edition

A-LIST, LLC titles are available for site license or bulk purchase by institutions, user groups, corporations, etc.

Book Editor: Thomas Rymer

Contents

Introduction

Dear reader:

If you have bought this book thinking you will find examples for working with databases, cryptography, office applications, or other similar serious stuff, you have made a big mistake. Go to the store where you bought the book and return it. Undoubtedly, the database subject is an important one, but my book deals with entirely different matter. It only considers *programming for fun*.

What This Book Is About

Books devoted to learning any programming language are, as a rule, too serious and rigid. This approach is justified with students learning the theoretical foundations of a language. But people learning a language on their own and those who want to expand their knowledge are better off employing a different methodology.

It is a common knowledge that with a creative approach, even the most boring and tedious job becomes easier. Fortunately, creativity in studying programming appears to be improving. Books are becoming available that deal not with abstract examples but with interesting and practical tasks. This book is my attempt to take an alternative approach to learning Visual Basic .NET. I have collected examples that will help you improve your grasp of the language by writing programs for games, jokes, intricate patterns, and striking effects.

Who This Book Is For

This book is intended primarily for programmers with average and advanced levels of skill. No programming basics — how to launch the program, create a project, etc. — are explained in it. Nevertheless, it can be of use to fledgling programmers because I explain the most difficult programming aspects in as much detail as possible. It helps if you have experience programming in VB 6.0 because many examples in the book are reworked from projects written in this language. In this book, I often deal with the specifics of migrating from VB 6.0 to VB .NET 2003.

Reader Requirements

All examples given in the book are written in VB .NET 2003. But 99.9 percent of the examples will also work under VB 2002 and under the newer versions of VB .NET because they are based on the fundamental programming principles that are not prone to cardinal changes.

Supplementary Information

Any time a new version of any programming language is introduced, programmers in that language develop headaches. They have to learn the new features made available by the latest version of the programming package. VB .NET was not an exception. Whereas changes upgrading VB 5.0 to VB 6.0 were rather cosmetic in nature, the move to the VB .NET version is nothing short of a revolution.

> ### A little laugh
>
> A population census taker asking a programmer:
>
> — What is your native language?
>
> — What do you mean, my native language?
>
> — Well, what language have you been learning since your childhood, using all your life?
>
> — BASIC.
>
> — No, not that. A real language.
>
> — Oh, a real language! In that case, it's C.

All this is in the past. VB .NET, combined with all the capabilities of the .NET Framework platform, is now as much a full-fledged language as C# or C++. Almost every aspect of VB .NET has undergone changes: There are new functions, new methods, new objects, new programming style, etc. But what should programmers do with their stock of extensively used examples written in the older versions of the language? There is only one answer: Learn the new version of the language and modify the examples. I ran into this problem myself and had to review my entire source-code collection. In this book, I used examples from my extensive library. Most examples were in VB 6.0, and I had to rewrite them practically anew to run under VB .NET. I also used examples from various Internet and book sources. In the course of the book, I reference these sources, from which you also can pick up a good deal of interesting information. I will list these sources in *Conclusion*.

It must be said that the examples used in this book are not the pinnacle of perfection. I started collecting them when I was just beginning to master the intricacies of programming. Now, several years later, I am going through the source codes and see something that can be optimized, something that needs to be rewritten, and something that is simply not needed and should be deleted. But I decided not to change these examples radically; rather, I leave the task of improving them to you, as homework. I advise you not to try to mechanically copy examples. Try to come up with your own version of the examples, fiddle with different parameters, etc. In general, take an active approach to learning the VB .NET 2003 language. Only in this way can you expect to attain full mastery of the programming language. And I will try to help you to the best of my modest abilities.

Using the Examples

You can find all the examples used in this book on the accompanying CD-ROM. The examples are grouped in folders by chapters. For example, folder 7 contains examples used in *Chapter 7*. Look for the file with the SLN extension in these folders. Launching this file in VB .NET 2003 (or Visual Studio .NET 2003), you will load all projects of the given chapter. To run a specific project, select the project's name and select the **Set as StartUp Project** command.

Acknowledgments

I put lots of time and energy into writing this book. Long and tedious was the time I spent selecting examples that would be interesting and entertaining. In addition, I had to find a happy medium in the narrating style: I wanted the book to not just be a trivial collection of examples but also provide entertaining reading.

There are many sites devoted to programming, to which programmers can send their programs for review. Some people call such sites file garbage dumps. I strongly disagree with this opinion. These sites can be compared with diamond mines: In the megabytes of code dirt downloaded from them, you can find gems of programming that are a pure pleasure to explore. To my great regret, I cannot name individually all the authors of the projects I have accumulated in my collection. The number of files I have downloaded and examined is simply beyond all calculation. But their authors all have my big thank-you!

My cat kindly let me use his pictures to illustrate some examples under the condition that I treat him to a double portion of his favorite liver — which I will definitely do.

PART I: STRINGS AND TEXTS

Chapter 1: String Effects

> Examples teach better than instructions or books.
>
> *N. I. Lobachevsky*

I will start this book with the simplest subject: strings. At first, it might seem like there is not much that you can do with them. But strings can actually be the source material for some very interesting effects. You should remember that a string consists of individual elements: characters. This fact, combined with the timer capabilities, can be used to display the necessary string not all at once, but only those parts of it and in such a manner as necessary. In this way, we can create such animation effects as a typewritten line, a ticker tape line, etc. Let's move on to putting these effects into practice.

1.1. A Typewritten Line

Create a new project and name it `TypingText` (Listing 1.1). Place the following controls on the form: a label, named `Label1`, two buttons, named `Button1` and `Button2`, and a timer, named `Timer1`.

> **TIP**
>
> In our examples, we will often leave the default names for the controls. For actual projects, however, I would advise you to use descriptive names. For example, a button can be named `butAnimString` (animation string).

Set the Text property value of the Label1 label to Entertaining Programming, the Text property value of the Button1 button to Start, and the Interval property value of the Timer1 timer to 500. Set the Text property value of the Button2 button to Button. You can add your own code for processing the click event of this button. Set the Text property value of our Form1 form to Typewritten Line. This text will be displayed in the form's title bar, thus indicating the purpose of our exercise. Leave the default values for the other properties of the controls. Now double-click the Button1 button to open the code window, where you will write the code that will be executed when the button is clicked.

Listing 1.1. A Typewritten Line Example

```
'----------------------------------------------
' TypingText © 2004 Alexander Klimov
'   ------------------------------------------

    Private Sub Button1_Click(ByVal sender As System.Object, ByVal e As _
System.EventArgs) Handles Button1.Click
        If Button1.Text = "Start" Then
            Timer1.Enabled = True
            Button1.Text = "Stop"
        Else
            Timer1.Enabled = False
            Button1.Text = "Start"
        End If
    End Sub

    Private Sub Timer1_Tick(ByVal sender As System.Object, ByVal e As _
System.EventArgs) Handles Timer1.Tick
        ' Left to right animation
        Dim title As String = "Entertaining Programming"
        Static c As Integer = 0
        Label1.Text = title.Substring(0, c)
        Me.Text = title.Substring(0, c)
        c += 1
        If c = title.Length() + 1 Then c = 0

        ' Right to left animation
        Dim title2 As String = "Button"
        Static i As Integer = title2.Length()
        Button2.Text = title2.Substring(0, i)
        i -= 1
        If i = -1 Then i = title2.Length()
    End Sub
```

Let's examine what the code we just wrote does. Clicking on the button labeled **Start** starts the timer and changes the button's label to **Stop**. Clicking the button again stops the timer and changes the button's label back to **Start**. All of the work required to create the effect takes place on the `Tick` event of the timer. First, we declare a string variable named `title` and set its value to `Entertaining Programming`. Next, we create a static variable `c` to serve as a counter. Using the `Substring` method of the `String` class, we build up the string, starting with the first character and finishing with the last. When the last character is reached, the counter is zeroed out, and the process starts anew. As you can see, it is not difficult at all to create the effect, but the impression it produces is interesting. The animation of the string output can be paused at any moment by clicking the `Button1` button. Clicking the button again resumes the animation from the point, at which it had been paused. To make the example more effective, I made it so that the form title bar is also animated, by inserting this piece of code:

```
Me.Text = title.Substring(0, c)
```

If you want to make a text string shrink instead of grow, this example can be changed easily to achieve the effect. To do this, you will have to create one more counter: `i`. The initial value of this counter is set to the length of the given text string. A character is deleted from the string for every click of the timer. When the counter value reaches 0, it is set to the string length value again. This modified code is applied to the text of the second button. And there you have it. You have written your first simple program, demonstrating that significant results can be achieved using simple methods. Next, we will consider some more complicated examples.

1.2. A Flashing Title Bar

Let's make the example a bit more complicated. The main feature is that the timer is created without using the visual programming tools. Being able to create objects by programming, without using the toolbar, comes in handy when there is no Visual Studio package available. Yes, you heard it right: Programs can be created with the help of an ordinary Notepad.

> **NOTE**
>
> The .NET Framework package contains a free project compiler. Writing code using Notepad is a fascinating exercise, although the term *extreme programming* is, perhaps, a more suitable description of the practice. In some cases, however, this skill may come in handy. For example, you may have access to a computer with .NET Framework installed, but without the Visual Studio .NET package. In this case, the only way to write a program is to write it with a text editor.

But let's move on to the example. We will change the way the text in the form title bar is animated a little. Now the string will not only grow, but it will also flash a few times,

Chapter 1: String Effects

further attracting the user's attention. This example is taken from my collection written in VB 6.0, and reworked making use of the new capabilities offered by VB.NET 2003. Create a new project and name it `FlashText`. Insert the following code in the code editor (Listing 1.2).

Listing 1.2. A Flashing Animated Line

```
'---------------------------------------
' FlashText © 2004 Alexander Klimov
'---------------------------------------
    Dim title As String = "Entertaining Programming"
    Dim b As Integer
    Dim p As Integer
    Dim I As Integer

    ' Creating two timers programmatically
    Dim tmr As New System.Timers.Timer
    Dim tmr2 As New System.Timers.Timer

    Private Sub Form1_Load(ByVal sender As Object, ByVal e As System.EventArgs) _
Handles MyBase.Load
        AddHandler tmr.Elapsed, AddressOf OnTimedEvent
        tmr.Interval = 200
        tmr.Enabled = True
        AddHandler tmr2.Elapsed, AddressOf OnTimedEvent2
        tmr2.Interval = 100
        tmr2.Enabled = False
        CheckAgain()
    End Sub

    Public Sub OnTimedEvent(ByVal source As Object, ByVal e As _
System.Timers.ElapsedEventArgs)
        Dim t As String
        t = Microsoft.VisualBasic.Left(title, b)
        MyClass.Text = t
        b = b + 1
        If b > I Then
            b = 0
            tmr.Enabled = False
            tmr2.Enabled = True
            p = 0
        End If
    End Sub

    Public Sub OnTimedEvent2(ByVal source As Object, ByVal e As _
System.Timers.ElapsedEventArgs)
```

```
    p = p + 1
    If p Mod 2 = 0 Then
        MyClass.Text = title
    Else
        MyClass.Text = ""
    End If
    If p = 10 Then
        tmr2.Enabled = False
        tmr.Enabled = True
    End If
End Sub

Sub CheckAgain()
    I = Len(title)
    b = 0
    p = 0
End Sub
```

Let's examine what the code you just wrote does. First, we declared two class-level variables and two timers. Note that we did not resort to the visual editor to add controls (in this case, the timers) to our project. When the form is loaded, the timers are turned on by the two event handlers for Elapsed events. I also assigned these timers certain properties when the form is loaded, and included the CheckAgain procedure, which will be discussed later. The event handler code for the first timer is simple and is practically the same as the code for the typewritten line in the first example. The only difference is that a second timer is added to it to make the form title bar flash. The CheckAgain procedure simply sets the old value for the title's length and zeros out the b and p variables. As you can see, this example is not actually complicated at all. The reason I started by calling it complicated is that programmers who have just switched from VB 6.0 to VB.NET will feel uncomfortable writing timer and event handler code at first.

1.3. A Scrolling Line

You have most likely seen displays where the same ad scrolls in and out in an endless loop. Let's try to reproduce this effect with the RunTitle project (Listing 1.3). All you need to do is place a timer on the form.

Listing 1.3. A Scrolling Line

```
'----------------------------------------
' RunTitle © 2004 Alexander Klimov
'----------------------------------------
```

```
    Private Sub Timer1_Tick(ByVal sender As System.Object, ByVal e As _
System.EventArgs) Handles Timer1.Tick
        Dim StrTemp As String
        StrTemp = Me.Text
        StrTemp = Microsoft.VisualBasic.Right( _
      StrTemp, Len(StrTemp) - 1) & Microsoft.VisualBasic.Left(StrTemp, 1)
        Me.Text = StrTemp
    End Sub

    Private Sub Form1_Load(ByVal sender As System.Object, ByVal e As System.EventArgs)
Handles MyBase.Load
        ' Need to add a few spaces at the end,
        ' to have a gap between successive lines.
        Me.Text = "Entertaining Programming        "
    End Sub
```

In this example, we remove the line's first character and add it to the end of the line. To put a gap between successive lines, a few spaces had to be added at the end of the line.

1.4. The Matrix Effect

Here is another text line effect, which I call the *Matrix* effect. If you have seen the movie, you remember the flickering letters when it starts. I tried to reproduce this effect in the Matrix project (Listing 1.4). For this example, you will have to create a timer Timer1. Set its Interval property value to 100, and the Enable property to True.

Listing 1.4. The Matrix Effect

```
'------------------------------------
' Matrix effect © 2004 Alexander Klimov
'------------------------------------
    Dim FXCounter As Integer = 0
    Dim FXCounter2 As Integer
    Dim SingleChr As String

    Private Sub Timer1_Tick(ByVal sender As System.Object, ByVal e As System.EventArgs) _
Handles Timer1.Tick

        ' The sample text that materializes in the end
    Dim StrTemp As String
        StrTemp = "MATRIX"

        ' Looping through all characters
        ' Right to left
```

```
    If FXCounter = 0 Then
        FXCounter2 = 31
        FXCounter = 1
    End If

    ' The character replacement position
    Dim iStart As Integer
    iStart = Len(StrTemp) - (FXCounter - 1)

    Try
        If FXCounter2 = 31 Then SingleChr = Mid$(StrTemp, iStart, 1)
        FXCounter2 = FXCounter2 + 1
        Mid(Me.Text, iStart, 1) = Chr(FXCounter2)
        If FXCounter2 = Asc(SingleChr) Then
            FXCounter2 = 31
            FXCounter = FXCounter + 1
        End If

    Catch ex As Exception When iStart = 0
        ' The error handler
        Timer1.Enabled = False
    End Try
End Sub

Private Sub Form1_Load(ByVal sender As System.Object, ByVal e As System.EventArgs) _
Handles MyBase.Load
    Me.Text = "Kitten"
End Sub
```

1.6. Conclusion

In the examples considered in this chapter, we treated strings as sets of characters. But they can also be treated as graphics objects. In this case, you can make letters of different colors, fill them with gradient colors, spin letters around their axis, or drag them along a curve. We will consider how to do all of this in the following chapters.

1.7. Suggestions and Recommendations

See if you can devise your own string effects. Here are some recommendations.

❑ Modify the example in *Section 1.3* to make the line scroll from left to right.
❑ In the same example, the Left and Right functions are used that were inherited from VB 6.0 for compatibility purposes. Try to modify the example using the methods of the System.String class.

Chapter 2: Text Games

In this chapter, you will see how to manipulate texts. You may wonder just what the difference is between strings of characters and texts. Good question. The division into strings and text is purely a matter of convention. I simply wanted to separate the two areas in which texts are used in programs. The string operations performed in *Chapter 1* can be applied, for example, in the form title bars. It should be clear, however, that we cannot change the font size or character colors or rotate the characters in different directions in form title bars. In application areas other than form title bars, however, we have more options for creating striking effects using different character sizes and colors. Here, therefore, we will work with texts.

2.1. Using Hatch and Gradient Brushes

The easiest way to obtain a particular effect when working with texts is to use hatch and/or gradient brushes. I will discuss brushes in detail in *Chapter 3*, which deals with graphics. For the time being, I will just provide a simple example project named `UsingBrushes` (Listing 2.1).

Listing 2.1. Using Hatch and Gradient Brushes

```
'------------------------------------
' UsingBrushes © 2004 Alexander Klimov
'------------------------------------
Imports System.Drawing.Drawing2D

    Private Sub Form1_Paint(ByVal sender As Object, ByVal e As _
System.Windows.Forms.PaintEventArgs) Handles MyBase.Paint
        Dim g As Graphics = e.Graphics
    Dim f As New Font("Tahoma", 48, FontStyle.Bold)
        Dim sBrick As String = "Brick Hatch"
        Dim sGradient As String = "Gradient Fill"

        ' Creating a brick style hatch brush
        Dim hbr As New HatchBrush(HatchStyle.HorizontalBrick, _
            Color.White, Color.Tomato)
        ' Outputting a line filled with bricks
        g.DrawString(sBrick, f, hbr, 0, 0)

        Dim rect As New Rectangle(10, 50, _
                    ClientSize.Width, ClientSize.Height)
        ' Creating a gradient brush
        Dim lgrb As New LinearGradientBrush(rect, _
                    Color.Violet, Color.SkyBlue, _
                    LinearGradientMode.BackwardDiagonal)
        g.DrawString(sGradient, f, lgrb, 0, 100)

    End Sub
```

In this example, I use two types of brushes: The first brush uses brick hatching, while the other uses gradient fill. The results are shown in Fig. 2.1.

Fig. 2.1. Using brushes with texts

2.2. The 3D Text

Text in forms is quite often flat, which is not particularly attractive. This can be fixed by giving the text a 3D appearance. There are two types of 3D effects: embossed and depressed. These effects are created by simply mixing text with another color that imitates shadow. This method is used widely in a diverse number of areas. But let's move on to practical work. Create a new VB .NET project named 3DText and place a button on the form. For starters, we'll create an embossing effect. For this, we will need to call the DrawString method twice. The first call draws the specified string in gray color on the form. The second draws the same string, but in white color and offset by one or two pixels above the first string (Listing 2.2).

Listing 2.2. Creating Embossed Text

```
'----------------------------------------
' 3DText © 2004 Alexander Klimov
'----------------------------------------
    Private Sub Form1_Paint(ByVal sender As Object, ByVal e As _
System.Windows.Forms.PaintEventArgs) Handles MyBase.Paint
        Dim sb As New SolidBrush(Color.Gray)
        Dim f As New Font("Tahoma", 48, FontStyle.Bold)
        Dim g As Graphics = e.Graphics
        g.DrawString("Kitten", f, sb, 10, 10)
        sb.Color = Color.White
        g.DrawString("Kitten", f, sb, 8, 8)
    End Sub
```

Launch the project and check out the embossed text effect that has been created (Fig. 2.2).

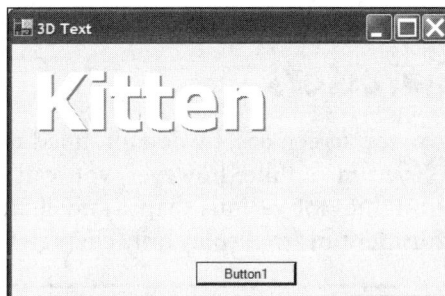

Fig. 2.2. Embossed 3D text

To create a shallow 3D effect, the second string has to be offset below the first. This effect is created using the Button1 button (Listing 2.3).

Listing 2.3. Creating Shallow 3D Text

```
    Private Sub Button1_Click(ByVal sender As System.Object, ByVal e As _
System.EventArgs) Handles Button1.Click
        Dim sb As New SolidBrush(Color.Gray)
        Dim f As New Font("Tahoma", 48, FontStyle.Bold)
        Dim g As Graphics = CreateGraphics()
        g.Clear(BackColor)
        g.DrawString("White Kitten", f, sb, 10, 10)
        sb.Color = Color.White
        g.DrawString("White Kitten", f, sb, 12, 12)
        g.Dispose()
    End Sub
```

Launch the project and click on the button. This should change the text from bas-relief to shallow relief (Fig. 2.3).

Fig. 2.3. Shallow 3D Text

2.3. Outlined Characters

Text characters displayed on the screen are, by default, filled with a color. If you want the characters to only be displayed in outline, however, you can opt for the DrawPath class. This class is used to create outlines for various shapes and characters. In the Outline project (Listing 2.4), we will consider how to display only character outlines on the screen.

Listing 2.4. Creating Character Outlines

```
'---------------------------------------
' Outline © 2004 Alexander Klimov
'---------------------------------------
```

```
Imports System.Drawing.Drawing2D

    Private Sub Form1_Paint(ByVal sender As Object, ByVal e As _
System.Windows.Forms.PaintEventArgs) Handles MyBase.Paint
        ' Creating a path
        Dim pth As New GraphicsPath

        ' Adding a string
        pth.AddString("I love cats", _
                    New FontFamily("Tahoma"), _
                    0, 70, New Point(30, 30), _
                    StringFormat.GenericDefault)

        ' Creating a blue pen
        Dim p As New Pen(Color.Blue, 2)

        ' Outputting outlined character text
        e.Graphics.DrawPath(p, pth)

        ' Clearing the path
        pth.Reset()

        ' Adding new text
        pth.AddString("I love dogs too", _
                    New FontFamily("Verdana"), _
                    0, 60, New Point(30, 120), _
                    StringFormat.GenericTypographic)

        ' Filling the path with a brush
        e.Graphics.FillPath(Brushes.Peru, pth)

        ' Outputting to the screen
        e.Graphics.DrawPath(p, pth)

        ' Releasing resources
        pth.Dispose()
    End Sub
```

This example is pretty easy to understand. First, we create an outline pth, into which we then add the first text. The outlines of the string characters are displayed on the screen. For the sake of comparison, the second text is displayed with its characters filled with the Peru color (Fig. 2.4). Nevertheless, you can still see the outlines of the characters in the second text.

Fig. 2.4. Character outlines

2.4. A Glowing Text

A striking effect is produced by text that is surrounded by a glowing halo. The method for creating a halo is similar to that for creating a 3D effect. I borrowed the halo idea from an example I found on a site by Robert W. Powell (**www.bobpowell.net**). Create a project named ElectricFX, and place a graphics object PicrtureBox1 in the form. The location and other properties for this control are not important, so leave the default values. All of the code is contained in the Paint event of the Form form. A reference to the System.Drawing.Drawing2D namespace must be added at the beginning of the code (Listing 2.5).

Listing 2.5. Creating an Electric Glow Effect

```
'-------------------------------------
' ElectricFX © 2004 Alexander Klimov
'-------------------------------------
Imports System.Drawing.Drawing2D

    Private Sub Form1_Paint(ByVal sender As Object, ByVal e As _
System.Windows.Forms.PaintEventArgs) Handles MyBase.Paint

        Me.BackColor = Color.Black

       ' Creating a drawing at the specified scale
       Dim bm As New Bitmap(CInt(Me.ClientSize.Width / 5), _
                        CInt(Me.ClientSize.Height / 5))

     ' Creating a GraphicsPath object
       Dim pth As New GraphicsPath

        ' Adding a string in the specified style
        pth.AddString("Electric glow effect", _
                New FontFamily("Tahoma"), _
                CInt(FontStyle.Bold), 48, _
```

```
                New Point(10, 20), _
                StringFormat.GenericTypographic)

    ' Creating a Graphics object
    Dim g As Graphics = Graphics.FromImage(bm)

    ' Creating a matrix to produce the effect
    Dim mx As Matrix
    mx = New Matrix(1.0F / 5, 0, 0, _
                1.0F / 5, -(1.0F / 5), _
                -(1.0F / 5))

    ' Selecting the smoothing mode
    g.SmoothingMode = SmoothingMode.AntiAlias

    ' Transforming the Graphics object
    g.Transform = mx

    ' Creating a pen
    Dim p As New Pen(Color.Tomato, 3)

    ' Drawing text along the created path
    g.DrawPath(p, pth)

    ' Filling the text for a better effect
    g.FillPath(Brushes.Yellow, pth)

    ' Releasing resources
    g.Dispose()

    ' Setting the smoothing mode for the outlines
    e.Graphics.SmoothingMode = SmoothingMode.AntiAlias
    e.Graphics.InterpolationMode = _
                InterpolationMode.HighQualityBicubic

    ' Expanding the picture to create the effect of fuzzy edges
    e.Graphics.DrawImage(bm, ClientRectangle, 0, 0, _
            bm.Width, bm.Height, GraphicsUnit.Pixel)

    ' Redrawing the original text
    e.Graphics.FillPath(Brushes.Black, pth)

    ' Releasing resources
    pth.Dispose()
End Sub
```

Let's take a look at some of the portions of the code. To create the halo around the text, I used the `InterpolationMode` property to make a fuzzy text edge effect. The technique for creating a halo involves drawing the text twice. First, a reduced copy of the image is created, which will then be stretched using the interpolation mode. A definite value has to be provided for the stretching coefficient. In our example, the stretching coefficient is set at 1:5. How does everything work here? First, an image in the given scale is created. A path is then created, and the necessary text added. The `Graphics` object can now be obtained from the `PictureBox` graphics object, and the matrix to compress the image can be created. The path is then filled with the desired color using the pen and, for a more impressive effect, the path is filled with the brush selected. Next, the image is stretched to create the blurry effect. Finally, the specified text is displayed again to create the ultimate desired effect (Fig. 2.5).

Fig. 2.5. The electric glow effect

2.5. Rotating Text

A number of methods from the `Graphics` class provide us with extensive capabilities for the manipulation of text. With one line of code you can rotate a text to any angle, flip it horizontally or vertically, tilt the characters, and so on. In Visual Basic 6.0, it took significant programming skills to carry out these text operations. It is difficult, if not impossible, to describe all of the text transformations that can be performed with the tools offered by VB .NET. More detailed information can be found in the documentation for the package. We will look at a few examples here. These will be static examples, but you can add a timer or loops to create animation effects. For example, the `RotatedText` project (Listing 2.6) shows how to draw a string rotated through 180 degrees.

Listing 2.6. Rotating a String through 180 Degrees

```
'--------------------------------------

' RotatedText © 2004 Alexander Klimov

'--------------------------------------

    Private Sub Button1_Click(ByVal sender As System.Object, ByVal e As _
System.EventArgs) Handles Button1.Click
        Dim g As Graphics
```

```
    g = CreateGraphics()

    ' Rotating the text through 180 degrees
    g.RotateTransform(180)
    g.DrawString("Entertaining Programming", _
              New Font(Font.FontFamily, 16), _
              Brushes.Green, -Width / 2, -Height / 2)

    g.Dispose()
End Sub
```

As you can see, the effect is achieved with only one call of the RotateTransform method (Fig. 2.6).

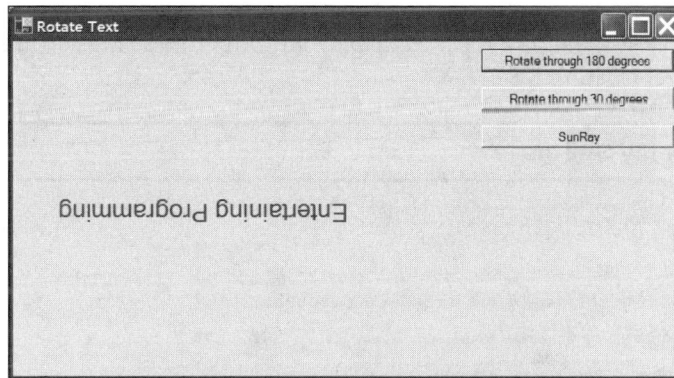

Fig. 2.6. Text rotated through 180 degrees

Accordingly, to rotate text through a smaller angle, the necessary angle is specified using the RotateTransform method (Listing 2.7).

Listing 2.7. Rotating String through 30 Degrees

```
    Private Sub butAngleText_Click(ByVal sender As System.Object, ByVal e As _
System.EventArgs) Handles butAngleText.Click

    Dim f As New Font("Arial", 14, FontStyle.Regular)
    Dim g As Graphics = CreateGraphics()
        g = CreateGraphics()

        ' Moving to the specified reference point
      g.TranslateTransform(30, 30)

        ' Rotating the string through 30 degrees
```

```
    g.RotateTransform(30)

    ' Outputting the string at the specified angle
  g.DrawString("Text rotated through 30 degrees", f, Brushes.Red, 0, 0)

    ' Resetting the transformation matrix
    g.ResetTransform()
    g.Dispose()
End Sub
```

The rotation can be performed not only through a positive angle (clockwise), but also through a negative angle (counterclockwise). Consequently, calling the `RotateTransform` method with a parameter value of `-10` will rotate the text counterclockwise. As for me, I just couldn't resist the temptation to display a number of strings around a point to create a sunray effect (Listing 2.8).

Listing 2.8. Sunray Strings

```
  Private Sub butSunText_Click(ByVal sender As System.Object, ByVal e As _
System.EventArgs) Handles butSunText.Click

  Dim f As New Font("Arial", 14, FontStyle.Regular)
  Dim g As Graphics = CreateGraphics()
  g = CreateGraphics()
    ' Clearing the form
    g.Clear(BackColor)

    ' Determining the form's center
  Dim cx As Integer = ClientSize.Width \ 2
    Dim cy As Integer = ClientSize.Height \ 2

    ' Moving to the specified reference point
    g.TranslateTransform(cx, cy)
    g.FillEllipse(Brushes.Yellow, -45, -45, 90, 90)

    Dim i As Integer
    For i = 0 To 359 Step 15
        g.DrawString("Sunray", f, Brushes.Yellow, 50, 0)
        ' Rotating the string through 20 degrees
        g.RotateTransform(20)
```

```
    Next

      ' Resetting the transformation matrix
    g.ResetTransform()
      g.Dispose()
End Sub
```

The text in the example is displayed in the `For … Next` loop, rotating the text by 20 degrees in each step. To keep the letters from sticking together, I moved the strings away from the center point a little and added a yellow spot to give it an appearance more like that of the sun (Fig. 2.7).

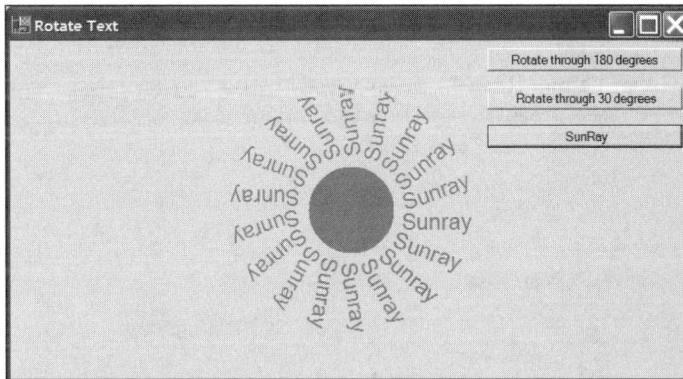

Fig. 2.7. Sunray strings

2.6. Meetings and Partings

The following effects look especially impressive in the **About** dialog windows, which contain information about the author, the program version, homepage and email ad dress, and so on. The basic points of the first example are as follows. Two strings are placed at a distance from each other. When the timer is started, the strings begin to draw closer to each other, pause for a short time when they meet, and then move apart again. The sequence is repeated for as long as the timer runs. Begin by creating a new project. Name it `Credits`, and give the form the name `frmAbout`. Place a timer `Timer1` in the form. All of the properties for the timer will be set using the code of Listing 2.9. As a result, they do not have to be edited using the Property Editor.

Listing 2.9. The Source Code for the Meetings and Partings example

---

```vb
'-------------------------------------
' Credits © 2004 2004 Alexander Klimov
'-------------------------------------
    Dim x1 As Single ' the coordinates for the first string
    Dim x2 As Single ' the coordinates for the second string
    Dim g As Graphics
    Dim f As Font
    Dim closuredistance As Single
    Private Const speed As Single = 0.1
    Dim moveamount As Single

    Private Sub Timer1_Tick(ByVal sender As System.Object, ByVal e As System.EventArgs) _
Handles Timer1.Tick
        g.Clear(Me.BackColor)
        g.DrawString("Entertaining", f, Brushes.Blue, x1, 10)
        g.DrawString("Programming", f, Brushes.BlueViolet, x2, 70)
        closuredistance = Math.Abs(x1 - x2)
        moveamount = speed * closuredistance

        If moveamount < 1 Then moveamount = 1

        x2 = x2 + moveamount
        x1 = x1 - moveamount

        If x2 > Me.Width Or x1 < -1000 Then
            x2 = -270
            x1 = 725
        End If
    End Sub

    Private Sub frmAbout_Load(ByVal sender As System.Object, ByVal e As _
System.EventArgs) Handles MyBase.Load
        g = Me.CreateGraphics()
        x1 = Me.Width
        x2 = 0

        f = New Font("Times New Roman", 14, FontStyle.Bold, _
                    GraphicsUnit.Point)
        Timer1.Interval = 40
        Timer1.Start()
    End Sub
```

The code is pretty straightforward. The `closuredistance` variable is assigned the distance between the strings, which is obtained by subtracting their coordinates as follows:

```
closuredistance = Math.Abs(x1 - x2)
```

The value that is obtained is then multiplied by a `speed` constant. The greater the distance between the strings, the greater the value for the `moveamount` variable and, consequently, the string approach speed. The approach speed drops as the strings get closer to each other. When the strings are moving apart, the opposite process takes place. The speed, at which the strings move away from each other, accelerates constantly. Although the code is relatively simple, it produces an impressive effect on the screen.

2.7. A Scrolling String

In *Chapter 1*, I showed you how to create a scrolling string effect in the form title bar. That example employed old functions included in VB 6.0. I will now demonstrate how to create an analogous example using the new methods of the `String` class. In order to provide the example with a little more flair, we will also fill the text with gradient color. Create a `RunText` project, and place a `Timer1` timer in the form (Listing 2.10).

Listing 2.10. A Scrolling Line Example

```
'-------------------------------------
' RunText © 2004 Alexander Klimov
'-------------------------------------
    ' The two gradient colors
    Private startColor1 As Color = Color.Green
    Private endColor2 As Color = Color.Gold
    ' The scrolling line font
    Private f As Font

    ' Adding a few spaces at the end of the string
    ' to have a gap between the successive lines
    Private sScrollText As String = "Announcements            "

Public Function RunningText()

    ' The algorithm for creating the effect
    ' Removing one character from the left
    ' and adding it to the string's right end
    sScrollText = sScrollText.Substring(1, _
        (sScrollText.Length - 1)) + sScrollText.Substring(0, 1)
    Invalidate()
```

```
    End Function

    Private Sub Timer1_Tick(ByVal sender As System.Object, ByVal e As System.EventArgs) _
Handles Timer1.Tick
        RunningText()
    End Sub

    Private Sub Form1_Paint(ByVal sender As Object, ByVal e As _
System.Windows.Forms.PaintEventArgs) Handles MyBase.Paint
        ' Creating a gradient brush
        Dim MyBrush As Brush = _
            New LinearGradientBrush( _
            ClientRectangle, startColor1, endColor2, 10)
        ' Setting the font properties
            f = New Font(Font.Name, 60, _
                    Font.Style, GraphicsUnit.Pixel)
        ' Outputting the string
        e.Graphics.DrawString(sScrollText, f, MyBrush, 0, 0)

        ' Releasing resources
        MyBrush.Dispose()
        f.Dispose()
    End Sub
```

Running the project produces a string that scrolls from right to left. Note that, as the string is moving, the color of the letters changes gradually.

2.8. The Scrolling String Improved

The previous scrolling string example was actually not a very good one. Changing the values of the coordinates in the DrawString method is a much more convenient way of creating this effect. The ScrollText project (Listing 2.11) demonstrates text that scrolls along both the vertical and horizontal axes. To generate this example, we will need a timer (tmrScroll) and two radio buttons (rbVert and rbHoriz).

Listing 2.11. Scrolling Text in the Horizontal and Vertical Directions

```
'---------------------------------------
' ScrollText © 2004 Alexander Klimov
'---------------------------------------
    ' For the vertical scrolling
    Dim y_vert As Single

    ' For the horizontal scrolling
```

```
Dim x_horiz As Single

Dim g As Graphics
Dim f As Font
Dim scroll As String = "Scrolling"

Private Sub tmrScroll_Tick(ByVal sender As System.Object, _
        ByVal e As System.EventArgs) Handles tmrScroll.Tick

    If rbHoriz.Checked Then
        ' Horizontal scrolling
     g.Clear(Me.BackColor)
        g.DrawString(scroll, f, Brushes.Black, x_horiz, y_vert)
        If x_horiz <= (0 - 90) Then
            x_horiz = Me.Width
        Else
            x_horiz -= 5
        End If
    Else
        ' Vertical scrolling
        g.Clear(Me.BackColor)
        g.DrawString(scroll, f, Brushes.Black, x_horiz, y_vert)

        If y_vert <= (0 - 10) Then
            y_vert = Me.Height
        Else
            y_vert -= 5
        End If

    End If
End Sub

Private Sub Form1_Load(ByVal sender As System.Object, _
        ByVal e As System.EventArgs) Handles MyBase.Load
    g = Me.CreateGraphics()

    y_vert = Me.Height

    x_horiz = Me.Width - 200

    tmrScroll.Interval = 100
    tmrScroll.Start()
    f = New Font("Times New Roman", 14, FontStyle.Bold, _
        GraphicsUnit.Point)
End Sub
```

The scrolling technique is very simple. You merely calculate the coordinates of the output string and, after a timed interval, subtract the specified number of pixels. In the given example, I used a fixed value for the Scrolling string:

```
If x_horiz <= (0 - 90) Then ...
```

I selected a parameter value of 90 by trial and error method. If you intend to write a universal code that can handle any string, you need to calculate the string's length using the MeasureString method.

2.9. The Star Wars Effect

VB .NET's powerful text manipulation capabilities can be used to change text in a large variety of ways. For example, in some movies the background story is provided in text on the screen before the events in the film itself begin. The text of these narrations often tapers towards the top of the screen. The most famous example of this was at the beginning of the Star Wars films. Here is how this effect can be created on your own computer (Listing 2.12).

Listing 2.12. Star Wars Text

```
'---------------------------------------
' Star Wars Text © 2004 Alexander Klimov
'---------------------------------------
Imports System.Drawing.Drawing2D

    Private Sub Form1_Paint(ByVal sender As Object, ByVal e As _
System.Windows.Forms.PaintEventArgs) Handles MyBase.Paint
        ' Creating a path
    Dim pth As GraphicsPath = New GraphicsPath
        Dim ff As FontFamily = New FontFamily("Tahoma")

        ' Adding text to the path
        Dim y As Integer
        pth.AddString("Jack and Jill", ff, 0, 70, _
                New Point(0, 90 * y), _
                StringFormat.GenericTypographic)

        pth.AddString("Went up the hill", ff, 0, 70, _
                New Point(0 - 100, 90 * 1), _
                StringFormat.GenericTypographic)
        pth.AddString("To fetch a little water", ff, 0, 70, _
                New Point(0 - 150, 90 * 2), _
                StringFormat.GenericTypographic)

        ' Creating an array for the warp transformation
        Dim points() As PointF = { _
```

```
New PointF(ClientSize.Width / 2 - ClientSize.Width / 4, 0), _
New PointF(ClientSize.Width / 2 + ClientSize.Width / 4, 0), _
New PointF(0, ClientSize.Height), _
New PointF(ClientSize.Width, ClientSize.Height)}

        ' Transforming the path
        pth.Warp(points, New RectangleF(0, 0, 820, 450))

        ' Filling the background
        e.Graphics.FillRectangle(Brushes.Black, ClientRectangle)

        ' Filling the path with yellow color
        e.Graphics.FillPath(Brushes.Yellow, pth)

      ' Releasing resources
        pth.Dispose()

    End Sub
```

If you examine the ends of each line (Fig. 2.8), you will see that each line tapers slightly at the top.

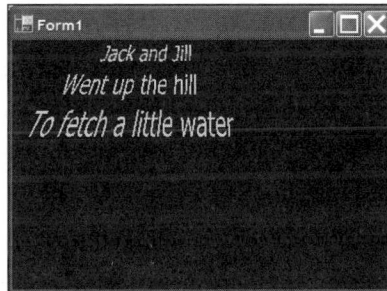

Fig. 2.8. The Star Wars intro text effect

2.10. Funny Fonts

Any text is displayed on the screen using the fonts that are installed in the user's system. At first, I thought that fonts would not be a very interesting subject, so I didn't plan to include them in the book. I was mistaken. Using a creative approach, even a seemingly dull subject like fonts can produce some interesting effects. In addition to the regular fonts that are installed on most computers, there are numerous fonts developed by enthusiasts and professional companies that are worthy of note. You might want to use one or more of these fonts in your applications. There are, however, risks involved. If the font used by your program is not installed in the user's system, Windows will try to substitute a font that is already installed and that matches the specified font most closely. The result may be far from satisfactory. In this case, you will have to let prospective users of your program know that they need to install the font in question if it is not already present on their machines. This, obviously, is not always convenient. Fortunately, there is a more effective method. Fonts can be added to programs dynamically. All you have to do is add an extra font file to the program. You don't even have to install your font in the user's system (which is a plus, as many users dislike cluttering up their system files). Fortunately, Visual Basic .NET 2003 contains the PrivateFontCollection class, which makes it possible to work with custom fonts. If you look at the image in Fig. 2.9 carefully, you will see that the characters are made from cat silhouettes! I downloaded a few fonts of this type from the **Cats Portal** site (**http://cats-portal.ru**). For the CatFont example (Listing 2.13), I used the PussyFoot font. But you do not have to use this font yourself. You can use any fonts of your own. Just don't forget to write out the full path to your font in the program code.

Listing 2.13. Using Custom Fonts in Applications

```
'-------------------------------------
' CatFont © 2004 Alexander Klimov
'-------------------------------------
Imports System.Drawing.Text

    Private Sub Form1_Paint(ByVal sender As Object, ByVal e As _
System.Windows.Forms.PaintEventArgs) Handles MyBase.Paint

        Dim count As Integer = 0
        Dim familyName As String = ""
        Dim fontFamilies() As FontFamily
        Dim private_FontColl As New PrivateFontCollection

        ' Adding your font to the applications (Specify your own path to the font file!)
        private_FontColl.AddFontFile("e:\download\pussyfoot.ttf")

        fontFamilies = private_FontColl.Families

        ' Calculating the number of the font families in the fontFamilies array
      count = fontFamilies.Length

        ' Obtaining the name of the first item in the collection
        familyName = fontFamilies(0).Name

        Dim ff As FontFamily = New FontFamily(familyName, _
                                        private_FontColl)
        Dim f As New Font(ff, 72, FontStyle.Regular)

        ' Outputting string I LOVE Visual Basic
```

```
        e.Graphics.DrawString("I", f, _
                            Brushes.Blue, 150, 20)
        e.Graphics.DrawString("love", f, _
                            Brushes.Red, 70, 120)
        e.Graphics.DrawString("Visual Basic", f, _
                            Brushes.Blue, 5, 220)
End Sub
```

Once again, don't forget to specify the full path to the font file. I placed my pussyfoot.ttf font in the e:\download folder, but you, most likely, will have a different path to your font.

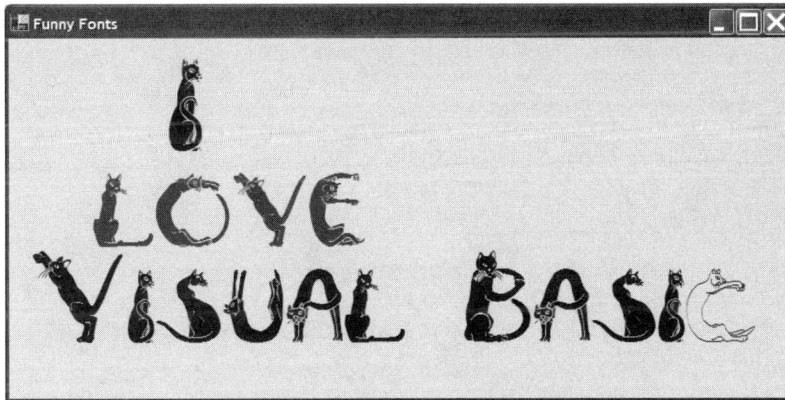

Fig. 2.9. Using non-standard fonts

In some cases, using non-standard fonts is fully justified and makes it possible to provide an application with its own particular charm.

A Little Laugh

A programmer is being examined by an eye doctor.
Doctor: — Can you read this line of the chart? (Points to BKEIQXS).
Programmer: — Doctor, you are using wrong code page.

2.11. Suggestions and Recommendations

❐ Modify the Scroll String project (*Section 2.8*) in such a way as to make the text move from top to bottom and from left to right.

❐ In the same project, instead of fixed values, use the values returned by the MeasureString method.

PART II: VISUAL BASIC .NET 2003 GRAPHICS CAPABILITIES

Chapter 3: The Fundamentals of the GDI+ Interface

The weakest point with regard to Visual Basic 6.0 is, perhaps, its poor graphics capabilities. The processing of large graphics objects can take dozens of minutes, and can sometimes even cause the computer to hang. Moreover, the built-in capabilities are sufficient to carry out only the simplest of operations. To perform more complex operations with graphics work requires calling Windows API functions. Everything is different with VB .NET. Working with graphics is a pure pleasure now. We will consider the most interesting examples.

GDI+ is the successor to GDI, as indicated by the plus sign in its name. I want to warn you right off the bat that, despite the broad capabilities provided by the new interface, we will still have to resort to unmanaged code in Windows API functions in some cases. This is understandable, as the .NET Framework developers simply cannot keep up with all of the graphics methods and properties that are in demand among programmers. Currently, GDI+ comprises the following six namespaces:

- ☐ `System.Drawing;`
- ☐ `System.Drawing.Design;`
- ☐ `System.Drawing.Drawing2D;`
- ☐ `System.Drawing.Imaging;`
- ☐ `System.Drawing.Printing;`
- ☐ `System.Drawing.Text.`

For our purposes, the first four namespaces, which deal directly with graphics and images, are likely of the greatest interest. Those programmers who worked extensively with GDI will be interested in learning about the main differences between the new and old technologies. First of all, the new interface does not make use of the *device context* and *device-context handle* concepts. These concepts have been replaced with the `Graphics` object, which contains all of the methods and properties necessary for drawing. In addition, the principles of the output of graphics to devices have changed. For example, before, a function for creating a pen could be called only once, after which the pen that was created could be used to draw an unlimited number of lines. Now, the pen to be used has to be specified explicitly every time a line is drawn on the screen. These two examples alone provide an idea of the significant changes that have been made in the graphics techniques. As a result, you should pay careful attention when studying this chapter.

3.1. The *Graphics* Class

The `Graphics` class is one of the most powerful and comprehensive classes for working with graphics within the .NET Framework hierarchy. It can be used to draw lines, curves, figures, and much more. Simply listing the properties and methods of this class would take several pages. I have selected the examples that are, in my opinion, the most interesting. Before moving onto working with these, you first have to learn the theory and become familiar with the main graphics objects. The first thing you need to remember is that, before drawing any object (a square, oval, line, etc.), you need to create a surface, on which to draw the object (what used to be called the *device context* in GDI). The role of the drawing surface can be played by the form itself, the entire screen, a control, as well as a printer. The drawing surface is created with the help of a `Graphics` object. This object can be accessed or created in the following ways:

❑ First of all, the form itself already contains a `Graphics` object, which can be addressed via drawing events (e.g., `Paint` event).
❑ If this object has to be addressed via a button event, the `CreateGraphics` method can be used.

These are the main techniques that I will use in this book. The other methods are used less often, so they will not be covered here. I would like to draw your attention to the `CreateGraphics` method. Beginners often repeat the same mistake over and over again, calling this method as follows:

```
Dim g As New Graphics
```

This code will not work and the code editor will issue an error message. The proper way to do this is as follows:

```
Dim g As Graphics
```

In this book, I will use the following technique often:

```
Dim g As Graphics = CreateGraphics()
```

Of course, if you are uncomfortable with the fact that only one letter is used to define an object, you can name your objects as you please. But I use this object so often in the examples here that using a single letter as a name simply saves time.

3.2. Pens

The drawing surface, logically enough, provides you with something to draw on. But you also need something to draw with. Just as in real life, you can draw with pens, brushes, or whole images (stamps). Let's compare these methods with our concepts of drawing. A pen is more convenient for drawing lines, curves, arcs, etc. In principle, a shape can be filled with color using a pen as well, but this is a rather tiresome and inefficient method. A pen can draw thick or thin lines, depending on the width of its tip, the amount of force applied, and the amount of ink inside. Inks of different colors can also be used. In machine language, these concepts take the following forms:

```
Dim p As New Pen(Color.Red)
Dim p2 As New Pen(Color.Blue, 5) ' wide nib
```

The first line of code creates a red pen that is one pixel wide. The second code line creates a blue pen that is five pixels wide.

3.2.1. The DrawLine Method

The `DrawLine` method is used to draw lines of various colors and widths. A line is drawn using a pen and the coordinates for the two endpoints. Because the pen color can be created using the `FromArgb` method, lines with different levels of transparency can be drawn, as demonstrated in the `DrawLineSample` project (Listing 3.1).

Listing 3.1. Drawing Lines

```
'-------------------------------------
' DrawLineSample © 2004 Alexander Klimov
'-------------------------------------
    Private Sub Form1_Paint(ByVal sender As Object, ByVal e As _
System.Windows.Forms.PaintEventArgs) Handles MyBase.Paint
        Dim g As Graphics = e.Graphics
        Dim clr As New Color
        Dim p As New Pen(clr, 5)

        ' Outputting several horizontal lines
        ' of different transparency
```

```
      Dim i As Integer
      For i = 10 To 210 Step 20
          p.Color = clr.FromArgb(255 - i, i, 255, 0)
          g.DrawLine(p, 10, i, 200, i)
      Next
End Sub
```

Running the program produces several horizontal lines of various transparencies. The effect can be enhanced by adding code to draw solid colored lines before the main code.

```
g.DrawLine(New Pen((Color.Red), 10), 20, 5, 20, 215)
g.DrawLine(New Pen((Color.Blue), 10), 190, 5, 190, 215)
```

3.3. Brushes

Brushes are handy for filling large areas with color. In this respect, the association with the brushes you would use to paint a room, rather than those typically used by an artist, is more appropriate. Unlike the Pen class, the Brush class is an abstraction and an instance of it cannot be created. At first, I constantly forgot about this, and would end up writing the following code:

```
Dim br as New Brush(Color.Black)
```

I would ultimately be left scratching my head for a long time trying to figure out where I had gone wrong. Profit from my experience — define a new brush properly, as follows:

```
Dim sb as New SolidBrush(Color.Black)
```

There are several types of brushes, both simple and advanced. All of them are contained in the System.Drawing and System.Drawing.Drawing2D namespaces. Brushes are an important part of the Windows graphics system. From the standpoint of entertainment, the TextureBrush, LinearGradientBrush, and PathGradientBrush classes are of the greatest interest. Depending on your imagination, other classes, like SolidBrush or HatchBrush, can also be used to achieve interesting effects. Once again, remember that all of these classes inherit from the main abstract class: Brush.

3.3.1. The SolidBrush Class

Before learning how to use the new brushes, let's first refresh our solid brush skills in the SolidBrushSample project (Listing 3.2).

Listing 3.2. Using Solid Brushes

```
'--------------------------------------
' SolidBrushSample  © 2004 Alexander Klimov
'--------------------------------------
  Private Sub butSimple_Click(ByVal sender As System.Object, ByVal e As _
System.EventArgs) Handles butSimple.Click
        Dim g As Graphics = CreateGraphics()
        Dim rect As New Rectangle(10, 10, _
              Me.ClientSize.Width - 20, _
              Me.ClientSize.Height - 20)
        ' Creating a green solid brush
        Dim sbr As Brush = New System.Drawing.SolidBrush(Color.Green)

        ' Using the brush to fill a rectangle
        g.FillEllipse(sbr, rect)

        ' Framing the rectangle with a 10-pixel wide frame
        g.DrawEllipse( _
           New Pen(Color.DarkMagenta, 10), rect)
        g.Dispose()
    End Sub
```

But a solid brush can also be semi-transparent. Here is an example, with three circles each filled with a different, semi-transparent color (Listing 3.3).

Listing 3.3. Using Semi-Transparent Brushes

```
  Private Sub butTransp_Click(ByVal sender As System.Object, ByVal e As _
System.EventArgs) Handles butTransp.Click
        Dim g As Graphics = CreateGraphics()
        ' Creating three semi-transparent brushes
        Dim trnsRedBrush As New SolidBrush(_
                     Color.FromArgb(150, 255, 0, 0))
        Dim trnsGreenBrush As New SolidBrush (_
                     Color.FromArgb(150, 0, 255, 0))
        Dim trnsBlueBrush As New SolidBrush (_
                     Color.FromArgb(150, 0, 0, 255))

        ' The base and height of a triangle
        ' to position the circles
        ' Each apex of the triangle is a center
        ' for one of the circles
```

```
' The base of the triangle equals the diameter of the circles.
Dim triBase As Single = 150
Dim triHeight As Single = CSng(Math.Sqrt((3 * (triBase * _
triBase) / 4)))

' Coordinates for the first circle
Dim x1 As Single = 40
Dim y1 As Single = 40

' Filling the circles
g.FillEllipse(trnsRedBrush, x1, y1 _
            2 * triHeight, 2 * triHeight)
g.FillEllipse(trnsGreenBrush, x1 + triBase / 2 _
            y1 + triHeight, 2 * triHeight, 2 * triHeight)
g.FillEllipse(trnsBlueBrush, x1 + triBase, _
            y1, 2 * triHeight, 2 * triHeight)

    g.Dispose()
End Sub
```

Experiment with running the program in various modes. For example, first click on the **Semitransparent Brushes** button. You will see the example that was just described (Fig. 3.1). This will involve three overlapping, semi-transparent circles. Take a look at the colors in the areas where the circles overlap. Now click on the button labeled **Simple Brush Example,** and then click on the first button again. Note that, with the green ellipse in the background, the semitransparent red circle becomes brown.

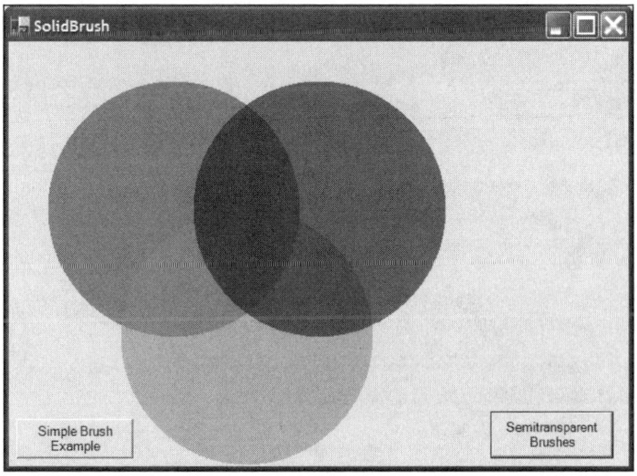

Fig. 3.1. Circles drawn with semitransparent brushes

3.3.2. *The* HatchBrush *Class*

The HatchBrush class comprises more than 50 different hatch brushes. Compared to the six brush styles in the Windows GDI, the difference is obvious, isn't it? The whole might of the new brush arsenal can be demonstrated by displaying all of the existing hatch brush styles in a HatchBrushStyles project (Listing 3.4).

Listing 3.4. Displaying All HatchBrush Class Styles

```
'------------------------------------
' HatchBrushStyles  © 2004 Alexander Klimov
'------------------------------------
Imports System.Drawing.Drawing2D

    Private Sub Form1_Paint(ByVal sender As Object, ByVal e As _
System.Windows.Forms.PaintEventArgs) Handles MyBase.Paint
        ' There are 53 styles altogether
    Const FIRST_STYLE As Integer = 0
        Const LAST_STYLE As Integer = 52
        Dim x As Integer = 10
        Dim y As Integer = 10

        Dim i As Integer
        For i = FIRST_STYLE To LAST_STYLE
            DrawAllHatch(e.Graphics, x, y, CType(i, HatchStyle))
        Next i
    End Sub

    Private Sub DrawAllHatch(ByVal g As Graphics, ByRef x As Integer, ByRef y As _
Integer, ByVal hatch_style As HatchStyle)
        ' Text width
        Const TEXT_WID As Integer = 170
        ' The size of the hatch brush sample rectangles
        Dim rect As New Rectangle(x + TEXT_WID, y, 40, 35)

        ' Using the simplest brush
        Dim hbr As New HatchBrush(hatch_style, Color.White)
        g.DrawString(CInt(hatch_style) & ". " & _
            hatch_style.ToString, _
            Me.Font, Brushes.Black, x, y)
        g.FillRectangle(hbr, rect)
```

```
    g.DrawRectangle(Pens.Black, x + TEXT_WID, y, rect.Width, rect.Height)

    y += rect.Height + 10
    If y + rect.Height > Me.ClientSize.Height Then
        x += TEXT_WID + rect.Width + 30
        y = 10
    End If
End Sub
```

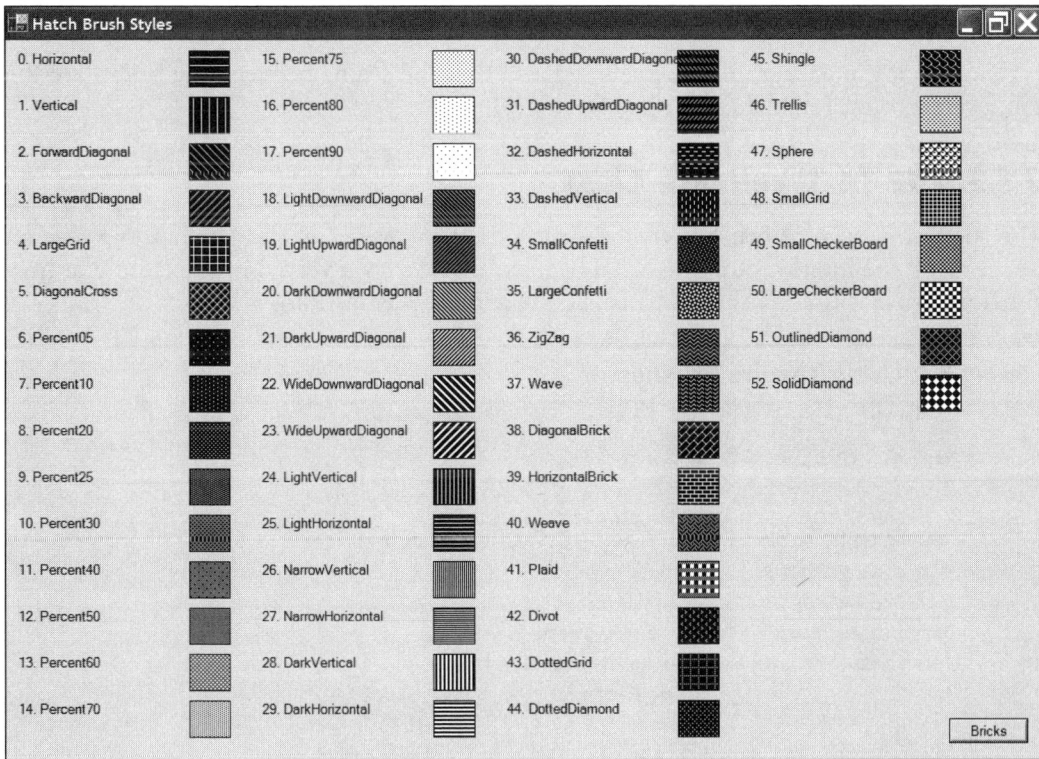

Fig. 3.2. All HatchBrush class styles

This example displays all of the hatch brush styles on the screen in small rectangles (Fig. 3.2). Note also that each rectangle is numbered and labeled with the name of the style. Personally, I like the `HorizontalBrick` style. Don't forget that the hatch colors can be any pair of colors, and not just of the black-and-white variety. Let's fill a form with red bricks (Listing 3.5).

Listing 3.5. Filling a Form with Bricks

```
    Private Sub butBricks_Click(ByVal sender As System.Object, ByVal e As _
System.EventArgs) Handles butBricks.Click
        ' Filling the form with bricks
        Dim hbr As New HatchBrush(_
                HatchStyle.HorizontalBrick, Color.Gray, Color.Tomato)
        Dim g As Graphics = CreateGraphics()

        g.FillRectangle(hbr, 0, 0, ClientSize.Width, ClientSize.Height)
        g.Dispose()
    End Sub
```

Note that the background color is red and that the seams between the bricks are the foreground color. I mixed these up at first.

3.3.3. *The* TextureBrush *Class*

The specific feature of brushes created using the TextureBrush class is that they use an image to fill the interior of a shape. To begin with, let's try a very simple example of how a texture brush is used: a TextureBrushSample project (Listing 3.6).

Listing 3.6. Using Texture Brushes

```
'-------------------------------------
' TextureBrushSample  © 2004 Alexander Klimov
'-------------------------------------
    Private Sub butSimpleTextureBrush_Click(ByVal sender As System.Object, ByVal e As _
System.EventArgs) Handles butSimpleTextureBrush.Click
        Dim g As Graphics
        g = CreateGraphics()
        Dim img As Image = PictureBox1.Image
        Dim tb As New System.Drawing.TextureBrush(img _
                        New Rectangle(0, 0, 60, 88))

        tb.WrapMode = Drawing2D.WrapMode.Tile.TileFlipY
        g.FillEllipse(tb, 0, 0, _
                2 * ClientSize.Width \ 3, 2 * ClientSize.Height \ 3)
        g.FillRectangle(tb, ClientSize.Width \ 3, _
                        ClientSize.Height \ 3, _
                        ClientSize.Width \ 2, _
                        2 * ClientSize.Height \ 3)
        g.Dispose()
    End Sub
```

In this example, we first create a texture brush, for which the texture is the image loaded in advance from the `PictureBox` graphics object. Texture brushes have several filling modes. For example, the `TileFlipY` mode used in the example flips the image horizontally and multiplies it, thus filling the ellipse and the rectangle. Note that, despite the fact that these two shapes overlap, the images within them do not. Apropos, texture brushes can be rotated, offset, and scaled. Insert the following line before the code that displays the shapes on the screen:

```
tb.RotateTransform(-35)
```

As you can see, the brush images have rotated through 35 degrees.

Texture brushes can be used not only to fill system-generated shapes, like rectangles or ellipses, but also to fill custom bitmap shapes (Fig. 3.3). This is done with the help of the `DrawPolygon` method (Listing 3.7).

Listing 3.7. Using a Texture Brush To Fill a Custom Shape

```
Private Sub butPolygon_Click(ByVal sender As System.Object, ByVal e As
System.EventArgs) Handles butPolygon.Click
        Dim pts() As Point = { _
            New Point(50, 25), _
            New Point(100, 25), _
            New Point(150, 100), _
            New Point(100, 175), _
            New Point(50, 175), _
            New Point(5, 100) _
        }

        ' Using the brush to fill a polygon
        Dim tb As New System.Drawing.TextureBrush(PictureBox1.Image)
        Dim g As Graphics
        g = CreateGraphics()
        g.Clear(Me.BackColor)
        g.FillPolygon(tb, pts)

        ' Creating a pen
        Dim a_pen As New Pen(Color.RoyalBlue, 2)
        a_pen.DashStyle = Drawing.Drawing2D.DashStyle.DashDotDot

        ' Drawing a polygon
        g.DrawPolygon(a_pen, pts)
        g.Dispose()
    End Sub
```

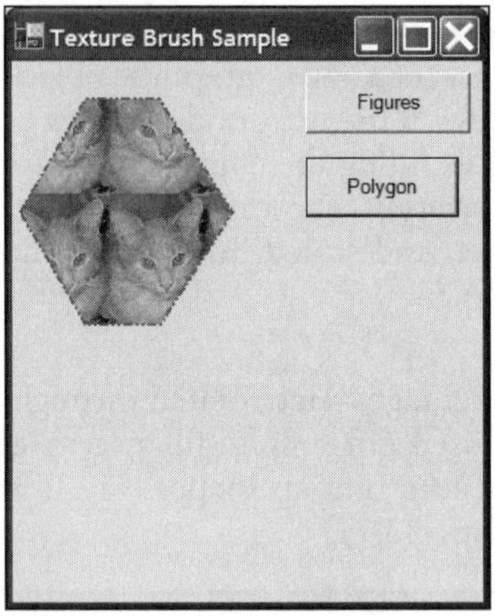

Fig. 3.3. Using texture brushes

The example just considered is too static. I suggest that we consider another way of using texture brushes. This time, we will draw various shapes on the form that will automatically be filled with the selected brush.

The main actions take place in the code for the MouseDown, MouseMove, and MouseUp events. Start by defining some global variables in a new project, TextureBrush2 (Listing 3.8).

Listing 3.8. Dynamic Shape Filling

```
'-------------------------------------
' TextureBrush2  © 2004 Alexander Klimov
'-------------------------------------

    Private AllPoints() As Point
    Private MaxPoint As Integer
    Private bDrawing As Boolean

    Private Sub Form1_MouseDown(ByVal sender As Object, ByVal e As _
System.Windows.Forms.MouseEventArgs) Handles MyBase.MouseDown
        bDrawing = True
        Dim g As Graphics = Me.CreateGraphics()
        g.Clear(Me.BackColor)

        MaxPoint = 0
        ReDim AllPoints(MaxPoint)
        AllPoints(MaxPoint).X = e.X
        AllPoints(MaxPoint).Y = e.Y
```

```
End Sub

    Private Sub Form1_MouseMove(ByVal sender As Object, ByVal e As _
System.Windows.Forms.MouseEventArgs) Handles MyBase.MouseMove
        If Not bDrawing Then Exit Sub
        MaxPoint += 1
        ReDim Preserve AllPoints(MaxPoint)
        AllPoints(MaxPoint).X = e.X
        AllPoints(MaxPoint).Y = e.Y

        Dim g As Graphics = Me.CreateGraphics()
        g.DrawLine(Pens.Black, _
            AllPoints(MaxPoint - 1), AllPoints(MaxPoint))
    End Sub

    Private Sub Form1_MouseUp(ByVal sender As Object, ByVal e As _
System.Windows.Forms.MouseEventArgs) Handles MyBase.MouseUp
        bDrawing = False
        If MaxPoint < 1 Then Exit Sub

        Dim g As Graphics = Me.CreateGraphics()
        Dim br As New TextureBrush(PictureBox1.Image)
        g.FillPolygon(br, AllPoints)
        g.DrawPolygon(Pens.Black, AllPoints)
        g.Dispose()
    End Sub
```

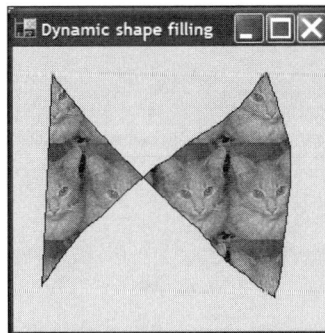

Fig. 3.4. Texture brush effects

Let's examine what this code does. When the user starts drawing, the left mouse button is pressed first, thereby triggering the MouseDown event. The handler for this event uses a bDrawing flag, which indicates that drawing has been enabled. The form is then cleared using the Clear method, and the mouse coordinates are placed in the AllPoints array.

Pressing and holding down the left mouse button, the user starts moving the mouse pointer. This is actually when the drawing is performed. Consequently, the MouseMove event needs to be handled. When the mouse pointer is being moved, its changing coordinates are written to the array and connected using the DrawLine method. All that is left to do now is fill the resulting shape with the selected texture brush, which is done by the MouseUp event handler when the mouse button is released. Launch the program, and draw any shape on the form. As soon as you finish drawing (release the left mouse button), the shape will fill with the texture brush, for which the texture is the image loaded in advance into the PictureBox graphics object (Fig. 3.4).

3.4. Rectangles

A single rectangle can be drawn using the DrawRectangle or FillRectangle methods. To draw a number of rectangles, the DrawRectangles or FillRectangles methods are more convenient. When methods with the Fill prefix are used, the specified rectangles are filled with a brush of a specified color. With other methods, the shape outline is drawn. The following project, named Figures, is a simple example of displaying blue squares diagonally (a square, after all, is also is a rectangle, in case you forgot) (Listing 3.9).

Listing 3.9. Drawing Rectangles

```
'---------------------------------------
' Figures   © 2004 Alexander Klimov
'---------------------------------------
    Private Sub Form1_Load(ByVal sender As Object, ByVal e As System.EventArgs) _
Handles MyBase.Load
        ClientSize = New Size(400, 400)
    End Sub

    Private Sub mnuDrawRectangles_Click(ByVal sender As System.Object, ByVal e As _
System.EventArgs) Handles mnuDrawRectangles.Click
        ' Outputting a series of squares diagonally
        Dim g As Graphics = CreateGraphics()
        Dim rs As Rectangle() = {New Rectangle(0, 0, 100, 100), _
                                 New Rectangle(100, 100, 100, 100), _
                                 New Rectangle(200, 200, 100, 100), _
                                 New Rectangle(300, 300, 100, 100)}
        g.FillRectangles(New SolidBrush(Color.Blue), rs)
        g.Dispose()
    End Sub
```

I specified the size of the client area of the form as 400×400 pixels on purpose, in order to have the squares fit exactly into the drawing area (Fig. 3.5).

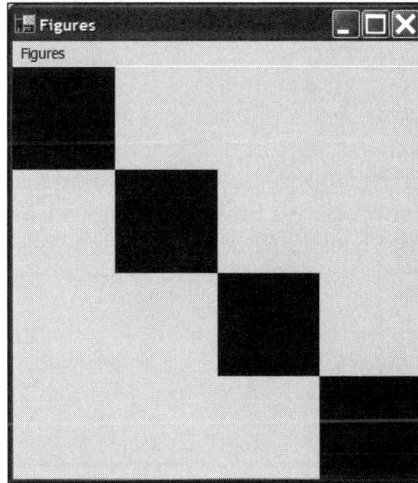

Fig. 3.5. Drawing squares

3.5. Ellipses

Now that you are acquainted with pens and brushes, you can start drawing other simple shapes. Ellipses are drawn with the help of the DrawEllipse and FillEllipse methods. There is no method in VB .NET 2003 for drawing a sequence of ellipses similar to the DrawRectangles method. But it is not that difficult to create this method yourself. The following example (Listing 3.10) shows how to do this by way of drawing several concentric ellipses (Fig. 3.6).

Listing 3.10. Drawing Ellipses

```
    Private Sub mnuEllipse_Click(ByVal sender As System.Object, ByVal e As _
System.EventArgs) Handles mnuEllipse.Click
        Dim g As Graphics = CreateGraphics()
        Dim p As New Pen(Color.Green)
        Dim i As Integer
        For i = 0 To 100 Step 5
            g.DrawEllipse(p, 10 + i, 10, 200 - 2 * i, 200)
        Next
        g.Dispose()
    End Sub
```

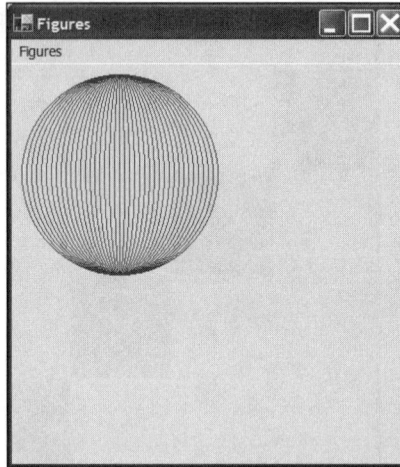

Fig.3.6. Drawing concentric ellipses

3.6. Sectors

If you like pies, then you already know what a sector is: It looks like a piece of pie. In fact, this is what sectors are called in graphics: pies. Accordingly, the `FillPie` method is used for drawing these. Perhaps you have seen the symbol that is used to warn that radioactive material is in vicinity (Fig. 3.7). Here is how a similar shape can be drawn (Listing 3.11).

Listing 3.11. Drawing Sectors

```
    Private Sub mnuPie_Click(ByVal sender As System.Object, ByVal e As _
System.EventArgs) Handles mnuPie.Click
        Dim g As Graphics = CreateGraphics()
        Dim sb As New SolidBrush(Color.Yellow)
        Dim i As Integer
        For i = 0 To 359 Step 120
            g.FillPie(sb, 30, 30, 110, 110, i, 60)
        Next
        g.Dispose()
    End Sub
```

Fig. 3.7. Drawing sectors

3.7. Arcs

Arcs are drawn using, sensibly enough, the `DrawArc` method. Calling the method twice, a moon can be drawn (Listing 3.12).

Listing 3.12. Drawing Arcs

```
   Private Sub mnuArc_Click(ByVal sender As System.Object, ByVal e As _
System.EventArgs) Handles mnuArc.Click
       Dim g As Graphics = CreateGraphics()
       g.DrawArc(New Pen(Color.Red), 100, 70, 300, 300, 90, -180)
       g.DrawArc(New Pen(Color.Red), 150, 70, 200, 300, 90, -180)
       g.Dispose()
   End Sub
```

3.8. Polygons

Polygons are defined by an array of points that are connected by straight lines, using the `DrawPolygon` method. The first point of the array is connected to the last automatically. The method, by itself, is neither interesting nor difficult. Therefore, we will consider how to create a polygon dynamically. For this, you will have to create an array holding ten points. The coordinates for the points can be changed by dragging the apexes with the mouse (Listing 3.13).

Listing 3.13. Creating a Polygon

```
'-------------------------------
' A dynamic polygon  © 2004 Alexander Klimov
'-------------------------------
Imports System.Math

    ' The variable enabling/disabling the moving status
    ' If it equals -1, moving is disabled
    Private CheckState As Integer = -1

    ' Declaring the array of points
    Private apts(9) As Point

    ' The size of the marks
    Private Const iSize As Integer = 6
    Private Const iCenter As Integer = iSize \ 2

    Private Sub Form1_Load(ByVal sender As System.Object, ByVal e As System.EventArgs) _
Handles MyBase.Load

        ' Specifying the polygon apexes
        apts(0).X = 80 : apts(0).Y = 20
        apts(1).X = 100 : apts(1).Y = 80
        apts(2).X = 160 : apts(2).Y = 80
        apts(3).X = 120 : apts(3).Y = 120
        apts(4).X = 140 : apts(4).Y = 180
        apts(5).X = 80 : apts(5).Y = 140
        apts(6).X = 20 : apts(6).Y = 180
        apts(7).X = 40 : apts(7).Y = 120
        apts(8).X = 5 : apts(8).Y = 80
        apts(9).X = 60 : apts(9).Y = 80
    End Sub

    Private Sub CreatePolygon(ByVal g As Graphics)
        ' Clearing the form from the previously-drawn lines
        g.Clear(BackColor)
        ' Drawing a polygon
        g.DrawPolygon(Pens.Red, apts)

        ' Drawing the markers for grabbing with the mouse
        Dim rectangles() As Rectangle
        ReDim rectangles(apts.GetUpperBound(0))
        For i As Integer = 0 To apts.GetUpperBound(0)
```

```
                ' Defining the size of the marks and their centers
            With rectangles(i)
                    .X = apts(i).X - iCenter
                    .Y = apts(i).Y - iCenter
                    .Width = iSize
                    .Height = iSize
            End With
        Next i

        ' Filling the marks with white color and outlining them in black
        g.FillRectangles(Brushes.White, rectangles)
        g.DrawRectangles(Pens.Black, rectangles)
    End Sub


    Private Sub Form1_Paint(ByVal sender As Object, ByVal e As _
System.Windows.Forms.PaintEventArgs) Handles MyBase.Paint
        CreatePolygon(e.Graphics)
    End Sub


    Private Sub Form1_MouseDown(ByVal sender As Object, ByVal e As _
System.Windows.Forms.MouseEventArgs) Handles MyBase.MouseDown
        Dim dx As Single
        Dim dy As Single

        For i As Integer = 0 To apts.GetUpperBound(0)
            If Abs(apts(i).X - e.X) < iCenter And _
               Abs(apts(i).Y - e.Y) < iCenter _
            Then
                ' Dragging the mark
                CheckState = i
                Exit For
            End If
        Next i
    End Sub


    Private Sub Form1_MouseMove(ByVal sender As Object, ByVal e As _
System.Windows.Forms.MouseEventArgs) Handles MyBase.MouseMove
        ' Doing nothing if there is no moving
        If CheckState = -1 Then Exit Sub

        ' Moving the apexes
        apts(CheckState).X = e.X
        apts(CheckState).Y = e.Y

        ' Redrawing
```

```
        CreatePolygon(Me.CreateGraphics())
    End Sub


    Private Sub Form1_MouseUp(ByVal sender As Object, ByVal e As _
System.Windows.Forms.MouseEventArgs) Handles MyBase.MouseUp
        CheckState = -1
    End Sub
```

Having launched the program, you will see a star-shaped polygon with white square marks at the apexes. Pointing the mouse to one of the marks, and then dragging it with the left mouse button moves the corresponding apex. So, we have created a simple polygon editor for ourselves (Fig. 3.8).

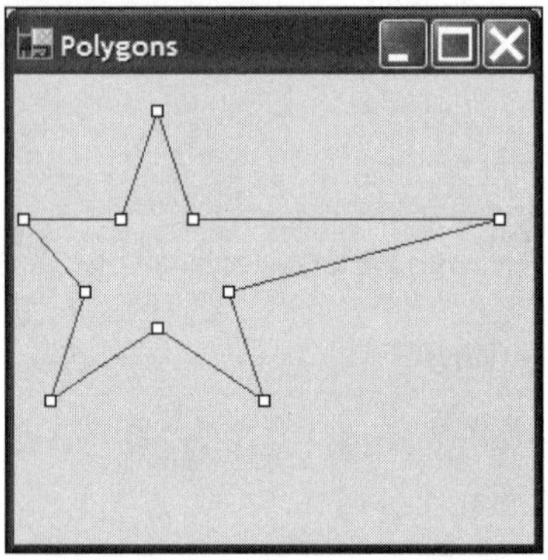

Fig. 3.8. Creating polygons

3.9. Bezier Curves

Bezier curves are created on the basis of four control points. They were invented by a French engineer, Pierre Bezier, for the automobile industry. Today, Bezier curves are used in a broad range of other scientific and industrial processes. Our interest in them, however, is strictly esthetic. Drawing Bezier curves is an interesting activity. The behavior of Bezier curves can be described in the following way: A curve starts at the first specified point and ends at the fourth. The two intermediate points act as magnets of a sort. The curve first tries to approach the first intermediate point and, without reaching it, moves on to the second intermediate point, moving away from it before ending at the last point. It is interesting to observe the behavior of such curves in an interactive mode. Let's create a Beziers project, in which we will specify four arbitrary control points, based on which the curve will be drawn automatically (Listing 3.14).

Listing 3.14. Drawing a Bezier Curve Based on Specific Points

```
'------------------------------------
' Beziers © 2004 Alexander Klimov
'------------------------------------
    ' A Bezier curve needs four control points
    Private m_Points(3) As Point
    Private LimitPoints As Integer = -1


    Private Sub Form1_MouseDown(ByVal sender As Object, ByVal e As _
System.Windows.Forms.MouseEventArgs) Handles MyBase.MouseDown
        Dim g As Graphics = CreateGraphics()

        If LimitPoints = 3 Then
            g.Clear(Me.BackColor)
            LimitPoints = 0
        Else
            LimitPoints += 1
        End If


        m_Points(LimitPoints).X = e.X
        m_Points(LimitPoints).Y = e.Y


        ' Drawing four dots
        For i As Integer = 0 To LimitPoints
            Dim rect As New Rectangle( _
                m_Points(i).X - 5, m_Points(i).Y - 5, 10, 10)
            g.FillEllipse(Brushes.Blue, rect)
        Next i

        If LimitPoints = 3 Then
            ' Drawing a Bezier curve
            g.DrawBezier(Pens.Red, _
                m_Points(0), m_Points(1), _
                m_Points(2), m_Points(3))
        End If

        g.Dispose()


    End Sub
```

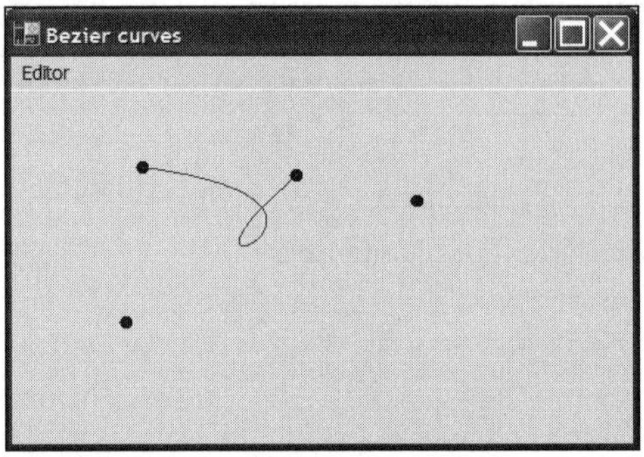

Fig. 3.9. Drawing a Bezier curve based on the specified points

Launch the program, and click four times on different places on the form. After the fourth click a Bezier curve will appear, drawn according to the specified control points. To make the process more visual, the control points in the example are depicted as blue dots (Fig. 3.9).

The example turned out to be an interesting one, but I was still not totally satisfied with it. I wanted to move the control points, thus changing the shape of the curve dynamically. So I decided to write a simple Bezier curve editor. The editing involves the following. A Bezier curve is output to the form. Clicking the left mouse button positions the mouse pointer at the starting point of the curve. Now, holding the left mouse button down, you can move the starting point to any place on the form. Clicking the right mouse button positions the mouse pointer at the end point of the curve. It can be moved around the form in the same way as the starting point. As the points are dragged, the appearance of the Bezier curve changes. The source code for this project is shown in Listing 3.15.

Listing 3.15. A Bezier Curve Editor

```
Dim startpoint As New Point(100, 100)
Dim control1 As New Point(200, 10)
Dim control2 As New Point(350, 20)
Dim endpoint As New Point(400, 100)

Private Sub Form1_MouseDown(ByVal sender As Object, _
        ByVal e As System.Windows.Forms.MouseEventArgs) _
        Handles MyBase.MouseDown

        ' When the left mouse button is depressed
        If e.Button = MouseButtons.Left Then
            Cursor.Position = PointToScreen(startpoint)
        ' When the right mouse button is depressed
        ElseIf e.Button = MouseButtons.Right Then
```

```
                Cursor.Position = PointToScreen(endpoint)
            End If
    End Sub


    Private Sub mnuEditBezier_Click(ByVal sender As System.Object, ByVal e As _
System.EventArgs) Handles mnuEditBezier.Click
        Dim g As Graphics = CreateGraphics()
        g.Clear(Me.BackColor)
        g.DrawBezier(Pens.Red, startpoint, control1, control2, endpoint)
    End Sub

    Private Sub Form1_MouseMove(ByVal sender As Object, _
        ByVal e As System.Windows.Forms.MouseEventArgs) _
        Handles MyBase.MouseMove

          If e.Button = MouseButtons.Left Then
             startpoint = New Point(e.X, e.Y)
             Invalidate()
          ElseIf e.Button = MouseButtons.Right Then
             endpoint = New Point(e.X, e.Y)
             Invalidate()
          End If
      End Sub


    Private Sub Form1_Paint(ByVal sender As Object, _
        ByVal e As System.Windows.Forms.PaintEventArgs) _
        Handles MyBase.Paint

        Dim g As Graphics = e.Graphics
        g.DrawBezier(_
            Pens.Red, startpoint, control1, control2, endpoint)
      End Sub
```

3.10. Suggestions and Recommendations

Try to expand on the capabilities of the Bezier curve editor described in *Section 3.9* to control the Bezier curve by not only using the end points, but also by using the two middle control points.

Chapter 4: Curves

Drawing curves is a very captivating pastime. The shapes formed by curves cast a hypnotizing spell on the observer. Some curve types have even been given their own names. Many prominent scientists have made the subject of curves their main topic of focus. Curves can be simple and compound. Let's consider them more closely. First of all, you already know that the VB .NET drawing functions are delivered via the methods of the `Graphics` class. As a rule, the names of these methods begin with the `Draw` or `Fill` prefixes. It is necessary to use `Pen` and `Brush` objects in these methods. The former are responsible for drawing lines, while the latter are used to fill shapes with color.

In addition to the basic methods, the trigonometric methods of the `Math` class are used for drawing curves. Those programmers who have switched from VB 6 should make particular note of this class. All of the trigonometric functions that existed in Visual Basic are now contained in this class. You should also remember that all calculations are performed in radians, not degrees. Moreover, the `Math` class already has a built-in constant `PI`. So, now, it is no longer necessary to declare this constant by yourself:

```
Const Pi = 3.14
```

You can simply use the constant like this in any expression:

```
Math.PI
```

Let's move on to some practical examples.

4.1. The *DrawLines* Method

Curves are often drawn using the `DrawLines` method. This method draws curves by first creating many short segments, which are then joined into a curve according to a specified formula. One of the overloaded `DrawLines` methods of the `Graphics` class appears as follows:

```
Sub DrawLines(ByVal pn As Pen, ByVal aptf as PointF( ))
```

The first parameter specifies which pen to use; the second parameter contains a floating-point array holding the coordinates. Note that this method can handle hundreds of thousands of coordinates. The more `PointF` structures are passed to the method, the smoother the curve will be. The method is very efficient and takes only fractions of a second to draw as many as a million short lines.

4.1.1. Sine Curves

Many will still remember the formula for drawing a sine curve you were taught in your high school trigonometry courses. For those who don't, here it is:

```
y = Sin(x)
```

An example of drawing sine curves in VB .NET is carried out in a `Curves` project (Listing 4.1).

Listing 4.1. Drawing a Sine Curve

```
'-------------------------------------
' Curves  © 2004 Alexander Klimov
'-------------------------------------
    Private Sub butSinusoid_Click(ByVal sender As System.Object, ByVal e As _
System.EventArgs) Handles butSinusoid.Click
        Dim g As Graphics = CreateGraphics()

        Dim cx As Integer
        Dim cy As Integer
        cx = MyBase.Width
        cy = MyBase.ClientSize.Height / 2

        Dim ptf(cx - 1) As PointF
        Dim cW As Integer

        ' The number of waves
        cW = txtWaves.Text

        ' Clearing the form
```

```
g.Clear(Me.BackColor)

Dim i As Integer
For i = 0 To cx - 1
    ptf(i).X = i
    ptf(i).Y = CSng(_
        (cy / 2) * (1 - Math.Sin(i * cW * Math.PI / (cx - 1))))
Next i
g.DrawLines(Pens.Red, ptf)
g.Dispose()
End Sub
```

Let's examine what this code does. In the first line, a `Graphics` object is created to draw curves:

```
Dim g As Graphics = CreateGraphics()
```

Then two variables — `cx` and `cy` — are created to hold the range of the allowed values. I picked these values by means of trial and error, in order to be sure that the sine curve will not leave the form boundaries. The `ptf` variable holds the array of point coordinates. For added convenience, I placed a text field, in which the number of the waves the sine curve is to have, is specified on the form:

```
cW = txtWaves.Text    ' The number of the waves
```

Now the loop is launched. The main work to display the sine curve on the screen is done by the following line of code:

```
ptf(i).Y = CSng((cy / 2) * (1 - Math.Sin(i * cW * Math.PI / (cx - 1))))
```

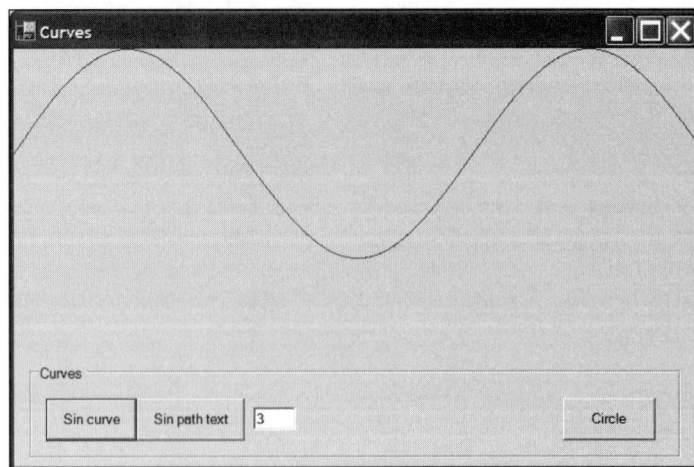

Fig. 4.1. Drawing a sine curve

At first glance, this code line seems to have nothing in common with the sine curve formula. But, in fact, all of the additional variables used in this code line either shift or flatten the sine curve that is drawn. You can experiment with different values for these variables. Depending on the values you enter, the height of the sine curve waves, their number, and location on the screen will change (Fig. 4.1).

4.1.2. Writing along a Sine Path

Having learned to draw a sine curve on the screen might provide you with some entertainment, but there are few practical applications. So why draw it? The answer is that sine curves are used extensively in the creation of various animation effects. Take a good look, for example, at a fluttering flag. Looking closely at the flag's edges, you will discover that they are shaped like a sine curve. Moreover, lines are not the only things that can be drawn along a sine curve's path. Other objects, including texts, can be used to follow the trail. Indeed, if the DrawString method uses the coordinates of a character in its parameters, why not take advantage of this capability? Place a button on the form in the previous example (Listing 4.1); name it butSinText. Modifying the example a little, we obtain the following code (Listing 4.2).

Listing 4.2. Writing along a Sine Curve Path

```
    Private Sub butSinText_Click(ByVal sender As System.Object, ByVal e As _
System.EventArgs) Handles butSinText.Click
        ' The procedure for writing along a sine curve path
    Dim g As Graphics = CreateGraphics()
        Dim cx As Integer
        Dim cy As Integer
        cx = MyBase.Width
        cy = MyBase.ClientSize.Height / 2

        Dim ptf(cx - 1) As PointF
        ' The number of waves
        Dim cW As Integer
        cW = txtWaves.Text

        ' Clearing the form
        g.Clear(Me.BackColor)

        Dim i As Integer
        For i = 0 To cx - 1 Step 10
            Dim br As New SolidBrush(Color.RoyalBlue)
```

```
      Dim title As String = _
         "Entertaining programming. The text is placed along the sine curve path."
      Dim ch As Char

      If i >= (title.Length) * 10 Then
          ch = " "
      Else
          ch = title.Chars(i / 10)
      End If

      ptf(i).X = i
      ptf(i).Y = CSng(_
          (cy / 2) * (1 - Math.Sin(i * cW * Math.PI / (cx - 1))))
      g.DrawString(ch, Me.Font, br, ptf(i))
    Next i

    g.Dispose()
End Sub
```

First of all, the step in the loop was changed as follows:

```
For i = 0 To cx - 1 Step 10
```

If this is not done, the text characters will simply overlap. Next, a variable to hold the text to be placed along the sine curve path was created:

```
Dim title As String = "Entertaining programming. The text is placed _
along the sine curve path."
```

Now the text has to be conditioned a little. First, we declare a new ch variable to hold individual text characters. Then we need to make sure that the counter does not exceed the allowable limits. If it does exceed the range of allowable values that is determined by the length of the text, a simple space will be displayed.

```
Dim ch As Char

        If i >= (title.Length) * 10 Then
            ch = " "
        Else
            ch = title.Chars(i / 10)
        End If
```

Instead of calling the DrawLines method, the DrawString method is called, to whose first parameter all of the characters of the text being displayed are passed.

```
g.DrawString(ch, Me.Font, br, aptf(i))
```

The results can be seen in Fig. 4.2.

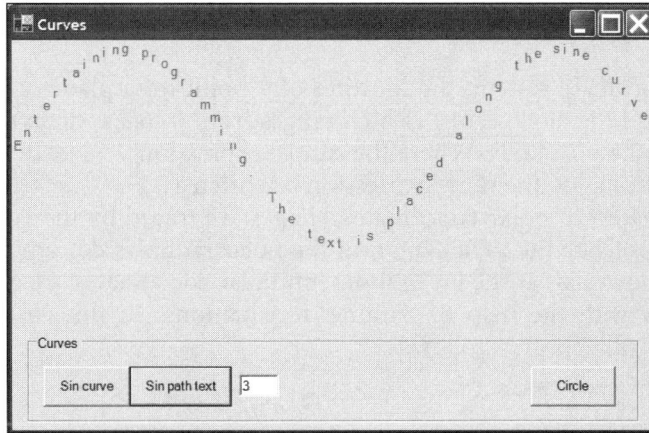

Fig. 4.2. Writing along a sine curve path

4.2. Curvilinear Coordinates

The examples sited above are too simple because they are based on the relatively primitive sine curve formula. But there are more complex curves, which are much more difficult to build using conventional formulas. For example, the following is the formula for a circle:

```
x2 + y2 = r2
```

If you try to display a graph for this function, you will run into a whole bunch of problems. First of all, you will have to extract the square root. Second, you need to keep an eye on the x variable in order not to move outside of the range of allowable values. Finally, the function itself is very nonlinear. Where the values for x are close to 0, the circle's points are located close to each other. As the values for x increase, the changes increase sharply, creating gaps in the circle displayed.

Here is where other coordinate systems come to the rescue. In addition to the orthogonal Cartesian coordinates with which we are all familiar, there are other ways in mathematics to specify a point's location on a plane. The most common of these are the *polar*, *cylindrical*, and *spherical* coordinate systems. All of these coordinate systems are related. They have a central point called the *pole*, from which spread out concentric circles (the polar coordinate system), cylinders (the cylindrical coordinate system), or spheres (the spherical coordinate system). A point's location is determined with the help of a ray radiating from the pole and intersecting with the corresponding circle, cylinder, or sphere at the specified point.

These coordinate systems are ideal for displaying shapes constructed around a single central point. Shapes formed in curvilinear coordinate systems are described with quite simple and succinct mathematical expressions and possess unique esthetic qualities. They are associated with the shapes we see around us in nature: flowers, butterflies, seashells, etc.

4.2.1. Polar Coordinates

In the polar coordinate system, the location of a point on a plane is determined by the polar radius R and the angle theta (which ranges from 0 to 2 radians), that the polar radius forms with the polar axis. Where the simple expression y = kx defines a straight line in Cartesian coordinates, the same expression rewritten as R = k * theta defines a spiral in polar coordinates. In polar coordinates, shapes are traced by the end of the revolving variable-length polar radius. The length of the polar radius is determined by the angle it forms with the polar axis at the given moment. Polar coordinates are converted to Cartesian coordinates with the help of parametric equations. In this case, the formula for drawing a circle will appear as follows:

```
X(theta) = R * Cos (theta)
Y(theta) = R * Sin(theta),
```

where theta is the angle ranging from 0 to 2 radians, and R is the radius of the circle. By setting the R variable to different values, we can obtain oblate or oblong ellipsoids. Consequently, curve formulas are much easier to calculate in the polar coordinate system than using Cartesian coordinates. But let's move on to the practical work. Listing 4.3 contains the code for drawing a circle.

Listing 4.3. Drawing a Circle

```
    Private Sub butCircle_Click(ByVal sender As System.Object, ByVal e As _
System.EventArgs) Handles butCircle.Click
        ' Drawing a circle
        Dim g As Graphics = CreateGraphics()
        Dim cx, cy As Integer
        cx = Me.ClientSize.Width / 3
        cy = Me.ClientSize.Width / 3
        Dim iNumPoints As Integer = 10000
        Dim ptf(iNumPoints) As PointF
        Dim i As Integer
        Dim redPen As New Pen(Color.Red)

        ' Clearing the form
        g.Clear(Me.BackColor)

        ' Moving the coordinate system
        g.TranslateTransform(200, 150)

        For i = 0 To iNumPoints
            Dim theta As Double = i * 2 * Math.PI / iNumPoints
            ptf(i).X = CSng((cx) / 2 * (Math.Cos(theta)))
```

```
        ptf(i).Y = CSng((cy) / 2 * (Math.Sin(theta)))
    Next i
    g.DrawLines(redPen, ptf)
    g.Dispose()
End Sub
```

In the example, I set the `iNumPoints` variable to 10,000. I believe that 10,000 points are more than enough to draw a circle on the screen. Some readers may ask why I would bother to draw a circle this way, given that there is already the built-in `DrawEllipse` method? In fact, there is a slight difference between these two methods. The `DrawEllipse` method draws a circle at once, while our method draws multiple short lines at the specified coordinates and then connects them into a circle. In Section 4.1.2, I already demonstrated how to place text along a line. The same approach can be used to display text along a circle path. But, most importantly, there are some curves for drawing, for which Visual Basic .NET 2003 has no readymade methods. These curves are what we will consider next.

4.2.2. A Four-Leaf Clover

Polar coordinates can be used to draw very complex and beautiful shapes, such a four-leaf clover, for example. The formula for drawing it is the following: `R = Cos (s*theta)`, with the `theta` angle ranging from 0 to 2 radian (from 0 to 360 degrees). Modifying the circle-drawing example produces the `Curves2` project (Listing 4.4).

Listing 4.4. Drawing a Four-Leaf Clover

```
'---------------------------------------
' Curves2  © 2004 Alexander Klimov
'---------------------------------------
    Private Sub butClover_Click(ByVal sender As System.Object, _
            ByVal e As System.EventArgs) Handles butClover.Click
        Dim g As Graphics = CreateGraphics()
        Dim cx, cy As Integer
        cx = Me.ClientSize.Width / 3
        cy = Me.ClientSize.Width / 3
        Dim iNumPoints As Integer = 2 * (cx + cy)
        Dim aptf(iNumPoints) As PointF

        g.Clear(BackColor)

        Dim i As Integer
        For i = 0 To iNumPoints
```

```
        Dim theta As Double = i * 2 * Math.PI / iNumPoints
        Dim r As Double = Math.Cos(2 * theta)
        aptf(i).X = CSng(_
          (cx - 1) / 2 * (1 + Math.Cos(theta) * Math.Cos _
          txtTheta.Text * theta)))
        aptf(i).Y = CSng(_
          (cy - 1) / 2 * (1 + Math.Sin(_
          theta) * Math.Cos(txtTheta.Text * theta)))
    Next i
    g.DrawLines(Pens.Red, aptf)
    g.Dispose()
End Sub
```

In the example, the value of the theta angle was preset at 2 by setting the Text property of the txtTheta text box to 2. Experiment a little with this value. You will watch as the program draws beautiful flowers (Fig. 4.3).

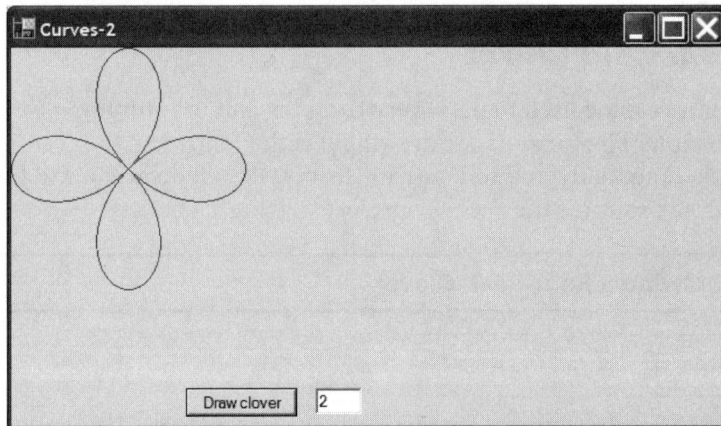

Fig. 4.3. Drawing a four-leaf clover

4.3. The Curve Family

For many years, scientists have collected information about formulas for drawing various shapes. Many shapes have been given their own names. The list of named curves is quite impressive and includes the following:

- Astroid
- Cardioid
- Deltoid
- Pascal's Limacon

- ❐ Archimedes' Spiral
- ❐ Logarithmic Spiral
- ❐ Cochleoid

- ❐ Strophoid
- ❐ Nephroid

Before starting to draw various curves, you need to create a project template. This will make it easier for you to examine the resulting curves. The curve-drawing project is named `DrawCurves`. Create a new project and add to it a new module, named `Transformation.vb`. This will be used to move the co-ordinate's origin to the center of the form (Listing 4.5). It is much more convenient to have it located here than in the upper left corner of the form.

Listing 4.5. Module Transformation.vb

```vb
'-----                 --------------------
' DrawCurves   © 2004 Alexander Klimov
'---------------------------------------
Imports System.Drawing.Drawing2D
Module Transformation

    ' The procedure to convert
    ' world coordinates wxmin, wymin, wxmax, and wymax
    ' into the device coordinates dxmin, dymin, dxmax, dymax

    Public Sub MapGraphicsWindow(ByVal g As Graphics, _
            ByVal wxmin As Single, ByVal wymin As Single, _
            ByVal wxmax As Single, ByVal wymax As Single, _
            ByVal dxmin As Single, ByVal dymin As Single, _
            ByVal dxmax As Single, ByVal dymax As Single)

        ' Returning to the initial state
        g.ResetTransform()

        ' Converting the world coordinates of the center
        g.TranslateTransform(-(wxmax + wxmin) / 2, _
                            -(wymax + wymin) / 2, _
                            MatrixOrder.Append)

        ' Scaling
        Dim sx As Single
        sx = CSng((dxmax - dxmin) / (wxmax - wxmin))
        Dim sy As Single
        sy = CSng((dymax - dymin) / (wymax - wymin))
```

```
        g.ScaleTransform(sx, sy, MatrixOrder.Append)

        ' Moving to the form's center
      g.TranslateTransform((dxmax + dxmin) / 2, _
                           (dymax + dymin) / 2, _
                           MatrixOrder.Append)
    End Sub
End Module
```

4.3.1. Proving Ground for the Experiments

After creating the module, return to the main form. Because there are many curves, I will describe only the most popular. Drawing will be carried out using menus. There is also an option for drawing the coordinate grid. The main template for the form appears as shown in Listing 4.6.

Listing 4.6. The Template for Drawing Curves

```
'-------------------------------------
' Drawing curves  © 2004 Alexander Klimov
'-------------------------------------
Imports System.Math

    Private Sub DrawAxes(ByVal g As Graphics)
        ' Drawing the coordinate axes
        Dim x As Double
        Dim y As Double

        ' Creating a black pen for drawing the coordinate axes
        Dim p_axes As New Pen(Color.Black, 0)

        g.DrawLine(p_axes, -2, 0, 2, 0)
        ' The X-axis scale
        For x = -2 To 2 Step 0.5
            g.DrawLine(p_axes, CSng(x), CSng(-0.1), CSng(x), CSng(0.1))
        Next x

    ' The Y-axis scale
    g.DrawLine(p_axes, 0, -2, 0, 2)
        For y = -2 To 2 Step 0.5
            g.DrawLine(p_axes, CSng(-0.1), CSng(y), CSng(0.1), CSng(y))
        Next y
```

```
    End Sub

    Private Sub mnuAxes_Click(ByVal sender As System.Object, ByVal e As _
System.EventArgs) Handles mnuAxes.Click
        ' The state of the check box
        mnuAxes.Checked = Not mnuAxes.Checked
    End Sub
```

4.3.2. A Multi-Leaf Clover

The template is now ready and you can move on to drawing curves. All you need to do for is to add a new menu item and write the procedure for drawing the curve. Let's start with drawing the already familiar four-leaf clover. Its formula is as follows:

```
R = Cos (2*theta)
```

The four-leaf is created using a separate procedure, which is called via the `Click` event of the `mnuFourLeaf` menu item (Listing 4.7).

Listing 4.7. Drawing a Multi-Leaf Clover

```
Private Sub DrawFourLeaf(ByVal g As Graphics)
    ' Drawing the multi-leaf clover
    Dim x As Double
    Dim y As Double
    Dim old_x As Double
    Dim old_y As Double
    Dim r As Double
    Dim t As Double
    Dim dt As Double
    Dim iFromTxt As Integer = CInt(txtSettings.Text)

    ' Drawing a curve
    t = 0
    dt = PI / 100
    old_x = 0
    old_y = 0
    Dim p_curve As New Pen(Color.Blue, 0)
    Do While t <= 2 * PI
        ' The formula for a four-leaf is: r = CSng(1 * Cos(2 * t))
        r = CSng(1 * Cos(iFromTxt * t))
        x = r * Cos(t)
```

```
        y = r * Sin(t)
        g.DrawLine(p_curve, CSng(old_x), CSng(old_y), _
                   CSng(x), CSng(y))
        old_x = x
        old_y = y
        t = t + dt
    Loop

End Sub


    Private Sub mnuFourLeaf_Click(ByVal sender As System.Object, ByVal e As _
System.EventArgs) Handles mnuFourLeaf.Click

        Dim g As Graphics = CreateGraphics()

        MapGraphicsWindow(g, _
                -2, -2, 2, 2, _
                0, ClientSize.Height - 1, _
                ClientSize.Width - 1, 0)

        ' Drawing the four-leaf clover
        g.Clear(BackColor)
        If mnuAxes.Checked = True Then
            DrawAxes(g)
        End If

        DrawFourLeaf(g)

        g.Dispose()
    End Sub
```

Actually, this code is not just useful for drawing four leaves, but can also be used to draw three, five, 25 — whatever you wish. For this reason, instead of using a constant in the curve formula, I used an iFromTxt variable, the value for which is set as the value of the Text property of the txtSettings text box, converted into an integer. The code for this is as follows:

```
Dim iFromTxt As Integer = CInt(txtSettings.Text)
```

The default value for the Text property is set to 2 in the property editor, which results in the drawing of a four-leaf clover. Try to set this variable to different values when running the program. You will see a whole bunch of different flowers (Fig. 4.4).

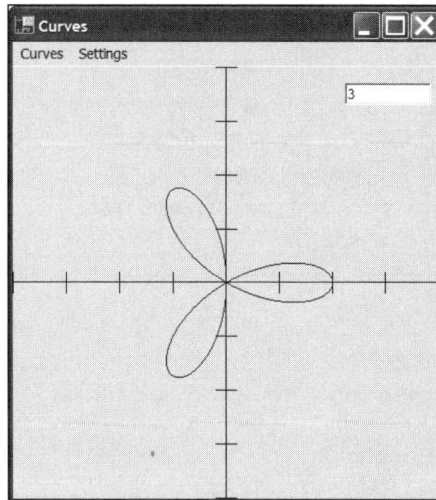

Fig. 4.4. The flower obtained by setting *txtSetting.Text = 3*

4.3.3. The Pirouetting Circle

Now let's take a circle and place it inside another circle. All of the curves traced by a point on a circle rolling inside another fixed circle belong to the hypocycloid family (from the Greek *hypo* — under, below and *kykloeides* — circular). What path do you think a point on one circle rolling inside another, fixed, circle will trace? Strange as it may sound, it might even be a straight line! This occurs when the radius of the inside circle is half that of the external circle. The first person to discover and describe this phenomenon was Nicolaus Copernicus. When the radius of the internal circle is one-third of the radius of the external circle, the curve traced is called the *Steiner Curve* or *deltoid*.

4.3.3.1. The Deltoid

The deltoid formula (Fig. 4.5) is the following:

```
x = 2 * a * cos(theta) + a * cos(2 * theta)
y = 2 * a * sin(theta) - a * sin(2 * theta)
```

The code for drawing a deltoid is provided in Listing 4.8. The variable a is the radius of the inside circle, which is one-third of the radius of the circle inside, of which it is rolling.

Listing 4.8. Drawing a Deltoid

```
Private Sub DrawDeltoid(ByVal g As Graphics)
    ' Drawing a deltoid
    Dim x As Double
```

```vb
        Dim y As Double
        Dim old_x As Double
        Dim old_y As Double
        Dim r As Double
        Dim t As Double
        Dim dt As Double
        Dim iFromTxt As Integer = CInt(txtSettings.Text)

        t = 0
        dt = PI / 100
        old_x = 0
        old_y = 0
        Dim p_curve As New Pen(Color.Blue, 0)
        Do While t <= 2 * PI
            ' The deltoid formula
            ' x = 2 a cos(theta) + a cos(2 theta)
            ' y = 2 a sin(theta) - a sin(2 theta)
            x = 1 * Cos(t) + 0.5 * Cos(2 * t)
            y = 1 * Sin(t) - 0.5 * Sin(2 * t)
            g.DrawLine(p_curve, CSng(old_x), CSng(old_y) _
                    CSng(x), CSng(y))
            old_x = x
            old_y = y
            t = t + dt
        Loop
    End Sub


    Private Sub mnuDeltoid_Click(ByVal sender As System.Object, ByVal e As _
System.EventArgs) Handles mnuDeltoid.Click
        Dim g As Graphics = CreateGraphics()

        MapGraphicsWindow(g, _
                -2, -2, 2, 2, _
                0, ClientSize.Height - 1, _
                ClientSize.Width - 1, 0)
        g.Clear(BackColor)
        If mnuAxes.Checked = True Then
            DrawAxes(g)
        End If

        DrawDeltoid(g)
        g.Dispose()
    End Sub
```

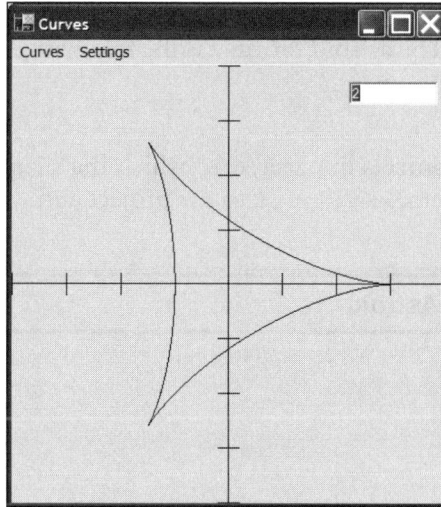

Fig. 4.5. Drawing a deltoid

4.3.3.2. The Astroid

Making the radius of the internal circle one-fourth of the radius of the external circle produces the astroid (Fig. 4.6). The curve's name originates from the word *astron*, which

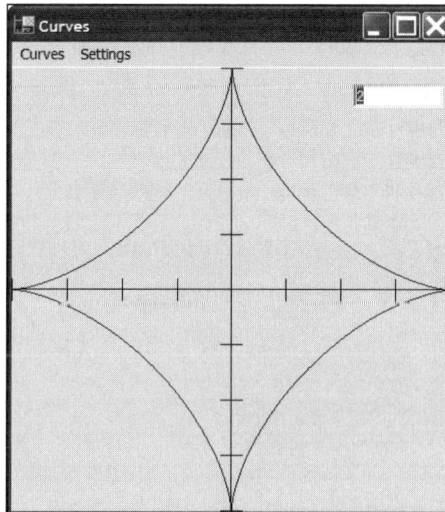

Fig. 4.6. Drawing an astroid

is Greek for a star. This curve has the appearance of a stylized star. Now you know how astronomy got its name. The astroid formula is the following:

```
x = a* cos(t)^3
y = a* sin(t)^3
```

where the a coefficient controls the degree, to which the shape is oblong. To draw an astroid, add a new menu item, mnuAstroid, to the project and write the corresponding code (Listing 4.9).

Listing 4.9. Drawing an Astroid

```
Private Sub DrawAstroid(ByVal g As Graphics)
    ' Drawing an astroid
    Dim x As Double
    Dim y As Double
    Dim old_x As Double
    Dim old_y As Double
    Dim r As Double
    Dim t As Double
    Dim dt As Double
    Dim iFromTxt As Integer = CInt(txtSettings.Text)

    t = 0
    dt = PI / 100
    old_x = 0
    old_y = 0
    Dim p_curve As New Pen(Color.Blue, 0)
    Do While t <= 2 * PI
        ' The astroid formula
        ' x = a cos(theta)^3
        ' y = a sin(theta)^3
        x = iFromTxt * Cos(t) ^ 3
        y = iFromTxt * Sin(t) ^ 3
        g.DrawLine(p_curve, CSng(old_x), CSng(old_y), _
                CSng(x), CSng(y))
        old_x = x
        old_y = y
        t = t + dt
    Loop

End Sub

    Private Sub mnuAstroid_Click(ByVal sender As System.Object, ByVal e As _
System.EventArgs) Handles mnuAstroid.Click
```

```
    Dim g As Graphics = CreateGraphics()

    MapGraphicsWindow(g, _
            -2, -2, 2, 2, _
            0, ClientSize.Height - 1, _
            ClientSize.Width - 1, 0)
    g.Clear(BackColor)
    If mnuAxes.Checked = True Then
        DrawAxes(g)
    End If

    DrawAstroid(g)
    g.Dispose()
End Sub
```

4.3.4. Epicycloids

Let's consider another case where a circle rolls around another circle, only this time it is rolling around the outside. All curves traced in this way belong to the *epicycloid* family (from the Greek *epi* — on, at). Two of the members of this family are the cardioid and Pascal's limacon.

4.3.4.1. The Cardioid

If the radius of the circle rolled around another circle is the same as the radius of the fixed circle, the curve traced by a point on the circumference of the moving circle is somewhat similar in shape to that of the heart (Fig. 4.7). Accordingly, this curve is called cardioid (from the Greek *kardia* - heart). The cardioid formula is the following:

```
r = 2a(1 + cos(theta))
```

The variable a is the radius of the two circles. In our example, the circle radius is set to 0.5 conventional units. Therefore, in the code editor, the formula will appear as follows:

```
r = CSng(1 * (1 + Cos(t)))
```

All that is left to do now is to add a new menu item and write the procedures, DrawCardioid and mnuCardioid.click for drawing the curve (Listing 4.10).

Listing 4.10. Drawing a Cardioid

```
Private Sub DrawCardioid(ByVal g As Graphics)
    ' Drawing a cardioid
    Dim x As Double
    Dim y As Double
    Dim old_x As Double
```

```vb
        Dim old_y As Double
        Dim r As Double
        Dim t As Double
        Dim dt As Double

        t = 0
        dt = PI / 100
        old_x = 0
        old_y = 0
        Dim p_curve As New Pen(Color.Black, 0)
        Do While t <= 2 * PI
            ' Cardioid r = 2a(1 + cos(theta)),
            ' where a is the radius of the two circles.
            r = CSng(1 * (1 + Cos(t)))
            x = r * Cos(t)
            y = r * Sin(t)
            g.DrawLine(p_curve, CSng(old_x), CSng(old_y), _
                    CSng(x), CSng(y))
            old_x = x
            old_y = y
            t = t + dt
        Loop

    End Sub


    Private Sub mnuCardioid_Click(ByVal sender As System.Object, ByVal e As _
System.EventArgs) Handles mnuCardioid.Click
        Dim g As Graphics = CreateGraphics()

        MapGraphicsWindow(g, _
                -2, -2, 2, 2, _
                0, ClientSize.Height - 1, _
                ClientSize.Width - 1, 0)
        g.Clear(BackColor)
        If mnuAxes.Checked = True Then
            DrawAxes(g)
        End If

        DrawCardioid(g)

        g.Dispose()
    End Sub
```

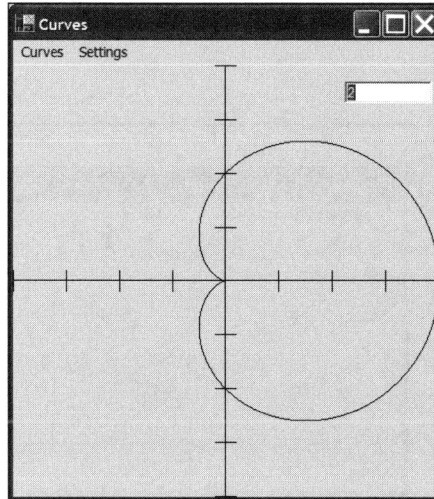

Fig. 4.7. Drawing a cardioid

4.3.4.2. Pascal's Limacon

What happens if the tracing point is located not on the circumference of the rolling circle, but inside it? Then we obtain a curve called Pascal's Limacon (Fig. 4.8). This curve was discovered by and named after Etienne Pascal, the father of the famous French scientist Blaise Pascal. The formula for drawing Pascal's limacon is the following:

```
r = b + 2a cos(theta)
```

The cardioid curve is a special case of the limacon. This can be ascertained easily by setting b = 2a. Because drawing this shape is not that different from drawing the previous ones, I will provide only a fragment of the code for doing this (Listing 4.11). The full listing can be found on the accompanying CD-ROM.

Listing 4.11. Drawing Pascal's Limacon

```
Do While t <= 2 ^ PI
    ' The limacon formula
'r = b + 2a cos(theta)
    r = CSng(0.3 + 1 * (Cos(t)))
    x = r * Cos(t)
    y = r * Sin(t)
    gr.DrawLine(p_curve, CSng(old_x), CSng(old_y) _
            CSng(x), CSng(y))
```

```
       old_x = x
       old_y = y
       t = t + dt
   Loop
```

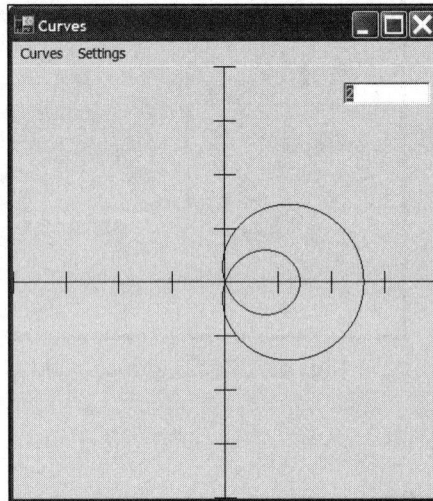

Fig. 4.8. Drawing Pascal's limacon

4.3.4.3. Other Curves

There are a couple of other curves worth mentioning. I recommend that you check them all out in the DrawCurves project on the accompanying CD-ROM.

❒ The *nephroid* is a curve traced by a point on the circumference of a circle rolling outside another circle that is twice its diameter. The nephroid formula is the following:

```
x = a (3 cos(theta) - cos(3 theta))
y = a (3 sin(theta) - sin(3 theta))
```

❒ The *lemniscate* is a curve similar in shape to the symbol for infinity. The lemniscate formula is as follows:

```
r^2 = a^2 cos(2 theta)
```

4.3.5. Archimedes' Spiral

We often see helical shapes around us in our everyday life. If you like taking bath, you have probably noticed that the water forms a vortex, a kind of a spiral, when draining from the bathtub. The preeminent Greek mathematician and inventor Archimedes studied spirals. As you probably know, it was in the bathtub where he exclaimed his famous "Eureka!" (albeit in relation to a matter other than spirals).

Imagine an ant crawling along the second hand of a clock at a constant speed. The path it traces is Archimedes' spiral. The shape was named after Archimedes because he used its properties to study the problem of angle trisection. The formula for Archimedes' spiral in polar coordinates is the following:

```
r = k*theta
```

Using the trifolium example (see project Curves2, Listing 4.4), modify the code a little to draw a spiral in the Spiral project (Listing 4.12):

```
aptf(i).X = CSng((cx) / 10 * (8 + Math.Cos(theta) * 0.09 * theta))
aptf(i).Y = CSng((cy) / 10 * (8 + Math.Sin(theta) * 0.09 * theta))
```

Listing 4.12. Spiral of Archimedes

```
'--------------------------------------
' Spiral  © 2004 Alexander Klimov
'--------------------------------------
Private Sub butArchim_Click(ByVal sender As System.Object, ByVal e As System.EventArgs) _
Handles butArchim.Click
        Dim g As Graphics = CreateGraphics()
        Dim cx, cy As Integer
        cx = ClientSize.Width / 2
        cy = ClientSize.Height / 2
        Const iNumRevs As Integer = 20
        Dim iNumPoints As Integer = 5000
        Dim aptf(iNumPoints) As PointF
        Dim theta, rScale As Double
        Dim i As Integer
        g.Clear(BackColor)

        For i = 0 To iNumPoints
            theta = i * 2 * Math.PI / (iNumPoints / iNumRevs)
            rScale = i / iNumPoints
            aptf(i).X = CSng(cx * (1 + rScale * Math.Cos(theta)))
            aptf(i).Y = CSng(cy * (1 + rScale * Math.Sin(theta)))
        Next i

        Dim blackPen As New Pen(Color.Black, 4)
        g.DrawLines(blackPen, aptf)
    End Sub
```

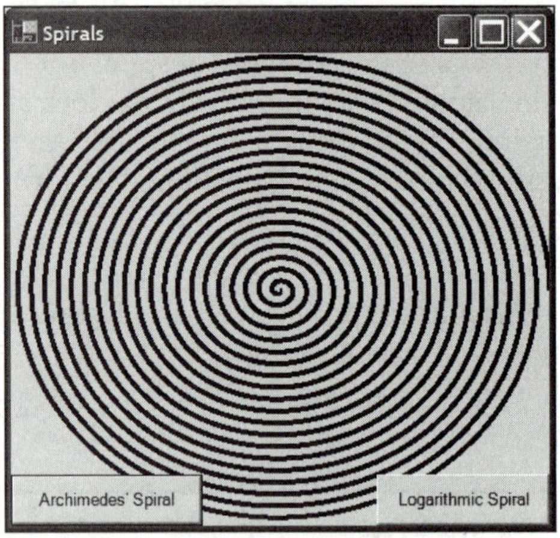

Fig. 4.9. Archimedes' Spiral

The results can be seen in Fig. 4.9. As you remember, the `DrawLines` method draws multiple short line segments to form a curve. But what happens if the number of these segments is sharply reduced? You will witness some very interesting effects. Try to set the `iNumPoints` variable to a smaller value — 15, for instance. You will end up with a peculiar, triangular spiral. Counting the number of straight lines in this triangle, you will see that it corresponds to the `iNumPoints` value.

4.3.6. The Logarithmic Spiral

Let's consider another case. Imagine that three equidistant ants (each sitting at one of the apexes of an equilateral triangle) have decided to get together. The first ant sets out to meet the second, the second one heads towards the third, and the third ant advances towards the first. Traveling at the same speed, at any moment in time each ant will always stay at the apex of a progressively smaller equilateral triangle similar to the original, in the process tracing a logarithmic curve. The logarithmic spiral formula is the following:

```
R = a^theta
```

A snail's shell is formed in a shape similar to that of the logarithmic spiral. The properties of the logarithmic spiral have been studied by many scientists and are applied in a number of different industrial uses. The Swiss mathematician Jacob Bernoulli even included in his will the request that it be engraved on his headstone. Converting the cited formula to the polar coordinate system, we obtain the following code for drawing the logarithmic spiral (Listing 4.13).

Listing 4.13. The Logarithmic Spiral

```
Private Sub butLogSpiral_Click(ByVal sender As System.Object, ByVal e As _
System.EventArgs) Handles butLogSpiral.Click
        Dim g As Graphics = CreateGraphics()
        Dim cx, cy As Integer
        cx = ClientSize.Width / 50
        cy = ClientSize.Height / 50
        Const iNumRevs As Integer = 8
        Dim iNumPoints As Integer = 5000
        Dim aptf(iNumPoints) As PointF
        Dim theta, rScale As Double
        Dim i As Integer
        g.Clear(BackColor)

        For i = 0 To iNumPoints
            theta = i * 2 * Math.PI / (iNumPoints / iNumRevs)
            rScale = i / iNumPoints
            aptf(i).X = CSng(cx * (20 + Math.Cos(theta) * 1.07 ^ theta))
            aptf(i).Y = CSng(cy * (20 + Math.Sin(theta) * 1.07 ^ theta))
        Next i

        Dim blackPen As New Pen(Color.Black, 4)
        g.DrawLines(blackPen, aptf)
End Sub
```

4.3.7. Cycloids

We have already seen the interesting shapes that can be created if the tracing point is located not on the circumference of a rolling circle, but inside or outside of it. All of these shapes belong to the general group of *cycloids*. Let's try to draw a few of these shapes. For this, we will need two parametric functions and a procedure to draw curves. I decided not to hard-program one of the parameters for the procedure, but to obtain it from a text box. Try to experiment with this value to see what different curves can be created (one of them is shown in Fig. 4.10). The code for the project, named `Hypocycloid`, is given in Listing 4.14.

Listing 4.14. Drawing Cycloids

```
'-------------------------------------
' Hypocycloid © 2004 Alexander Klimov
'-------------------------------------
    ' The procedure for drawing cycloids
    Private Sub DrawCycloid(ByVal g As Graphics, _
```

```vb
        ByVal cx As Integer, ByVal cy As Integer _
        ByVal start_t As Single, ByVal stop_t As Single, _
        ByVal dt As Single)

    Dim num_pts As Integer
    Dim pts() As PointF
    Dim pt As Integer
    Dim t As Single
    Dim px As Single
    Dim py As Single

    num_pts = (stop_t - start_t) / dt
    ReDim pts(num_pts)

    ' Determining the center for drawing
    px = cx + X(start_t)
    py = cy + Y(start_t)

    ' Determining all points for the curve
    t = start_t
    For pt = 0 To num_pts - 1
        pts(pt).X = cx + X(t)
        pts(pt).Y = cy + Y(t)
        t += dt
    Next pt

    pts(num_pts) = pts(0)

    ' Connecting all the points
    g.DrawLines(New Pen(Color.Black), pts)
End Sub


' Parametric function X(t).
Private Function X(ByVal t As Single) As Single
    X = (20000 * (2 * Cos(t) + Cos(t * txtParam.Text)) / 30) / 10
End Function

' Parametric function Y(t).
Private Function Y(ByVal t As Single) As Single
    Y = (20000 * (2 * Sin(t) + Sin(t * txtParam.Text)) / 30) / 10
End Function


Private Sub Form1_Paint(ByVal sender As Object, ByVal e As _
System.Windows.Forms.PaintEventArgs) Handles MyBase.Paint
```

```
    ' Outputting when the form is loaded
    DrawCycloid(e.Graphics, _
        Me.Width \ 2, Me.Height \ 2, _
        0, 14 * PI, 0.1)
End Sub


Private Sub txtParam_TextChanged(ByVal sender As System.Object, ByVal e As _
System.EventArgs) Handles txtParam.TextChanged
    Dim g As Graphics = CreateGraphics()
    g.Clear(Me.BackColor)
    DrawCycloid(g, _
            Me.Width \ 2, Me.Height \ 2, _
            0, 14 * PI, 0.1)
    g.Dispose()

End Sub
```

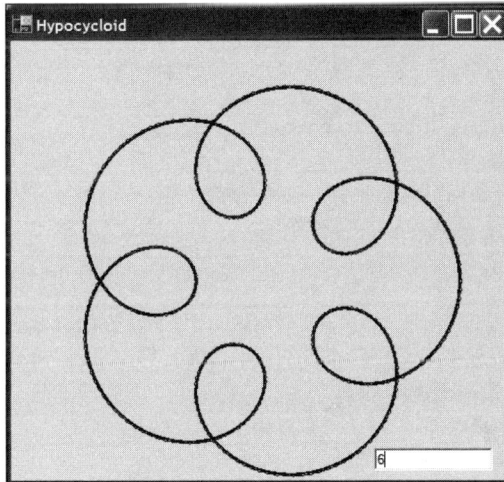

Fig. 4.10. A cycloid shape

4.3.8. The Spider Web

Let's try a couple more experiments with curves. Imagine a circle with points placed on it at a certain constant interval. Connect each of these points with a point shifted in phase a certain number of times, N.

The points of the chord intersections will form an intricate moire pattern. For example, with N = 1, nothing will be drawn, because the start and end points of the lines coincide.

Increasing the value of the N variable, however, will produce patterns with nodes, where the number of nodes equals N−1. The most interesting thing happens when N = 2. In this case, the shape drawn is the already familiar cardioid. At N = 3 the shape is a two-node nephroid. If 360 can be divided evenly by the value for N−1, the image displays a degree of orderliness, as can be seen in the Spiderweb project (Listing 4.15).

Listing 4.15. Creating Traceries

```
'---------------------------------------
' Spiderweb  © 2004 Alexander Klimov
'---------------------------------------
    Private Sub butGetPautina_Click(ByVal sender As System.Object, ByVal e As _
System.EventArgs) Handles butGetPautina.Click
        Static N As Double
        ' The spiderweb coordinates
        Dim xx As Integer = 350
        Dim yy As Integer = 270

        ' The spiderweb radius
        Dim R As Integer = 270
        N = TextBox1.Text
        Dim g As Graphics = CreateGraphics()
        g.Clear(BackColor)

        Dim i As Integer
        For i = 0 To 360 Step 2
            Dim T As Double
            T = i * PI / 180
            ' The coordinates of the first points of the pair on the circle
            Dim x As Double
            x = R * System.Math.Cos(T)
            Dim y As Double
            y = R * System.Math.Sin(T)
            ' The coordinates of the offset points of the pair
            Dim x2 As Double
            x2 = R * System.Math.Cos(N * T)
            Dim y2 As Double
            y2 = R * System.Math.Sin(N * T)

            ' Connecting the points
            g.DrawLine(Pens.Blue, _
                    CInt(x + xx), CInt(y + yy), _
                    CInt(x2 + xx), CInt(y2 + yy))
        Next i
    End Sub
```

You can set N to different values using the text box, and check out the resulting patterns. You can also opt for another approach, and let the program change the N value at a timer event (Listing 4.16). This will produce a series of changing traceries. It is quite an interesting spectacle, somewhat similar to a kaleidoscope.

Listing 4.16. Creating Traceries Using a Timer

```
    Private Sub butTimer_Click(ByVal sender As System.Object, ByVal e As _
System.EventArgs) Handles butTimer.Click
        Timer1.Start()
    End Sub


    Private Sub Timer1_Tick(ByVal sender As System.Object, ByVal e As _
System.EventArgs) Handles Timer1.Tick
        Static N As Double

        ' The spider web coordinates
        Dim xx As Integer = 350
        Dim yy As Integer = 270

        ' The spider web radius
        Dim R As Integer = 270

        N = N + 0.03
        Dim g As Graphics = CreateGraphics()
        g.Clear(BackColor)

        Dim i As Integer
        For i = 0 To 360 Step 2
            Dim T As Double
            T = i * PI / 180
            Dim x As Double
            x = R * System.Math.Cos(T)
            Dim y As Double
            y = R * System.Math.Sin(T)
            Dim x2 As Double
            x2 = R * System.Math.Cos(N * T)
            Dim y2 As Double
            y2 = R * System.Math.Sin(N * T)
            g.DrawLine(Pens.Blue, CInt(x + xx), CInt(y + yy), _
                    CInt(x2 + xx), CInt(y2 + yy))
        Next i
    End Sub
```

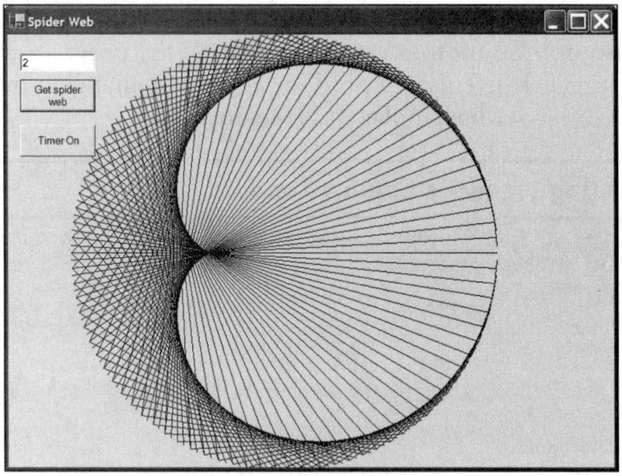

Fig. 4.11. A spiderweb

Running the program produces some eye-catching patterns (Fig. 4.11). A program like this just cries out to be used as a screen saver.

4.4. Suggestions and Recommendations

There are a great number of other interesting curves. I advise you to do some research on curves, obtain formulas for some curves not covered in this chapter, and build their graphs on your computer.

Chapter 5: Gradient Brushes

Gradient, as used in the graphics field, is a smooth transition from one color to another. Surfaces filled with gradient colors produce spectacular visual effects. The subject of creating gradients used to be quite popular on VB programming forums. There were even commercial ActiveX controls for creating gradient-colored surfaces. The general method for creating a gradient fill is to fill the area with numerous thin lines, changing their color progressively. But the gradient capabilities of VB .NET are so powerful, diverse, and at the same time easy to use, that it simply makes no sense to use the old methods from VB 6.0. In this chapter, we will consider several of the new gradient brush techniques.

5.1. The *LinearGradientBrush* Class

The `LinearGradientBrush` is derived from the abstract `Brush` class and is used to create gradient brushes for filling in a straight line. There are several overloaded versions of this class. Here is a short list:

- ❏ `Public Sub New(Point, Point, Color, Color)` — The start and end points of the linear gradient are specified, along with the start and end colors.
- ❏ `Public Sub New(Rectangle, Color, Color, LinearGradientMode)` — The rectangle for limiting the gradient, the start and end points, and the direction of the gradient are specified.

❑ `Public Sub New(Rectangle, Color, Color, Single)` — The rectangle for limiting the gradient, the start and end points, and the direction angle of the gradient are specified.

We will start our familiarization with this class by creating a simple example (the `LinearGradientBrushSample` project) that draws a circle with a horizontal gradient fill (Listing 5.1).

Listing 5.1. Creating a Gradient Fill

```
'---------------------------------------
' LinearGradientBrushSample © 2004 Alexander Klimov
'---------------------------------------
Private Sub Form1_Paint(ByVal sender As Object, ByVal e As
System.Windows.Forms.PaintEventArgs) Handles MyBase.Paint
        Dim g As Graphics = e.Graphics
        Dim rect As New Rectangle(10, 10, 90, 90)
        Dim p As New Pen(Color.RoyalBlue)
        g.DrawEllipse(p, rect)
        Dim lgb As New LinearGradientBrush(rect, _
           Color.RoyalBlue, Color.DeepSkyBlue, _
           LinearGradientMode.Horizontal)
        g.FillEllipse(lgb, rect)
End Sub
```

First, we create a pen and a limiting rectangle for creating a circle. Then, using the familiar `DrawEllipse` method, we draw a circle at the specified point and fill it with a gradient color. In the above example, the horizontal gradient was used. But, in addition to the horizontal gradient, the `LinearGradientBrush` class comprises several other gradient styles. These are the following:

❑ `BackwardDiagonal` is a gradient from upper right to lower left.
❑ `ForwardDiagonal` is a gradient from upper left to bottom right.
❑ `Horizontal` is a gradient from left to right.
❑ `Vertical` is a gradient from top to bottom.

Gradient fills can be applied not only to graphics elements, like ellipses or rectangles, but also to texts. This makes perfect sense, because fonts are actually graphic objects, to which many of the graphics methods can be applied. Let's add the code given in Listing 5.2 to the previous example (Listing 5.1).

Listing 5.2. Creating Gradient-Filled Text

```
' Gradient-filled text
Dim rec As New RectangleF(50, 80, 300, 90)
Dim lgbText As New LinearGradientBrush(rec, _
    Color.Red, Color.Yellow, LinearGradientMode.ForwardDiagonal)

Dim f As Font
f = New Font("Tahoma", 36, Font.Style.Bold, GraphicsUnit.Pixel)
g.DrawString("Visual Basic. NET", f, lgbText, 10, 110)
```

This code produces text filled with a gradient brush under the ellipse. Let's breathe some life into this example. By default, the gradient color changes perpendicularly to a specified line. One of the constructor versions makes it possible to change the angle of the gradient direction. This ability, combined with a timer, can be used to change the angle of the gradient dynamically. This will produce the effect of a rotating disco light. The code for this effect is provided in Listing 5.3.

Listing 5.3. An Animation Effect Using Gradient

```
Private Sub Timer1_Tick(ByVal sender As System.Object, ByVal e As System.EventArgs) _
Handles Timer1.Tick
    ' The gradient angle
    Static angle As Integer

    Dim g As Graphics
    g = CreateGraphics()
    Dim rect As New Rectangle(150, 10, 90, 90)
    Dim p As New Pen(Color.RoyalBlue, 1)

    g.DrawEllipse(p, rect)

    Dim lbr As New LinearGradientBrush(rect, _
        Color.RoyalBlue, Color.DeepSkyBlue, angle)
    g.FillEllipse(lbr, rect)

    angle += 10
    If angle >= 360 Then
        angle = 0
    End If
    g.Dispose()
End Sub
```

In the example, we declare an `angle` variable to hold the gradient direction angle. The value of the variable is changed by 10 degrees after a certain time period, thus creating the rotating-light effect. Unfortunately, it is impossible to produce this effect on paper, so I cannot show it to you in the book. You will have to try the project on your computer to really be able to appreciate it.

5.2. Who Needs Photoshop?

Once, while surfing the Internet, I ran across an example for creating a button for a web page using the popular Adobe Photoshop graphics editor. The following describes the process:

1. Create a square image. The image size in the example was 80 × 80 pixels (but it is better to make the button smaller if it is intended for a web page). Using the marquee tool, select a circular area. To make the right circle, press and hold down the <Shift> button while selecting the circle area.

2. Select a dark background color and a lighter foreground color. Using the **Gradient** tool, fill in the selected area. The angle of the fill depends on the desired lighting angle. In the example, an angle of 45 degrees was used, from upper left to bottom right. To obtain the exact 45-degree gradient fill, press and hold the <Shift> key while filling in the area.

3. Now, select a smaller circle inside the large one. (If the selection of the larger circle is still in place, the smaller circle can be contrasted by executing the **Select/Modify/Contrast** menu sequence.) Next, fill the smaller circle with the same color gradient, but in the opposite direction: from the bottom right to the upper left.

4. The finishing touch is supplying the button with a label. The label should to be made in a contrasting color. Also, to achieve the best results, the **Anti-Aliasing** item in the print tool options must be checked.

When reading these lines, I thought that the same results could be achieved without resorting to the graphics editor. Don't you have the same desire that I did, to want to try the described operations using Visual Basic .NET 2003? The results of my experiments are given in the Photoshop project (Listing 5.4).

Listing 5.4. Drawing a Fancy Button

```
'---------------------------------------

' Photoshop © 2004 Alexander Klimov

'---------------------------------------

Imports System.Drawing.Drawing2D

    Private Sub Button1_Click(ByVal sender As System.Object, ByVal e As _
System.EventArgs) Handles Button1.Click
```

```
        Dim g As Graphics = CreateGraphics()
        Dim grBrush As LinearGradientBrush
        Dim rect As New Rectangle(20, 20, 70, 70)
        Dim startColor As Color = Color.LightBlue
        Dim endColor As Color = Color.Blue

        grBrush = New LinearGradientBrush(rect _
            startColor, endColor, LinearGradientMode.ForwardDiagonal)
        g.FillEllipse(grBrush, rect)
        grBrush = New LinearGradientBrush(rect, _
            endColor, startColor, LinearGradientMode.ForwardDiagonal)
        g.FillEllipse(grBrush, New Rectangle(30, 30, 50, 50))

        g.Dispose()
    End Sub
```

So, following the instructions, I created a circle with the ForwardDiagonal gradient fill. Inside of this circle, I placed a smaller one, filling it with the opposite direction gradient. The final result was a cute 3D button, looking somewhat like a button on a dress (Fig. 5.1). If you have some descriptions of how to create various effects using graphics editors, try to implement those effects using VB .NET's graphics capabilities. I am sure you will have lots of fun with this.

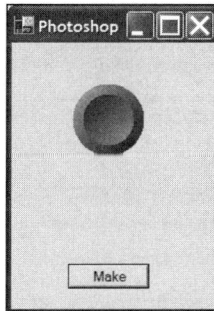

Fig. 5.1. Drawing a fancy button

5.3. The *PathGradientBrush* Class

The PathGradientBrush class is analogous to the LinearGradientBrush class, except that it fills in shapes not along a straight line, but along a specified path. Using this class produces very interesting results, creating the illusion of 3D shapes. An example is given in the PathGradientBrushSample project (Listing 5.5).

Listing 5.5. Creating a 3D Illusion

```vb
'---------------------------------------
' PathGradientBrushSample © 2004 Alexander Klimov
'---------------------------------------


    Private Sub Form1_Paint(ByVal sender As Object, ByVal e As _
System.Windows.Forms.PaintEventArgs) Handles MyBase.Paint
        Dim wid As Integer = Me.ClientSize.Width
        Dim hgt As Integer = Me.ClientSize.Height
        Dim pts() As Point = { _
            New Point(wid * 0.5, hgt * 0.1), _
            New Point(wid * 0.7, hgt * 0.3), _
            New Point(wid * 0.9, hgt * 0.5), _
            New Point(wid * 0.7, hgt * 0.7), _
            New Point(wid * 0.5, hgt * 0.9), _
            New Point(wid * 0.3, hgt * 0.7), _
            New Point(wid * 0.1, hgt * 0.5), _
            New Point(wid * 0.3, hgt * 0.3)}

        Dim g_path As New GraphicsPath
        g_path.AddClosedCurve(pts, 0.5)

        ' Defining a brush
        Dim g_brush As New PathGradientBrush(g_path)
        Dim surround_colors() As Color = {Color.Pink}
        g_brush.SurroundColors = surround_colors
        g_brush.CenterColor = Color.White
        g_brush.CenterPoint = New PointF(wid * 0.4, hgt * 0.4)

        ' Filling the shape
        e.Graphics.FillPath(g_brush, g_path)

        ' Outlining the shapes
        e.Graphics.DrawPath(Pens.Plum, g_path)

    End Sub
```

In this example, I attempted to depict something similar to a pillow. As can be seen from the example (Fig. 5.2), the gradient fill is formed by an array of points, which is then passed to the PathGradientBrush method.

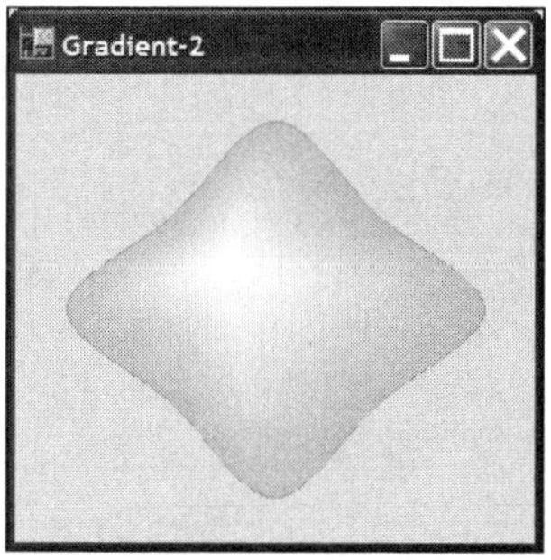

Fig. 5.2. Creating an illusion of 3D using a gradient fill

5.4. Balloons, Balls, and Bubbles

The 3D pillow example was somewhat of an abstraction. It is doubtful that you will have to create similar objects in your programs. But the ability to create 3D effects with the help of the `PathGradientBrush` class is most definitely worth adding to your arsenal of graphics tools. This class is most commonly used to create convex circles, imitating balls, balloons, bubbles, and other similar objects. An example is given in the `Balls` project (Listing 5.6).

Listing 5.6. Drawing balloons

```
'-------------------------------------
' Balls © 2004 Alexander Klimov
'-------------------------------------
Imports System.Drawing.Drawing2D

    Private Sub Form1_Paint(ByVal sender As Object, _
        ByVal e As System.Windows.Forms.PaintEventArgs) _
        Handles MyBase.Paint

    ' Creating a new path
    Dim gp As New GraphicsPath

        ' Drawing the first balloon
    gp.AddEllipse(10, 10, 100, 100)

    ' Creating a gradient brush
    Dim pgBrush As New PathGradientBrush(gp)

    ' Defining colors for the center of the balloon
```

```
pgBrush.CenterPoint = New PointF(70, 25)
    pgBrush.CenterColor = Color.SeaShell

    ' Defining the color of the balloon
    Dim clr() As Color = {Color.FromArgb(255, 255, 0, 0)}
    pgBrush.SurroundColors = clr

    ' Outputting the results to the screen
    e.Graphics.FillPath(pgBrush, gp)

    ' Repeating the procedure for the second balloon
    Dim gp2 As New GraphicsPath
    gp2.AddEllipse(120, 10, 100, 150)
    Dim pgBrush2 As New PathGradientBrush(gp2)
    pgBrush2.CenterPoint = New PointF(180, 45)
    pgBrush2.CenterColor = Color.SeaShell
    Dim clr2() As Color = {Color.FromArgb(255, 50, 155, 100)}
    pgBrush2.SurroundColors = clr2
    e.Graphics.FillPath(pgBrush2, gp2)

    ' A string to hold the balloons together
    e.Graphics.DrawLine(Pens.Black, 60, 110, _
            CInt(ClientSize.Width / 2 - 1), _
            ClientSize.Height - 1)
    e.Graphics.DrawLine(Pens.Black, 170, 160, _
            CInt(ClientSize.Width / 2 - 1), _
            ClientSize.Height - 1)

End Sub
```

Here, the important thing to pay attention to is determining the center of the fill. By moving this point away from the center of the ellipse, the effect of highlights on the surface of the balloons is created (Fig. 5.3).

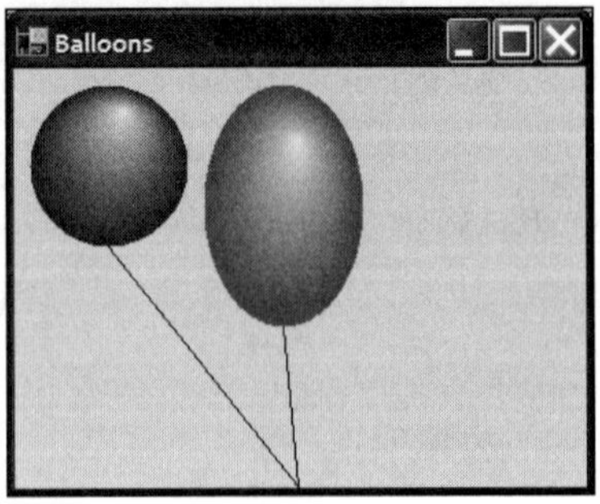

Fig. 5.3. Balloons

5.5. The Mosaic Gradient

Working with gradients is a lot of fun. I recommend that you study on your own the VB. NET documentation covering this area. In conclusion, I will show you another use of the gradient employing the mosaic brush. I borrowed this example from the *"Programming Microsoft Windows with Microsoft Visual Basic .NET"* book, by Charles Petzold. I strongly recommend that you read this book, in which the author provides several excellent examples demonstrating the use of this technique. I especially liked the example with hexagons. I would like to offer you a slight modification of this example, which I call the Honeycomb project (Listing 5.7).

Listing 5.7. Honeycombs

```
'---------------------------------------
' Honeycomb  © 2004 Alexander Klimov
'---------------------------------------
Imports System.Drawing.Drawing2D

    ' The size of one cell (the side and the radius)
    Const CellSize As Single = 30

    Private Sub Form1_Paint(ByVal sender As Object, _
            ByVal e As System.Windows.Forms.PaintEventArgs) _
            Handles MyBase.Paint

        ' Calculating a half of the hexagon height
        Dim HalfCell As Single = CSng(CellSize * Math.Sin(Math.PI / 3))

        ' The points for the hexagon, including the additional width
        Dim aptf() As PointF = {New PointF(CellSize, 0), _
                        New PointF(CellSize * 1.5, 0), _
                        New PointF(CellSize, 0), _
                        New PointF(CellSize / 2, -HalfCell), _
                        New PointF(-CellSize / 2, -HalfCell), _
                        New PointF(-CellSize, 0), _
                        New PointF(-CellSize * 1.5, 0), _
                        New PointF(-CellSize, 0), _
                        New PointF(-CellSize / 2, HalfCell), _
                        New PointF(CellSize / 2, HalfCell)}
```

```vb
' The size of the form
Dim cx As Integer = ClientRectangle.Width - 1
Dim cy As Integer = ClientRectangle.Height - 1

' Defining the first brush
Dim pgBrush As PathGradientBrush = _
            New PathGradientBrush(aptf, WrapMode.Tile)
' The color of the honeycombs
Dim clr() As Color = {Color.Yellow}
pgBrush.SurroundColors = clr

' Shifting the cell and defining the second brush
Dim i As Integer
For i = 0 To aptf.GetUpperBound(0)
    aptf(i).X += CellSize * 1.5F
    aptf(i).Y += HalfCell
Next i

Dim pgBrush2 As PathGradientBrush = _
                New PathGradientBrush(aptf, WrapMode.Tile)
pgBrush2.SurroundColors = clr

' Outputting the cells to the screen
Dim g As Graphics = e.Graphics
g.FillRectangle(pgBrush, 0, 0, cx, cy)
g.FillRectangle(pgBrush2, 0, 0, cx, cy)

End Sub

Private Sub Form1_Resize(ByVal sender As Object, ByVal e As System.EventArgs) _
Handles MyBase.Resize
    Refresh()
End Sub
```

In my opinion, the pattern (Fig. 5.4) is simply beautiful and just beseeches to be used as wallpaper. Experiment with various values for the brush colors and cell sizes.

Fig. 5.4. Honeycombs

5.6. Suggestions and Recommendations

The gradient brushes subject is one that can help unleash your creativity. Using various combinations of colors, styles, and shapes, beautiful pictures can be created worthy of being used as wallpaper for your desktop or for Internet pages. See if you can invent your own patterns with the help of gradient brushes.

Chapter 6: Transformations

Another advantage of using VB .NET instead of Visual Basic 6.0 is the powerful support in the form of image transformation functions it offers offered. The entire graphic content of the screen can be changed with one line of code. The possibilities are so great that I am simply at a loss as to which to demonstrate first. I guess I will start with the simple stuff.

6.1. World Transformations

World transformations make it possible to perform all kinds of transformations with text and graphics. The world transformations presuppose the following rules:

- ❏ Straight lines always remain straight.
- ❏ Parallel lines always stay parallel.
- ❏ Equal-sized objects always remain of an equal size.

But let's move on to the practical work. Create a new project and name it `WorldTransform`. Write the following code to handle the `Form_Paint` event (Listing 6.1):

Listing 6.1. World transformations

```
'-------------------------------------
' WorldTransform © 2004 Alexander Klimov
'-------------------------------------
```

```
    Private Sub Form1_Paint(ByVal sender As Object, ByVal e As _
System.Windows.Forms.PaintEventArgs) Handles MyBase.Paint
        Dim cx As Integer = ClientSize.Width
        Dim cy As Integer = ClientSize.Height
        Dim SomeText As String
        SomeText = "Jellicle Cats are black and white," _
            & vbNewLine & _
            "Jellicle Cats are rather small;" _
            & vbNewLine & _
            "Jellicle Cats are merry and bright," _
            & vbNewLine & _
            "And pleasant to hear when they caterwaul."
        Dim g As Graphics = e.Graphics

        g.DrawString(SomeText, Font, Brushes.Black, _
                        New RectangleF(0, 0, cx, cy))

    End Sub
```

Build the project and run the program. You will see a regular form window with the text of an excerpt from "The Song of the Jellicles" by Thomas Stearns Eliot in it. So what? But try adding the following line of code before the `DrawString` method that outputs the string:

```
' Rotating the text through 30 degrees
g.RotateTransform(30)
```

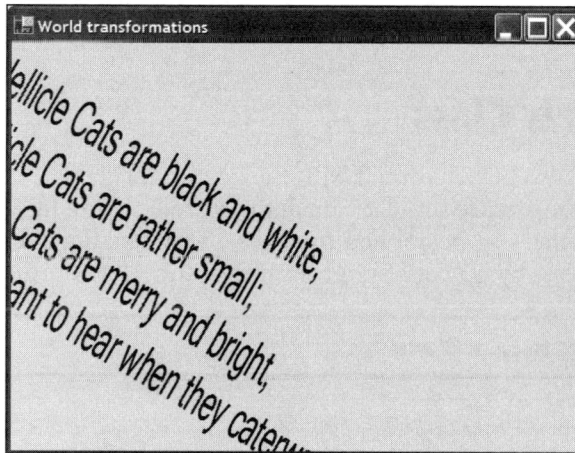

Fig. 6.1. Rotating text through 30 degrees

Recompile the project, and launch the program again. A single line of code, and one that is not that long, rotated the text through 30 degrees! (Fig. 6.1). VB 6.0 veterans will attest to the fact that a similar effect could only be achieved in that version by resorting to the Windows API system functions. By the way, the effect of several successive RotateTransform method calls is cumulative. The final rotation angle produced by calling this method several times will equal the sum of the angles specified for each call.

There are other, just as interesting methods where this one comes from. For example, try to add the ScaleTransform method before calling the DrawString method:

```
' Scaling up the characters
g.ScaleTransform(2, 4)
```

The resulting text is twice the height and four times the width of the original. The TranslateTransform method translates the coordinates of the characters being output along the coordinate axes:

```
g.TranslateTransform(50, 10)
```

Combining all of the described methods produces very interesting net results. Note that negative values can also be used as the parameters. This will make the resulting text a mirror copy of the original:

```
g.TranslateTransform(cx/2, cy/2)
g.ScaleTransform(1, -1)
g.DrawString(SomeText, Font, Brushes.Black, New RectangleF(0, 0, cx, cy))
```

First, we set the coordinates for the start of the text output at the center of the form. Next, using negative parameters, the text is flipped. Try to use other combinations, such as the following:

```
g.ScaleTransform(-1, 1)
```

or:

```
g.ScaleTransform(-1, -1)
```

6.2. The *Matrix* Class

Transformations can also be performed with the help of the Matrix class. It is mandatory for all Matrix movie fans to use this class in all their projects. Joking aside, this is indeed a very interesting class that can be applied to achieve very striking effects. Let's start to get acquainted with the class by way of a simple example: the Matrix project (Listing 6.2).

Listing 6.2. Using the Matrix Class

```
'---------------------------------------
' Matrix  © 2004 Alexander Klimov
'---------------------------------------

        Private Sub Form1_Paint(ByVal sender As Object, _
```

```
        ByVal e As System.Windows.Forms.PaintEventArgs) _
        Handles MyBase.Paint

    Dim myPen As New Pen(Color.Blue, 1)
    Dim myPen2 As New Pen(Color.Red, 1)
    Dim rotatePoint As New PointF(150.0F, 50.0F)

    ' Drawing a blue rectangle
    e.Graphics.DrawRectangle(myPen, 150, 50, 180, 100)

    ' Creating a matrix and rotating through 30 degrees
Dim myMatrix As New System.Drawing.Drawing2D.Matrix
    myMatrix.RotateAt(30, rotatePoint, MatrixOrder.Append)


' After applying the matrix,
' drawing another, red, rectangle

    e.Graphics.Transform = myMatrix
    e.Graphics.DrawRectangle(myPen2, 150, 50, 180, 100)
End Sub
```

The essence of the example is very simple. First, we draw a blue rectangle. Then we create a Matrix object and use its RotateAt method to obtain information for a 30-degree rotation. Next, the transformation information is passed to the Graphics object and, finally, a red rectangle of the same size is drawn. As you can see, the transformation has rotated the first rectangle 30 degrees clockwise around its upper left corner. Of course, matrix transformations can also be applied to text (Listing 6.3).

Listing 6.3. Applying Matrix to Texts

```
  Private Sub Button1_Click(ByVal sender As System.Object, ByVal e As _
System.EventArgs) Handles Button1.Click

    Static angle As Long     ' The rotation angle in degrees

    ' Creating a matrix for rotation around the 70, 70 point
    Dim rotation_matrix As New System.Drawing.Drawing2D.Matrix
    angle += 20
    rotation_matrix.RotateAt(angle, New PointF(70, 70))

    ' Creating Graphics object and transforming it
    Dim g = Me.CreateGraphics()
```

```
    g.Transform = rotation_matrix
    g.clear(Color.Black)
    g.DrawString("Matrix", Font, Brushes.Green, _
            New RectangleF(70, 70, 150, 150))
End Sub
```

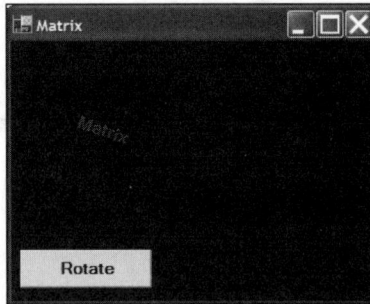

Fig. 6.2. Rotating text using a matrix

In this example I placed the code in a button click event handler routine. Now, every time the button is clicked, the text rotates 20 degrees clockwise (Fig. 6.2).

6.3. Rotating a Line

An animation of a rotating line can be easily created using the methods just described. An example is shown in the RotatiedLine project (Listing 6.4).

Listing 6.4. Rotating a Line around Its Center

```
'-------------------------------------
' RotatedLine  © 2004 Alexander Klimov
'-------------------------------------
Imports System.Drawing.Drawing2D
    ' A global variable for the rotation angle
    Public f As Integer

    Private Sub Form1_Paint(ByVal sender As Object, ByVal e As _
System.Windows.Forms.PaintEventArgs) Handles MyBase.Paint

        Dim g As Graphics = e.Graphics
        ' An auxiliary circle inside of which the line is rotated
        ' g.DrawEllipse(New Pen(Color.Violet, 3), 30, 30, 150, 150)

        Dim gp As New GraphicsPath
```

```
    gp.AddLine(105, 30, 105, 180)

    Dim rotationTransform As New Matrix(1, 0, 0, 1, 1, 1)
    Dim rotationPoint = New PointF(105.0F, 105.0F)

    rotationTransform.RotateAt(f, rotationPoint)
    gp.Transform(rotationTransform)

    g.DrawPath(New Pen(Color.BlueViolet, 3), gp)

    f = f + 10
    If f = 360 Then
        f = 0
    End If
End Sub

Private Sub Timer1_Tick(ByVal sender As System.Object, ByVal e As System.EventArgs) _
Handles Timer1.Tick
    Invalidate()
End Sub
```

In this example, a line segment rotates inside a circle. If you want the circle to show, remove the comment from this code line:

```
'g.DrawEllipse(New Pen(Color.Violet, 3), 30, 30, 150, 150)
```

Halving the line gives us a simple clock hand. But the subject of clocks deserves separate treatment.

6.3.1. Clocks

The transformation methods can be used to design more complex programs. Once, while writing this book, I glanced at the wall clock. For some reason, its second hand caught my attention. I wondered: Why not write a program to draw an analog wall clock? So I did, producing the AnalogClock example (Listing 6.5). Since a clock has three hands that do basically the same thing — move around in a circle — I defined a separate class for this task: cHands.

Listing 6.5. The Class to Draw Clock Hands

```
'--------------------------------------
' AnalogClock © 2004 Alexander Klimov
'--------------------------------------

Imports System.Drawing.Drawing2D

    ' The class to draw clock handsPublic Class cHands
```

```
Private angle As Integer = 0
Public gp As New GraphicsPath
Public bfilled As Boolean = False

' The procedure to calculate the  rotation angle
Public Sub SetAngle(ByVal newAngle As Integer, ByVal imgCenter As PointF)
    Dim rotate As Integer = newAngle - Angle
    Dim trans As New Matrix
    trans.RotateAt(rotate, imgCenter)
    gp.Transform(trans)
    Me.Angle = newAngle
End Sub

' The drawing procedure
Public Sub DrawClock(ByVal imgDraw As Graphics)
    If bfilled Then
        imgDraw.FillPath(Brushes.DeepPink, gp)
        imgDraw.DrawPath(Pens.Yellow, gp)
    Else
        imgDraw.DrawPath(New Pen(Color.DimGray, 1), gp)
    End If
End Sub
End Class
```

First, I declared a new, cHands, class in the project. In the first three code lines of this class, I declared three variables: angle defining the rotation angle of the hands; a graphics object, gp; and a Boolean, bfilled. The SetAngle procedure simply subtracts the value of the new angle from the old angle, and rotates the hand through the obtained angle using the RotateAt method. The DrawClock procedure draws the outlines of the hour and the minute hands for a better visual perception, and then fills them with the specified color. It is enough to draw the second hand with a brush one-pixel thick. Using this class, we can easily draw the clock hands and furnish them with the necessary properties. It is clear that we need a timer for our project. Place it on the main form, leave it its default name Timer1, and set its Enabled property to True. Our clock will be drawn not on the form itself, but in a picture box. Add a PictureBox control to the form. Name it picClock. This concludes the visual programming part of the project. It is time to add some more code to the project (Listing 6.6).

Listing 6.6. Creating a Clock

```
'---------------------------------------
' AnalogClock © 2004 Alexander Klimov
'---------------------------------------

Imports System.Drawing.Drawing2D
```

```
' Variables responsible for drawing the clock's hands and its center
Private hHour As New cHands
Private hMinute As New cHands
Private hSecond As New cHands
Private center = New PointF(150, 150)

Private Sub initclock()

    ' The picture box size is 300 x 300 pixels
    Me.ClientSize = New Size(300, 300)

    ' An array to hold several points. The points are connected to each other.
    ' The result is a template for the clock and minute hands.
    Dim drawHour As Point() = { _
      New Point(Int(picClock.Width / 2), Int(picClock.Height / 2)), _
      New Point(Int(picClock.Width / 2 - 5), 80), _
      New Point(Int(picClock.Width / 2), 50), _
      New Point(Int(picClock.Width / 2 + 5), 80), _
      New Point(Int(picClock.Width / 2), Int(picClock.Height / 2))}

    ' Adding these points to the object using the AddLines property
    ' of the GraphicsPath object
    hHour.gp.AddLines(drawHour)
    ' Filling the hour hand
    hHour.bfilled = True

    ' Drawing the minute hand in the same manner
    Dim drawMinute As Point() = { _
                    New Point(Int(picClock.Width / 2), _
                    Int(picClock.Height / 2)), _
                    New Point(Int(picClock.Width / 2 - 5), 60), _
                    New Point(Int(picClock.Width / 2), 30), _
                    New Point(Int(picClock.Width / 2 + 5), 60), _
                    New Point(Int(picClock.Width / 2), _
                    Int(picClock.Height / 2))}

    hMinute.gp.AddLines(drawMinute)
    hMinute.bfilled = True

    ' The second hand. This one is not filled
    hSecond.gp.AddLine(center, _
        New PointF(Int(picClock.Width / 2), 20))
End Sub

    Private Sub Timer1_Tick(ByVal sender As System.Object, ByVal e As System.EventArgs) _
Handles Timer1.Tick
```

```
        picClock.Invalidate()
    End Sub

    Private Sub picClock_Paint(ByVal sender As Object, ByVal e As _
System.Windows.Forms.PaintEventArgs) Handles picClock.Paint
        DrawFace(e.Graphics)
        hHour.setAngle((360 / 12) * Val(Format(Now, "hh")), center)

        hMinute.SetAngle((360 / 60) * Val(Format(Now, "mm")), center)
        hSecond.SetAngle((360 / 60) * Val(Format(Now, "ss")), center)

        hHour.DrawClock(e.Graphics)
        hMinute.DrawClock(e.Graphics)
        hSecond.DrawClock(e.Graphics)
    End Sub

    Private Sub DrawFace(ByVal g As Graphics)
        Dim path As String = _
            Mid(Application.ExecutablePath, 1, _
            InStrRev(Application.ExecutablePath, "\"))
        Dim bBoundClock As New HatchBrush(_
            HatchStyle.LargeConfetti, Color.Green, Color.White)

        g.FillEllipse(bBoundClock, New Rectangle(5, 5, 290, 290))
        g.FillEllipse(Brushes.WhiteSmoke, New Rectangle(15, 15, 270, 270))
        g.FillEllipse(Brushes.Green, New Rectangle(140, 140, 20, 20))

        Dim f As New Font("Arial", 10, FontStyle.Bold)
        Dim stringSize = g.MeasureString("BHV", f)
        g.DrawString("My Clock", f, Brushes.BlueViolet, _
                    (300 - stringSize.width) / 2, 200)

        bBoundClock.Dispose()
        ' Do not delete the g object!
    End Sub
End Class
```

To spare myself the trouble of carrying out tedious calculations, I set the size of the program window to a fixed 300 × 300 pixels, thus placing the center of the form at the (150, 150) point. The hour and the minute hands are drawn with the aid of the array of points, which are added to the lines using the AddLines method, and then filled with color. Because of its thickness or, rather, its lack thereof, the second hand does not need to be filled. Here, a single line will do. Note that the formula to calculate the angle for the hour hand is different from the formula to calculate the angle for the minute and the second hands. I hope that you realize that a clock face is divided into 12 hour segments and into 60 segments used to indicate both minutes and seconds. Therefore, we divide the circle into 12 or 60 equal parts, and then multiply the result by the current time. The obtained result is passed to the `SetAngle` procedure, which calculates the necessary angle, and the hands are drawn in their proper places using the `DrawClock` procedure.

To draw the clock face, a `LargeConfetti` style `HatchBrush` hatch brush is used. The first call of the `FillEllipse` method draws the green-peppered clock outline, the second call draws the white clock face, and the third call draws the green hand spindle. To make the clock more realistic, I added a manufacturer's name. I don't know what your plans concerning going into the wall clock business are, but I hope that if you do, you will remember me and share some of the profits. The main part of the program is now complete. Build the project, launch the program, and enjoy your clock (Fig. 6.3). You should see the second hand going around, with the hour and minute hands indicating the current hour and minutes according to the time set on your system clock.

Fig. 6.3. The clock

By the way, when putting the project together, I was not paying attention and made the mistake of placing the call to the `DrawFace` procedure at the very end. As a result, there were no clock hands when I started the program. Fortunately, thanks to the fact that the project was not one of Bill Gates' monster jobs combined with my silly habit of trying programs out every time after adding a new line of code, I managed to locate the reason for the missing hands quickly. But such carelessness can cause you to waste precious time searching for stupid mistakes. I am sometimes sent programs by authors who are baffled by the fact that, despite everything being right, the program does not work. They ask me to find the problem. Most often it turns out to be the result of plain absentmindedness and inattentiveness.

NOTE

The above should not be interpreted as an invitation to send me programs for debugging. Do not send me letters asking why your examples do not work. The chances are 99 percent that your letter will wind up in the trash can.

But let's get back to our clock. What I presented is just a general algorithm for creating an analog clock program. But the degree, to which it can be improved upon, is only limited by your imagination. For example, the clock hands can be given a whimsical appearance through the use of Bezier curves. So get back to the drawing board and let your fantasies fly.

6.3. Shears

Another interesting transformation type is the *shear*. In the `Shear` project, I demonstrate two simple examples of the horizontal and vertical shear (Listing 6.7). The shear effect is obtained by manipulating values in the `Matrix` class.

Listing 6.7. Shear

```
'-----------------------------
' Shear © 2004 Alexander Klimov
'-----------------------------
Imports System.Drawing.Drawing2D

    Private Sub Form1_Paint(ByVal sender As Object, ByVal e As _
System.Windows.Forms.PaintEventArgs) Handles MyBase.Paint
        Dim myMatrix As New Matrix
        Dim f As New Font("Tahoma", 18, FontStyle.Bold)

        myMatrix = New Matrix(1, 0, -0.5, 1, 0, 0)
        e.Graphics.Transform = myMatrix
        e.Graphics.DrawString(_
          "Stop pulling the cat by the tail", f, Brushes.Blue, 60, 30)

        e.Graphics.ResetTransform()
        myMatrix = New Matrix(1, 0, 0.5, 1, 0, 0)
        e.Graphics.Transform = myMatrix
        e.Graphics.DrawString(_
          "Stop pulling the cat by the tail", f, Brushes.Blue, 10, 70)

        ' Drawing a red color rectangle
        e.Graphics.ResetTransform()
        e.Graphics.Transform = New Matrix(1, 0.5, 0, 1, 0, 1)
        e.Graphics.DrawRectangle(Pens.Red, 80, 80, 160, 100)
    End Sub
```

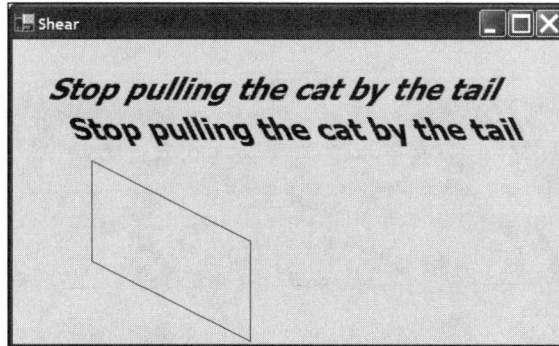

Fig. 6.4. Horizontal and vertical shears

Executing the program draws two strings, one tilted to the left, and the other to the right. They demonstrate the horizontal shear. Even though the characters are tilted to the side, they are all lined up. The red parallelogram demonstrates a vertical shear applied to a standard rectangle (Fig. 6.4).

6.4. Suggestions and Recommendations

Transformations are a new concept for Visual Basic programmers and offer great potential. I must confess that I have not delved into the subject too deeply yet myself. By the way, it does not say anywhere that only vertical or horizontal shear can be used. These two transformations can be combined to produce a shear in both directions.

Chapter 7: Shapes

Our world is filled with a multitude of shapes, to which we pay no attention because we have been surrounded by them since childhood. Let's try to rediscover their intriguing properties and reproduce them with the help of Visual Basic .NET 2003.

7.1. Drawing a Star

Five-pointed star shapes are everywhere around us. The US flag has fifty five-pointed stars on it, and the flags and symbols of many other countries include stars. The five-pointed star (the pentagram) was popular in ancient times and some peoples believe that five-pointed star amulets provide protection against illnesses.

7.1.1. Drawing a Star: Method 1

Try to draw a star yourself. Project `Stars` (Listing 7.1) shows how to do this.

Listing 7.1. Drawing a Star

```
'----------------------------------------
' Stars © 2004 Alexander Klimov
'----------------------------------------
Imports System.Drawing.Drawing2D
```

```
    Private Sub butStar1_Click(ByVal sender As System.Object, ByVal e As _
System.EventArgs) Handles butStar1.Click

        Dim cx As Integer = 150
        Dim cy As Integer = 150
        Dim apt(4) As Point

        Dim i As Integer
        For i = 0 To apt.GetUpperBound(0)
            Dim theta As Double = (i * 1.2 - 0.5) * Math.PI
            apt(i).X = CInt(cx * (1 + 0.7 * Math.Cos(theta)))
            apt(i).Y = CInt(cy * (1 + 0.7 * Math.Sin(theta)))
        Next i

        Dim g As Graphics = CreateGraphics()
        Dim br As New SolidBrush(Color.Red)
        g.DrawLine(New Pen(Color.Red, 3), apt(0), apt(1))
        g.DrawLine(New Pen(Color.Blue, 3), apt(1), apt(2))
        g.DrawLine(New Pen(Color.Blue, 3), apt(2), apt(3))
        g.DrawLine(New Pen(Color.Blue, 3), apt(3), apt(4))
        g.DrawLine(New Pen(Color.Green, 3), apt(0), apt(4))
        g.FillPolygon(br, apt, FillMode.Alternate)
        g.Dispose()
    End Sub
```

Compile the project and launch the program. You will see it draw a star with red points (Fig. 7.1). Let's examine how the code works. First, we declare two variables: cx and cy. These variables define the offset of the starting point for drawing relative to the coordinate origin. Then we have a loop that draws five lines to build the star. This piece of code needs to be considered in detail.

First, we need to specify the initial angle and its displacement for each iteration of the loop, with the following formula:

```
Dim theta As Double = (i * 1.2 - 0.5) * Math.PI
```

To have the star stand straight on two points, the first point needs to be shifted by 90 degrees, as follows:

```
0.5 * Math.PI
```

which is 90 degrees expressed in radians (the initial displacement angle).

The 0.7 value is the size of the star points. The size of the star can be varied by changing this parameter. Math.Cos(theta) is rotating the vector.

```
apt(i).X = CInt(cx * (1 + 0.7 * Math.Cos(theta)))
apt(i).Y = CInt(cy * (1 + 0.7 * Math.Sin(theta)))
```

Then the lines are drawn one after another, with the first and the second lines being of different colors, for better visualization. The `FillMode` method partially fills the star as follows:

```
g.FillPolygon(br, apt, FillMode.Alternate)
```

Using this method makes it possible to dispense with five calls to the `DrawLine` method. The `Winding` parameter can be used to fill the star completely as follows:

```
g.FillPolygon(br, apt, System.Drawing.Drawing2D.FillMode.Winding)
```

Fig. 7.1. Drawing a Star: Method 1

7.1.2. Drawing a Star: Method 2

The second method creates a star by drawing its outlines. Place another button on the form and add the following code to its click event (Listing 7.2).

Listing 7.2. Another Way to Draw a Star

```
Private Sub butStar2_Click(ByVal sender As System.Object, ByVal e As _
System.EventArgs) Handles butStar2.Click
        Dim g As Graphics = CreateGraphics()
        Dim cx As Integer = ClientRectangle.Width / 2
        Dim cy As Integer = ClientRectangle.Height / 2
        Dim outerR As Integer = 120
        Dim innerR As Integer = 46
        Dim pn As New Pen(Color.Red, 3)
        Dim pn2 As New Pen(Color.Blue, 3)

        Dim i As Integer
        For i = 0 To 10
            If i Mod 2 = 1 Then
```

```
        g.DrawLine(pn, _
CInt(cx + Math.Ceiling(outerR * Math.Cos((i + 1) * Math.PI / 5))), _
CInt(cy + Math.Ceiling(outerR * Math.Sin((i + 1) * Math.PI / 5))), _
CInt(cx + Math.Ceiling(innerR * Math.Cos(i * Math.PI / 5))), _
CInt(cy + Math.Ceiling(innerR * Math.Sin(i * Math.PI / 5))))

    Else
        g.DrawLine(pn2, _
CInt(cx + Math.Ceiling(outerR * Math.Cos(i * Math.PI / 5))), _
CInt(cy + Math.Ceiling(outerR * Math.Sin(i * Math.PI / 5))), _
CInt(cx + Math.Ceiling(innerR * Math.Cos((i + 1) * Math.PI / 5))), _
CInt(cy + Math.Ceiling(innerR * Math.Sin((i + 1) * Math.PI / 5))))

    End If
  Next

  g.Dispose()
End Sub
```

The first three lines of code should require no explanation. Next are the radiuses of the external and internal circles, on which the star's five vertices and five valleys will lie. Because the vertices and valleys alternate, these points are separated into odd and even, and connected with lines (Fig. 7.2).

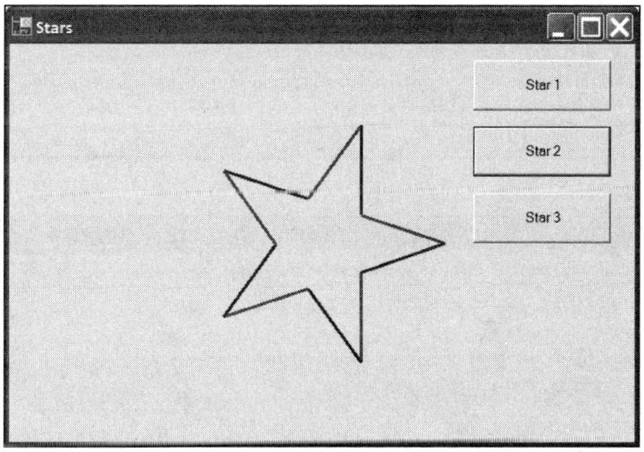

Fig. 7.2. Drawing star outline

7.1.3. A Gradient Star

Let's return to the first star project. Modifying its code a little, you can draw a star with gradient fill (Fig. 7.3). This method is based on one of the examples from *"Programming Microsoft Windows with Microsoft Visual Basic .NET"*, by Charles Petzold (Listing 7.3).

Listing 7.3. Creating a Star with Gradient Fill

```
Private Sub butStar3_Click(ByVal sender As System.Object, ByVal e As _
System.EventArgs) Handles butStar3.Click
    Dim cx As Integer = 150
    Dim cy As Integer = 150

    Dim apt(4) As Point

    Dim i As Integer
    For i = 0 To apt.GetUpperBound(0)
        Dim theta As Double = (i * 1.2 - 0.5) * Math.PI
        apt(i).X = CInt(cx * (1 + 0.7 * Math.Cos(theta)))
        apt(i).Y = CInt(cy * (1 + 0.7 * Math.Sin(theta)))
    Next i

    Dim pgBrush As New PathGradientBrush(apt)
    pgBrush.CenterColor = Color.SeaShell
    pgBrush.SurroundColors = New Color() {Color.Red}

    Refresh()

    Dim g As Graphics = CreateGraphics()
    g.FillPolygon(pgBrush, apt, FillMode.Winding)
    g.Dispose()
End Sub
```

Fig. 7.3. A Gradient Star

7.2. The Yin and Yang Shape

The Yin and Yang symbol is an ancient oriental sign. According to the ancient Chinese philosophy, Yin is associated with dark, moist, receptive, earthy, and feminine, whereas Yang is bright, dry, active, heavenly, and masculine. Yin and Yang exist in almost constant interaction. A distinctive feature of this shape is that it consists of two shapes, which, together, form a circle (Fig. 7.4). This is difficult to imagine if you consider each shape separately. The Yin-Yang project is my attempt to draw this figure (Listing 7.4).

Listing 7.4. Drawing the Yin-Yang Shape

```
'----------------------------------------
' Yin-Yang © 2004 Alexander Klimov
'----------------------------------------
    Private Sub Button1_Click(ByVal sender As System.Object, ByVal e As _
System.EventArgs) Handles Button1.Click
        ' Drawing the Yin-Yang Shape
        Dim g As Graphics = CreateGraphics()
        Dim black_pen As SolidBrush = New SolidBrush(Color.Black)
        Dim white_pen As SolidBrush = New SolidBrush(Color.White)
        g.FillEllipse(black_pen, 100, 100, 200, 200)
        System.Threading.Thread.Sleep(1000)
        ' Making a one-second pause
        g.FillEllipse(white_pen, 150, 100, 100, 100)
        System.Threading.Thread.Sleep(1000)
        g.FillPie(white_pen, 100, 100, 200, 200, -90, 180)
        System.Threading.Thread.Sleep(1000)
        g.FillEllipse(black_pen, 150, 200, 100, 100)
        System.Threading.Thread.Sleep(1000)
        g.FillEllipse(black_pen, 185, 135, 30, 30)
        g.FillEllipse(white_pen, 185, 235, 30, 30)
        g.Dispose()
    End Sub
```

As can be seen by examining the code, the shape is formed by superimposing one black circle, one white circle, and one white pie (the FillPie method) over one large black circle. The algorithm to create the shape is very simple. First, a large circle filled in black is drawn on the form. Then the circle is conditionally divided into two equal parts horizontally. A white circle half the diameter of the large one is placed into the upper part. Now, the large circle is conditionally divided into two parts vertically, and one of them is filled white. Next, at the bottom of the large circle, a black circle of the same size as the white at the top is drawn. Finally, two small circles of the opposite color are drawn in the centers of the two small circles. To make the process easier to observe, I placed a one-second pause between the calls to the methods drawing the shape.

Fig. 7.4. Drawing the Yin-Yang shape

7.3. Fractals

Fractals are special shapes that enchant you with their beauty and mystique. Fractals can be encountered in most unexpected areas: meteorology, philosophy, geography, biology, mechanics, etc. A search using the term "fractals" in any search engine will produce numerous references to beautiful images that are using them. A basic definition of a fractal is an object whose structure is the same at any scale. Large objects have the same structure as small ones.

A simple example of a fractal is graph paper. A large sheet of this paper can be considered as a big square, which is, in turn, divided into smaller squares. The process is repeated for each square until the squares have one-millimeter sides. A grid of smaller squares is not particularly interesting to look at. There are other ways to fragment the initial shape, which will be considered a little later.

The creation of the term is attributed to Benoit Mandelbrot. Mandelbrot himself derived the word *fractal* from the Latin *fractus*, which means broken. One of the definitions for fractal is a geometric shape made up of shapes, each of which is a reduced-scale replica of the whole, or at least a very close approximation. In one of his examples Mandelbrot suggested looking at the sea line from an airplane, from a man, and through a magnifying loop. In all cases the pattern will be the same, only of a different scale. The first germs of the ideas for fractal geometry sprouted back in the 19th century. Georg Cantor used a simple recursive procedure to transform a line segment into a set of disjointed points (the so-called *Cantor dust*). To produce the Cantor dust, start with a line segment, divide it into three equal parts, remove the middle part, and repeat the procedure indefinitely. Giuseppe Peano drew a special type of line — the Peano Curve — using the following algorithm. The curve is built by starting with a line segment, dividing it into three equal parts, and then building a square on each side of the middle part. The process is repeated indefinitely for each line of the pattern. The Peano curve is unique in that it fills the entire surface. It has been proven that for each surface point there is a corresponding Peano curve point. The Peano curve and the Cantor dust did not fit within the conventional mathematical concepts. They had no distinct dimensionality. The Cantor dust was seemingly built on the base of a one-dimensional line, but consisted of points (zero dimensionality). The Peano curve was also built on the base of a one-dimensional line, but the final result was a two-dimensional plane. Until the 20th century, no attempt was made to systemize these strange objects. They were purely the subject of data collection.

This continued until Benoit Mandelbrot, already mentioned, got into the business that is considered the father of the modern fractal geometry. Working as a mathematical analyst at the IBM Thomas J. Watson Research Center, he was studying electronic circuit noises that could not be described statistically. Having gradually correlated the facts, he discovered a new area in mathematics: fractal geometry. So why are fractals so beautiful? Mathematics is filled with beauty throughout. You only have to see it. Here is what Mandelbrot himself wrote in his book *"The Fractal Geometry of Nature:"*

"Why is geometry often called cold and dry? One of the reasons is its being unable to describe the shape of clouds, mountains, or trees. Clouds are not spheres, mountains are not angles, a coastline is not a circle, tree bark is not smooth, and a lightning is not a straight line..."

7.3.1. Programming Fractals

The following is the general algorithm for building fractals:

```
A large-scale object is drawn
Parts of this object are replaced with reduced-scale copies of the object
```

It is obvious that the above is a description of a recursive process. Let's build our first fractal. The algorithm for this is the following:

```
The procedure to draw a square
    At each corner of the square a smaller square is drawn
    A square is drawn, if there are no squares of smaller size.
End of the procedure
```

The `Fractals` project implements this algorithm in VB .NET 2003 code (Listing 7.5).

Listing 7.5. Drawing a Simplest Fractal

```
'------------------------------------
' Fractals © 2004 Alexander Klimov
'------------------------------------

    Sub Square(ByRef x As Integer, ByRef y As Integer, ByRef Size As Integer)

        ' To exit the procedure
```

```
    If Size < 20 Then Exit Sub

    Dim g As Graphics = CreateGraphics()
    g.DrawRectangle(Pens.Red, x, y, Size, Size)
    ' The upper left corner
    Square(x - Size / 4, y - Size / 4, Size / 2)

    ' The upper right corner
    Square(x + Size - Size / 4, y - Size / 4, Size / 2)

    ' The bottom left corner
    Square(x - Size / 4, y + 3 * Size / 4, Size / 2)

    ' The bottom right corner
    Square(x + Size - Size / 4, y + 3 * Size / 4, Size / 2)

    g.Dispose()
End Sub


Private Sub mnuSquare_Click(ByVal sender As System.Object, ByVal e As _
System.EventArgs) Handles mnuSquare.Click
    Refresh()
    Square(200, 200, 250)
End Sub
```

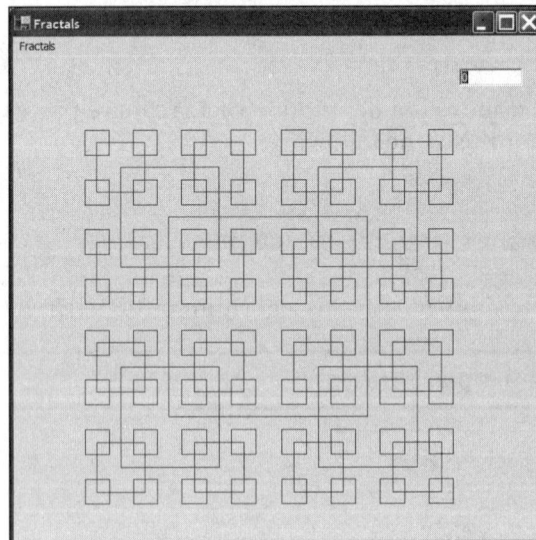

Fig. 7.5. A simplest fractal from squares

After each iteration of the loop, four new squares are drawn, the size of each being a quarter of the size of the previous square. The result is shown in Fig. 7.5.

7.3.2. A Patterned Tablecloth

Now that you understand the main principles for building fractals, you can diversify them, adding your own elements. A very interesting pattern is obtained by connecting the corners of an imaginary square and placing in its center two crossed lines, half the length of the square's side at a 45-degree angle to the crossing diagonals. The square is then broken into four parts, and the same procedure is applied to each of these. The process is repeated as many times as necessary (Listing 7.6). The result is a sort of a weave-pattern tablecloth (Fig. 7.6).

Listing 7.6. Creating a Patterned Tablecloth

```
'---------------------------------------
' A patterned tablecloth
'---------------------------------------

    Sub Pattern(ByRef x As Integer, ByRef y As Integer, ByRef size As Integer)
        ' To exit the procedure
        If size < 5 Then Exit Sub

        Dim g As Graphics = CreateGraphics()

        ' The diagonals
        g.DrawLine(Pens.Red, x, y, x + size, y + size)
        g.DrawLine(Pens.Red, x + size, y, x, y + size)

        ' The vertical line
        g.DrawLine(Pens.Blue, CInt(x + size / 2), y, CInt(x + size / 2), CInt(y + size))
        ' The horizontal line
        g.DrawLine(Pens.Blue, CInt(x), CInt(y + size / 2), CInt(x + size), CInt(y + size / 2))

        Pattern(x - 3 * size / 4, y + size / 4, size / 2)
        Pattern(x + 5 * size / 4, y + size / 4, size / 2)
        Pattern(x + size / 4, y - 3 * size / 4, size / 2)
        Pattern(x + size / 4, y + 5 * size / 4, size / 2)

        g.Dispose()
    End Sub

    Private Sub mnuTablecloth_Click(ByVal sender As System.Object, ByVal e As _
System.EventArgs) Handles mnuTablecloth.Click
        Refresh()
        Pattern(200, 200, 120)
    End Sub
```

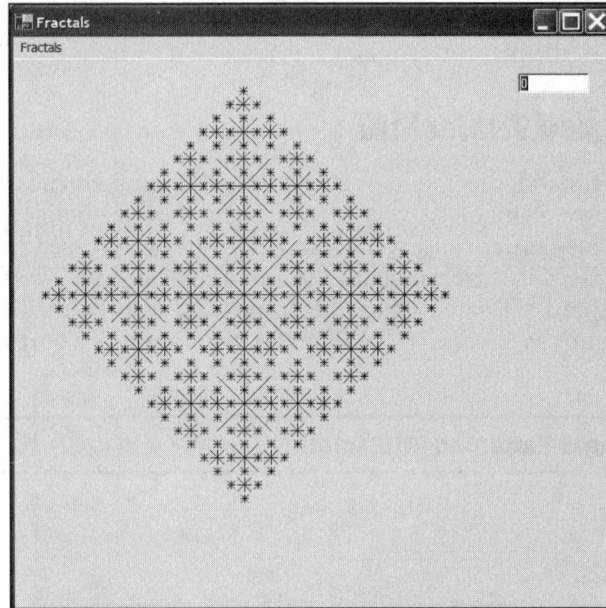

Fig. 7.6. A tablecloth weaved with fractals

7.3.3. Types of Fractals

Fractals are classified into several groups. The largest groups are the following:

- Geometric fractals
- Algebraic fractals
- Systems of iterated functions
- Stochastic fractals

7.3.4. Geometric Fractals

The history of fractals originated with geometric fractals. This type of fractal is obtained by creating simple geometric constructions. A usual algorithm for constructing geometric fractals is the following: You start with a pattern, a collection of line segments, to be used as the base for the fractal. Next, a set of rules is applied to this pattern to transform it into some geometric shape. The same set of rules is applied to each part of the resulting shape. With each step, the shapes become more and more complex, producing a geometric fractal in the end. The Peano curve considered earlier is a geometric fractal. Classical examples of geometric fractals are the *Koch Snowflake*, *Dragon Curve*, and *Sierpinski Triangle*.

7.3.4.1. The Koch Snowflake

The Koch Snowflake is the most interesting and best-known of these geometric fractals. Start with an equilateral triangle, and replace each of its sides with four line segments, each 1/3 the length of the original side. To fit these segments between the vertices, the middle two segments of the newly-created four are jackknifed outward to form a smaller triangle. The procedure is repeated for each new line. Consequently, with each iteration, the length of the broken line increases by a third. Performing an infinite number of iterations produces the Koch snowflake fractal (Fig. 7.7). It turns out that our broken line of infinite length encompasses a finite area. The process can also be visualized as superimposing two equal size triangles (Listing 7.7).

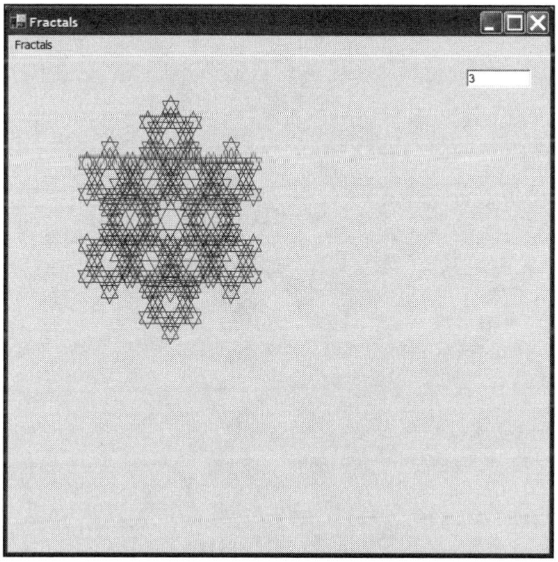

Fig. 7.7. The Koch Snowflake

Listing 7.7. Constructing the Koch Snowflake

```
'----------------------------------------
' The Koch Snowflake
'----------------------------------------
    Sub Koch(ByVal xpos, ByVal ypos, ByVal size)
        Dim x()
        Dim y()

        ReDim x(12), y(12)
        Dim shift As Single
```

```vbnet
Dim i As Integer
If size < 20 Then Exit Sub
shift = size / 8
x(1) = xpos
y(1) = ypos + 4 * shift
x(2) = xpos + shift
y(2) = ypos + 2 * shift
x(3) = xpos + 3 * shift
y(3) = y(2)
x(4) = xpos + 2 * shift
y(4) = ypos
x(5) = x(3)
y(5) = ypos - 2 * shift
x(6) = x(2)
y(6) = y(5)
x(7) = xpos
y(7) = ypos - 4 * shift
x(8) = xpos - shift
y(8) = y(5)
x(9) = xpos - 3 * shift
y(9) = y(5)
x(10) = xpos - 2 * shift
y(10) = ypos
x(11) = x(9)
y(11) = y(2)
x(12) = x(8)
y(12) = y(2)

Dim g As Graphics = CreateGraphics()
' Drawing the first triangle
g.DrawLine(Pens.Red, x(1), y(1), x(5), y(5))
g.DrawLine(Pens.Red, x(5), y(5), x(9), y(9))
g.DrawLine(Pens.Red, x(9), y(9), x(1), y(1))

' Drawing the second triangle
g.DrawLine(Pens.Red, x(3), y(3), x(7), y(7))
g.DrawLine(Pens.Red, x(7), y(7), x(11), y(11))
g.DrawLine(Pens.Red, x(11), y(11), x(3), y(3))

' Comment the following code lines out
' to see the initial two triangles

Koch(xpos, ypos, 2 * shift)
For i = 1 To 12
    Koch(x(i), y(i), 3 * shift)
Next
g.Dispose()
```

```
      End Sub

    Private Sub mnuKoch_Click(ByVal sender As System.Object, ByVal e As _
System.EventArgs) Handles mnuKoch.Click
        Refresh()
        Koch(200, 200, 200)
    End Sub
```

7.3.4.2. The Dragon Curve

The Dragon Curve belongs to the class of self-similar recursively constructed geometric structures. A zero-order curve is just a straight line. Folding it at a right angle, we obtain a first-order curve (Fig. 7.8). Continue folding the resulting line segments at right angles, iterating the angle direction inward and outward. Figs. 7.9 and 7.10 show the second- and third-order curves, respectively. A drawing of a curve of a large enough order is somewhat reminiscent of a dragon, hence the name. The procedure used to draw a dragon curve could be like that shown in Listing 7.8.

Listing 7.8. Creating the Dragon Curve

```
'-------------------------------------
' The Dragon Curve
'-------------------------------------
    Sub Dragon(ByRef x1 As Integer, ByRef y1 As Integer, ByRef x2 As Integer, ByRef y2 _
As Integer, ByRef k As Integer)
        Dim xn As Integer
        Dim yn As Integer
        Dim g As Graphics = CreateGraphics()

        If k > 0 Then
            xn = (x1 + x2) / 2 + (y2 - y1) / 2
            yn = (y1 + y2) / 2 - (x2 - x1) / 2
            Call Dragon(x1, y1, xn, yn, k - 1)
            Dragon(x2, y2, xn, yn, k - 1)
        Else
            g.DrawLine(Pens.Red, x1, y1, x2, y2)
        End If

        g.Dispose()
    End Sub

    Private Sub mnuDragon_Click(ByVal sender As System.Object, ByVal e As _
System.EventArgs) Handles mnuDragon.Click
        Refresh()
        Dragon(200, 300, 500, 300, CInt(TextBox1.Text))
    End Sub
```

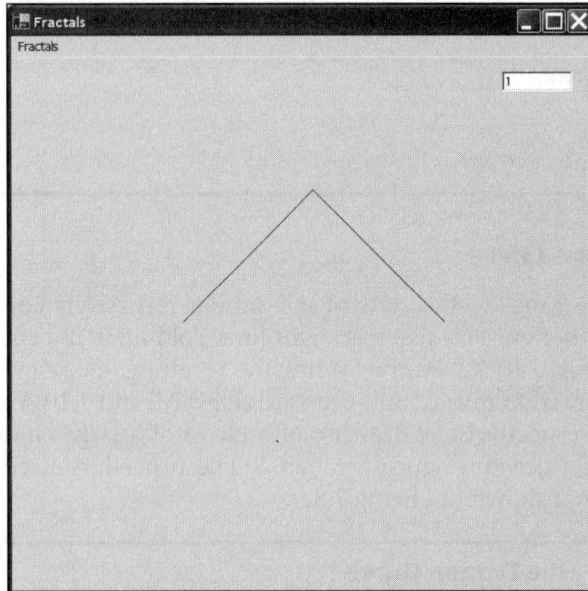

Fig. 7.8. The first-degree curve

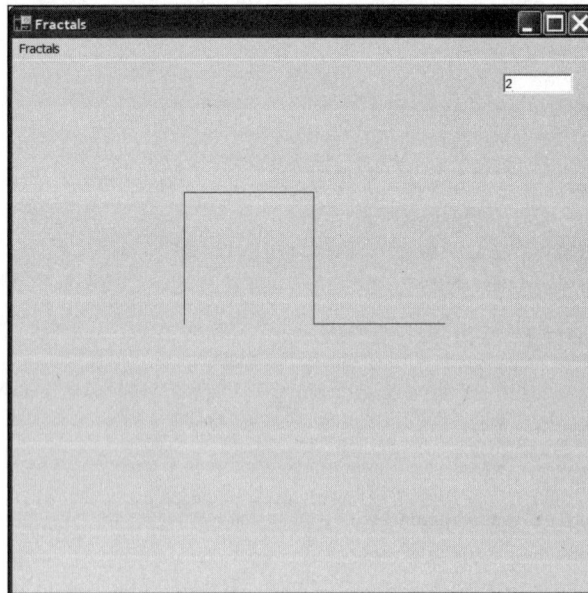

Fig. 7.9. The second-degree curve

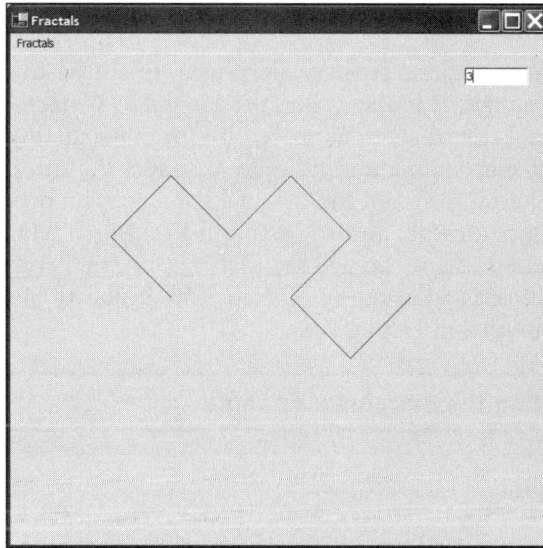

Fig. 7.10. The third-degree curve

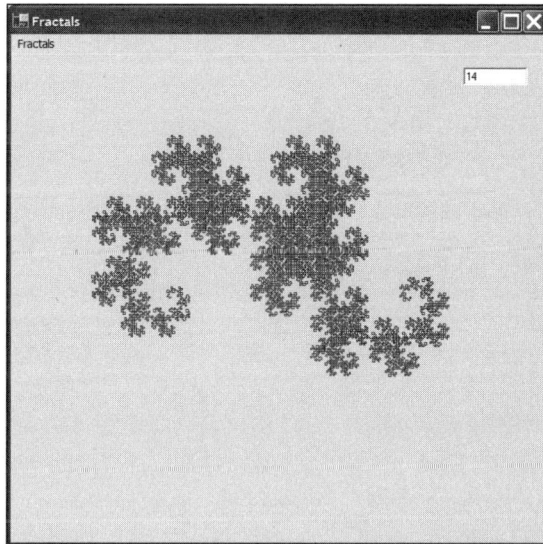

Fig. 7.11. The Harter-Heightway fractal

To draw the dragon curve with different order coefficients, I placed a variable into the code that takes its value from the text field. To draw the Harter-Heightway fractal (a subset of the dragon curve), enter 14 into the text field (Fig. 7.11).

7.3.4.3. The Sierpinski Triangle

In 1915, a Polish mathematician, Waclaw Sierpinski, invented the fractal that bears his name: the *Sierpinski Triangle*. It is also called the *Sierpinski Gasket*. This triangle is one of the earliest known fractal examples. The procedure for constructing the Sierpinski Triangle is the following. Take an equilateral triangle. Connect the midpoints of its sides. Cut out the resulting center triangle from the original triangle. The procedure is repeated for each of the three triangles created, and so forth, on to infinity. Magnifying any of the resulting triangles and examining it, we will see that it is an exact copy of the original triangle. The Sierpinski triangle is an example of exact self-similarity in fractals. A program to draw this triangle is provided in Listing 7.9.

Listing 7.9. Constructing the Sierpinski Triangle

```
'----------------------------------------
' The Sierpinski Triangle
'----------------------------------------
    Private Sub DrawTriangle(ByVal x1 As Single, ByVal y1 As Single, ByVal x2 As _
Single, ByVal y2 As Single, ByVal x3 As Single, ByVal y3 As Single)
        ' Drawing a triangle
        Dim g As Graphics = CreateGraphics()
        g.DrawLine(Pens.Red, x1, y1, x2, y2)
        g.DrawLine(Pens.Red, x2, y2, x3, y3)
        g.DrawLine(Pens.Red, x3, y3, x1, y1)
        g.Dispose()
    End Sub

    Private Sub DrawSerpinski(ByVal x1 As Single, ByVal y1 As Single, ByVal x2 As _
Single, ByVal y2 As Single, ByVal x3 As Single, ByVal y3 As Single, ByVal counter As Integer)
        Dim x1n, y1n, x2n, y2n, x3n, y3n As Single

        If counter > 0 Then
            x1n = (x1 + x2) / 2
            y1n = (y1 + y2) / 2
            x2n = (x2 + x3) / 2
            y2n = (y2 + y3) / 2
            x3n = (x3 + x1) / 2
            y3n = (y3 + y1) / 2
            DrawTriangle(x1n, y1n, x2n, y2n, x3n, y3n)

            DrawSerpinski(x1, y1, x1n, y1n, x3n, y3n, counter - 1)
            DrawSerpinski(x2, y2, x1n, y1n, x2n, y2n, counter - 1)
            DrawSerpinski(x3, y3, x2n, y2n, x3n, y3n, counter - 1)
        End If
```

```
    End Sub

    Private Sub Button1_Click(ByVal sender As System.Object, ByVal e As _
System.EventArgs) Handles Button1.Click
        Dim g As Graphics = CreateGraphics()
        g.Clear(BackColor)
        DrawTriangle(320, 10, 600, 470, 40, 470)
        DrawSerpinski(320, 10, 600, 470, 40, 470, TextBox1.Text)
        g.Dispose()
    End Sub
```

To make the example more visual, I decided to make the order of the drawn fractal variable, and added a text box on the form, in which the order can be specified. The default value is set to 6 (Fig. 7.12). To see the fractal built starting from the lowest order, you can enter the values 1, 2, 3, etc. into this field. Note that the higher the number, the higher the load on the processor. My computer hung when I tried to set the order to 22.

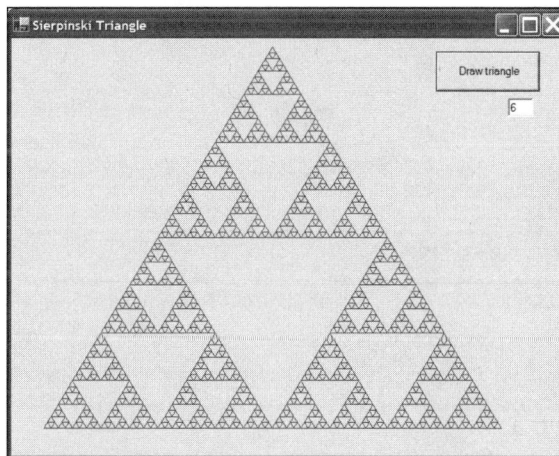

Fig. 7.12. The Sierpinski triangle

7.3.5. Algebraic Fractals

Algebraic fractals comprise another large group. They were given this name because they are constructed based on algebraic formulas. We will demonstrate algebraic fractals with the help of the classical Mandelbrot set. I decided not to try to re-invent the wheel by preparing the code myself because I found a ready example on the site **www.vb-helper.com** (Listing 7.10).

Listing 7.10. Creating the Mandelbrot Set

```vb
'--------------------------------------
' The Mandelbrot Set
' The example is taken from site www.vb-helper.com
' Author: Rod Stevens
'--------------------------------------
Imports System.Math

    Private m_DrawingBox As Boolean
    Private m_X1, m_Y1, m_X2, m_Y2 As Integer
    Private m_ZoomingBitmap As Bitmap
    Private m_ZoomingGraphics As Graphics

    ' Graphical variables
    Private m_Bitmap As Bitmap
    Private m_Graphics As Graphics

    ' Coordinates
    Private Const MIN_X As Double = -2.2
    Private Const MAX_X As Double = 1
    Private Const MIN_Y As Double = -1.2
    Private Const MAX_Y As Double = 1.2
    Private m_Wxmin As Double = MIN_X
    Private m_Wxmax As Double = MAX_X
    Private m_Wymin As Double = MIN_Y
    Private m_Wymax As Double = MAX_Y

    Public Const MaxIterations As Integer = 128

    ' Colors
    Public m_NumColors As Integer
    Private m_Colors() As Color

    Private Sub Form1_Load(ByVal sender As System.Object, ByVal e As System.EventArgs) _
Handles MyBase.Load
        ' Drawing the first image
        ' Loading the colors
        m_NumColors = 15
        ReDim m_Colors(m_NumColors)
        For i As Integer = 0 To m_NumColors - 1
            m_Colors(i) = Color.FromArgb( _
                QBColor(i + 1) + &HFF000000)
        Next i
```

```
        ' Drawing the fractal
        DrawMandelbrot()
    End Sub


    Private Sub Form1_Resize(ByVal sender As Object, ByVal e As System.EventArgs) _
Handles MyBase.Resize
        ' Redrawing when the form size changes
        If m_Colors Is Nothing Then
            m_NumColors = 15
            ReDim m_Colors(m_NumColors)
            For i As Integer = 0 To m_NumColors - 1
                m_Colors(i) = Color.FromArgb( _
                    QBColor(i + 1) + &HFF000000)
            Next i
        End If


        If Me.WindowState = FormWindowState.Minimized Then Exit Sub

        ' If the form is simply moved but no size change
        If Not (m_Bitmap Is Nothing) Then
            If m_Bitmap.Width = PictureBox1.ClientSize.Width And _
                m_Bitmap.Height = PictureBox1.ClientSize.Height _
                Then Exit Sub
        End If

        ' Drawing the fractal
        DrawMandelbrot()
    End Sub


    Private Sub PictureBox1_Click(ByVal sender As System.Object, ByVal e As _
System.EventArgs) Handles PictureBox1.Click

    End Sub


    Private Sub PictureBox1_MouseDown(ByVal sender As Object, ByVal e As _
System.Windows.Forms.MouseEventArgs) Handles PictureBox1.MouseDown
        ' Starting drawing a rubber rectangle
        m_DrawingBox = True
        m_X1 = e.X
        m_Y1 = e.Y
        m_X2 = m_X1
        m_Y2 = m_Y1

        ' Making a copy of the current image
        m_ZoomingBitmap = New Bitmap(m_Bitmap)
```

```
    m_ZoomingGraphics = Graphics.FromImage(m_ZoomingBitmap)
End Sub

    Private Sub PictureBox1_MouseMove(ByVal sender As Object, ByVal e As _
System.Windows.Forms.MouseEventArgs) Handles PictureBox1.MouseMove
        ' Continuing drawing the rubber rectangle
        If Not m_DrawingBox Then Exit Sub

        ' Saving the angles
        m_X2 = e.X
        m_Y2 = e.Y

        ' Drawing a new rectangle
        Dim gr As Graphics = PictureBox1.CreateGraphics()
        Dim rect As New Rectangle
        rect.X = Min(m_X1, m_X2)
        rect.Y = Min(m_Y1, m_Y2)
        rect.Width = Abs(m_X2 - m_X1)
        rect.Height = Abs(m_Y2 - m_Y1)
        m_ZoomingGraphics.DrawImage(m_Bitmap, 0, 0)
        m_ZoomingGraphics.DrawRectangle(Pens.White, rect)

        ' Outputting the result
        PictureBox1.Image = m_ZoomingBitmap
    End Sub

    Private Sub PictureBox1_MouseUp(ByVal sender As Object, ByVal e As _
System.Windows.Forms.MouseEventArgs) Handles PictureBox1.MouseUp
        ' Finishing drawing the rubber rectangle
        m_DrawingBox = False

        ' Releasing resources
        PictureBox1.Image = Nothing
        m_ZoomingBitmap.Dispose()
        m_ZoomingGraphics.Dispose()
        m_ZoomingBitmap = Nothing
        m_ZoomingGraphics = Nothing

        ' Saving the new angles
        m_X2 = e.X
        m_Y2 = e.Y

        ' Placing the selected coordinates in order
        Dim x1, x2, y1, y2, factor As Double
```

```
        x1 = Min(m_X1, m_X2)
        x2 = Max(m_X1, m_X2)
        y1 = Min(m_Y1, m_Y2)
        y2 = Max(m_Y1, m_Y2)

        ' Converting the screen coordinates
        factor = (m_Wxmax - m_Wxmin) / PictureBox1.ClientSize.Width
        m_Wxmax = m_Wxmin + x2 * factor
        m_Wxmin = m_Wxmin + x1 * factor

        factor = (m_Wymax - m_Wymin) / PictureBox1.ClientSize.Height
        m_Wymax = m_Wymin + y2 * factor
        m_Wymin = m_Wymin + y1 * factor

        ' Drawing the fractal
        DrawMandelbrot()
End Sub


' Adjusting the size
Private Sub AdjustAspect()
        Dim want_aspect, Picturebox1_aspect As Double
        Dim hgt, wid, mid As Double

        want_aspect = (m_Wymax - m_Wymin) / (m_Wxmax - m_Wxmin)
        Picturebox1_aspect = _
          PictureBox1.ClientSize.Height / PictureBox1.ClientSize.Width
        If want_aspect > Picturebox1_aspect Then
            wid = (m_Wymax - m_Wymin) / Picturebox1_aspect
            mid = (m_Wxmin + m_Wxmax) / 2
            m_Wxmin = mid - wid / 2
            m_Wxmax = mid + wid / 2
        Else
            hgt = (m_Wxmax - m_Wxmin) * Picturebox1_aspect
            mid = (m_Wymin + m_Wymax) / 2
            m_Wymin = mid - hgt / 2
            m_Wymax = mid + hgt / 2
        End If
End Sub


' The procedure to draw the fractal
Private Sub DrawMandelbrot()
        ' Doing nothing if the graphics size is zero
        If PictureBox1.ClientSize.Width < 1 Or _
          PictureBox1.ClientSize.Height < 1 Then Exit Sub
```

```vb
' Creating graphics objects
If Not (m_Graphics Is Nothing) Then
    PictureBox1.Image = Nothing
    m_Graphics.Dispose()
    m_Bitmap.Dispose()
End If
m_Bitmap = New Bitmap(PictureBox1.ClientSize.Width, _
PictureBox1.ClientSize.Height)
m_Graphics = Graphics.FromImage(m_Bitmap)

' Clearing the image
m_Graphics.Clear(Color.Black)
PictureBox1.Image = m_Bitmap
PictureBox1.Refresh()

Const MAX_MAG_SQUARED As Double = 4.0

AdjustAspect()

Dim clr As Integer
Dim ReaC, ImaC, dReaC, dImaC, ReaZ, ImaZ, ReaZ2, ImaZ2 As Double

Dim wid As Integer = PictureBox1.ClientSize.Width
Dim hgt As Integer = PictureBox1.ClientSize.Height
dReaC = (m_Wxmax - m_Wxmin) / (wid - 1)
dImaC = (m_Wymax - m_Wymin) / (hgt - 1)

ReaC = m_Wxmin
For i As Integer = 0 To wid - 1
    ImaC = m_Wymin
    For j As Integer = 0 To hgt - 1
        ReaZ = 0
        ImaZ = 0
        ReaZ2 = 0
        ImaZ2 = 0
        clr = 0
        Do While clr < MaxIterations And _
                ReaZ2 + ImaZ2 < MAX_MAG_SQUARED
            ReaZ2 = ReaZ * ReaZ
            ImaZ2 = ImaZ * ImaZ
            ImaZ = 2 * ImaZ * ReaZ + ImaC
            ReaZ = ReaZ2 - ImaZ2 + ReaC
            clr = clr + 1
        Loop
```

```
            m_Bitmap.SetPixel(i, j, _
                m_Colors(clr Mod m_NumColors))

            ImaC = ImaC + dImaC
        Next j
        ReaC = ReaC + dReaC

        If i Mod 10 = 0 Then PictureBox1.Refresh()
    Next i

    PictureBox1.Refresh()

    Me.Text = "Mandelbrot (" & _
        Format$(m_Wxmin) & ", " & _
        Format$(m_Wymin) & ")-(" & _
        Format$(m_Wxmax) & ", " & _
        Format$(m_Wymax) & ")"
End Sub


    Private Sub mnuFullScale_Click(ByVal sender As System.Object, ByVal e As _
System.EventArgs) Handles mnuFullScale.Click
        m_Wxmin = MIN_X
        m_Wxmax = MAX_X
        m_Wymin = MIN_Y
        m_Wymax = MAX_Y

        DrawMandelbrot()
    End Sub
```

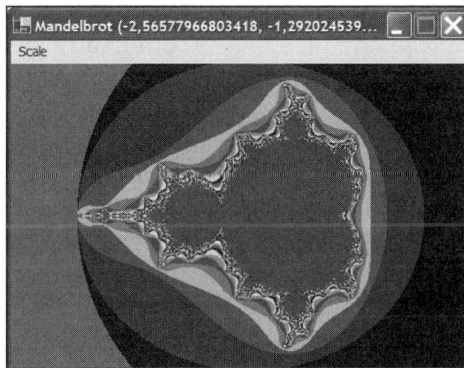

Fig. 7.13. The Mandelbrot set

We can take a small piece of the Mandelbrot set image from Fig. 7.13 and scale it up to fill the screen. What we see is a manifestation of quasi self-similarity. This quasi self-similarity will be manifested at any stage of zooming in.

7.3.6. L-Systems

Aficionados of fractals and mathematic images are familiar with fantastic images of plants obtained using special programs. These are so-called *L-systems.* They are built based on two principles. The first principle is the so-called "turtle graphics" (the draw) operator of the GWBASIC patriarch and its progenies, Turbo Basic and QBasic. In these programs, movements are drawn in a series of steps as increments relative to the current point. This behavior can also be modeled by specifying the movements as coordinate increments. The second principle is the crux of the method: Each individual movement is replaced with the entire image. For example, let's start with a Y-shaped fork. In the next step, each of the three branches is replaced with the same fork, turning the fork itself into a branch. The following iterations produce a shaggy bush, then a pretty fuzzy fractal tree. Changing the starting image produces most various plant images, ranging from umbrella-like dill, to spiky tumbleweed, to a bunch of seaweed.

The essence of L-coding comes down to the following. Imagine some virtual programmable device made of a pen, a pen-controlling mechanism, and a sheet of paper. The pen-controlling mechanism can execute several commands. These are the following: It can lower the pen to the paper and draw a straight line segment of a specified length in the direction, in which the pen is currently oriented: the F command. It can change the orientation of the pen relative to the current orientation by a certain relative angle, clockwise or counterclockwise: the commands + and - . It can also remember (push on stack) its current state and recall (pop off stack) a previously remembered state: the commands [and], respectively. In the given context, the state means the (x, y, a) triplet, where x and y are the coordinate of the pen, and a is the pen-orientation angle. Consequently, specifying a certain initial direction, defining the relative rotation angle of 90 degrees, and specifying the length of the segment, the F+F+F+F command sequence can be used to draw a square. In the same way, specifying the relative rotation angle of 60 degrees, the F++F++F command sequence can be used to draw an equilateral triangle.

Assume also that, in addition to the characters for the five enumerated commands, other characters can be inserted into programs for our virtual device that the control mechanism will simply ignore. That is, if we enter the command F+BF+CCF+CF, the device will draw a square anyway. Finally, let's equip our device with an add-on with the following function. Before the program is sent to the controlling mechanism, the add-on can parse it a specified number of times. During each parsing, it can change any characters in the program sequence according to certain previously specified rules. The initial program character sequence is now called the *axiom.* Let our axiom be FB+, the rule B < F+FB, and the number of parsings, for example, two. Having processed the axiom, the add-on will place the FF+FF+FB+ sequence on the device's input. That's about all there is to it. The virtual device just described can be used to construct the most diverse fractal shapes, from traditional mathematical fractals, such as, for example, the Koch Snowflake or the Hilbert Curve, to structures remarkably like land and sea plants. Let's consider what symbols are generally used to code L systems.

The letter F designates a move forward, the + sign designates clockwise rotation, the – sign designates counterclockwise rotation. The rotation angle is specified in a program and is constant for all rotations. The letter B designates returning without drawing. We do not need drawing on the way back, as the return mechanism is more important. Let's designate the point, to which we need to return, as [and the point, from which the return is made, as]. Then a Y-fork can be programmed as follows:

- ❏   F — Move forward
- ❏   [— Remember the current position
- ❏   + — Rotate left through 22.5 degrees
- ❏   F — Move forward after the rotation
- ❏   ] — Return to the remembered position
- ❏   [— Remember the current position
- ❏   – — Return left relative to the direction in the remembered point
- ❏   F — Move forward after the rotation
- ❏   ] — Return to the remembered position

These movements are amenable to coding. A more complex operation of coding the next step can also be implemented, replacing each straight segment of the fork with the same fork. Two steps will draw three steps, and three steps will draw four steps. It is rather tiresome to draw each step by replacing the program coding, and this is where we take advantage of recursion. This is just the tool for this type of job! By declaring the necessary variables and passing the values of the return point coordinates, we can draw any tree according to a previously-specified formula with the help of a self-calling procedure. The program provided for your perusal (the LSystem project, Listing 7.11) will allow you to delight in the growth of a tree on the screen in a fractally-unpredictable manner. Launching the program, you will see it drawing a branch bent down by the wind. The recursion depth (the same as the fuzziness of the branch) can be changed by changing the value of the Kmax variable (Fig. 7.14). By changing the movement formula, you can create the most amazing and fantastic images.

Listing 7.11. Constructing an L-System

```
'-------------------------------------
' LSystem © 2004 Alexander Klimov
'-------------------------------------
    Dim F(50) As String
```

```
Dim X(10) As Single
Dim Y(10) As Single
Dim Fi(10) As Single
Dim Xtemp(10) As Single
Dim Ytemp(10) As Single
Dim Fitemp(10) As Single
Dim Xtemp2(10) As Single
Dim Ytemp2(10) As Single
Dim Fitemp2(10) As Single
Dim Fi0 As Single

Dim k As Integer
Dim Kmax As Integer
Dim branch As Integer
Dim i(10) As Integer
Dim Xnew As Single
Dim Ynew As Single

Private Sub Form1_Load(ByVal sender As System.Object, ByVal e As System.EventArgs) _
Handles MyBase.Load
        k = 1
        Kmax = 5  ' Number of cycles

        branch = 300 / Kmax ^ 2.5  ' The size of an element
        X(0) = 800  ' The coordinate of the drawing starting point
        Y(0) = 600
        Fi(0) = 0 ' The drawing starting angle
        Fi0 = 3.14 / 8 ' Angle rotation

        ' The drawing procedure
        F(1) = "-"   ' This designates rotation left.
        F(2) = "f"   ' This designates a step forward.
        F(3) = "+"   ' This designates rotation right.
        F(4) = "f"
        F(5) = "+"
        F(6) = "["
  ' Remembering the current position to return to when coming to the ] character
        F(7) = "+"
        F(8) = "f"
        F(9) = "-"
        F(10) = "f"
        F(11) = "-"
        F(12) = "]"  ' Returning to the position remembered at the [ character
        F(13) = "-"
        F(14) = "["
```

```
        F(15) = "-"
        F(16) = "f"
        F(17) = "+"
        F(18) = "f"
        F(19) = "+"
        F(20) = "f"
        F(21) = "]"
End Sub
Sub Cicl()

        X(k) = X(k - 1)
        Y(k) = Y(k - 1)
        Fi(k) = Fi(k - 1)

        For i(k) = 1 To 50
            If F(i(k)) = "-" Then Fi(k) = Fi(k) - Fi0
            If F(i(k)) = "f" Then
                If k = Kmax Then
                    Drw()
                    X(k) = Xnew
                    Y(k) = Ynew
                Else
                    k = k + 1
                    Cicl()
                    k = k - 1
                    X(k) = X(k + 1)
                    Y(k) = Y(k + 1)
                End If
            End If

            If F(i(k)) = "+" Then Fi(k) = Fi(k) + Fi0
            If F(i(k)) = "[" Then Xtemp(k) = X(k) : Ytemp(k) = Y(k) : Fitemp(k) = Fi(k)
            If F(i(k)) = "]" Then X(k) = Xtemp(k) : Y(k) = Ytemp(k) : Fi(k) = Fitemp(k)
            If F(i(k)) = "[[" Then Xtemp2(k) = X(k) : Ytemp2(k) = Y(k) : Fitemp2(k) = Fi(k)
            If F(i(k)) = "]]" Then X(k) = Xtemp2(k) : Y(k) = Ytemp2(k) : Fi(k) = Fitemp2(k)

        Next i(k)
End Sub

Sub Drw()
    Xnew = X(k) + branch * Math.Sin(Fi(k))
    Ynew = Y(k) - branch * Math.Cos(Fi(k))
    Dim g As Graphics = CreateGraphics()
    g.TranslateTransform(-450, -150)
```

```
        g.DrawLine(Pens.Green, X(k), Y(k), Xnew, Ynew)
        g.Dispose()

    End Sub


    Private Sub Timer1_Tick(ByVal sender As System.Object, ByVal e As _
System.EventArgs) Handles Timer1.Tick
        Cicl()
        Timer1.Enabled = False
    End Sub
```

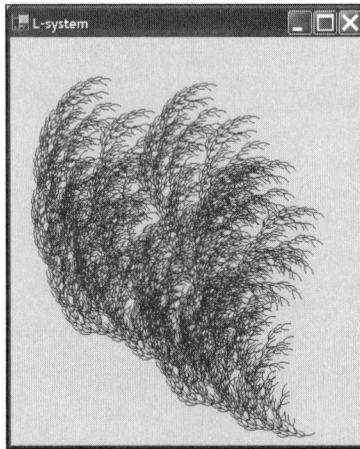

Fig. 7.14. A branch drawn using an L system

You should note that this program is almost the exact analog of a project written in VB 6.0. All I had to change was just one line to output a line using the `DrawLine` method. This demonstrates the deep kinship between VB .NET 2003 and the older version of this language.

7.4. Suggestions and Recommendations

Take a good look at the objects that surround you and try to write a program to draw them. Shapes obtained using L systems may turn out to be the most interesting.

Chapter 8: Images

GDI+ provides powerful image processing capabilities using the `Bitmap` class. This class has numerous properties and methods. I have selected those that are practically unavailable in VB 6.0.

8.1. Smoothing Images

One of the most important and useful features of the `Graphics` class is the ability to smooth out images when their size changes. You most likely have had to enlarge or reduce images in graphics editors at least sometimes and are also likely not too happy with the image distortion caused by these operations. Advanced graphics editors can smooth out distortions of this type by subjecting areas with sharp color transitions to additional processing. Let's take a look at how the distortions accompanying changes in the size of an image can be moderated by way of a practical example. We will load a test image into a program, change its size, and display the result on the screen. To illustrate the example, I created an `Antialias` project and placed three `Picture Box` and two `Button` controls on the main form. A test image is loaded in one of the picture boxes, named `picSource`. The other two picture boxes are left empty. First, we will reduce the test image to half of its size, and then copy it into the `picNoChange` picture box without any additional processing (Listing 8.1).

Listing 8.1. An Image Distortion Example

```
'-------------------------------------
' Antialias © 2004 Alexander Klimov
'-------------------------------------

    Private Sub Button1_Click(ByVal sender As System.Object, ByVal e As _
System.EventArgs) Handles Button1.Click
        ' The source image
        Dim img As New Bitmap(picSource.Image)

        ' The size for the new image
        Dim wid As Integer = picSource.Width \ 2
        Dim hgt As Integer = picSource.Height \ 2
        Dim bmp_to As New Bitmap(wid, hgt)

        ' Copying the reduced image without additional processing
        Dim g As Graphics = Graphics.FromImage(bmp_to)
        g.DrawImage(img, 0, 0, wid - 1, hgt - 1)

        ' Outputting the result
        picNoChange.Image = bmp_to
    End Sub
```

As you can see, the reduced image is less sharp then the original (Fig. 8.1). Now, let's try to apply one of the smoothing methods to the reduced image (Listing 8.2).

Listing 8.2. A Smoothed-out Image Example

```
    Private Sub Button2_Click(ByVal sender As System.Object, ByVal e As _
System.EventArgs) Handles Button2.Click
        Dim img As New Bitmap(picSource.Image)

        Dim wid As Integer = picSource.Width \ 2
        Dim hgt As Integer = picSource.Height \ 2
        Dim bmp_to As New Bitmap(wid, hgt)

        ' Copying the image applying a smoothing method
        Dim g As Graphics = Graphics.FromImage(bmp_to)
        g.InterpolationMode = _
            Drawing2D.InterpolationMode.HighQualityBilinear
        g.DrawImage(img, 0, 0, wid - 1, hgt - 1)
        picChange.Image = bmp_to
    End Sub
```

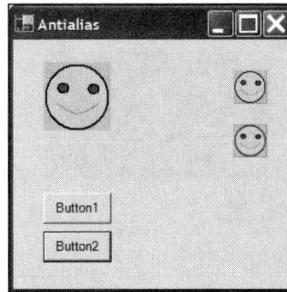

Fig. 8.1. A smoothed-out image

8.2. The *MakeTransparent* Method

One of the interesting methods of the `Bitmap` class is `MakeTransparent`. This method, as the name suggests, allows you to make a specified image color transparent. The simplest way to implement this effect is as follows. I used the standard Windows' Paint image editor to create a test image. The image consists simply of a green-filled background, on which the word "CAT" is written in aquamarine. In a new project, named `MakeTransparent`, I placed two `PictureBox` controls, named `picFrom` and `picTo` on the form. I assigned my image to the `Image` property of the `picFrom` picture box. I also placed two buttons on the form, leaving their default properties unchanged. The green color of the image can be considered to be its background, as it takes its larger part. Let's try to make the background color transparent. This can be done (Fig. 8.2) using the code of Listing 8.3.

Listing 8.3. Making the Background Transparent

```
'---------------------------------------
' MakeTransparent © 2004 Alexander Klimov
'---------------------------------------
    Private Sub Button1_Click(ByVal sender As System.Object, ByVal e As _
System.EventArgs) Handles Button1.Click
        Dim bmp_fr As New Bitmap(picFrom.Image)
        Dim g As Graphics = Graphics.FromImage(bmp_fr)
        Dim backColor As Color = bmp_fr.GetPixel(3, 3)

        ' Making the background color transparent
        bmp_fr.MakeTransparent(backColor)

        ' Outputting the results to the screen
        picTo.Image = bmp_fr
    End Sub
```

Fig. 8.2. Image with the transparent background color

To determine the color of the background, I used the GetPixel method, which allows you to identify the color in a specified point. Because most of the image is filled with green color, it is almost certain that the point with the coordinates (3, 3) will be of the green color that we need. The code in the Button1 click event handler makes the green color transparent, so it does not show on the screen, leaving only the text. The natural question arises of whether it is possible to make the color of the letters transparent, instead of the background. The simple answer is "yes," as can be seen in Fig. 8.3. This is achieved using the Button2 click event handler (Listing 8.4).

Listing 8.4. Making Letters Transparent

```
    Private Sub Button2_Click(ByVal sender As Object, ByVal e As System.EventArgs) _
Handles Button2.Click
        Dim bmp_fr As New Bitmap(picFrom.Image)
        Dim g As Graphics = Graphics.FromImage(bmp_fr)

        ' These are the coordinates of one of the letters' points.
        Dim foreColor As Color = bmp_fr.GetPixel(60, 47)

        ' Making the color of this point transparent
        bmp_fr.MakeTransparent(foreColor)

        ' Outputting the results to the screen
        picTo.Image = bmp_fr
    End Sub
```

I determined the coordinates of a point in a letter using the Paint program, where the coordinates of any point on the canvas are displayed in the right part of the status bar, located at bottom of the program's main window. I used these coordinates in my example.

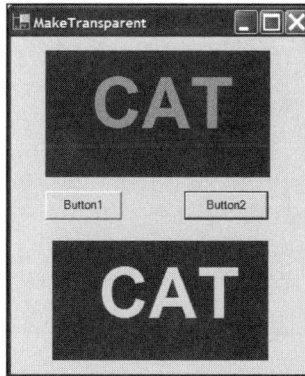

Fig. 8.3. An image with transparent letter color

8.2.1. Superimposing Images

If you have understood how we went about making any color in an image transparent, you will have no problems understanding the following example. The basics of the example are as follows. Suppose that we have two images. One is a picture and the other contains plain text as in the example just considered. Simply superimposing the text, with its background in place, over the picture will produce less-than-appealing results. But what if we remove the background of the text image (i.e., make it transparent), and only then superimpose the text? Let's try it. The example is demonstrated in the MakeTransparent2 project (Listing 8.5).

Listing 8.5. Superimposing Text on a Picture

```
'-------------------------------------
' MakeTransparent2  © 2004 Alexander Klimov
'-------------------------------------
    Private Sub butMakeTrans_Click(ByVal sender As System.Object, ByVal e As _
System.EventArgs) Handles butMakeTrans.Click
        ' Processing the image with text
        Dim bmp_txt As New Bitmap(picText.Image)
        Dim g As Graphics = Graphics.FromImage(bmp_txt)
        Dim backColor As Color = bmp_txt.GetPixel(1, 1)

        ' Making the background color transparent
        bmp_txt.MakeTransparent(backColor)

        ' Copying the text into the main image
```

```
Dim bmp_cat As New Bitmap(picImage.Image)
Dim gr As Graphics = Graphics.FromImage(bmp_cat)
gr.DrawImage(bmp_txt, _
    (bmp_cat.Width - bmp_txt.Width) \ 2, _
    bmp_cat.Height - bmp_txt.Height)

' Outputting the results to the screen
picImage.Image = bmp_cat

End Sub
```

First, we make the background color of the text image transparent (see the previous example, Listing 8.3). Then, we copy the resulting text image into the main image, which contains a picture of a cat. The effect we have obtained is similar to that produced by photomontage (Fig. 8.4).

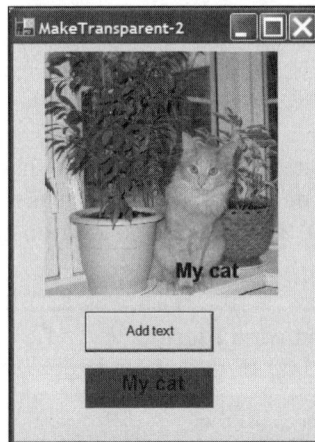

Fig. 8.4. Superimposing text on a picture

8.2.2. Watermarks

The example above can be expanded by superimposing a semi-transparent image on another. This creates a watermark effect. We know watermarks mainly as a practice used with currency and securities to prevent counterfeiting. Watermarks are also used extensively in graphics files as a security feature to protect intellectual property. The Watermark project (Listing 8.6) is very similar to the previous example to superimpose an image. The detailed comments in the source code will help you understand this example.

Listing 8.6. Creating Watermarks

```
'---------------------------------------
' Watermark © 2004 Alexander Klimov
'---------------------------------------
    ' The procedure for placing a watermark on an image
    Private Sub DrawWatermark(ByVal watermark As Bitmap, _
        ByVal basic As Bitmap, ByVal x As Integer, ByVal y _
        As Integer)
        ' The coefficient of the alpha-channel transparency
        Const ALPHA As Byte = 85

        ' Looping through all pixels
        ' of the watermark image
        ' changing their color's alpha component
        ' and making their opacity a third of the total
        Dim clr As Color
        For py As Integer = 0 To watermark.Height - 1
            For px As Integer = 0 To watermark.Width - 1
                clr = watermark.GetPixel(px, py)
                watermark.SetPixel(px, py, _
                    Color.FromArgb(ALPHA, clr.R, clr.G, clr.B))
            Next px
        Next py

        ' Making the background of the watermark image transparent
        ' by taking a pixel from the upper left corner
        Dim backColor As Color = watermark.GetPixel(3, 3)
        ' and making this color transparent
        watermark.MakeTransparent(backColor)

        ' Copying the obtained result into the base image
        Dim g As Graphics = Graphics.FromImage(basic)
        g.DrawImage(watermark, x, y)
    End Sub

    Private Sub butWatermark_Click(ByVal sender As System.Object, ByVal e As _
System.EventArgs) Handles butWatermark.Click
        ' The watermark image
        Dim watermarkImage As New Bitmap(picWatermark.Image)

        ' The main image for the experiment
        Dim basicImage As New Bitmap(picImage.Image)

        ' The coordinates to output the watermark
```

```
Dim x As Integer = basicImage.Width - watermarkImage.Width
Dim y As Integer = basicImage.Height - watermarkImage.Height

watermarkImage = New Bitmap(picWatermark.Image)

' Superimposing the watermark image on the base image
DrawWatermark(watermarkImage, basicImage, x, y)

' Outputting the results to the screen
picImage.Image = basicImage

End Sub
```

Launching the program and clicking the button will produce a watermark image, superimposed on the base image (Fig. 8.5). I made the watermark transparency two-thirds of the total (0 — complete transparency, 255 — complete opacity). Naturally, you can select whatever transparency coefficient you like.

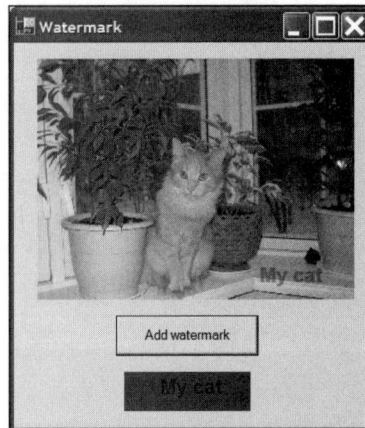

Fig. 8.5. Creating watermarks

8.3. Applying Effects to Images

Simply looking at pictures is not that interesting. It is much more fun to apply some special effects to them. Graphics editors like Adobe Photoshop or Paint Shop Pro allow you to apply many special effects to images. These effects are created by processing image areas according to special algorithms. Let's take a look at some of these. An image may be considered as a collection of many pixels of different colors. Patterns of multicolored pixels compose the final image that is output to the screen. The GetPixel method makes it possible to access any image pixel and determine its characteristics. Once we have the necessary data, the SetPixel method can be used to modify the image. Note that processing all of the pixels in large images can take a significant amount of time, especially on less powerful computers. The Pixel project (Listing 8.7) shows how to convert a color image into a grayscale image.

Listing 8.7. Converting a Color Image into a Grayscale Image

```
'---------------------------------------
' Pixel  © 2004 Alexander Klimov
'---------------------------------------
    Private Sub butGrayScale_Click(ByVal sender As System.Object, ByVal e As _
System.EventArgs) Handles butGrayScale.Click
        Dim clr As Integer ' color
        Dim wid As Integer ' width
        Dim hei As Integer ' height

        ' The coordinates of the pixels
        Dim x As Integer
        Dim y As Integer

        ' Creating a Bitmap object from a picture box
        Dim myBitmap As Bitmap = picImage.Image

        wid = myBitmap.Width - 1
        hei = myBitmap.Height - 1

        ' Looping through all pixels of the image
        ' and changing their color to gray
        For y = 0 To hei
            For x = 0 To wid
                With myBitmap.GetPixel(x, y)
                    clr = 0.3 * .R + 0.6 * .G + 0.1 * .B
                End With
                myBitmap.SetPixel(x, y, _
                    Color.FromArgb(255, clr, clr, clr))
            Next x
        Next y

        ' Outputting the result
        picImage.Image = myBitmap

    End Sub
```

Converting to the gray color is performed according to the following formula:

```
0.299*RED+0.587*GREEN+0.114*Blue
```

This formula takes into account how the human eye perceives colors. The NTSC television standard is based on this formula, which is also widely used in graphics.

8.3.1. The Color Model

There is another method for converting images: the `SetColorMatrix` method of the `ColorMatrix` class. This class is defined in the `System.Drawing.Imaging` namespace and allows the color model to be changed with the help of a 5 × 5 RGBA color-conversion matrix. Each element of the matrix is a coefficient ranging from 0 to 1. Complete color intensity equals 1 (i.e., the 255 value correlates to the value 1). You may ask why our matrix is 5 × 5, and not 4 × 4, to correspond to the standard color representation. The reason is that the last value is used for non-linear conversions and usually equals 1. Let's see how this class is used in practice. We will try to change the intensity of each of the component colors by a certain value and observe the results. The code for this project, named `ColorMatrixSample`, is provided in Listing 8.8.

Listing 8.8. Using a Matrix to Convert Images

```vb
'-------------------------------------
' ColorMatrixSample © 2004 Alexander Klimov
'-------------------------------------

Imports System.Drawing.Drawing2D
Imports System.Drawing.Imaging


    Private Sub Button1_Click(ByVal sender As System.Object, ByVal e As _
System.EventArgs) Handles Button1.Click
        Dim img As Image = PictureBox1.Image

        Dim copy As Bitmap = New Bitmap(img.Width, img.Height)

        Dim ia As ImageAttributes = New ImageAttributes
        Dim cm As ColorMatrix = New ColorMatrix
        cm.Matrix00 = cm.Matrix11 = cm.Matrix22 = 0.99F


        ia.SetColorMatrix(cm)


        Dim g As Graphics
        g = Graphics.FromImage(copy)
        g.DrawImage(img, New Rectangle(0, 0, img.Width, img.Height), 0, 0, img.Width, _
img.Height, GraphicsUnit.Pixel, ia)
```

```
      PictureBox1.Image = copy
      g.Dispose()
      img.Dispose()
   End Sub
```

The picture used in the example is Autumn.jpg, from the Windows XP's \Windows\Web\Wallpaper folder. The leaves on the trees are yellow, the realistic color for this season. Applying the matrix with the specified settings has made all of the leaves a rich green color and turned season in the park from autumn to summer right in front of our eyes! Unfortunately, this effect cannot be reproduced on paper; so I urge you to carry out this project and check out the converted picture.

Let's try a few more experiments to reinforce your newly-acquired knowledge. A short while back, we looked at the effect produced by converting a color image into a gray one by looping through each of its pixels. The same can be done using the ColorMatrix class and applying the already familiar formula (Listing 8.9).

Listing 8.9. Converting a Color Image into a Grayscale Image

```
   Private Sub butGray_Click(ByVal sender As System.Object, ByVal e As _
System.EventArgs) Handles butGray.Click
         ' Converting a color image into a grayscale image
         Dim img As Image = PictureBox1.Image

         Dim copy As Bitmap = New Bitmap(img.Width, img.Height)

         Dim ia As ImageAttributes = New ImageAttributes

         ' The algorithm for converting to grayscale
         Dim cm As ColorMatrix = New ColorMatrix(New Single()() _
               {New Single() {0.3, 0.3, 0.3, 0, 0}, _
                New Single() {0.59, 0.59, 0.59, 0, 0}, _
                New Single() {0.11, 0.11, 0.11, 0, 0}, _
                New Single() {0, 0, 0, 1, 0}, _
                New Single() {0, 0, 0, 0, 1}})

         ia.SetColorMatrix(cm)

         Dim g As Graphics
         g = Graphics.FromImage(copy)
         g.DrawImage(img, _
            New Rectangle(0, 0, img.Width, img.Height), 0, 0, _
            img.Width, img.Height, GraphicsUnit.Pixel, ia)
```

```
        PictureBox1.Image = copy
        g.Dispose()
        img.Dispose()
    End Sub
```

Another common image-processing operation is making a negative of an image. This is achieved by changing the values of the main colors to the opposite ones (Listing 8.10).

Listing 8.10. Turning an Image Negative

```
    Private Sub butNegative_Click(ByVal sender As System.Object, ByVal e As _
System.EventArgs) Handles butNegative.Click
        ' Turning image negative

        Dim img As Image = PictureBox1.Image
        Dim copy As Bitmap = New Bitmap(img.Width, img.Height)
        Dim ia As ImageAttributes = New ImageAttributes

        ' The algorithm for converting to negative
        Dim cm As ColorMatrix = New ColorMatrix(New Single()() _
              {New Single() {-1, 0, 0, 0, 0}, _
               New Single() {0, -1, 0, 0, 0}, _
               New Single() {0, 0, -1, 0, 0}, _
               New Single() {0, 0, 0, 1, 0}, _
               New Single() {0, 0, 0, 0, 1}})

        ia.SetColorMatrix(cm)

        Dim g As Graphics
        g = Graphics.FromImage(copy)
        g.DrawImage(img, _
           New Rectangle(0, 0, img.Width, img.Height), 0, 0, _
           img.Width, img.Height, GraphicsUnit.Pixel, ia)
        PictureBox1.Image = copy
        g.Dispose()
        img.Dispose()
    End Sub
```

The final example we will consider is that of making images semi-transparent. Here, we will make use of the Matrix33 property, which gets or sets the element at the 3rd row and 3rd column of the ColorMatrix object. By setting it to 0.5, we specify that we want to convert the Alpha (transparency) component (Listing 8.11).

Listing 8.11. Creating a Semi-Transparent Image

```
    Private Sub butHalfTrans_Click(ByVal sender As System.Object, ByVal e As _
System.EventArgs) Handles butHalfTrans.Click
        ' Creating a semi-transparent image

        Dim img As Image = PictureBox1.Image
        Dim copy As Bitmap = New Bitmap(img.Width, img.Height)
        Dim ia As ImageAttributes = New ImageAttributes

        ' The algorithm to obtain semi-transparency
        Dim cm As ColorMatrix = New ColorMatrix(New Single()() _
            {New Single() {1, 0, 0, 0, 0}, _
             New Single() {0, 1, 0, 0, 0}, _
             New Single() {0, 0, 1, 0, 0}, _
             New Single() {0, 0, 0, 0.5, 0}, _
             New Single() {0, 0, 0, 0, 1}})

        ia.SetColorMatrix(cm)

        Dim g As Graphics
        g = Graphics.FromImage(copy)
        g.DrawImage(img, _
            New Rectangle(0, 0, img.Width, img.Height), 0, 0, _
            img.Width, img.Height, GraphicsUnit.Pixel, ia)
        PictureBox1.Image = copy
        g.Dispose()
        img.Dispose()
    End Sub
```

Having looked at all of these examples led me to want to create some unusual effect. I believe that an image gradually appearing from another image is unusual enough. Let's get rolling.

8.3.2. The Gradual Appearance of One Image out of Another

The idea, on which this effect is based, is very simple. You already know how to control the transparency of images. In this way, you can increase the transparency of one image gradually, thus allowing another image, located in the same area of the form, to appear. The effect can be enhanced by adding the ability to change the color components of the ColorMatrix matrix randomly. The example is demonstrated in the ColorMatrixFX project (Listing 8.12).

Listing 8.12. An Emerging Image

```
'-------------------------------------
' ColorMatrixFX  © 2004 Alexander Klimov
'-------------------------------------
Imports System.Drawing.Drawing2D
Imports System.Drawing.Imaging

    ' The transparency level
    Private transparent As Single = 0.1F

    ' The transparency change step
    Private trStep As Single = 0.1F

    ' The color matrix array
    Private apts(,) As Single = {{1.0F, 0.0F, 0.0F, 0.0F, 0.0F}, _
                                 {0.0F, 1.0F, 0.0F, 0.0F, 0.0F}, _
                                 {0.0F, 0.0F, 1.0F, 0.0F, 0.0F}, _
                                 {0.0F, 0.0F, 0.0F, transparent, 0.0F}, _
                                 {0.0F, 0.0F, 0.0F, 0.0F, 1.0F}}

    Private backImg As Image
    Private frontImg As Image

    Private cm As New ColorMatrix
    Private ia As New ImageAttributes
    Private r As New Rectangle
    Private rnd As New Random

    Private Sub Form1_Paint(ByVal sender As Object, ByVal e As _
System.Windows.Forms.PaintEventArgs) Handles MyBase.Paint
        DrawFX(e, transparent)
    End Sub

    Private Sub Form1_Load(ByVal sender As Object, ByVal e As System.EventArgs) _
Handles MyBase.Load
        ' To reduce the form flicker
        MyClass.SetStyle(ControlStyles.UserPaint, True)
        MyClass.SetStyle(ControlStyles.AllPaintingInWmPaint, True)
        MyClass.SetStyle(ControlStyles.DoubleBuffer, True)

        backImg = PictureBox1.Image
```

```
        frontImg = PictureBox2.Image
        r = New Rectangle(0, 0, MyClass.ClientSize.Width, _
                        ClientSize.Height)

        Dim i, j As Integer
        For i = 0 To 4
            For j = 0 To 4
                cm.Item(i, j) = apts(i, j)
            Next
        Next
    End Sub


    Private Sub Timer1_Tick(ByVal sender As System.Object, ByVal e As System.EventArgs) _
Handles Timer1.Tick
        If transparent < 0 Or transparent > 1 Then
            trStep *= -1
            cm.Matrix01 = Convert.ToSingle(rnd.NextDouble)
            cm.Matrix12 = Convert.ToSingle(rnd.NextDouble)
            cm.Matrix23 = Convert.ToSingle(rnd.NextDouble)
        End If

        transparent += trStep
        cm.Matrix33 = transparent
        Refresh()
    End Sub


    Private Sub DrawFX(ByVal e As PaintEventArgs, ByVal trsp As Single)
        Dim g As Graphics = e.Graphics
        g.DrawImage(backImg, r)

        ia.SetColorMatrix(cm)
        g.DrawImage(frontImg, r, 0, 0, _
          frontImg.Width, frontImg.Height, _
          GraphicsUnit.Pixel, ia)
    End Sub
```

I assume that you can figure out how the code works for yourself. The main processing takes place in the handler of the timer's Tick event, which also calls the procedure declared, DrawFX. Fig. 8.6 shows one moment of one image appearing from another. The image files are located on the accompanying CD-ROM.

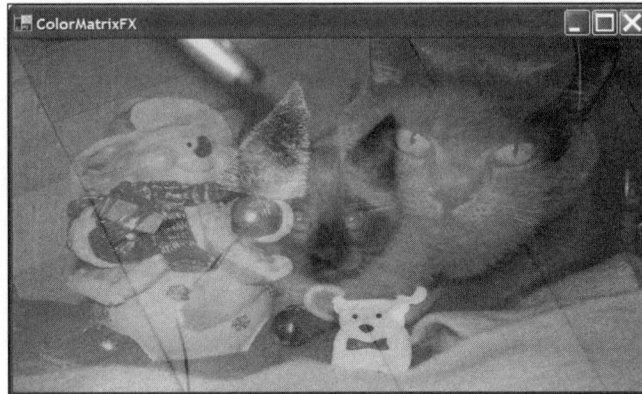

Fig. 8.6. An emerging image

8.4. The *DrawImage* Method

The `DrawImage` method of Visual Basic .NET 2003 is a very powerful graphics tool. Its weak analog in the old Visual Basic 6.0 is the `PaintPicture` method. The mighty `DrawImage` method has 30 overloaded versions. Just describing all of them would almost fill a chapter of its own, so we will consider only the most interesting examples. One version appears as follows:

```
Overloads Public Sub DrawImage( _
    ByVal image As Image, _
    ByVal destPoints() As Point _
)
```

This version of the method uses an array of three points as parameters. These points are the upper left, upper right, and bottom left corners of the image. Consequently, with the help of these points, a parallelogram can be created.

8.4.1. Parallelogram

The code to construct a parallelogram is very easy and short. First, create a new project and name it `Warp`. All of the processing takes place when painting the form (Listing 8.13).

Listing 8.13. Creating a Parallelogram

```
'----------------------------------------
' Warp © 2004 Alexander Klimov
'----------------------------------------
    Private Sub Form1_Paint(ByVal sender As Object, ByVal e As _
System.Windows.Forms.PaintEventArgs) Handles MyBase.Paint
```

```
' Loading an image from a file
Dim img As Image = Image.FromFile(Application.StartupPath() _
                    & "..\..\cat2.jpg")

' Declaring an array for points
' defining the corners of the image
Dim w As Single = img.Width
Dim h As Single = img.Height
Dim corners As Point() = { _
                    New Point(w * 0.5, 0), _
                    New Point(w, h * 0.5), _
                    New Point(0, h * 0.5)}

' Outputting the image to the screen
e.Graphics.DrawImage(img, corners)
End Sub
```

Let's examine what this code does. First, we load an image from a file into the `img` variable. Next, we declare an array to hold three points. For convenience, I used the dimensions of the picture itself. After slight manipulations with these, I obtained points corresponding to the middle of the image's horizontal and vertical dimensions. I then assigned the three points the coordinates I had obtained. The rest is all simple. The `DrawImage` method is called, with the image and the new coordinates as its parameters, and the deformed image is displayed on the screen (Fig. 8.7).

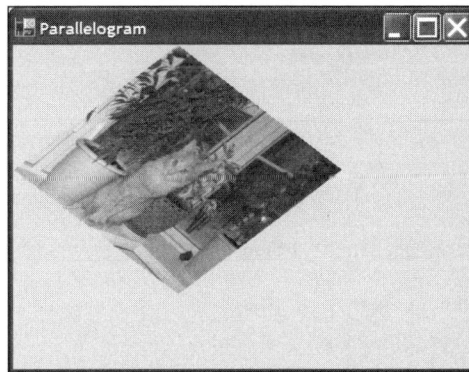

Fig. 8.7. Parallelogram

8.4.2. Dragging Images

I borrowed the idea for the next example from the Rod Stephens' site (**www.vb-helper.com**), where many other interesting examples can also be found. The example outputting a distorted image is too simple; I only used it as an introduction to the subject. But you can use this example to make the program interactive. For example, you can let the user modify the image using the mouse. Since an image can be deformed by moving its corners, the coordinates of these corners can be modified dynamically. To make the example more visual, I used special red circle markings. You can place the mouse cursor on any of these markings and drag it to another place. The program will recalculate the new coordinates of the selected point and change the image dynamically. I do not, however, recommend using very large images for examples. The program processes a huge amount of data in the background and an image that is too large will be updated very slowly. But let's move on to the example. Create a new project named Drag and place two PictureBox controls on the form. Name them picSource and picDest. The picSource control will hold the source image. Load any image in it using the Image property, and make it invisible by setting the Visible property to False. This concludes the visual programming part. Now, open the code editor tab and add the following code to the project (Listing 8.14).

Listing 8.14. Changing Images Dynamically

```
'-------------------------------------
' Drag © 2004 Alexander Klimov
' Based on an idea of Rod Stephens (www.vb-helper.com)
'-------------------------------------
    ' The radius of the marking circles
    Private Const CORNER_RADIUS As Integer = 7
    Private BmSource As Bitmap
    Private BmDest As Bitmap
    Private Corners As Point()
    Private DragCorner As Long

    Private Sub Form1_Load(ByVal sender As System.Object, ByVal e As System.EventArgs) _
Handles MyBase.Load
        BmSource = New Bitmap(picSource.Image)
        BmDest = New Bitmap( _
                        CInt(BmSource.Width), _
                        CInt(BmSource.Height))

        Corners = New Point() { _
                        New Point(0, 0), _
                        New Point(BmSource.Width, 0), _
                        New Point(0, BmSource.Height)}

        DragCorner = -1

        ' Outputting the image
```

```
        WarpImage()
End Sub


' Drawing the image
Private Sub WarpImage()
    ' Creating a Graphics object for the image
    Dim gr_dest As Graphics = Graphics.FromImage(BmDest)

    ' Copying the source image into the destination image
    gr_dest.Clear(picDest.BackColor)
    gr_dest.DrawImage(BmSource, Corners)

    ' Drawing three marking circles
    Dim i As Long
    For i = 0 To 2
        Dim pn As New Pen(Color.Red, 3)
        gr_dest.DrawEllipse(pn, _
            Corners(i).X - CORNER_RADIUS, _
            Corners(i).Y - CORNER_RADIUS, _
            2 * CORNER_RADIUS, 2 * CORNER_RADIUS)
    Next i

    ' Showing the result
    picDest.Image = BmDest
End Sub


' Dragging the corners
Private Sub picDest_MouseDown(ByVal sender As Object, ByVal e As _
System.Windows.Forms.MouseEventArgs) Handles picDest.MouseDown
    Dim i As Long

    ' If the mouse pointer is inside one of the markings
    For i = 0 To 2
        If (Math.Abs(Corners(i).X - e.X) < CORNER_RADIUS) And _
            (Math.Abs(Corners(i).Y - e.Y) < CORNER_RADIUS) _
        Then
            ' start dragging the corner
            DragCorner = i
            Exit For
        End If
    Next i
End Sub


Private Sub picDest_MouseMove(ByVal sender As Object, ByVal e As _
System.Windows.Forms.MouseEventArgs) Handles picDest.MouseMove
```

```
    ' Checking whether a corner is being dragged
    If DragCorner < 0 Then Exit Sub

    Corners(DragCorner).X = e.X
    If Corners(DragCorner).X < 0 Then
        Corners(DragCorner).X = 0
    ElseIf Corners(DragCorner).X > BmDest.Width Then
        Corners(DragCorner).X = BmDest.Width
    End If
    Corners(DragCorner).Y = e.Y
    If Corners(DragCorner).Y < 0 Then
        Corners(DragCorner).Y = 0
    ElseIf Corners(DragCorner).Y > BmDest.Height Then
        Corners(DragCorner).Y = BmDest.Height
    End If

    WarpImage()
End Sub


' Done dragging
Private Sub picDest_MouseUp(ByVal sender As Object, ByVal e As _
System.Windows.Forms.MouseEventArgs) Handles picDest.MouseUp
    DragCorner = -1
End Sub
```

Let's examine how this code works. First, I declared several global variables. The CORNER_RADIUS variable holds the value of the radius for the marking circles. These markings are used to drag the image's corners. The BmSource and BmDest variables will hold graphic objects: the source and destination images. The Corners variable is an array for the points, and the DragCorner variable is an indicator that an image corner can be dragged. When the form is loaded, the BmSource and BmDest variables are assigned the preloaded image and an array is defined to hold the three points used in the program. The coordinates of the upper left, upper right, and bottom left corners of the image are used for the example. The WrapImage procedure carries out the modification of the image. Let's examine this procedure in detail. First, a Graphics object is created for the image, and the source image is copied into it. To assist in tracking the whereabouts of the points, three marking circles are drawn with the following code:

```
    ' Drawing three marking circles
    For i = 0 To 2
        Dim pn As New Pen(Color.Red, 3)
        gr_dest.DrawEllipse(pn, _
            Corners(i).X - CORNER_RADIUS, _
```

```
            Corners(i).Y - CORNER_RADIUS, _
            2 * CORNER_RADIUS, 2 * CORNER_RADIUS)
    Next i
```

Finally, the result is output into the `picDest` picture box control. The most interesting processing takes place in the handlers of the `picDest_MouseDown` and `picDest_MouseMove` events. When the left mouse button is depressed, the coordinates of the mouse pointer are determined and, if at this moment the mouse pointer is within one of the marking circles, the corresponding corner of the image is dragged. The dragging is performed by the handler of the `picDest_MouseMove` event. It reconfigures the corners of the image dynamically to the current mouse coordinates.

8.4.3. Placing Images on the Sides of a Cube

You have probably already realized the implications of the image dragging example. If you look at how a cube is drawn on a flat surface, you will see that it is nothing other but a collection of adjoining parallelograms that represent its sides. Consequently, it is a cinch to draw a cube with whatever images you want on its sides. This kind of cube looks cool on the monitor. Let's carry out this task in a new project named `DrawCube`. For starters, you will need three graphics files to load in the form when the program starts. Find any three pictures that strike your fancy on you computer, and memorize (or, better yet, write down) the paths to them. I used three pictures of my cat, named them 1.jpg, 2.jpg, and 3.jpg, and placed them in the bin folder for the project. I did this only for my own convenience. You can name your pictures whatever you want and place them in whatever folders you want. Just make sure that you specify the correct paths for them. The code to display the cube on the screen is located in the handler of the `Click` event of the `butDrawCube` button (Listing 8.15).

Listing 8.15. Placing Images on the Faces of a Cube

```
'---------------------------------------
' DrawCube   © 2004 Alexander Klimov
'---------------------------------------
    Private Sub butDrawCube_Click(ByVal sender As System.Object, ByVal e As _
System.EventArgs) Handles butDrawCube.Click
        ' Creating a Graphics object for the cube with images
        Dim g As Graphics
        g = CreateGraphics()
        g.TranslateTransform(100, 200)

        Dim m_Images(2) As Image
        Dim app_path As String
        app_path = Application.StartupPath
```

```
    m_Images(0) = Image.FromFile(app_path & "\1.jpg")
    m_Images(1) = Image.FromFile(app_path & "\2.jpg")
    m_Images(2) = Image.FromFile(app_path & "\3.jpg")

    ' Three points defining the front facet of the cube
    Dim face1(2) As Point
    face1(0) = New Point(-50, -20)
    face1(1) = New Point(250, -20)
    face1(2) = New Point(-50, 230)

    ' The top facet
    Dim face2(2) As Point
    face2(0) = New Point(70, -140)
    face2(1) = New Point(370, -140)
    face2(2) = New Point(-50, -20)

    ' The side facet
    Dim face3(2) As Point
    face3(0) = New Point(250, -20)
    face3(1) = New Point(370, -140)
    face3(2) = New Point(250, 230)

    ' Outputting the images to the screen
    g.DrawImage(m_Images(1), face1)
    g.DrawImage(m_Images(2), face2)
    g.DrawImage(m_Images(0), face3)
    g.Dispose()
End Sub
```

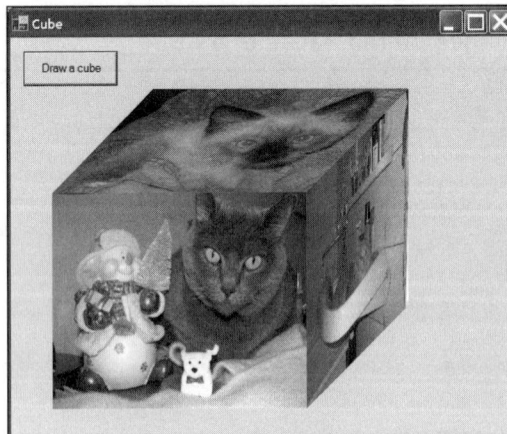

Fig. 8.8. A cube with images

Build the project, run the program, and admire the results (Fig. 8.8). Cool, isn't it? First, the images are loaded into the m_Images array, and the three cube faces are then created. Each face is a parallelogram and can be defined using an array of three points. The important thing here is to juxtapose the parallelograms in such a way so that they form a cube on the screen.

8.4.4. Rotating an Image through a Specified Angle

The technique considered in the previous two examples is also used to rotate an image through a certain angle. The main problem that needs to be addressed in this task is to calculate the new positions of the corners using trigonometric formulas. The image is then output on the screen at these new coordinates. The RotateAngle project is implements the image-rotation example. Place two PictureBox, and 1 each of Label, TextBox, and Button controls on the form. Load any image into the picFrom picture box control. All processing is carried out by the code located in the handler of the click event for the butRotate button (Listing 8.16).

Listing 8.16. Rotating an Image through a Specified Angle

```
'-----------------------------------------------
' RotateAngle © 2004 Alexander Klimov
'-----------------------------------------------
Imports System.Math

    Private Sub butRotate_Click(ByVal sender As System.Object, ByVal e As _
System.EventArgs) Handles butRotate.Click
        ' Obtaining access to the image from the picFrom object
        Dim bm_from As New Bitmap(picFrom.Image)

        ' Declaring an array of points for the corners of the picture
        Dim wid As Single = bm_from.Width
        Dim hgt As Single = bm_from.Height
        Dim corners As Point() = { _
            New Point(0, 0), _
            New Point(wid, 0), _
            New Point(0, hgt), _
            New Point(wid, hgt)}

        ' Finding the center of the image
        Dim cx As Single = wid / 2
        Dim cy As Single = hgt / 2
        Dim i As Long
```

```vb
    For i = 0 To 3
        corners(i).X -= cx
        corners(i).Y -= cy
    Next i

    ' Starting to rotate
    Dim theta As Single = Single.Parse(txtAngle.Text) * PI / 180.0
    Dim sin_theta As Single = Sin(theta)
    Dim cos_theta As Single = Cos(theta)
    Dim X As Single
    Dim Y As Single
    For i = 0 To 3
        X = corners(i).X
        Y = corners(i).Y
        corners(i).X = X * cos_theta + Y * sin_theta
        corners(i).Y = -X * sin_theta + Y * cos_theta
    Next i

    Dim xmin As Single = corners(0).X
    Dim ymin As Single = corners(0).Y
    For i = 1 To 3
        If xmin > corners(i).X Then xmin = corners(i).X
        If ymin > corners(i).Y Then ymin = corners(i).Y
    Next i
    For i = 0 To 3
        corners(i).X -= xmin
        corners(i).Y -= ymin
    Next i

    ' Creating new Bitmap and Graphics objects
    Dim bm_to As New Bitmap(CInt(-2 * xmin), CInt(-2 * ymin))
    Dim g_to As Graphics = Graphics.FromImage(bm_to)

    ' Because the DrawImage method uses two points
    ' redefining the array by deleting the last point
    ReDim Preserve corners(2)

    ' Drawing the obtained image to picTo
    ' and outputting the results to the screen
    g_to.DrawImage(bm_from, corners)
    picTo.Image = bm_to
End Sub
```

Build the project and launch the program. You can enter any numerical value in the text field. The image is rotated counterclockwise for positive angle values and clockwise for negative angle values.

8.4.5. Using a Timer to Spin an Image

Having learned how to rotate an image through any angle, you are now ready for a project to spin an image. Create a new project, and name it Spin. Just as in the previous example, place a btnStart button and two picture box controls on the form. Set the Text property of the button to Start. Name one of the picture boxes picFrom (it will hold the source image) and the other picTo (this is where the image will be processed). Set the SizeMode property of both picture boxes to AutoSize. Load an image into the picFrom control. In my example, I used a picture of a cat sitting in a sink. Also place a Timer control on the form. Set the Interval property of the timer to 1. The visual part of the project is now done, so you can begin writing the code. For starters, declare the global variables (Listing 8.17).

Listing 8.17. Spinning an Image

```
'---------------------------------------
' Spin  © 2004 Alexander Klimov
'---------------------------------------
    ' For copying the image from the source
    Private bmp_from As Bitmap
    Private fromWid As Integer
    Private fromHgt As Integer
    Private fromCx As Single
    Private fromCy As Single
    Private fromCorners As PointF()

    ' For the image being spun
    Private bmp_to As Bitmap
    Private toWid As Integer
    Private toHgt As Integer
    Private toCx As Single
    Private toCy As Single

    Private FramesDrawn As Long
    Private ToBackColor As Color

    Private Sub Form1_Load(ByVal sender As System.Object, ByVal e As System.EventArgs) _
Handles MyBase.Load
        bmp_from = New Bitmap(picFrom.Image)
```

```
        fromWid = bmp_from.Width
        fromHgt = bmp_from.Height
        fromCx = fromWid / 2
        fromCy = fromHgt / 2
        fromCorners = New PointF() {
            New PointF(0, 0), _
            New PointF(fromWid, 0), _
            New PointF(0, fromHgt), _
            New PointF(fromWid, fromHgt)}

        toWid = Math.Sqrt(fromWid * fromWid + fromHgt * fromHgt)
        toHgt = toWid
        toCx = toWid / 2
        toCy = toHgt / 2
        bmp_to = New Bitmap(toWid, toHgt)

        Dim i As Long
        For i = 0 To 3
            fromCorners(i).X -= fromCx
            fromCorners(i).Y -= fromCy
        Next i

        ToBackColor = picTo.BackColor
    End Sub

    Private Sub Timer1_Tick(ByVal sender As System.Object, ByVal e As System.EventArgs) _
Handles Timer1.Tick

        FramesDrawn += 1

        ' Increasing the angle
        Const dtheta = 3 * Math.PI / 180.0
        Static theta As Single = 0
        theta += dtheta

        ' Placing the coordinates of the image corners into the array
        Dim corners() As PointF = fromCorners

        ' One corner is not needed; removing it.
        ReDim Preserve corners(2)

        ' Spinning
        Dim sin_theta As Single = Math.Sin(theta)
        Dim cos_theta As Single = Math.Cos(theta)
```

```
        Dim X As Single
        Dim Y As Single
        Dim i As Long
        For i = 0 To 2
            X = corners(i).X
            Y = corners(i).Y
            corners(i).X = X * cos_theta + Y * sin_theta
            corners(i).Y = -X * sin_theta + Y * cos_theta
        Next i

        For i = 0 To 2
            corners(i).X += toCx
            corners(i).Y += toCy
        Next i

        ' Creating a new image and a Graphics object
        Dim g_to As Graphics = Graphics.FromImage(bmp_to)

        ' Outputting the results to the screen
        g_to.Clear(ToBackColor)
        g_to.DrawImage(bmp_from, corners)

        picTo.Image = bmp_to
    End Sub
    Private Sub btnStart_Click(ByVal sender As Object, ByVal e As System.EventArgs) _
Handles btnStart.Click
        ' Starting or stopping spinning
        Static start_time As DateTime

        If Timer1.Enabled Then
            ' Stopping spinning
            Dim stop_time As DateTime
            stop_time = Now
            Timer1.Enabled = False
            btnStart.Text = "Start"

        Else
            ' Starting spinning
            Timer1.Enabled = True
            btnStart.Text = "Stop"
            FramesDrawn = 0
            start_time = Now
        End If
    End Sub
```

When the form is loaded, the variables containing the size of the image and the coordinates for its center and corners are initialized. The image is spun by the code in the handler for the timer's `Click` event, which is started and stopped by the `btnStart` button. While you're at this, try to comment out the code responsible for the background color of the picture box. This will produce a quite interesting effect.

8.5. Saving Images

Although it is possible to work with images in other formats in VB 6.0, they can only be saved in the cumbersome BMP format. To save images in formats other than BMP, you have to resort to complicated third-party programs. VB .NET makes it surprisingly easy to convert one graphics format into another. All you have to do is to do is specify the necessary format in the `ImageFormat` class. All of the most popular formats are supported: BMP, GIF, JPG, TIFF, ICO, and a few others. The `SaveImage` project (Listing 8.18) demonstrates how to save an image from a picture box object to the computer disk in each of the four most common formats (BMP, GIF, JPG, and PNG).

Listing 8.18. Saving Images to the Disk

```
    Private Sub butSave_Click(ByVal sender As System.Object, ByVal e As _
System.EventArgs) Handles butPng.Click
        Dim file_path As String = Application.ExecutablePath
        file_path = file_path.Substring(0, _
            file_path.LastIndexOf("\bin")) & _
          "\test."

        ' Using the image from the picture box
        Dim pic As Bitmap = picTest.Image

        ' Saving the image in different formats
        pic.Save(file_path & "bmp", ImageFormat.Bmp)
        pic.Save(file_path & "jpg", ImageFormat.Jpeg)
        pic.Save(file_path & "gif", ImageFormat.Gif)
        pic.Save(file_path & "png", ImageFormat.Png)
    End Sub
```

Do not forget to include this code line at the beginning of the project to import the necessary namespace:

```
Imports System.Drawing.Imaging
```

This example by itself demonstrates the degree, to which VB .NET 2003 has advanced beyond the capabilities of VB 6.0, its predecessor.

8.6. The *ImageAnimator* Class

VB .NET 2003 also supports animated images, so you no longer need to install third party components to work with these. Moreover, the `ImageAnimator` class makes it possible not only to display animations, but also work with individual animation frames. Let's consider this class in detail. It offers four methods altogether. The `CanAnimate` method is used to determine whether an image is animated. The `Animator` project (Listing 8.19) is a simple example of working with an animated image on a form.

Listing 8.19. Working with Animated Images

```
'-------------------------------------
'Animator © 2004 Alexander Klimov
'-------------------------------------
Imports System.Drawing

    ' Creating a Bitmap object from a file
    Private animatedImage As New Bitmap(Application.StartupPath _
        & "..\..\anicat.gif")
    Private currentlyAnimating As Boolean = False

    ' The animation procedure
    Public Sub AnimateImage()
        If Not currentlyAnimating Then
            ' Starting animation
            ImageAnimator.Animate(animatedImage, _
            New EventHandler(AddressOf Me.OnFrameChanged))
            currentlyAnimating = True
        End If
    End Sub

    Private Sub OnFrameChanged(ByVal o As Object, ByVal e As EventArgs)
        ' A forced call of the Paint event
        Me.Invalidate()
    End Sub

    Protected Overrides Sub OnPaint(ByVal e As PaintEventArgs)
        ' Starting animation
        AnimateImage()

        ' Obtaining the next frame
        ImageAnimator.UpdateFrames()

        ' Outputting the frame to the screen
```

```
        e.Graphics.DrawImage(Me.animatedImage, New Point(130, 30))
    End Sub

    Private Sub butStop_Click(ByVal sender As System.Object, ByVal e As _
System.EventArgs) Handles butStop.Click
        ' Stopping animation
        ImageAnimator.StopAnimate(animatedImage, _
            New EventHandler(AddressOf Me.OnFrameChanged))
    End Sub
```

I first declared a `Bitmap` object, into which I then loaded the animated imaged from the anicat.gif file (if necessary, you should change the file path). Then I created an `AnimateImage` procedure to carry out the animation, which calls the `Animate` method.

8.6.1. Animation Frames

As already mentioned, the `ImageAnimator` class can be used not only to play back animated images, but also to extract individual animation frames. Let's explore how this is done using the `Animator2` project. You will need to place three picture-box controls and one button on the form. The anicat.gif animated image is located in the project folder. If necessary, you can change the path to the image file for your version of the project. The program extracts three frames from the animated image: the first, the third, and the last, and outputs them to the screen in picture-box controls. Listing 8.20 gives the code of the event handler for the click event of the button that outputs the frames to be displayed on the screen.

Listing 8.20. Extracting Individual Animation Frames

```
'---------------------------------------
' Animator2  © 2004 Alexander Klimov
'---------------------------------------
Imports System.Drawing.Drawing2D
Imports System.Drawing

    Private Sub butGetFrames_Click(ByVal sender As System.Object, ByVal e As _
System.EventArgs) Handles butGetFrames.Click
        ' Loading the image and extracting frames from it
        Me.Cursor = Cursors.WaitCursor
        Dim anim As New Animation(Application.StartupPath _
          & "..\..\anicat.gif")
        Me.Cursor = Cursors.Default

        ' Outputting the first frame
```

```
        PictureBox1.Image = anim.Frame(0)
        ' Outputting the third frame
        PictureBox2.Image = anim.Frame(2)
        ' Outputting the last frame
        PictureBox3.Image = anim.Frame(anim.FrameCount - 1)
    End Sub
```

As you can see, the code references a new class, Animation (Listing 8.21), which carries out the bulk of the work to extract the animation frames.

Listing 8.21. Defining the Animation Class

```
Class Animation
    Implements IDisposable

    Dim m_img As System.Drawing.Image
    Dim m_Frames As New System.Collections.ArrayList
    Dim m_FrameCount As Integer

    Sub New(ByVal imgPath As String)
        ' Loading the image
        m_img = System.Drawing.Image.FromFile(imgPath)

        ' An error handler
        If ImageAnimator.CanAnimate(m_img) = False Then
            m_img.Dispose()
            Throw New ArgumentException("This is not an animated image.")
        End If

        ' The number of frames
        Dim frame_count As New Imaging.FrameDimension(m_img.FrameDimensionsList _
            (0))
        m_FrameCount = m_img.GetFrameCount(frame_count)

        ' Extracting all animation frames
        AddCurrentFrame()
        ImageAnimator.Animate(m_img, New EventHandler(AddressOf _
            OnFrameChanged))

        Do
        Loop Until GetAll
    End Sub

    ' Returning the total number of frames
```

```vbnet
Public ReadOnly Property FrameCount() As Integer
    Get
        Return m_FrameCount
    End Get
End Property


' Returning the image of the frame stored in the array
Public ReadOnly Property Frame(ByVal index As Integer) As Bitmap
    Get
        Return DirectCast(m_Frames(index), Bitmap)
    End Get
End Property


Public Sub Dispose() Implements System.IDisposable.Dispose
    StopAnimate()
End Sub


' The procedure for changing frames
Private Sub OnFrameChanged(ByVal sender As Object, ByVal e As EventArgs)
    ' Stopping when the last frame has been reached
    If GetAll Then
        StopAnimate()
        Exit Sub
    End If

    ' Changing the frame and storing it in the array
    ImageAnimator.UpdateFrames(m_img)
    AddCurrentFrame()
End Sub


' The procedure for adding the current frame to the array
Private Sub AddCurrentFrame()
    ' Creating a Bitmap object
    Dim bmp As New Bitmap(m_img.Width, m_img.Height)
    ' Creating a Graphics object
    Dim g As Graphics = Graphics.FromImage _
        (DirectCast(bmp, System.Drawing.Image))
    g.DrawImage(m_img, 0, 0)
    ' Adding the frame to the array
    m_Frames.Add(bmp)
End Sub


' Returning True after all frames have been extracted
Private ReadOnly Property GetAll() As Boolean
```

```
        Get
            Return m_Frames.Count = FrameCount
        End Get
    End Property

    ' Stopping the animation and releasing all resources
    Private Sub StopAnimate()
        ImageAnimator.StopAnimate(m_img, _
            New EventHandler(AddressOf OnFrameChanged))
        m_img.Dispose()
    End Sub
End Class
```

All the necessary explanations for the code are provided in the comments. Launch the project and click the button. Each of the picture boxes will display a frame from the animated image (Fig. 8.9).

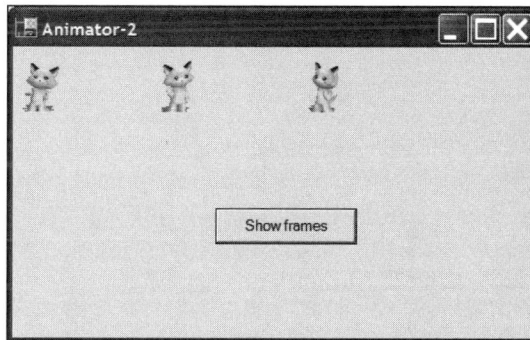

Fig. 8.9. Extracting frames from an animated image

8.7. Suggestions and Recommendations

The graphics capabilities of Visual Basic .NET are so enormous that it is impossible to describe all of the possible techniques and tricks in a few chapters. I suggest that you look for additional information in other programming books and on the Internet.

PART III: KEYBOARD AND MOUSE

Chapter 9: Keyboard

The keyboard is one of the main components of any computer system. Even the mouse, which is seemingly indispensable for GUIs, is less important for system operation. If you disconnect the mouse, the computer will still boot and, yes, you can continue working without it. But try disconnecting the keyboard: The POST will issue an error message and the system will refuse to boot. In this chapter, we will consider several interesting examples involving the keyboard.

First, we'll provide a short description of this input device. Depending on the model, your keyboard has about 100 different keys. Regardless of the model, however, all keyboards have a standard set of keys in common. These are the three rows of the alphanumeric keys, the modifier keys (e.g., <Shift>, <Alt>, and <Ctrl>), the function keys, and the numerical keypad (for desktop keyboards). In addition, the keyboard has light-emitting diode (LED) indicators that light up when certain keys are pressed. This concludes our brief introduction to the keyboard, so we will now move on to concrete examples.

9.1. Switching the Keyboard Layouts

If you use a language other than English in your work or for some other reason, then you still have to enter text in that language, even if you have an English version of Windows installed on your system. Consequently, you have to switch keyboard input languages periodically. As a rule, all you need to do is simultaneously press the <Shift>+<Alt> keys to switch to the other language. This is the default combination, but other key combinations can be assigned to perform this task. But programs that automatically switch the input language have become popular of late. They work by analyzing the words that are being typed to determine the language that is being used. So, if these programs can switch keyboard-input languages, why can't we do the same? The way this can be done is demonstrated in the `KeyboardLayout` project (Listing 9.1). It makes use of the `CurrentInputLanguage` property of the `InputLanguage` class, which belongs to the `System.Glogalization` namespace.

Listing 9.1. Switching Keyboard Layouts

```
'-------------------------------------
' KeyboardLayout © 2004 Alexander Klimov
'-------------------------------------

Imports System.Globalization

    Private Sub Button1_Click(ByVal sender As System.Object, _
            ByVal e As System.EventArgs) Handles Button1.Click

        'InputLanguage.CurrentInputLanguage = InputLanguage.FromCulture( _
                                        'New CultureInfo("es"))
        InputLanguage.CurrentInputLanguage = InputLanguage.FromCulture( _
                                        New CultureInfo("en-US"))
    End Sub
```

The code contains two modes for switching the keyboard-input language. If you need to switch from the American English keyboard layout to one for Spanish, remove the comments from the first line of code and comment out the second line of code. If you use another keyboard layout (German, French, Chinese, etc.) you can find the corresponding keyboard layout codes in the VB .NET documentation.

9.2. Playing Color Music on the Keyboard

Most keyboards have LED indicators that allow users to track the state of the <Caps Lock>, <Num Lock> and <Scroll Lock> keys. For example, if the Caps Lock indicator is lit up, it means that the <Caps Lock> key has been activated and all letters will be typed in upper case (if the <Shift> key is held down, however, letters will be typed in lower case). But a programmer can also do what a user can. How about putting on a light show on the keyboard? The indicators can be turned on and off to accompany a tune programmatically. I will show how to do this in the `LockKeys` project (Listing 9.2). All you have to do is to place one button on the form.

Listing 9.2. Turning Key Indicators On/Off Programmatically

```
'--------------------------------------
' LockKeys  © 2004 Alexander Klimov
'--------------------------------------
    ' Declaring an API function
    Private Declare Sub keybd_event Lib "user32" _
            (ByVal bVk As Byte, _
             ByVal bScan As Byte, _
             ByVal dwFlags As Integer, _
             ByVal dwExtraInfo As Integer)

    ' Constants for the function
    Const VK_NUMLOCK As Short = &H90S
    Const VK_SCROLL As Short = &H91S
    Const VK_CAPITAL As Short = &H14S
    Const KEYEVENTF_EXTENDEDKEY As Short = &H1S
    Const KEYEVENTF_KEYUP As Short = &H2S

    Private Sub Button1_Click(ByVal sender As System.Object, ByVal e As _
System.EventArgs) Handles Button1.Click
        ' The <Num Lock> key
        ' Simulating a key press
        keybd_event(VK_NUMLOCK, &H45S, KEYEVENTF_EXTENDEDKEY Or 0, 0)

        ' Releasing the key
        keybd_event(VK_NUMLOCK, &H45S, _
            KEYEVENTF_EXTENDEDKEY Or KEYEVENTF_KEYUP, 0)

        ' The <Caps Lock> key
        ' Simulating a key press
        keybd_event(VK_CAPITAL, &H45S, KEYEVENTF_EXTENDEDKEY Or 0, 0)

        ' Simulating a key release
        keybd_event(VK_CAPITAL, &H45S, _
            KEYEVENTF_EXTENDEDKEY Or KEYEVENTF_KEYUP, 0)

        ' The <Scroll Lock> key
        ' Simulating pressing and releasing the key
        keybd_event(VK_SCROLL, &H45S, KEYEVENTF_EXTENDEDKEY Or 0, 0)
        keybd_event(VK_SCROLL, &H45S, _
            KEYEVENTF_EXTENDEDKEY Or KEYEVENTF_KEYUP, 0)
    End Sub
```

In order to be able to control the key indicators programmatically, the Windows API keybd_event function has to be declared, along with the necessary constants. To imitate the pressing and releasing of a key, this function needs to be called twice in the click event handler for the Button1 button. Calling the event handler repeatedly toggles the indicators on and off, so there is no need to write a separate procedure for each action.

9.3. Determining the Status of the Keyboard Keys

You already know how to turn on or off the indicators for the <Caps Lock>, <Num Lock>, and <Scroll Lock> keys programmatically. But how can the current status of these key be determined? Here you can make use of the Windows API GetKeyboardState function, which is used to determine the state of any keyboard key. The KeyState project using this function is shown in Listing 9.3.

Listing 9.3. Determining the Current Status of Keyboard Keys

```
'-------------------------------------
' KeyState  © 2004 Alexander Klimov
'-------------------------------------
' The WinAPI function
        Private Declare Function GetKeyboardState Lib "user32" _
                            (ByRef pbKeyState As Byte) As Integer

    ' The constants
    Const VK_NUMLOCK As Short = &H90S
    Const VK_SCROLL As Short = &H91S
    Const VK_CAPITAL As Short = &H14S

    Private Sub Button1_Click(ByVal sender As System.Object, ByVal e As _
System.EventArgs) Handles Button1.Click
        Dim CapsLockState As Boolean
        Dim keys(255) As Byte

        GetKeyboardState(keys(0))

        CapsLockState = keys(VK_CAPITAL)

        If CapsLockState Then
            TextBox1.Text = "CAPSLOCK"
        Else
            TextBox1.Text = "capslock"
        End If
    End Sub
```

The function provides a snapshot of the status of all of the keyboard's keys. Consequently, we have to compare the bit of the necessary key to determine the current status of the key. In the present example, we show you how to find out the current status of the <Caps Lock> key.

9.4. Screenshots of the Screen or Active Window

You probably know that pressing the <Print Screen> key copies the contents of the entire screen to the clipboard. Pressing <Alt>+<Print Screen> only copies the contents of the current window to the clipboard. In either case, the contents of the clipboard can now be pasted into any graphics editor (e.g., into Windows' Paint). It is sometimes necessary for a program to take a snapshot of the screen or the current window. It is possible to write a procedure to simulate the pressing of the necessary keys. The `PrintScreen` project (Listing 9.4) demonstrates how the methods of the `SendKeys` class can be used to do this. After you create a blank project, place a button and a picture box on the form. The picture box will be used to place the screenshot from the clipboard into it.

Listing 9.4. Screenshots

```
'---------------------------------------
' PrintScreen  © 2004 Alexander Klimov
'---------------------------------------
    Function GetScreenshot() As Image
        Return GetScreenshot(False)
    End Function


    Function GetScreenshot(ByVal activeWindow As Boolean) As Image
        ' A screenshot of the active window
        If activeWindow Then
            SendKeys.SendWait("%{PRTSC}")
        Else
            SendKeys.SendWait("{PRTSC 2}")
        End If


        ' There is a screenshot in the clipboard
        Return DirectCast _
            Clipboard.GetDataObject().GetData(DataFormats.Bitmap), _
            Image)
    End Function


    Private Sub butGetScreenShot_Click(ByVal sender As System.Object, ByVal e As _
System.EventArgs) Handles butGetScreenShot.Click
```

```
    picScreenShot.Image = GetScreenshot()

    ' For a screenshot of the active window use the True value
    picScreenShot.Image = GetScreenshot(True)
End Sub
```

As you can see, we have defined two versions of the function. The first function has no parameters and takes a screenshot of the entire screen. The second function uses one parameter, to specify that only a screenshot of the active window needs to be taken (the same as with the <Alt> key pressed). A more complex example of creating screenshots will be shown in *Chapter 19*.

9.5. Using the Calculator

Since we have already become involved with the methods of the SendKeys class, let's consider another related example. It is possible to send simulated key strokes not only to the native program, but also to other running programs. Suppose that we have the standard calculator included in Windows running. We can make this program active and send it the necessary key-stroke combination. The SendToCalculator project (Listing 9.5) implements such an example.

Listing 9.5. Sending Simulated Keys to Calculator

```
'------------------------------------
' SendToCalculator  © 2004 Alexander Klimov
'------------------------------------
    Private Sub Form1_Load(ByVal sender As System.Object, ByVal e As System.EventArgs) _
Handles MyBase.Load
        ' Making the Calculator window active
        AppActivate("Calculator")

        ' Sending the necessary key press combination
        SendKeys.SendWait("2*2{ENTER}")
    End Sub
```

Don't forget to launch Calculator before running the program. Otherwise, you will receive an error message. The program executes when the main form is loaded. At this moment, Calculator becomes active and shows the results from multiplying 2 by 2 (Fig. 9.1).

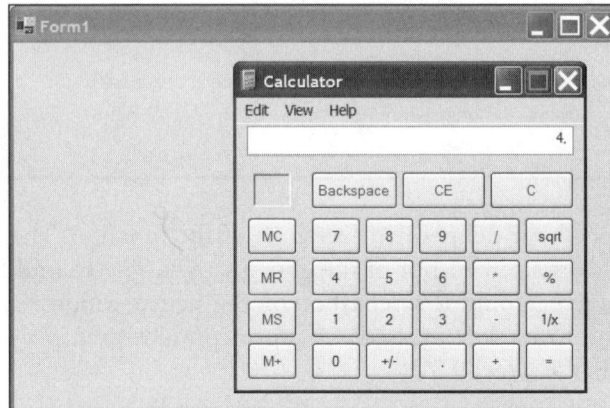

Fig. 9.1. Multiplying two numbers in Calculator

9.6. Suggestions and Recommendations

❒ Using Listing 9.3 as a guide, write a procedure to obtain the status of the <Num Lock> and <Scroll Lock> keys.

❒ For the example in Listing 9.5 to work, Calculator must already have been started. Try to make the example more complicated and make your program launch Calculator itself.

Chapter 10: Mouse

This chapter deals with the computer input device that we all know and love as the mouse. Strangely enough, as soon as I began writing this chapter, my cat, Ginger, jumped up on my lap and began staring at the monitor. As you probably know, a standard mouse has eyes, ears, and a tail. Ginger, get outta here, please! Sorry. Any mouse has at least two buttons, while newer models can have three, or even five, buttons. Most contemporary mice are also equipped with a scrolling wheel. See if you can leave the mouse alone for a while and work using the keyboard only. I am certain that 90 percent of you will feel uncomfortable without the familiar rodent shape in your palm. Although Microsoft recommends that programmers mirror mouse operations with the keyboard keys, there are many programs that work with the mouse only.

10.1. Drawing

The mouse can be used for drawing. You have, most likely, done this numerous times in the Paint graphics editor that comes with any Windows version. But we will now try to write our own graphics editor. First, let's break the process of drawing with the mouse down into its constituent parts. The drawing process begins with placing the mouse pointer in the area intended for drawing. This can be the client area of the program window or a picture-box control. The next step is to press a mouse button. Both the left and the right mouse buttons can be used. Depending on the developer's intentions, the left and the right mouse buttons can be used to perform different drawing functions. Holding the button down, the mouse pointer is moved to another point in the drawing area, trailing the drawn line, which allows us to control the mouse movements. The final operation is to release the button, which, naturally, terminates the drawing process. The sequence just described is performed as many times as necessary. Consequently, from the programming standpoint, drawing consists of processing the MouseDown, MouseMove, and MouseUp mouse events. Having this knowledge in our arsenal, we are all set to write a graphics editor. We will start with a simple example, with only the form and a button, where we will use the button to clear the form. The source code for the project, named SimplePaint, is provided in Listing 10.1.

Listing 10.1. Drawing Using the Mouse

```
'---------------------------------------
' SimplePaint  © 2004 Alexander Klimov
'---------------------------------------
    ' The mouse coordinates at the moment the button is depressed.
    Dim x_md, y_md As Integer

    ' Drawing with a blue pen 3-pixel thick
    Dim p As New Pen(Color.Blue, 3)

    ' Tracking the state of the button being down
    ' to know when the user finishes drawing
    Dim bPaint As Boolean

    Private Sub Form1_MouseDown(ByVal sender As Object, ByVal e As _
    System.Windows.Forms.MouseEventArgs) Handles MyBase.MouseDown
        ' Starting to draw
        bPaint = True

        ' The mouse coordinates at the moment the button is depressed.
        x_md = e.X
        y_md = e.Y
    End Sub

    Private Sub Form1_MouseMove(ByVal sender As Object, ByVal e As _
    System.Windows.Forms.MouseEventArgs) Handles MyBase.MouseMove
        If bPaint Then
            ' Creating a Graphics object for drawing
            Dim g As Graphics = CreateGraphics()

            ' Determining the mouse coordinates during the mouse movement
```

```
        Dim x_mm As Integer = e.X
        Dim y_mm As Integer = e.Y

        ' Drawing
        g.DrawLine(p, x_md, y_md, x_mm, y_mm)

        ' Passing the mouse coordinates to the global variables
        x_md = x_mm
        y_md = y_mm
        g.Dispose()
      End If
    End Sub

    Private Sub Form1_MouseUp(ByVal sender As Object, ByVal e As _
System.Windows.Forms.MouseEventArgs) Handles MyBase.MouseUp
      bPaint = False
    End Sub

    Private Sub Button1_Click(ByVal sender As System.Object, ByVal e As _
System.EventArgs) Handles butClear.Click
      Dim g2 As Graphics = CreateGraphics()
      g2.Clear(MyBase.BackColor)
      g2.Dispose()
    End Sub
```

Fig. 10.1 shows a drawing of a mouse that only took me a few seconds to create. You don't think it looks like a mouse? You simply have no idea of what the real art is!

Fig. 10.1. A drawing produced using the graphics editor

A little laugh

A programmer comes home and his cat runs up and starts fawning all over him, purring, and licking his hands. His wife wonders:

— What in the world has come over the cat? — she asks. — Why is she licking your hand?

— Why not? — he answers. — She can smell a mouse!

10.2. Drawing Straight Lines

In addition to freehand drawing, any graphics editor allows you to draw straight lines. The code for drawing straight lines is practically the same as the freehand process just considered. But I have changed it somewhat to demonstrate other ways of doing this. In particular, instead of separate variables for the mouse coordinates, I used the `Point` structure. The resulting code for the `LinesGDIPlus` project is shown in Listing 10.2.

Listing 10.2. Drawing Straight Lines

```
'-------------------------------------
' LinesGDIPlus  © 2004 Alexander Klimov
'-------------------------------------
    Private g As Graphics

    Private DrawPen As Pen
    Private ErasePen As Pen

    Private ptsStart As Point
    Private ptsPrevious As Point
    Dim bPaint As Boolean

    InitializeComponent()

    ' Custom initialization after calling InitializeComponent()
    g = Me.CreateGraphics()

    ' A pen for erasing the previous line
    ErasePen = New System.Drawing.Pen(Me.BackColor)
    ' A pen for drawing the main line
    DrawPen = New System.Drawing.Pen(Color.Blue)

    Private Sub Form1_MouseDown(ByVal sender As Object, ByVal e As _
System.Windows.Forms.MouseEventArgs) Handles MyBase.MouseDown
```

```
        bPaint = True

        ' Saving the starting mouse coordinates
        ptsStart.X = e.X
        ptsStart.Y = e.Y

        ' Saving the end coordinates
        ptsPrevious = ptsStart
    End Sub

    Private Sub Form1_MouseMove(ByVal sender As Object, ByVal e As _
System.Windows.Forms.MouseEventArgs) Handles MyBase.MouseMove
        If bPaint Then
            ' The current mouse coordinates
            Dim ptsCurrent As Point

            ' Saving the current coordinates of the line's end point
            ptsCurrent.X = e.X
            ptsCurrent.Y = e.Y

            ' Drawing a line, after erasing old lines.
            g.DrawLine(ErasePen, _
                ptsStart.X, ptsStart.Y, ptsPrevious.X, ptsPrevious.Y)
            g.DrawLine(DrawPen, _
                ptsStart.X, ptsStart.Y, ptsCurrent.X, ptsCurrent.Y)

            ' Saving the last point of the line to be used in drawing the next line
            ptsPrevious = ptsCurrent
        End If
    End Sub

    Private Sub Form1_MouseUp(ByVal sender As Object, ByVal e As _
System.Windows.Forms.MouseEventArgs) Handles MyBase.MouseUp
        bPaint = False
    End Sub
```

First, I declared a number of global variables. The ErasePen and DrawPen variables are used to erase and draw lines. The coordinates for the mouse pointer are stored in the ptsStart and ptsPrevious structures. The graphics object and the pens are initialized in the constructor of the New form. The MouseDown, MouseMove, and MouseUp events are processed using the event handler code from the previous example.

The performance of our new graphics editor, however, leaves a bit to be desired with regard to its level of professionalism. Launch the program and do the following. Draw a straight line. No problems so far. But watch carefully what happens next! Click the mouse near the line and, holding the button down, move the pointer to another area of the screen. A thin line will be drawn by the pointer. Without releasing the button, move the mouse pointer to another point in the drawing area. Try to wiggle the mouse pointer around the line's starting point and to touch the first line. You will see that, when the new line intersects with the old line, the latter is partially erased. This happens because GDI+ does not support the XOR operation, which restores the portions of the old drawing that are erased by the new drawing. This problem is solved by using the Windows API graphics functions, which we will look at in the next project.

10.3. Drawing Lines Using Windows API Functions

The `LinesAPI` (Listing 10.3) project makes use of several Windows API functions, as well as the `Point` structure, which is used by some functions. Let's explore this structure in more detail. First of all, it must be declared before declaring functions — doing otherwise will result in an error. Second, in order to avoid conflicts with the .NET's `System.Drawing.Point` structure, our structure's name must be changed, for example to `POINTAPI`.

> **NOTE**
> The `POINTAPI` name had also to be used in VB 6.0, because it has a keyword named `Point`.

Listing 10.3. Drawing Lines Using Windows API Functions

```
'---------------------------------------
'   LinesAPI © 2004 Alexander Klimov
'---------------------------------------
    Private Structure POINTAPI
        Public x As Int32
        Public y As Int32
    End Structure

    Private Declare Auto Function SetROP2 Lib "gdi32.dll" _
        Alias "SetROP2" (ByVal hDC As IntPtr, _
        ByVal nDrawMode As Int32) As Int32

    Private Declare Auto Function MoveToEx Lib "gdi32.dll" _
        Alias "MoveToEx" (ByVal hDC As IntPtr, _
        ByVal x As Int32, ByVal y As Int32, _
```

```
        ByRef lpPoint As POINTAPI) As Boolean

    Private Declare Auto Function LineTo Lib "gdi32.dll" _
        Alias "LineTo" (ByVal hDC As IntPtr, _
        ByVal x As Int32, ByVal y As Int32) As Boolean

    Private Declare Auto Function CreatePen Lib "gdi32.dll" _
        Alias "CreatePen" (ByVal nPenStyle As Int32, _
        ByVal nWidth As Int32, ByVal crColor As Int32) As IntPtr

    Private Declare Auto Function SelectObject Lib "gdi32.dll" _
        Alias "SelectObject" (ByVal hDC As IntPtr, _
        ByVal hObject As IntPtr) As IntPtr

    Private Declare Function DeleteObject Lib "gdi32.dll" _
        Alias "DeleteObject" (ByVal hObject As IntPtr) As Boolean

    Private Const R2_NOT As Int32 = 6
    Private Const R2_XORPEN As Int32 = 7
    Private Const PS_DOT As Int32 = 2
    Private g As Graphics

    Private ptsStart As POINTAPI
    Private ptsPrevious As POINTAPI
    Dim bPaint As Boolean

    Public Sub New()
        MyBase.New()

        InitializeComponent()

        g = Me.CreateGraphics()
    End Sub


  Private Sub Form1_MouseDown(ByVal sender As Object, ByVal e As _
System.Windows.Forms.MouseEventArgs) Handles MyBase.MouseDown
        bPaint = True

        ptsStart.x = e.X
        ptsStart.y = e.Y

        ptsPrevious = ptsStart
    End Sub


    Private Sub Form1_MouseUp(ByVal sender As Object, ByVal e As _
System.Windows.Forms.MouseEventArgs) Handles MyBase.MouseUp
        bPaint = False
```

```
    End Sub

    Private Sub Form1_MouseMove(ByVal sender As Object, ByVal e As _
System.Windows.Forms.MouseEventArgs) Handles MyBase.MouseMove
        If bPaint Then
            ' The handle for the device context for drawing
            Dim hDC As IntPtr
            ' The previous mode, returned by the SetROP2 function
            Dim Mix As Int32
            ' Temporary variables
            Dim ptsCurrent As POINTAPI
            Dim ptsOld As POINTAPI
            ' The values returned by the MoveToEx and LineTo functions
            Dim Success As Boolean

            ' Saving the current coordinates of the line's last point
            ptsCurrent.x = e.X
            ptsCurrent.y = e.Y

            ' Obtaining the device context handle
            hDC = g.GetHdc()
            ' Setting a new graphics mode -
            ' inverting the current color
            Mix = SetROP2(hDC, R2_NOT)

            ' Moving to the line's starting point
            Success = MoveToEx(hDC, ptsStart.x, ptsStart.y, ptsOld)

            ' Clearing the previous line
            Success = LineTo(hDC, ptsPrevious.x, ptsPrevious.y)

            ' Moving to the line's starting point again
            Success = MoveToEx(hDC, ptsStart.x, ptsStart.y, ptsOld)

            ' Drawing a new line
            Success = LineTo(hDC, ptsCurrent.x, ptsCurrent.y)

            ' Releasing resources
            g.ReleaseHdc(hDC)

            ' Saving the current coordinates of the line's end point
            ' for the next erasing operation
            ptsPrevious = ptsCurrent
        End If

    End Sub
```

The main point that has to be noted is using the SetRop2 function with the R2_NOT constant. The benefit of using this function is that it inverts colors automatically, so you do not have to worry about pens to redraw lines that cross. I found another example on the **http://msdn.microsoft.com** site that allows pens of different style, to be used. All you have to do is comment out the code for the MouseMove event handler and insert the following code:

```
If bPaint Then
    Dim hDC As IntPtr
    Dim Mix As Int32
    Dim ptsCurrent As POINTAPI
    Dim ptsOld As POINTAPI
    Dim Success As Boolean

    ' Pen handles
    Dim hPen As IntPtr
    Dim hOldPen As IntPtr

    ptsCurrent.x = e.X
    ptsCurrent.y = e.Y

    hDC = g.GetHdc()

    ' Creating a dotted pen one pixel wide.
    hPen = CreatePen(PS_DOT, 1, &HFF0000)

    ' Associating hPen with the current device context
    hOldPen = SelectObject(hDC, hPen)

    ' Setting the graphics mode
    Mix = SetROP2(hDC, R2_XORPEN)

    Success = MoveToEx(hDC, ptsStart.x, ptsStart.y, ptsOld)

    Success = LineTo(hDC, ptsPrevious.x, ptsPrevious.y)

    Success = MoveToEx(hDC, ptsStart.x, ptsStart.y, ptsOld)

    Success = LineTo(hDC, ptsCurrent.x, ptsCurrent.y)

    ' Restoring the previous pen
    hPen = SelectObject(hDC, hOldPen)

    ' Deleting the pen for drawing lines
```

```
        Success = DeleteObject(hPen)

        ' Releasing resources
        g.ReleaseHdc(hDC)

        ptsPrevious = ptsCurrent
    End If
```

But this does not exhaust the options for drawing straight lines. There is a third method, which is also described on the Microsoft site. A description of line-drawing methods would not be complete without this example.

10.4. Drawing Lines Using the *DrawReversibleLine* method

The `System.Window.Forms` namespace contains the `ControlPaint` class, which is used for working with the standard controls. Pertinent to our activities is the `DrawReversibleLine` method, which is used to draw a line. You must take note of the fact, however, that the drawing area for this method is not limited by the form boundaries. It extends over the entire screen. Consequently, you will have to take care to keep the mouse pointer within the required limits. In the demonstration project (Listing 10.4), the drawing area is not limited, as drawing over the entire screen area produces an interesting effect and you may find a use for it in your projects. The new project is named `LinesControlPaint`. This time, the right mouse button, instead of the left, is used for drawing, just to give your index finger a bit of a rest.

Listing 10.4. The Third Method for Drawing Straight Lines

```
'----------------------------------------
' LinesControlPaint   © 2004 Alexander Klimov
'----------------------------------------
    Private ptsStart As Point
    Private ptsPrevious As Point


    Private Sub Form1_MouseDown(ByVal sender As Object, ByVal e As _
System.Windows.Forms.MouseEventArgs) Handles MyBase.MouseDown
        ' If the right button has been depressed
        If e.Button = MouseButtons.Right Then
            ' Saving the current coordinates of the line's start point
            ptsStart.X = e.X
```

```
            ptsStart.Y = e.Y

            ' Saving the previous current coordinates of the line's end point
            ptsPrevious = ptsStart
        End If
    End Sub

    Private Sub Form1_MouseMove(ByVal sender As Object, ByVal e As _
  System.Windows.Forms.MouseEventArgs) Handles MyBase.MouseMove
        ' If the right button has been depressed
        If e.Button = MouseButtons.Right Then
            ' Variables for the coordinates of the lines' end point
            Dim ptsCurrent As Point

            ' Saving the coordinates
            ptsCurrent.X = e.X
            ptsCurrent.Y = e.Y

            ' Drawing a new line
            ControlPaint.DrawReversibleLine(PointToScreen(ptsStart), _
                PointToScreen(ptsPrevious), Color.Coral)
            ControlPaint.DrawReversibleLine(PointToScreen(ptsStart), _
                PointToScreen(ptsCurrent), Color.Coral)

            ' Saving the current coordinates of the line's end point
            ' for the next MouseMove handler call
            ptsPrevious = ptsCurrent
        End If
    End Sub
```

The comments in the program's body explain the line-drawing process in detail. There is not much to it. And now, for the demonstration of the promised effect. Start the program, depress the right mouse button, and move the mouse pointer beyond the limits of the form. You will see that the line extends past the form's boundaries (Fig. 10.2). See if you can make your form look like a hedgehog, or give it a mustache. So now you have learned three methods to draw a line. I personally like the method using Windows API functions. The method that is more suitable for solving your line-drawing problems is a matter for you to decide. While you are still doing this, we will move on to the next stage: drawing shapes.

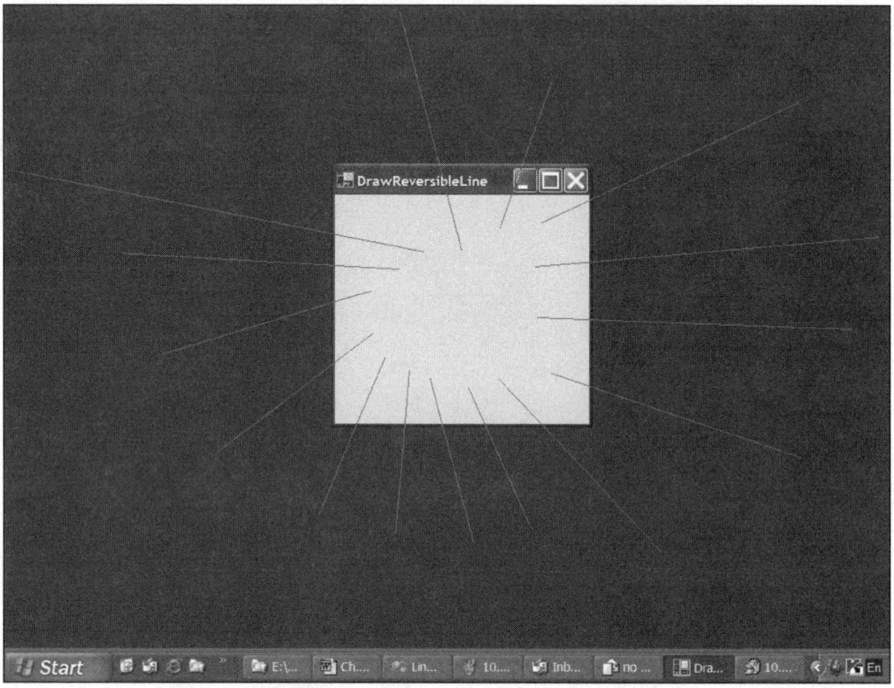

Fig. 10.2. Drawing lines past the form boundaries

10.5. Overlaying Images

In the following example, we will consider how to create the effect of overlaying one image with another. The source code for the project, called `Overlay`, is provided in Listing 10.5. Moreover, you will draw the shape of the image yourself with the mouse pointer. The new project will need four picture-box controls. The `MouseDown`, `MouseMove`, and `MouseUp` mouse events will still be used to select the drawing area. This time, however, these will be control events and not form events. Our task is to preserve the array of all points created by the movement of the mouse pointer. We will use this array to create a path containing a portion of the selected image, and then add this portion to the other image at the same coordinates.

Listing 10.5. Overlaying Images

```
'--------------------------------------
' Overlay  © 2004 Alexander Klimov
'--------------------------------------
Imports System.Drawing.Drawing2D
```

```
' An array of points
Private apoints() As Point
Private m_MaxPoint As Integer

Private Sub Form1_Load(ByVal sender As System.Object, ByVal e As System.EventArgs) _
Handles MyBase.Load
    picFromClone.Image = DirectCast(picFrom.Image.Clone, Bitmap)
    picToClone.Image = DirectCast(picTo.Image.Clone, Bitmap)
End Sub

Private Sub picFrom_MouseDown(ByVal sender As Object, ByVal e As _
System.Windows.Forms.MouseEventArgs) Handles picFrom.MouseDown

    ' Clearing the previous area selections
    picFrom.Image = DirectCast(picFromClone.Image.Clone, Bitmap)

    ' Saving the starting point
    m_MaxPoint = 0
    ReDim apoints(m_MaxPoint)
    apoints(m_MaxPoint).X = e.X
    apoints(m_MaxPoint).Y = e.Y
End Sub

Private Sub picFrom_MouseMove(ByVal sender As Object, ByVal e As _
System.Windows.Forms.MouseEventArgs) Handles picFrom.MouseMove
    ' If nothing is selected, doing nothing
    If apoints Is Nothing Then Exit Sub

    ' Saving the new point
    m_MaxPoint += 1
    ReDim Preserve apoints(m_MaxPoint)
    apoints(m_MaxPoint).X = e.X
    apoints(m_MaxPoint).Y = e.Y

    ' Drawing a line made up from the points
    Dim g As Graphics = picFrom.CreateGraphics
    g.DrawLine(Pens.Yellow, _
        apoints(m_MaxPoint).X, _
        apoints(m_MaxPoint).Y, _
        apoints(m_MaxPoint - 1).X, _
        apoints(m_MaxPoint - 1).Y)
End Sub

Private Sub picFrom_MouseUp(ByVal sender As Object, ByVal e As _
System.Windows.Forms.MouseEventArgs) Handles picFrom.MouseUp
```

```
' If nothing is selected, doing nothing
If apoints Is Nothing Then Exit Sub

' Closing the path
If (apoints(0).X <> apoints(m_MaxPoint).X) Or _
    (apoints(0).Y <> apoints(m_MaxPoint).Y) _
Then
    ' Saving the new point
    m_MaxPoint += 1
    ReDim Preserve apoints(m_MaxPoint)
    apoints(m_MaxPoint).X = apoints(0).X
    apoints(m_MaxPoint).Y = apoints(0).Y
End If

' Adding all points to the path
Dim area_path As New GraphicsPath(FillMode.Winding)
area_path.AddLines(apoints)

' Setting the selection borders
Dim selectbmp As Bitmap = DirectCast(picFromClone.Image.Clone, Bitmap)
Dim g_select As Graphics = Graphics.FromImage(selectbmp)
g_select.DrawPath(Pens.Orange, area_path)
picFrom.Image = selectbmp

' Copying the selected image to the other image
Dim resultbmp As Bitmap = DirectCast(picToClone.Image.Clone, Bitmap)
Dim g_result As Graphics = Graphics.FromImage(resultbmp)

' Clipping the path
g_result.SetClip(area_path)
' Copying the image
g_result.DrawImage(picFromClone.Image, 0, 0)

' Outputting the result
picTo.Image = resultbmp

' Refreshing the data
apoints = Nothing

End Sub
```

As can be seen in Fig. 10.3, the gourmet dish has been copied from the table to the apartment where a cat named Christine lives. Have fun, Christine!

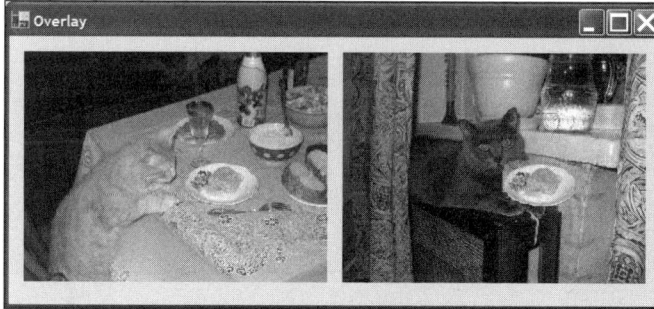

Fig. 10.3. Overlaying one image with another

10.6. A Web

The mouse can be used not only to draw primitive lines and squares, but also webs! You will have to make the following preparations for the Web project (Listing 10.6). Set the form's background color to black, because our web will be white. Set the value of the form's Cursor property to Cross. Also, place a label control on the form and set its Text property to Holding a mouse button down, move the mouse pointer around. Now you can start writing the code. First, declare two form-class-level variables.

Listing 10.6. Drawing a Web

```
'-------------------------------------
' Web   © 2004 Alexander Klimov
'-------------------------------------
    Private pts As Point = Point.Empty

    ' A flag to enable web drawing
    Dim bDraw As Boolean

    Private Sub Form1_MouseDown(ByVal sender As Object, ByVal e As _
System.Windows.Forms.MouseEventArgs) Handles MyBase.MouseDown
        bDraw = True
    End Sub

    Private Sub Form1_MouseMove(ByVal sender As Object, ByVal e As _
System.Windows.Forms.MouseEventArgs) Handles MyBase.MouseMove
        If bDraw Then
            Dim g As Graphics = CreateGraphics()
            DrawWeb(g, BackColor, pts)
            pts = New Point(e.X, e.Y)
```

```
        DrawWeb(g, Color.White, pts)
        g.Dispose()
    End If
End Sub

Private Sub Form1_MouseUp(ByVal sender As Object, ByVal e As _
System.Windows.Forms.MouseEventArgs) Handles MyBase.MouseUp
    bDraw = False
    Dim g As Graphics = CreateGraphics()
    g.Clear(BackColor)
    g.Dispose()
End Sub

Private Sub DrawWeb(ByVal g As Graphics, ByVal clr As Color, ByVal pt As Point)
    Dim cx As Integer = ClientSize.Width
    Dim cy As Integer = ClientSize.Height
    Dim p As New Pen(clr)

    g.DrawLine(p, pt, New Point(0, 0))
    g.DrawLine(p, pt, New Point(cx \ 4, 0))
    g.DrawLine(p, pt, New Point(cx \ 2, 0))
    g.DrawLine(p, pt, New Point(3 * cx \ 4, 0))
    g.DrawLine(p, pt, New Point(cx, 0))
    g.DrawLine(p, pt, New Point(cx, cy \ 4))
    g.DrawLine(p, pt, New Point(cx, cy \ 2))
    g.DrawLine(p, pt, New Point(cx, 3 * cy \ 4))
    g.DrawLine(p, pt, New Point(cx, cy))
    g.DrawLine(p, pt, New Point(3 * cx \ 4, cy))
    g.DrawLine(p, pt, New Point(cx \ 2, cy))
    g.DrawLine(p, pt, New Point(cx \ 4, cy))
    g.DrawLine(p, pt, New Point(0, cy))
    g.DrawLine(p, pt, New Point(0, cy \ 4))
    g.DrawLine(p, pt, New Point(0, cy \ 2))
    g.DrawLine(p, pt, New Point(0, 3 * cy \ 4))
End Sub
```

Moving the mouse pointer calls the DrawWeb procedure that draws the web. Note that this procedure is called twice. The first call erases the previous web, while the second call draws a new web on the form. The idea behind the web-drawing procedure is to draw lines from the current mouse pointer position to the form's borders. Holding a mouse button down, move the mouse pointer around. You will see that the web's center follows the mouse pointer (Fig. 10.4).

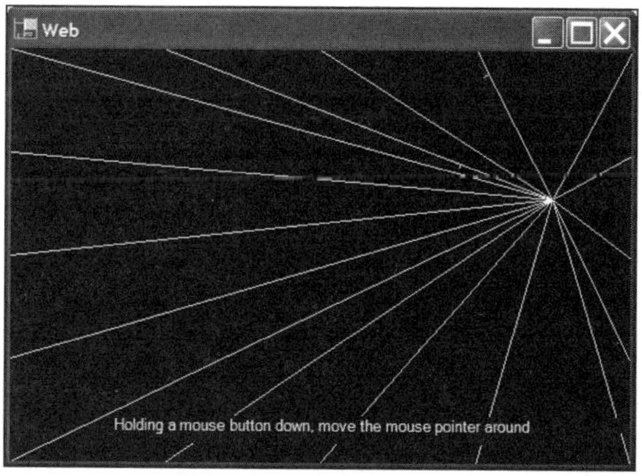

Fig. 10.4. Drawing a web

10.7. Moving the Mouse Pointer

The mouse pointer is moved using the Cursor.Position property, which allows the mouse cursor to be set to a new position. The PathData.Points property can be used to make the mouse pointer move along any intricate path. This property makes is possible to obtain the coordinates of all of the points making up the path. In this way, a circular path can be created, and the mouse pointer made to move along this path. The MovingMouse project (Listing 10.7) shows how this is done.

Listing 10.7. Moving the Mouse Pointer

```
'------------------------------------
' MovingMouse © 2004 Alexander Klimov
'------------------------------------
Imports System.Drawing.Drawing2D

    Sub MouseFigure(ByVal times As Integer)
        ' The procedure to move the mouse pointer
        ' along the specified path
        ' The "times" paremeter is the number of repetitions.
        Dim gp As New GraphicsPath

        ' The screen size
        Dim ScreenSize As Rectangle = Screen.GetBounds( _
                                      New Point(0, 0))

        ' Selecting a rectangle anywhere in the screen area
```

```vb
Dim rect As New Rectangle( _
            CInt(ScreenSize.Width / 2) - 100, _
            CInt(ScreenSize.Height / 2) - 100, 200, 200)

' Adding a circle to the path
gp.AddEllipse(rect)

' Breaking the circle into a series of lines
gp.Flatten()

' The loop to repeat the mouse pointer movements
Dim repeat As Integer
For repeat = 0 To times - 1

    Dim i As Integer
    ' Passing through all points of the path
    For i = 0 To gp.PathData.Points.Length - 1

        ' Making a brief stop
        System.Threading.Thread.Sleep(10)

        ' Moving the cursor
        Cursor.Position = New Point( _
                        CInt(gp.PathData.Points(i).X), _
                        CInt(gp.PathData.Points(i).Y))
    Next
Next

    ' Releasing resources
    gp.Dispose()
End Sub

Private Sub Button1_Click(ByVal sender As System.Object, ByVal e As _
System.EventArgs) Handles Button1.Click
    MouseFigure(5)
End Sub
```

Launch the program, and click the button labeled **Start moving**. The mouse pointer will move in a circular path five times. The effect can be enhanced by making the pointer leave a trail. Open the **Control Panel**, and open the **Mouse** item. Select the **Pointer Options** tab, and set the **Display pointer trails** option. This method of making the mouse pointer move along a specified path can be used in demonstration applications. For example, if you have decided to create a tutorial explaining the windows concept and you need to outline the window's borders with the pointer. This task can be performed easily by modifying the previous example a little bit, as is shown in Listing 10.8.

Listing 10.8. Form Borders

```
Sub AroundForm()
    ' The procedure to outline the window borders with the mouse pointer
    Dim gp As New GraphicsPath

    gp.AddLine(Me.DesktopLocation.X + 1, _
            Me.DesktopLocation.Y + 1, _
            Me.DesktopLocation.X + Me.Size.Width - 1, _
            Me.DesktopLocation.Y - 1)

    gp.AddLine(Me.DesktopLocation.X + Me.Size.Width - 1, _
            Me.DesktopLocation.Y - 1, _
            Me.DesktopLocation.X + Me.Size.Width - 1, _
            Me.DesktopLocation.Y + Me.Size.Height - 1)

    gp.AddLine(Me.DesktopLocation.X + Me.Size.Width - 1, _
            Me.DesktopLocation.Y + Me.Size.Height - 1, _
            Me.DesktopLocation.X + 1, _
            Me.DesktopLocation.Y + Me.Size.Height + 1)

    gp.AddLine(Me.DesktopLocation.X + 1, _
            Me.DesktopLocation.Y + Me.Size.Height + 1, _
            Me.DesktopLocation.X + 1, _
            Me.DesktopLocation.Y + 1)

    Dim i As Integer
    ' Passing through all points of the path
    For i = 0 To gp.PathData.Points.Length - 1

        ' Making a brief stop
    System.Threading.Thread.Sleep(500)

        ' Moving the cursor
        Cursor.Position = New Point( _
                            CInt(gp.PathData.Points(i).X), _
                            CInt(gp.PathData.Points(i).Y))
    Next

    ' Releasing resources
```

```
    gp.Dispose()
End Sub


Private Sub Button2_Click(ByVal sender As System.Object, ByVal e As _
System.EventArgs) Handles Button2.Click
    AroundForm()
End Sub
```

10.8. Suggestions and Recommendations

❏ The mouse is used in so many different areas that you will have to review this subject constantly. For example, you can write a graphics editor using examples 10.1, 10.2, and 10.3, and then expand its capabilities to working not only with graphics primitives, but with images as well.

❏ I will demonstrate a program in *Chapter 18* that makes a cat follow the mouse pointer with its eyes. Don't miss this one!

PART IV: FORMS AND CONTROLS

Chapter 11: Forms

A form is the foundation for developing graphical user interface programs. It is on the form that all controls are placed, text displayed, and images drawn. Programmers usually concentrate on these areas. But the form itself offers great potential for solving many different problems. Consequently, before considering how to use controls in unconventional ways, we will first consider the possibilities the form has to offer.

11.1. The Invisible Form

Most of you are undoubtedly familiar with the "Alice's Adventures in Wonderland," by the English writer Lewis Carrol. One of the book's characters was the Cheshire Cat, who had the singular feature of being able to disappear into the thin air. Let's try to get the form to pull this Cheshire Cat trick. The VB .NET 2003 forms have a new property: Opacity, which controls the transparency of the form. Using some imagination with this property can spice up your programs. The TransparentForm project provides an example of using form transparency. Create a new project, and place the following controls on it: a horizontal scroll bar to control the form's transparency, a button to exit the program, and a timer to create the disappearance effect when exiting the program. The main code is in the handler of the Scroll event of the scroll bar control (Listing 11.1).

Listing 11.1. Making the Form Transparent

```
'---------------------------------------
' TransparentForm  © 2004 Alexander Klimov
'---------------------------------------
    Private Sub HScrollBar1_Scroll(ByVal sender As System.Object, ByVal e As _
System.Windows.Forms.ScrollEventArgs) Handles HScrollBar1.Scroll
        Me.Opacity = 0.1 + HScrollBar1.Value / 100
        Me.Text = Me.Opacity.ToString
    End Sub
```

Run the program, and move the scrollbar slider back and forth a little. The form will change from being fully opaque to being practically invisible (Fig. 11.1). The current value of the form's transparency is shown in its title bar. I set the value at the lowest possible transparency, 0.1, to prevent the form from disappearing altogether. The variable transparency effect can also be used when exiting the program. In this case, the application makes its window transparent before shutting down (Listing 11.2).

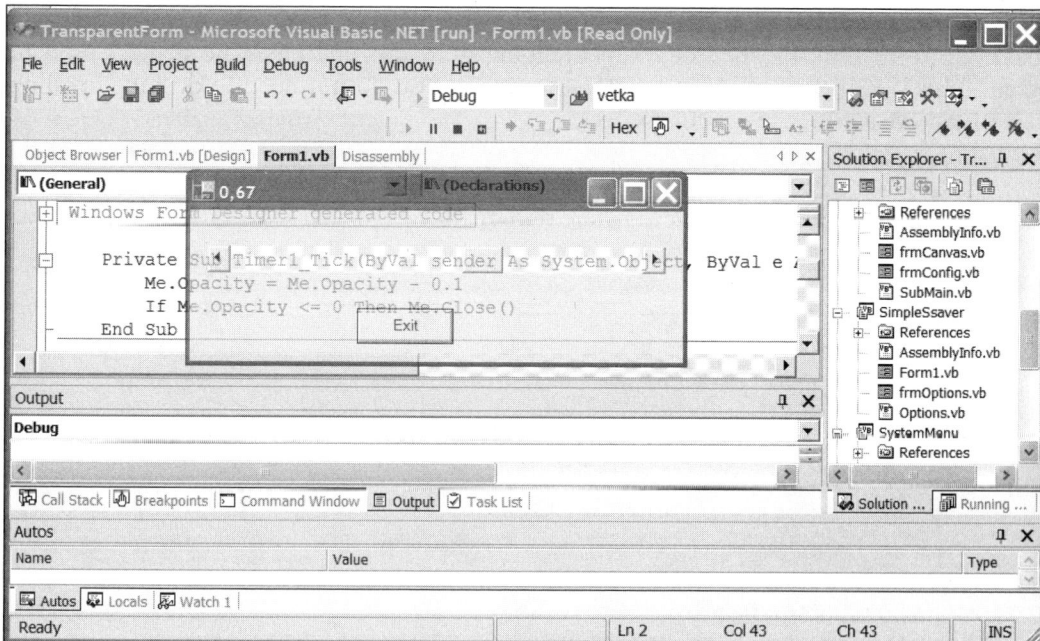

Fig. 11.1. A semitransparent form

Listing 11.2. The Cheshire Cat Form

```
    Private Sub Timer1_Tick(ByVal sender As System.Object, ByVal e As System.EventArgs) _
Handles Timer1.Tick
        Me.Opacity = Me.Opacity - 0.1
        If Me.Opacity <= 0 Then Me.Close()
    End Sub


    Private Sub butExit_Click(ByVal sender As System.Object, ByVal e As _
System.EventArgs) Handles butExit.Click
        Timer1.Enabled = True
    End Sub
```

11.2. Semitransparency During Dragging

Let's consider another example, in which the form's transparency changes. In certain cases, the mouse down event on the form title bar needs to be processed. In this case, the window is sent the WM_NCLBUTTONDOWN Windows message. When the button is released, the window is sent the WM_NCLBUTTONUP Windows message. These messages can be intercepted and used to perform some custom tasks. For example, we can make the form semitransparent when dragging it by the title bar. The project used to achieve this is named `TitleBarClick` (Listing 11.3). You do not need to do much coding in it to achieve a rather spectacular effect.

Listing 11.3. Semitransparency during Dragging

```
'-------------------------------------------
' TitleBarClick  © 2004 Alexander Klimov
'-------------------------------------------
    Private Const WM_NCLBUTTONDOWN As Long = &HA1
    Private Const WM_NCLBUTTONUP As Long = &HA0


Protected Overrides Sub WndProc(ByRef m As System.Windows.Forms.Message)
        ' If the left mouse button is down on the form title bar
    If CLng(m.Msg) = WM_NCLBUTTONDOWN Then
            ' Setting the level of the form's transparency
        If Me.Opacity <> 0.5 Then Me.Opacity = 0.5
            ' The button is released
    ElseIf CLng(m.Msg) = WM_NCLBUTTONUP Then
        If Me.Opacity <> 1.0 Then Me.Opacity = 1.0
```

```
        End If

        MyBase.WndProc(m)
    End Sub

End Class
```

Launch the program, and try to drag the form around the screen. You will see that, as soon as you click the mouse on the title bar, the form becomes semitransparent and remains as such while it is being dragged and until the button is released.

11.3. The Active Form

Since we are on the subject of using form semitransparency, here is another related example. Having several windows open on the screen at one time may cause the user a certain amount of discomfort. I suggest the following way of making your desktop less cluttered by open windows. When a window becomes inactive, the message to this effect is intercepted and the window is made semitransparent. When, conversely, the window becomes active, it is made fully opaque. This effect is implemented in the `ActiveForm` project (Listing 11.4).

Listing 11.4. Checking the Form's State

```
'-------------------------------------
' ActiveForm  © 2004 Alexander Klimov
'-------------------------------------
    Protected Overrides Sub WndProc(ByRef m As System.Windows.Forms.Message)
        MyBase.WndProc(m)

        Const WM_ACTIVATEAPP As Integer = &H1C
        If m.Msg = WM_ACTIVATEAPP Then
            If m.WParam.ToInt32() <> 0 Then
                ' The window has become active
                If Me.Opacity <> 1.0 Then Me.Opacity = 1.0
            Else
                ' The window has become inactive
                ' Setting the level of the form's transparency
                If Me.Opacity <> 0.5 Then Me.Opacity = 0.5
            End If
        End If
    End Sub
```

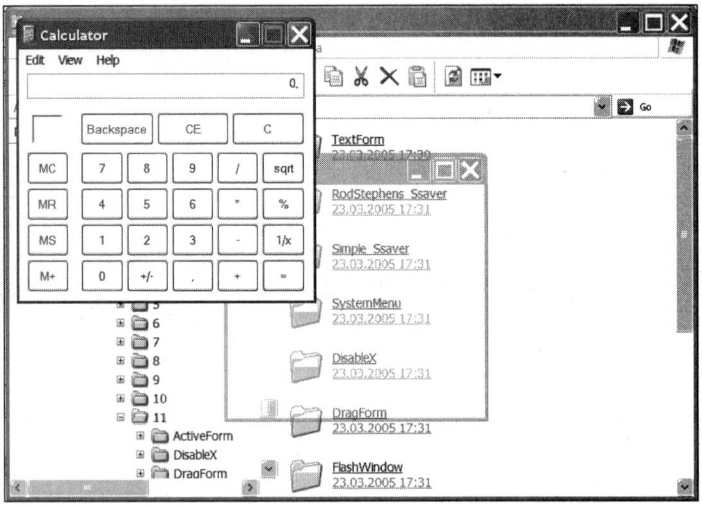

Fig. 11.2. The inactive window is semitransparent

Run the program along with a few others. When you switch to another program, you will see that, having lost the focus, your application form becomes semitransparent (Fig. 11.2). In my opinion, this is a very neat way to use the semitransparency. Bill Gates ought to give it a try in future Windows versions.

11.4. The Form as Text

We are all used to the form having a rectangular shape, either with straight corners, like in the pre-Windows XP versions, or with corners that are rounded, like in Windows XP. However, if you do not like the standard look, you can create a window of whatever shape you like. You can have it appear as text, for example. Let's try doing this. The example is implemented in the TextForm project (Listing 11.5). It is based on using the very powerful and interesting GraphicsPath class and the Region method.

Listing 11.5. Creating a Form Looking Like Text

```
'----------------------------------------
' TextForm  © 2004 Alexander Klimov
'----------------------------------------
Imports System.Drawing.Drawing2D

    Private Sub Form1_Paint(ByVal sender As Object, ByVal e As _
System.Windows.Forms.PaintEventArgs) Handles MyBase.Paint
        MyBase.BackColor = Color.Cyan
```

```
        Dim gp As New GraphicsPath
        Dim m_Text As String = "Kitten"
        gp.AddString(m_Text, New FontFamily("Tahoma"), _
                FontStyle.Bold, 70, New Point(35, 5), _
                StringFormat.GenericDefault)
        MyBase.Region = New Region(gp)
    End Sub


    Private Sub Form1_DoubleClick(ByVal sender As Object, ByVal e As System.EventArgs) _
Handles MyBase.DoubleClick
        MyBase.Close()
    End Sub
```

I start by setting the form's color to Cyan and creating an instance of the GraphicsPath class. I used the word "Kitten" for the text, the shape of which the window will take. But, if you are an eager dog fancier, you can use the word "Puppy." Using the AddString method, I set all the necessary font properties: the name, style, output coordinates, and format. Take note of the second parameter of the Point structure; I will return to it a little later. Setting the Region property to the created path will now discard all portions of the form that are not within the specified text.

Let's return to the parameter of the Point structure, mentioned earlier. Unless you set the FormBorderStyle property value to None, you should see portions of the form's title bar in the first four letters of the form. This will help you to handle certain tasks. In particular, the form can be dragged by these portions of the title bar just as a normal form is by the full-sized title bar. By right-clicking on it, you can call the system menu and select the **Close** command to exit the program (Fig. 11.3). It is possible, of course, to create a form without the title bar or to select a lower portion of the form, leaving the title bar out of the remaining portions of the form. But, in this case, you will have to make provisions for various contingencies. For example, the program can be exited by a double click. How a form can be dragged by any of its parts will be shown later in this chapter. Using similar Add prefix methods instead of the AddString method makes it possible to create forms that appear not only as text, but as various shapes.

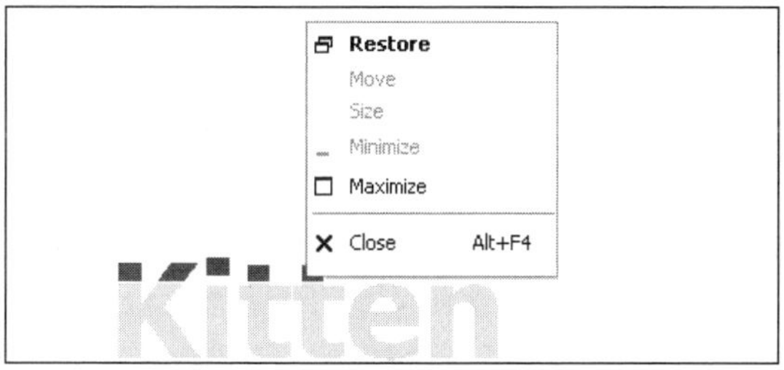

Fig. 11.3. Creating a form looking as text

11.5. Dragging Windows by Parts Other Than the Title Bar

As you know, windows can be dragged around the screen by grabbing them by the title bar with the mouse pointer. Sometimes, however, a situation arises when you have to drag a window by some other part. The window, for example, may not have a title bar. Once again, we can take advantage of the Windows API functions to solve this problem. The example is demonstrated in the DragForm project (Listing 11.6). After creating a template project, place a label and a button control on the form. Set the following properties to the following values:

☐ The form properties: FromBorderStyle = None
☐ The Label control properties:
  ● Name = lblDescription
  ● BackColor = LightBlue
  ● Text = Holding down the left mouse button, drag the form to another screen location
☐ The Button control properties:
  ● Name = butExit
  ● Next = Exit

The label tells the user what needs to be done to view the effect. In our example, because the form can only be dragged by a part of the window itself (grabbing other controls is not processed), the label is highlighted by another color to make it stand out. Our form has no title bar and, consequently, no cross button to close the program at the right end of the title bar. To close the program, I added a button named **Exit**.

Listing 11.6. Dragging a Form by Parts Other than the Title Bar

---

```
'-------------------------------------
' DragForm  © 2004 Alexander Klimov
'-------------------------------------
  ' API functions and constants
  Private Declare Function ReleaseCapture Lib "user32" () As Long

  Private Declare Function SendMessage Lib "user32" Alias "SendMessageA _
        (ByVal hwnd As IntPtr _
         ByVal wMsg As Integer, _
         ByVal wParam As Integer, _
```

```
        ByVal lParam As Integer) As Integer

    Private Const WM_NCLBUTTONDOWN As Integer = &HA1
    Private Const HTCAPTION As Integer = 2

    Private Sub Form1_MouseDown(ByVal sender As Object _
        ByVal e As System.Windows.Forms.MouseEventArgs _
        Handles MyBase.MouseDown

      ' Only when the left mouse button is depressed
      If e.Button = MouseButtons.Left Then
          ReleaseCapture()
          SendMessage(Me.Handle, WM_NCLBUTTONDOWN, HTCAPTION, 0)
      End If
    End Sub
```

Because forms are usually dragged using the left mouse button, the code for the `MouseDown` event checks for the following condition:

```
If e.Button = MouseButtons.Left
```

If the condition is met, the Window API functions, which allow forms to be dragged not only by the title bar, but also by any part of the client area, are called. Run the program and try dragging the window by grabbing it by any of its parts.

11.6. The System Menu

Any form that has a title has a system menu. We never give a second thought to its standard appearance, but it can be changed. This can be done by calling Windows API functions. Create a new project and name it `SystemMenu`. Because we will override some properties of the form, we need to create a new class, `CustomSystemMenu`, containing the code given in Listing 11.7.

Listing 11.7. Creating a New Class To Change the System Menu

```
'--------------------------------------
' The class for creating a system menu  © 2004 Alexander Klimov
'--------------------------------------
Public Class CustomSystemMenu
    Inherits System.Windows.Forms.NativeWindow
    Implements IDisposable

    ' Windows API functions
```

```
Private Declare Function GetSystemMenu Lib "user32" _
                        (ByVal hwnd As Int32, _
                        ByVal bRevert As Boolean) As Int32
Private Declare Function AppendMenu Lib "user32" _
        Alias "AppendMenuA" (ByVal hMenu As Int32, _
                        ByVal wFlags As Int32, _
                        ByVal wIDNewItem As Int32, _
                        ByVal lpNewItem As String) As Int32


' The constants
Private Const MF_STRING As Int32 = &H0        ' A menu item
Private Const MF_SEPARATOR As Int32 = &H800  ' A separator

' A Windows message
Private Const WM_SYSCOMMAND As Int32 = &H112

' The new identifier for the system menu
Private Const ID_ABOUT As Int32 = 1000

' The system menu handle
Private hSystemMenu As Int32

' The window handle
Private hParentHandle As Int32

' The text for the modified menu item
Private strAboutText As String = String.Empty

Public Event ShowMsgBox()

' The constructor to create the new menu item
' Parameters:
' intWinHandle : The parent window to process messages
' and to add the new menu item
Public Sub New(ByVal intWinHandle As Int32, _
        ByVal strMenuItemText As String)

    Me.AssignHandle(New IntPtr(intWinHandle))

    hParentHandle = intWinHandle
    strAboutText = strMenuItemText

    ' Obtaining the system menu handle
```

```vb
        hSystemMenu = GetSystemMenu(hParentHandle, 0)

        If CheckNewItem() = False Then
            Throw New Exception(_
          "Error creating a new system menu item.")
        End If

    End Sub


    ' Processing the WM_SYSCOMMAND message
    Protected Overrides Sub WndProc(ByRef m As System.Windows.Forms.Message)

        Select Case m.Msg
            Case WM_SYSCOMMAND
                MyBase.WndProc(m)

                If m.WParam.ToInt32 = ID_ABOUT Then
                    If hSystemMenu <> 0 Then
                        RaiseEvent ShowMsgBox()
                    End If
                End If

            Case Else
                MyBase.WndProc(m)
        End Select

    End Sub


    ' Releasing resources
    Public Sub Dispose() Implements System.IDisposable.Dispose

        If Not Me.Handle.Equals(IntPtr.Zero) Then
            Me.ReleaseHandle()
        End If

    End Sub


    ' Checking on the new menu item in the system menu
    Private Function CheckNewItem() As Boolean
        Try
            Return AppendToSystemMenu(hSystemMenu, strAboutText)
        Catch ex As Exception
            Return False
```

```
    End Try
End Function


' Adding a separator and the new item to the system menu
' Parameters:
' intHandle: The system menu handle
' strText: Adding text
Private Function AppendToSystemMenu(ByVal intHandle As Int32, _
                       ByVal strText As String) As Boolean

    Try
        ' Adding the separator
        Dim intRet As Int32 = AppendMenu _
                intHandle, MF_SEPARATOR, 0, String.Empty)

        ' Now adding our new item
        intRet = AppendMenu(intHandle, MF_STRING, ID_ABOUT, strText)

        If intRet = 1 Then
            Return True
        Else
            Return False
        End If

    Catch ex As Exception
        Return False
    End Try
End Function

End Class
```

This class uses the GetSystemMenu and AppendMenu Windows API functions to add a separator and a new menu item to the system menu. It also intercepts the Windows WM_SYSCOMMAND message that is sent to the window when the system menu is used. Let's now consider the main window of the program: Form1. Here, a mySystemMenu variable is declared within the class scope. It can be initialized in the New procedure as follows:

```
mySystemMenu = New CustomSystemMenu(Me.Handle.ToInt32,
"&About the program...")
```

All that is left to do is process the ShowMsgBox event that will occur when the new menu item is selected. The code for this event handler is shown in Listing 11.8.

Listing 11.8. Processing the New System Menu Item

```
'-------------------------------------
' SystemMenu  © 2004 Alexander Klimov
'-------------------------------------


' Declaring a variable
   Private WithEvents mySystemMenu As CustomSystemMenu

   Public Sub New()
      MyBase.New()

      'This call is required by the Windows Form Designer.
      InitializeComponent()

      'Add any initialization after the InitializeComponent() call
      mySystemMenu = New CustomSystemMenu(Me.Handle.ToInt32, "&About the program...")
   End Sub

   Private Sub mySystemMenu_ShowMsgBox() _
                        Handles mySystemMenu.ShowMsgBox
      ' Processing the click on the new menu item
      MsgBox( _
         "Entertaining Programming" & vbNewLine & "A. Klimov")
   End Sub
```

Fig. 11.4. A new item in the system menu

Run the program, click on the application icon at the extreme left of the title bar, and verify that there is a new item in the system menu (Fig. 11.4). Clicking on the new menu item should open a standard message box window containing the message. Of course, in your projects you will not be content with such a simple message, and will create a full-fledged dialog window, in which you can declare your genius to the whole world. Just don't forget to place, in very small print if you prefer, a note of thanks to the author for the idea and the solution.

11.7. A Flashing Title Bar

You are probably familiar with the situation where the title bar on a window that does not currently have the focus starts flashing. This is just the window's not-so-subtle way of getting your attention to make it active. This effect is implemented by calling the `FlashWindow` or the `FlashWindowEx` functions. Here, I will consider the newer and more powerful `FlashWindowEx` function. The example is implemented in the `FlashWindow` project (Listing 11.9). One button will be enough for this project. Name it `butFlash` and set its `Text` property to `Start Flashing`. Now, switch into the code editor. The first thing that needs to be done is to link the `System.Runtime.InteropServices` namespace.

Listing 11.9. Using the `FlashWindowEx` Function

```
'---------------------------------------
' FlashWindow  © 2004 Alexander Klimov
'---------------------------------------
Imports System.Runtime.InteropServices

    ' Constants for the structure
    Private Const FLASHW_STOP As Integer = 0
    Private Const FLASHW_CAPTION As Integer = &H1
    Private Const FLASHW_TRAY As Integer = &H2
    Private Const FLASHW_ALL As Integer = (FLASHW_CAPTION Or FLASHW_TRAY)
    Private Const FLASHW_TIMER As Integer = &H4
    Private Const FLASHW_TIMERNOFG As Integer = &HC
    Private FLASHW_FLAGS As Integer

    ' A structure for the function
    Private Structure FLASHWINFO
        Dim cbSize As Integer
        Dim hwnd As IntPtr
        Dim dwFlags As Integer
        Dim uCount As Integer
        Dim dwTimeout As Integer
    End Structure

    Private Declare Function FlashWindowEx Lib "user32" _
```

```
                (ByRef pflashwininfo _
                As FLASHWINFO) As Integer


    Private Sub butFlash_Click(ByVal sender As System.Object, ByVal e As _
System.EventArgs) Handles butFlash.Click
        Dim intRetval
        Dim fwi As FLASHWINFO

        With fwi
            .cbSize = Marshal.SizeOf(fwi)
            .hwnd = Me.Handle
            .dwFlags = FLASHW_TRAY
            .dwTimeout = 0
            .uCount = 5
        End With

        intRetval = FlashWindowEx(fwi)
    End Sub
```

The FlashWindowEx function uses information contained in the FLAHSINFO structure. This structure uses a number of constants. I decided to consider all of these constants, even though only one, FLASHW_TRAY, is actually used in our example. When this constant is used, only the window's button on the taskbar flashes. When you click the butFlash button, the program window will flash five times (variable uCount = 5). Launch the program and click the button. The program's button on the taskbar should start flashing.

11.8. Disabling the ✖ Button on the Form Title Bar

A common question on various forums is: How do I disable the ✖ button on the form title bar and how can I remove the **Close** command from the system menu? To perform this task, we have to resort to calling the Windows API system menu functions again. In this case, we need: GetSystemMenu, GetMenuItemCount, DrawMenuBar, and RemoveMenu. The code for the project, DisableX, is provided in Listing 11.10.

Listing 11.10. Disabling the ✖ Button on the Form Title Bar

```
'------------------------------------
' DisableX  © 2004 Alexander Klimov
'------------------------------------
    ' Constants
```

```vbnet
Const MF_BYPOSITION = &H400&
Const MF_REMOVE = &H1000&

' WinAPI functions
Private Declare Function GetSystemMenu Lib "user32" (_
      ByVal hwnd As Integer, ByVal bRevert As Integer) As Integer

Private Declare Function GetMenuItemCount Lib "user32" _
      (ByVal hMenu As Integer) As Integer

Private Declare Function DrawMenuBar Lib "user32" _
      (ByVal hwnd As Integer) As Integer

Private Declare Function RemoveMenu Lib "user32" _
      (ByVal hMenu As Integer, ByVal nPosition As Integer, _
      ByVal wFlags As Integer) As Integer

Private Sub Form1_Load(ByVal sender As System.Object, ByVal e As System.EventArgs) _
Handles MyBase.Load
      Dim hSysMenu As Integer
      Dim nCnt As Short

      ' Obtaining the form system menu handle
      ' (Restore, Move, Maximize, Minimize, Close)
      hSysMenu = GetSystemMenu(Handle.ToInt32, False)

      If hSysMenu Then
          ' Counting the number of items in the system menu
          nCnt = GetMenuItemCount(hSysMenu)
                  If nCnt Then
          ' The count starts at 0
          ' Item "Close" is the last item
          RemoveMenu(hSysMenu _
                  nCnt - 1, MF_BYPOSITION Or MF_REMOVE)
          ' Removing the separator
          RemoveMenu(hSysMenu _
                  nCnt - 2, MF_BYPOSITION Or MF_REMOVE)

          ' Redrawing the menu
          DrawMenuBar(Handle.ToInt32)
        End If
    End If
```

```
        End Sub

    Private Sub Button1_Click(ByVal sender As System.Object, ByVal e As _
System.EventArgs) Handles Button1.Click
            Application.Exit()
        End Sub
```

As a rule, the **Close** command is the last one in the system menu. This command is usually preceded by an item separator. Consequently, we simply need to count up all the commands in the menu and remove the last two. Running the project, you will see that the ☒ button is disabled. But now we have a problem: We cannot close the window and exit the program. To deal with this situation, a button has to be added to the form with the following code for its Click event handler:

```
    Application.Exit()
```

11.9. Screensavers

Screensavers were invented in those ancient times when the technical characteristics of monitors were less than ideal, and they could be damaged if left to display a static image for an extended period of time. To remedy this deficiency, some bright mind came up with the idea of launching a program displaying a moving image if there has been no input from the keyboard or the mouse for a prevoiusly-determined space of time — the screensaver. Today, monitor quality is significantly better, so screensavers are used mostly for fun or to hide your work from overly curious coworkers, in which case the screensaver is protected with a password.

It is a cinch to create a screensaver in Visual Basic .NET. In essence, a screensaver is a usual window program with some specific features. First of all, the screensaver extension is SCR, instead of the standard EXE. Second, no other instances of the program may be launched. Third, the mouse pointer must not appear on the screen when the program is running. Fourth, upon any key press or mouse move (not to mention a mouse-button press) the program must automatically terminate. Moreover, it is desirable to be able to preview a screensaver and to configure its settings in a window accessible through the **Display** item in the **Control Panel**. These are the main principles of any screensaver. As you can see, they are not particularly difficult.

Theoretically, any program can perform the screensaver functions. Nevertheless, certain rules must be followed. The screensaver's window must fill the entire screen, it cannot have a title bar, and it must display a dynamic image. In addition to everything just mentioned, screensavers can have the following command line switches:

❏ /p — displays a special screensaver-preview window. Clicking on the **Preview** button should launch the screensaver itself.

❑ /c — clicking on the **Parameters** button opens a special dialog window for configuring the screensaver.

❑ /s — the screensaver is launched in the regular operating mode.

Now that you know the basic rules, you can start on creating your own screensavers.

11.9.1. A Simple Screensaver

We will start by creating a very simple screensaver based on an example I found on the Microsoft site. It demonstrates the basic screensaver-creating principles, which is quite enough for our purposes in getting acquainted with the concepts involved. In the second example, I will demonstrate a more involved design. Create a new blank project and name it SimpleSsaver. Immediately set the following form properties:

❑ BackColor = Black
❑ ControlBox = False
❑ FormBorderStyle = None
❑ MaximizeBox = False
❑ MinimizeBox = False
❑ ShowInTaskBar = False
❑ WindowState = Maximized

We will create our screensaver in stages, periodically test-running the program to check for errors and to get a better understanding of how it works. After setting the necessary form properties, we need to declare several global variables that will be needed for various operations (Listing 11.11).

Listing 11.11. The First Stages in Creating the Screensaver

```
'-------------------------------------
' SimpleSsaver © 2004 Alexander Klimov
'-------------------------------------

    ' Declaring global variables
    ' A Graphics object on which to draw
    Private g As Graphics

    ' A Random object for outputting random shapes
    Private m_Random As New Random

    ' For the first use of the MouseMove event
    Private m_IsActive As Boolean = False

    ' To detect mouse movements
```

```
Private m_MouseLocation As Point

' An Options object containing the information about the user's choice
Private m_Options As New Options
```

As you will remember, a screensaver must terminate automatically upon a mouse move or the pressing of a mouse button. This means that event handlers for the MouseMove and MouseDown events have to be written (Listing 11.12).

Listing 11.12. Processing Mouse Events

```
Private Sub Form1_MouseMove(ByVal sender As Object, ByVal e As _
System.Windows.Forms.MouseEventArgs) Handles MyBase.MouseMove
    ' The screensaver must terminate upon a mouse move.
    ' But the MouseMove event is caused by very slight movements.
    ' Consequently, we track events
    ' when the mouse actually moves
    ' a few pixels before closing the screensaver.
    ' If the coordinates of the MouseLocation are 0,0,
    ' then moving to the current position
    ' and saving for future use.
    ' Otherwise, checking when the mouse
    ' moves at least 10 pixels.
    If Not m_IsActive Then
        Me.m_MouseLocation = New Point(e.X, e.Y)
        m_IsActive = True
    Else
        If Math.Abs(e.X - Me.m_MouseLocation.X) > 10 Or _
            Math.Abs(e.Y - Me.m_MouseLocation.Y) > 10 Then
            ' If the mouse moves, exiting the program
            Application.Exit()
        End If
    End If
End Sub

Private Sub Form1_MouseDown(ByVal sender As Object, ByVal e As _
System.Windows.Forms.MouseEventArgs) Handles MyBase.MouseDown
    ' Exiting the program when a mouse button is pressed
    Application.Exit()
End Sub
```

Build the project, run the program to make sure that everything works properly, and then move on. Just about any screensaver will likely use a timer to change the image on the screen. Place a `Timer` control on the form and enable it in the `Form_Load` event. At the same time, create a `Graphics` object, which we will need soon (Listing 11.13).

Listing 11.13. Adding a Timer

```
    Private Sub Form1_Load(ByVal sender As Object, ByVal e As System.EventArgs) _
Handles MyBase.Load
        ' Creating a Graphics object on which to draw
        g = CreateGraphics()

        ' Enabling the timer
        Timer1.Enabled = True
    End Sub


    Private Sub Timer1_Tick(ByVal sender As System.Object, ByVal e As System.EventArgs) _
Handles Timer1.Tick
        DrawFigures()
    End Sub
```

All that the timer does is outputting figures to the screen. For this, we create a separate procedure, `DrawFigures()` (Listing 11.14).

Listing 11.14. The Procedure for Drawing Figures

```
    Private Sub DrawFigures()
        ' The procedure to draw figures of different colors and sizes

        ' Obtaining the screen size
        Dim cx As Integer = Me.Width
        Dim cy As Integer = Me.Height

        ' Coordinates of random points
        Dim x1, x2, y1, y2 As Integer

        ' Rectangles for drawing figures
        Dim myRect As Rectangle

        ' The color for figures
        Dim myColor As Color

        ' Generating random numbers for the points' coordinates
        x1 = m_Random.Next(0, cx)
```

```
x2 = m_Random.Next(0, cx)

y1 = m_Random.Next(0, cy)
y2 = m_Random.Next(0, cy)

' Building a rectangle on the random coordinates
myRect = New Rectangle(Math.Min(x1, x2), Math.Min(y1, y2), _
        Math.Abs(x1 - x2), Math.Abs(y1 - y2))

' Selecting a random color
myColor = Color.FromArgb(255, m_Random.Next(255), _
    m_Random.Next(255), m_Random.Next(255))

'Drawing an ellipse
g.FillEllipse(New SolidBrush(myColor), myRect)
End Sub
```

We will add more code lines to this procedure in the future, but for now you can run the program to check out how it works. As you can see, you now have a perfectly functioning screensaver that draws ellipses of various colors and sizes randomly on the black background.

Now, it is time to forget everything that I have just told you. In fact, the program starts executing not with the Form_Load event, but with the Main procedure. This is a very important procedure (Listing 11.15), as it processes the command-line parameters mentioned earlier.

Listing 11.15. Processing the Command-Line Parameters

```
<STAThread()> Shared Sub Main(ByVal args As String())
    ' The program execution starts with this procedure.
    ' It processes the command line parameters
    ' and the user's settings via the Parameters button
    ' on the Screensaver tab of the Display applet.
    ' If the parameters are not used,
    ' the screensaver launches in the regular operating mode.
    If args.Length > 0 Then
        ' If the parameters are used,
        ' Windows recognizes the following switches:
        '    "/s", "/p" or "/c"

        ' Preview settings
        If args(0).ToLower = "/p" Then
```

```
                ' Leaving alone for the time being

                '  Simply exiting the program
                Application.Exit()
        End If

        ' If the program has a configuration window
        If args(0).ToLower.Trim().Substring(0, 2) = "/c" Then
                ' Creating a frmOptions form and displaying it
                Dim userOptionsForm As New frmOptions
                userOptionsForm.ShowDialog()

                ' Exiting the application
                Application.Exit()
        End If

        ' If the screensaver is not previewed
        If args(0).ToLower = "/s" Then

                ' Creating the main form and displaying it
                Dim screenSaverForm As New Form1
                screenSaverForm.ShowDialog()

                ' Exiting when the form is closed
                Application.Exit()
        End If

    Else
        ' Running the screensaver. This situation is employed
        ' when the user starts the program by a double-click.
        ' The command line parameters are not processed.

        ' Creating the frmScreenSaver form and displaying it
        Dim screenSaverForm As New Form1
        screenSaverForm.ShowDialog()

        ' Exiting when the form is closed
        Application.Exit()
    End If
End Sub
```

I supplied detailed comments with the procedure's code, so there should be no problems in understanding how it functions. One thing that has to be pointed out is that a new form is accessed in this procedure — frmOptions — in which the user can configure the screensaver's various parameters, such as the shape and color of the figures, the speed with which they are displayed, etc. A new form, on which several controls are placed, is therefore added to the project. The configuration window is shown in Fig. 11.5. Of interest to us is the code for the **OK** button and for the Load event of the configuration form. It is this code that handles the saving of the user settings to the disk and their reading from the file (Listing 11.16).

Listing 11.16. Saving and Reading the Settings

```
    Private Sub btnOK_Click(ByVal sender As System.Object, ByVal e As System.EventArgs) _
Handles btnOK.Click
        ' This code saves the settings to
        ' and reads them from the disk.

        Dim myOptions As New Options

        If Me.optEllipses.Checked Then
            myOptions.Shape = "Ellipses"
        Else
            myOptions.Shape = "Rectangles"
        End If

        myOptions.IsTransparent = Me.chkTransparent.Checked
        myOptions.Speed = Me.cboSpeed.Text

        ' Saving the settings to the disk
        myOptions.SaveOptions()

        ' Closing the object
        Me.Close()

    End Sub


    Private Sub frmOptions_Load(DyVal sender As System.Object, ByVal e As _
System.EventArgs) Handles MyBase.Load
        ' Loading the current settings and
        setting the values for various controls.

        Dim myOptions As New Options
        myOptions.LoadOptions()

        Me.cboSpeed.Text = myOptions.Speed
```

```
Me.chkTransparent.Checked = myOptions.IsTransparent

If myOptions.Shape = "Ellipses" Then
    Me.optEllipses.Checked = True
Else
    Me.optRectangles.Checked = True
End If

End Sub
```

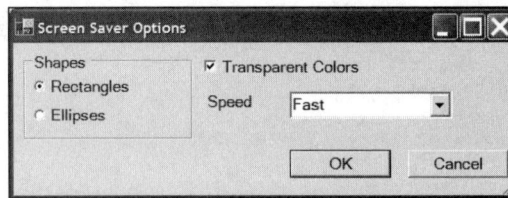

Fig. 11.5. The configuration window

As you have probably figured out by looking at the code, our screensaver can draw not only ellipses, but also rectangles, as well as configure the transparency of the figures and the speed, with which they are displayed. Therefore, we modify the DrawFigures procedure as follows:

```
Private Sub DrawFigures()
...
    ' If the user wants to use transparency,
    ' giving him/her this capability.
    If m_Options.IsTransparent Then
        myColor = Color.FromArgb(m_Random.Next(255), m_Random.Next(255), _
            m_Random.Next(255), m_Random.Next(255))
    Else
        ' If no transparency is needed,
        ' the alfa-component is set to 255.
        myColor = Color.FromArgb(255, m_Random.Next(255), _
            m_Random.Next(255), m_Random.Next(255))
    End If

    'Drawing an ellipse
    If m_Options.Shape = "Ellipses" Then
        g.FillEllipse(New SolidBrush(myColor), myRect)
    Else
        ' Drawing a rectangle
        g.FillRectangle(New SolidBrush(myColor), myRect)
    End If
```

A global variable holding the object for the user settings also has to be added:

```
' The Options object containing the information about the user's choice
Private m_Options As New Options
```

Now, the `Form1_Load` event handler needs to be modified:

```
 Private Sub Form1_Load(ByVal sender As Object, ByVal e As System.EventArgs) _
Handles MyBase.Load
    ...
    ' Loading saved settings.
    ' Note that if the settings file does not exist
    ' it will be created
    m_Options.LoadOptions()

    ' Setting the display speed
    Select Case m_Options.Speed
        Case "Slow"
            Timer1.Interval = 500
        Case "Fast"
            Timer1.Interval = 100
        Case Else
            Timer1.Interval = 200
    End Select
    ...
End Sub
```

All screensaver settings can be saved in either a regular text file or in the registry. Microsoft, for example, suggests using the XML capabilities in the screensaver example that I used as the base for my program. It should be noted that the corporation is actively promoting this language for common use. Perhaps you ought to take a close look at this language in order to use it in future projects. For the time being, however, let's move on to the final stage of our example. To create an XML configuration file, we need to add a new class to the project. Give it the name `Options` (file Options.vb). I provided all the necessary explanations in the comments for the class code, which I believe will be enough for you to get a grasp of how it works (Listing 11.17).

Listing 11.17. The Screensaver Options File

```
'********************
' file Options.vb
' Screensaver options
'********************
Option Strict On

Imports System.Xml.Serialization
```

```vb
Imports System.Xml
Imports System.IO

' This class contains settings information

<Serializable()> Public Class Options

    ' Setting variables and default values
    Private m_Speed As String = "Fast"
    Private m_Shape As String = "Ellipses"
    Private m_IsTransparent As Boolean = True

    ' Setting the configuration file location
    Private OptionsPath As String = _
        Environment.CurrentDirectory & "\ScreenSaver_Options.opt"

    ' --- Class property ---

    ' Whether the screensaver uses transparent
    ' colors to display figures.
    Public Property IsTransparent() As Boolean
        Get
            Return m_IsTransparent
        End Get
        Set(ByVal Value As Boolean)
            m_IsTransparent = Value
        End Set
    End Property

    ' Figures displayed
    Public Property Shape() As String
        Get
            Return m_Shape
        End Get

        Set(ByVal Value As String)
            m_Shape = Value
        End Set
    End Property

    ' The speed, with which figures are displayed
    Public Property Speed() As String
        Get
```

```
            Return m_Speed
        End Get

        Set(ByVal Value As String)
            m_Speed = Value
        End Set
End Property


' --- Class methods ---

' If the configuration file exists,
' the function returns "true", otherwise "false."
Public Function IsOptionFileExisting() As Boolean
        Dim myIO As New System.IO.FileInfo(OptionsPath)
        Return myIO.Exists()
End Function

' The function loads user settings.
' First, a check is made whether the configuration file exists
' if the file exists, the settings are loaded from it.
' If no file exists, it is created containing default values.
Public Sub LoadOptions()

        Dim myOptions As New Options    ' An Options object

        ' Checking for an existing file or creating a new one
        If myOptions.IsOptionFileExisting() Then

            ' Loading settings
            ' Creating XmlSerializer to obtain the values of the settings
            Dim mySerializer As New XmlSerializer(GetType(Options))

            ' Creating StreamReader to specify the configuration file
            Dim myTextReader As New StreamReader(OptionsPath)

            ' Creating XmlTextReader to read the settings
            Dim myXmlReader As New Xml.XmlTextReader(myTextReader)

            ' First, making sure the file supports the necessary format
            If mySerializer.CanDeserialize(myXmlReader) Then

                myOptions = CType(mySerializer.Deserialize(myXmlReader), Options)
            Else
```

```
            ' Saving the new configuration file
            myOptions.SaveOptions()
        End If

        ' Closing the IO object
        myXmlReader.Close()
        myTextReader.Close()

        ' Setting various settings using the info from the file
        ' (or using default values if there is no file)
        Me.Speed = myOptions.Speed
        Me.IsTransparent = myOptions.IsTransparent
        Me.Shape = myOptions.Shape

    End If
End Sub

' The procedure for saving the new settings
Public Sub SaveOptions()

    Dim myWriter As New System.IO.StreamWriter(OptionsPath)

    Dim myXmlSerializer As New XmlSerializer(Me.GetType())

    myXmlSerializer.Serialize(myWriter, Me)

    myWriter.Close()

End Sub

End Class
```

Our first screensaver is finally completed. All that is left to do is to perform a number of important operations to install it on the system. First, create an executable file (execute the **Build/Build ScreenSaver** menu sequence). Find this file (it should be in the bin folder of you project folder) and change its extension to SCR. Right-click on the file and select the **Install** command. You can also copy the file manually to the \Windows\System32 folder. Now, open the **Display** applet in the **Control Panel**, and select the **Screen Saver** tab. Find the name of your screensaver in the dropdown list, and click the **Settings** button. In the settings dialog window that opens, set the necessary options, and close the window. You can now click the **Preview** button and observe your screensaver in action.

11.9.2. Another Screensaver

I don't believe one example is enough to allow you to fathom all of the peculiarities involved in creating screensavers. Moreover, Microsoft has not used all of the standard screensaver features. In particular, the screensaver does not process one of the command line parameters, which is used to display the screensaver on the miniature screen on the **Screen Saver** tab of the **Display** applet. We also have not written a procedure to terminate the screensaver when a keyboard key is pressed. Therefore, I will provide another example, partially borrowed from the site maintained by Rod Stephens (**www.vb-helper.com**). The project name for this example is RodStephens_Ssaver. Because all screensavers are based on the same principles, I will not go into detail about each line of code, limiting myself to describing only some of them. I will also comment important points in the code. The screensaver displays balls bouncing off the sides of the monitor's screen (the bounce process will be described in other chapters).

The first thing that makes this screensaver different is that the Main procedure has been separated into an individual module, called SubMain.vb. The constants and the Windows API functions necessary for the example are also declared and defined in this module (Listing 11.18).

Listing 11.18. Bouncing Balls

```
'---------------------------------------
' The original version is located on Rod Stephens' site.
' http://www.vb-helper.com
'---------------------------------------
Module SubMain
    Public Const SWP_NOACTIVATE = &H10
    Public Const SWP_NOZORDER = &H4
    Public Const SWP_SHOWWINDOW = &H40
    Public Const GWL_STYLE = -16
    Public Const WS_CHILD = &H40000000
    Public Const GWL_HWNDPARENT = -8
    Public Const HWND_TOP = 0

    Public Structure RECT
        Public left As Integer
        Public top As Integer
        Public right As Integer
        Public bottom As Integer
    End Structure

    Public Declare Function GetClientRect Lib "user32" ( _
```

```
        ByVal hwnd As Integer, _
        ByRef lpRect As RECT) As Integer

Public Declare Function GetWindowLong Lib "user32" Alias "GetWindowLongA" ( _
        ByVal hwnd As Integer, _
        ByVal nIndex As Integer) As Integer

Public Declare Function SetWindowLong Lib "user32" Alias "SetWindowLongA" ( _
        ByVal hwnd As Integer, _
        ByVal nIndex As Integer, _
        ByVal dwNewInteger As Integer) As Integer

Public Declare Function SetWindowPos Lib "user32" ( _
        ByVal hwnd As Integer, _
        ByVal hWndInsertAfter As Integer, _
        ByVal x As Integer, _
        ByVal y As Integer, _
        ByVal cx As Integer, _
        ByVal cy As Integer, _
        ByVal wFlags As Integer) As Integer

Public Declare Function SetParent Lib "user32" ( _
        ByVal hWndChild As Integer, _
        ByVal hWndNewParent As Integer) As Integer

Public Enum ActionType
        actConfigure
        actPreview
        actRun
End Enum

Public m_Action As ActionType
Public Sub Main(ByVal args As String())
        ' Processing the command line parameters
        If args.Length = 0 Then
            m_Action = ActionType.actRun
        Else
            Select Case args(0).ToLower().Substring(0, 2)
                Case "/p"
                    m_Action = ActionType.actPreview
                Case "/c"
                    m_Action = ActionType.actConfigure
                Case "/s"
                    m_Action = ActionType.actRun
```

```
            Case Else
                m_Action = ActionType.actRun
        End Select
    End If


    Select Case m_Action
        Case ActionType.actRun
            ' Regular mode
            Dim canvas As New frmCanvas
            Application.Run(canvas)
        Case ActionType.actConfigure
            ' The settings window
            Dim dlg_config As New frmConfig
            Application.Run(dlg_config)
        Case ActionType.actPreview
            ' The preview window
            Dim canvas As New frmCanvas
            SetForm(canvas, args(1))
            Application.Run(canvas)
    End Select
End Sub

' Changing the form's parent for the preview window
Private Sub SetForm(ByRef frm As Form, ByRef arg As String)
    Dim style As Integer
    Dim preview_hwnd As Integer = Integer.Parse(CType(arg, String))
    Dim r As New RECT

    ' Obtaining the dimensions of the preview window
    GetClientRect(preview_hwnd, r)

    With frm
        .WindowState = FormWindowState.Normal
        .FormBorderStyle = FormBorderStyle.None
        .Width = r.right
        .Height = r.bottom
    End With

    ' Adding the WS_CHILD style
    style = GetWindowLong(frm.Handle.ToInt32, GWL_STYLE)
    style = style Or WS_CHILD
    SetWindowLong(frm.Handle.ToInt32, GWL_STYLE, style)

    ' Changing the parent for the window
```

```
        SetParent(frm.Handle.ToInt32, preview_hwnd)

        ' Setting the preview window to the GWL_PARENT value
        SetWindowLong(frm.Handle.ToInt32, GWL_HWNDPARENT, preview_hwnd)

        ' Form's positions in the preview window
        SetWindowPos(frm.Handle.ToInt32, 0, r.left, 0, r.right, r.bottom, _
            SWP_NOACTIVATE Or SWP_NOZORDER Or SWP_SHOWWINDOW)
    End Sub
End Module
```

You should examine the SetForm procedure carefully. This is where the clone of the screensaver that will be shown in the **Display** applet is formed. The frmConfig form is the screensaver's configuration window (Listing 11.19). It provides a text field, in which the user can set the number of balls to be displayed (users are so keen on configuring programs themselves).

Listing 11.19. The Code for the frmConfig Form

```
Public Class frmConfig
    Inherits System.Windows.Forms.Form


#Region " Windows Form Designer generated code "
...
#End Region


    ' Displaying the current settings
    Private Sub Config_Load(ByVal sender As System.Object, ByVal e As System.EventArgs) _
Handles MyBase.Load
        txtNumBalls.Text = GetSetting("Bouncer", "Settings", "NumBalls", "20")
    End Sub


    ' Saving the new settings
    Private Sub cmdOk_Click(ByVal sender As System.Object, ByVal e As System.EventArgs) _
Handles cmdOk.Click
        Try
            SaveSetting("Bouncer", "Settings", "NumBalls", CLng(txtNumBalls.Text))
        Catch exc As Exception
        End Try


        Close()
```

```
    End Sub

    Private Sub cmdCancel_Click(ByVal sender As System.Object, ByVal e As _
System.EventArgs) Handles cmdCancel.Click
        Close()
    End Sub
End Class
```

The number of balls selected by the user is written to the registry when the **OK** button is clicked. Clicking the **Cancel** button simply closes the window. The main code for the program is contained in the frmCanvas form (Listing 11.20). Since there is nothing conceptually new involved, I won't bother describing it.

Listing 11.20. The Code for the frmCanvas Form

```
Public Class frmCanvas
    Inherits System.Windows.Forms.Form

    Private m_Xmax As Integer
    Private m_Ymax As Integer

    ' (X, y) - the coordinates of the left corner
    ' of the rectangle, in which balls are drawn
    ' D - the diameter of a ball
    Private m_NumBalls As Long
    Private m_Color() As Color
    Private m_D() As Single
    Private m_X() As Single
    Private m_Y() As Single
    Private m_Vx() As Single
    Private m_Vy() As Single

    Private m_BufferBitmap As Bitmap
    Private m_BufferGraphics As Graphics
    Private m_Graphics As Graphics
    Private m_Random As New Random

    ' Hiding the cursor and enabling the timer
    Private Sub frmCanvas_Load(ByVal sender As Object, ByVal e As System.EventArgs) _
Handles MyBase.Load

        If m_Action = ActionType.actRun Then
            Cursor.Hide()
```

```
    Else
        RemoveHandler Me.KeyDown, AddressOf frmCanvas_KeyDown
        RemoveHandler Me.MouseMove, AddressOf frmCanvas_MouseMove
        RemoveHandler Me.MouseDown, AddressOf frmCanvas_MouseDown
    End If

    ' Saving the screen size
    m_Xmax = Width
    m_Ymax = Height

    ' Getting the number of the balls
    m_NumBalls = CLng(GetSetting("Bouncer", "Settings", "NumBalls", "20"))

    ' Creating the balls
    ReDim m_Color(m_NumBalls)
    ReDim m_D(m_NumBalls)
    ReDim m_X(m_NumBalls)
    ReDim m_Y(m_NumBalls)
    ReDim m_Vx(m_NumBalls)
    ReDim m_Vy(m_NumBalls)

    Const MAX_VEL As Single = 0.025
    Const MIN_D_FACTOR As Single = 0.025
    Const MAX_D_FACTOR As Single = 0.1
    For i As Integer = 0 To m_NumBalls - 1
        m_Color(i) = Color.FromArgb(&HFF000000 Or QBColor(m_Random.Next(1, 15)))
        m_D(i) = RandomSingle(m_Ymax * MIN_D_FACTOR, m_Ymax * MAX_D_FACTOR)
        m_X(i) = RandomSingle(1, m_Xmax - m_D(i))
        m_Y(i) = RandomSingle(1, m_Ymax - m_D(i))
        m_Vx(i) = RandomSingle(-m_Ymax * MAX_VEL, m_Ymax * MAX_VEL)
        m_Vy(i) = RandomSingle(-m_Ymax * MAX_VEL, m_Ymax * MAX_VEL)
    Next i

    m_BufferBitmap = New Bitmap(m_Xmax, m_Ymax)
    m_BufferGraphics = Graphics.FromImage(m_BufferBitmap)

    ' Creating a Graphics object for the form
    m_Graphics = CreateGraphics()

    tmrMove.Enabled = True
End Sub


' Returning a random number
```

```
    Private Function RandomSingle(ByVal min_value As Single, ByVal max_value As Single) _
As Single
        Return min_value + (max_value - min_value) * m_Random.NextDouble()
    End Function
```

Study the code on your own and design a screensaver that will knock the whole world dead. I wish you the best of luck!

11.10. Suggestions and Recommendations

The form is a rather conservative item of the graphical interface. It is, therefore, difficult to suggest anything interesting in this area. Screensavers are a whole different ballgame. Here you can let loose your fantasies. Check out the screensavers on your computer and try to write analogous programs. You don't have to achieve an absolute resemblance. Racking your brain to solve the principal problems is much more important.

Chapter 12: Controls

Controls are objects placed on the form (buttons, labels, text boxes, etc.) or in a special container (a timer, for example). You would be hard-pressed to find a program that does not use at least one control. The number of built-in controls has been increasing with each new version of Visual Basic. Moreover, programmers can create their own controls for solving particular tasks, or purchase them from other developers. In this chapter, we will consider a few rather unorthodox ways of using controls in programs.

12.1. Custom-Shaped Controls

We will start with an abstract control. Sometimes, I find the standard appearance of controls rather boring. The soul craves for something unusual. Why not, for example, make an oval button or a triangular one? We can get help here from the `Region` property, which discards the areas of the control that are not needed. I once created an ActiveX `OvalButton` control for VB 6.0, which you can still find on my site. To create this control, I had to dig through tons of documentation and use Windows API functions. But it was all made worth it by the huge popularity the button enjoyed. There were also analogous commercial versions of the control, but those days are long gone now. Today, creating a custom-shaped control is an amazingly easy task. Proof of this can be seen in the example of the `RoundControls` project (Listing 12.1). Place a button named `butRound` on the project form. We will use this button for our experiments, trying to make it oval. This will happen when the button itself is pressed.

Listing 12.1. Making a Button Oval

```
'------------------------------------
' RoundControls  © 2004 Alexander Klimov
'------------------------------------
Imports System.Drawing.Drawing2D

    Private Sub butRound_Click(ByVal sender As System.Object, _
            ByVal e As System.EventArgs) Handles butRound.Click

        Dim gp As New GraphicsPath
        Dim g As Graphics = CreateGraphics()

        ' Creating a rectangle the size of the button
        Dim newRectangle As Rectangle = butRound.ClientRectangle

        ' Reducing the size of the rectangle
        newRectangle.Inflate(-3, -3)

        ' Creating an ellipse of the obtained size
        gp.AddEllipse(newRectangle)
        butRound.Region = New Region(gp)

        ' Drawing framing for a round button
        g.DrawEllipse(New Pen(Color.Gray, 2), butRound.Left + 1, _
                butRound.Top + 1, _
                butRound.Width - 3, butRound.Height - 3)

        ' Releasing resources
        g.Dispose()
    End Sub
```

A short explanation is required. The size of the rectangle had to be reduced in order to hide the button's framing. This makes the button look neater. This is how simple it is to create a free-shaped control. The same thing can also be done with other controls.

12.2. Unconventional-Looking Controls

Sometimes, you just can't help wishing that the standard-looking controls could be exchanged for some with brighter individuality. Here is a short example of modifying the standard CheckBox control (project RedCheckBox, Listing 12.2). Place a regular CheckBox control on the form and write the following code.

Listing 12.2. Unconventional CheckBox

```
'---------------------------------------
' RedCheckBox    © 2004 Alexander Klimov
'---------------------------------------
    Private Sub Form1_Paint(ByVal sender As Object, ByVal e As _
System.Windows.Forms.PaintEventArgs) Handles MyBase.Paint
        Dim g As Graphics = e.Graphics
        Dim p As New Pen(Color.Red, 3)
        Dim ctrl As Control

        For Each ctrl In Me.Controls
            If TypeOf ctrl Is CheckBox Then
                g.DrawRectangle(p, New _
                    Rectangle(ctrl.Location, ctrl.Size))
            End If
        Next
    End Sub
```

Launching the program, you will see that the CheckBox control is now framed in red. Naturally, this technique can be applied to practically any other control.

12.3. The *TextBox* Control

The TextBox control is one of the most-often used controls in applications. Its application areas are text editors, fields to enter passwords, information messages, calculators, and so on.

12.3.1. Automatic Scrolling to the Text End

If a new text needs to be added at the end of the text in a multiline text box, the insertion point needs to be placed at end of the text. This can easily be done with a mere three lines of code, as demonstrated in the TextBoxSamples project (Listing 12.3).

Listing 12.3. Automatic Scrolling to the Text End

```
'---------------------------------------
' TextBoxSamples   © 2004 Alexander Klimov
'---------------------------------------
    Private Sub Button1_Click(ByVal sender As System.Object, ByVal e As _
System.EventArgs) Handles Button1.Click
        ' Adding text
```

```
        TextBox1.AppendText(" The added text.")
        ' Place the selection at the end of the text and set the focus.
        TextBox1.SelectionStart = TextBox1.Text.Length
        TextBox1.Focus()
    End Sub
```

The same technique can also be applied to the `RichTextBox` control.

12.3.2. Moving the Focus to the Next or Previous Control

You have most likely seen programs, in which the focus automatically moves to another control after a certain number of characters have been entered into a text box. This technique can be implemented using the `Control.SelectNextControl()` method. Suppose that when seven characters have been entered into a text box, the focus needs to be moved to another text box. The code to do this is given in Listing 12.4.

Listing 12.4. Moving the Focus to Another Control

```
    Private Sub txtNext1_TextChanged(ByVal sender As System.Object, ByVal e As  _
System.EventArgs) Handles txtNext1.TextChanged
        Const MAX_LENGTH As Integer = 7
        If txtNext1.Text.Length = MAX_LENGTH Then
            SelectNextControl(txtNext1, True, True, False, False)
        End If
    End Sub

    Private Sub txtNext2_TextChanged(ByVal sender As System.Object, ByVal e As  _
System.EventArgs) Handles txtNext2.TextChanged
        Const MAX_LENGTH As Integer = 7
        If txtNext2.Text.Length = MAX_LENGTH Then
            SelectNextControl(txtNext2, True, True, False, False)
        End If
    End Sub

    Private Sub txtNext3_TextChanged(ByVal sender As System.Object, ByVal e As  _
System.EventArgs) Handles txtNext3.TextChanged
        Const MAX_LENGTH As Integer = 7
        If txtNext3.Text.Length = MAX_LENGTH Then
            MsgBox("Thank You")
            Close()
        End If
    End Sub
```

As you can see, when the number of characters entered in the first text box reaches seven, the focus automatically moves from this control to another text box. The same thing happens in the second text box, with the focus moving to the third.

12.3.3. Counting Lines in a Multiline Text Box

If the `Multiline` property of a `TextBox` control is set to true, the `Lines` property returns an array of strings that contains the text in the text box. But this property has a slight short-coming: It does not take into account word divisions. In practice, it appears to be the case that the `Lines` property takes into account only the lines divided by a special symbol: the `vbNewLine` constant. But, if the `WordWrap` property of the text box is set to `True`, words that do not fit into the given text box length are automatically wrapped over to a new line. The `Lines` property does not take this fact into account. In this circumstance, the Windows API `EM_GETLINECOUNT` message comes in handy. It is sent by the `SendMessage` function to the appropriate control. Let's consider this case in relation to a specific example in the `NumberLines` project. Place a text box on the form, and set its `Multiline` property to `True`. Also place a button on the form. Name it `butCount`, and set its `Text` property to `Count`. We will use it to count the lines in the text box (Listing 12.5).

Listing 12.5. Counting Lines in a Text Box

```
'-------------------------------------
' NumberLines  © 2004 Alexander Klimov
'-------------------------------------
    Const EM_GETLINECOUNT As Integer = &HBA
    Declare Function SendMessage Lib "user32" _
        Alias "SendMessageA" (ByVal hwnd As IntPtr, _
        ByVal wMsg As Integer, _
        ByVal wParam As Integer, _
        ByVal lParam As Integer) As Integer


    Private Sub Form1_Load(ByVal sender As System.Object, ByVal e As System.EventArgs) _
Handles MyBase.Load
        TextBox1.Text = " Jellicle Cats have cheerful faces, Jellicle Cats have bright
black eyes; They like to practice their airs and graces And wait for the Jellicle Moon
to rise."
    End Sub


    Private Sub butCount_Click(ByVal sender As System.Object, ByVal e As _
System.EventArgs) Handles butCount.Click
        ' Number of lines in the text
        Dim NumberLines As Integer
```

```
        NumberLines = SendMessage(TextBox1.Handle, _
                            EM_GETLINECOUNT, 0, 0)
        MsgBox("Number of lines: " & NumberLines)
        MsgBox(TextBox1.Lines.GetUpperBound(0))
    End Sub
```

I intentionally placed an excerpt from the "The Song of the Jellicles," by T.S. Eliot, in one line to allow you to see the difference. Launching the program, you will see that a text this long cannot fit onto one line in the text box, and will automatically wrap into several lines. (The WordWrap property of the text box must be set to True.) The number of lines will depend on the width of the text box. Clicking the button will produce two messages. The first will provide information about the real number of lines in the text box, counted using the WM_GETLINECOUNT Windows message. The second message says that the text field contains no lines at all, because it can find no new line characters in the text.

12.3.4. Blocking the Text Box Context Menu

Any standard text box has a context menu with the standard edit commands: **Undo**, **Cut**, **Copy**, **Paste**, **Delete**, and **Select All**. If you need to block this menu in your program, you will have to override the WndProc method, which processes all Windows messages for text box controls. Create a new project, and name it TextContextMenu. Add a new class, named DisabledContextMenu, to the project, and override the WndProc as shown in Listing 12.6.

Listing 12.6. Blocking the Context Menu

```
'-------------------------------------
' TextContextMenu  © 2004 Alexander Klimov
' file DisabledContextMenu.vb
'-------------------------------------
Public Class DisabledContextMenu
    Inherits TextBox
    Private Const WM_CONTEXTMENU As Integer = &H7B

    Protected Overrides Sub WndProc(ByRef m As System.Windows.Forms.Message)
        If m.Msg <> WM_CONTEXTMENU Then
            MyBase.WndProc(m)
        End If
    End Sub
End Class
```

Go back to the main form and add two text boxes to it. Switch to the code editor and expand the line #Region " Windows From Designer generated code". Find the following lines in the expanded region:

```
Friend WithEvents TextBox1 As System.Windows.Forms.TextBox
Friend WithEvents TextBox2 As System.Windows.Forms.TextBox
```

Replace the second line with this one:

```
Friend WithEvents TextBox2 As DisabledContextMenu
```

A bit further below find this line:

```
Me.TextBox2 = New System.Windows.Forms.TextBox
```

Replace it with the following line:

```
Me.TextBox2 = New DisabledContextMenu
```

Launch the program and try to right-click on the second text box. You will see that the context menu for this text box does not appear. This means that the text box filters all of the Windows messages it receives, and does not let the specified WM_CONTEXTMENU message through for further processing.

12.3.5. Disabling the <Ctrl>+<X> Key Combination

It is not necessary to disable the entire context menu. You can, for example, disable only a certain key combination. For example, the <Ctrl>+<X> key combination places the selected text in the clipboard. This action is analogous to the context-menu **Cut** command. Let's try to override the WndProc method in such a way as to disable this key combination. Add a new class, CtrlX (Listing 12.7), to the TextContextMenu project just considered. The overriding of the WndProc method is carried out the same manner as in the previous example.

Listing 12.7. Disabling the <Ctrl>+<X> Key Combination in a Text Box

```
'--------------------------------------
' Disabling key combinations  © 2004 Alexander Klimov
' file CtrlX.vb
'--------------------------------------
Public Class CtrlX
    Inherits TextBox
    Private Const WM_CHAR As Integer = &H102

    Protected Overrides Sub WndProc(ByRef m As System.Windows.Forms.Message)
        ' If the <Ctrl> key is pressed
        If MyClass.ModifierKeys And Keys.Control Then
```

```
        Select Case m.Msg
            Case WM_CHAR
                ' Disabling Ctrl+X
                Select Case m.WParam.ToInt32
                    Case 24 'X is the 24th letter of the alphabet
                        ' Doing nothing
                        ' in order to not to process the message
                    Case Else
                        MyBase.WndProc(m)
                End Select
            Case Else
                MyBase.WndProc(m)
        End Select
    Else
        MyBase.WndProc(m)
    End If
End Sub
End Class
```

Add another text box, TextBox3, to the form. In the code editor, do the following changes:

```
' Comment out the line and add a new version of it.
'Friend WithEvents TextBox3 As System.Windows.Forms.TextBox
Friend WithEvents TextBox3 As CtrlX
...
Me.TextBox3 = New TextContextMenu.CtrlX
```

Run the program and try to right-click on the third text box. You will see that the context menu works as usual. Now try to select some text, and then cut it with the <Ctrl>+<X> key combination. You will see that this will not work. Thus, we have successfully overridden the WndProc method.

12.3.6. Digits Only

The task of entering only digits in a text box is often encountered in practice. There are many ways to solve this problem. I would like to suggest for your consideration an example that I wrote in Visual Basic 6.0, using Windows' built-in functions. The TextBox control has the ES_NUMBERS style, which is used to block the input of any characters that are not digits. But this is not enough to solve the problem. There is a way around this limitation. Simply paste the text from the clipboard into the text box. Therefore, the data in the clipboard has also to be checked. But let's move on to the example. We have to override the WndProc method in such a way so that non-numerical data cannot be pasted from the clipboard. Like in the previous examples, add a new class, DigitOnly, to the project, DigitTextBox (Listing 12.8).

Listing 12.8. The Class Allowing Only Digits To Be Entered

```
'---------------------------------------
' DigitTextBox  © 2004 Alexander Klimov
' File DigitOnly.vb
'---------------------------------------
Imports System.Text.RegularExpressions
Imports System.Runtime.InteropServices
Public Class DigitOnly
    Inherits TextBox

    Public Sub New()
        ' Creating a template for the regular expression
        ' A range of digits from 0 to 9
        Me.regex = New Regex("[0-9]", RegexOptions.Compiled)
    End Sub
    ' The style of the text box. Only digits can be entered.
    Private Const ES_NUMBER As Integer = &H2000

    ' The constant used by the clipboard functions
    Private Const CF_TEXT As Integer = 1

    ' A Windows message
    Private Const WM_PASTE As Integer = &H302

    ' The regular expression
    Private regex As regex

    ' Windows API functions
    <DllImport("user32", SetLastError:=True)> _
        Private Shared Function OpenClipboard(ByVal hWndNewOwner As IntPtr) As Boolean
    End Function

    <DllImport("user32", SetLastError:=True)> _
    Private Shared Function IsClipboardFormatAvailable(ByVal format As Integer) As Boolean
    End Function

    <DllImport("user32", SetLastError:=True)> _
    Private Shared Function GetClipboardData(ByVal format As Integer) As IntPtr
    End Function

    <DllImport("user32", SetLastError:=True)> _
    Private Shared Function CloseClipboard() As Boolean
    End Function
```

```vbnet
<DllImport("kernel32", SetLastError:=True)> _
Private Shared Function GlobalLock(ByVal hMem As IntPtr) As IntPtr
End Function

<DllImport("kernel32", SetLastError:=True)> _
Private Shared Function GlobalUnlock(ByVal hMem As IntPtr) As Boolean
End Function

' Overriding the WndProc method
Protected Overrides Sub WndProc(ByRef m As System.Windows.Forms.Message)
    Select Case m.Msg
        ' Processing the paste message
    Case WM_PASTE
            ' Checking the format of the data in the clipboard
            If IsClipboardFormatAvailable(CF_TEXT) Then
                ' Opening the clipboard
                If OpenClipboard(IntPtr.Zero) Then
                    ' Obtaining the clipboard handle in the specified format
                    Dim hTxt As IntPtr = GetClipboardData(CF_TEXT)

                    ' Allocating a memory block
                    Dim hMem As IntPtr = GlobalLock(hTxt)

                    ' Working with the string
                    Dim cliptxt As String = Marshal.PtrToStringAnsi(hMem)

                    ' Releasing the memory block
                    GlobalUnlock(hTxt)

                    ' Closing the clipboard
                    CloseClipboard()

                    ' Comparing the clipboard data with the regular expression
                    If regex.Match(cliptxt).Success Then
                        'm.Result = IntPtr.Zero
                        MyBase.WndProc(m)
                    Else
                        'MyBase.WndProc(m)
                        m.Result = IntPtr.Zero
                    End If
                End If
            Else
                MyBase.WndProc(m)
            End If
        Case Else
            MyBase.WndProc(m)
    End Select
End Sub

' Setting the "Numbers Only" style
```

```
Protected Overrides ReadOnly Property CreateParams() As System.Windows.Forms.CreateParams
    Get
        Dim cp As CreateParams = MyBase.CreateParams
        cp.Style = cp.Style Or ES_NUMBER
        Return cp
    End Get
End Property
End Class
```

Now, switch to the project's main form and add two text boxes. The first, txtDigit, will be a testing ground for our experiments. Set its Text property to blank. Leave the Text property of the second text box, txtAnyTxt, its default TextBox2 value. In the code editor, make the following changes:

```
Friend WithEvents txtDigit As DigitOnly
Me.txtDigit = New DigitTextbox.DigitOnly
```

Run the program. Try entering various characters in the first text box from the keyboard. You will notice that the text box rejects letters and accepts digits with no problems. Moving on to the second stage of the experiments, copy a digit, let's say 2, from the second text box in the clipboard and try to paste it into the first text box (Fig. 12.1). No problem so far. Now, copy some text and try to paste it. You will see that the text field does not accept data containing letters. Thus, we have created a functional control with new properties.

Some code portions are explained in the brief comments that accompany them. If you need additional information about the Windows API functions used in order to gain a better understanding of the logic behind the program, you will have to find it on your own. I would like to explain the regular expression in more detail. I used the [0-9] notation, which includes digits from 0 to 9, as a template. As the alternative, the /d expression could have been used. In my opinion, the first notation is more informative and easier to remember.

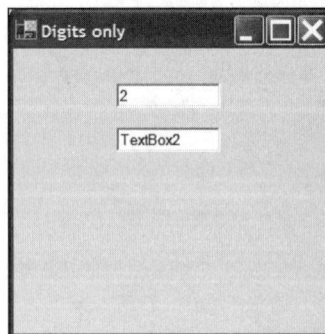

Fig. 12.1. The project's main form

12.4. The *Label* Control

12.4.1. Animated Labels

Here is another example from my collection of examples written in VB 6.0. The idea of the example is the following: Place two labels, each with different font and text-color properties, on the main form of the AniLabel project. Also place there a butFirst button, labeled First Effect, and a timer. Using the timer, the labels are compressed to their minimal size and then expanded again. In between these two processes, some of the label's properties can be changed. For example, the text of the labels or the character color can be altered. The source code for the program is provided in Listing 12.9.

Listing 12.9. Animated Labels

```
'---------------------------------------
' AniLabel © 2004 Alexander Klimov
'---------------------------------------
    Dim A As Integer ' The shrink and expansion step of the labels
    Dim LH As Integer ' The height of the labels

Private Sub Form1_Load(ByVal sender As System.Object, ByVal e As System.EventArgs) _
Handles MyBase.Load
        ' Calculating the height and the change step of the label
        LH = Label1.Height
        A = LH / 10
    End Sub


    Private Sub butFirst_Click(ByVal sender As Object, ByVal e As System.EventArgs) _
Handles butFirst.Click
        Timer1.Enabled = True
    End Sub

    Public Sub LabelMove(ByRef L As System.Windows.Forms.Label, ByRef N As Short, _
ByRef H As Short)
        ' If the label's height minus the change step is greater than 0
        ' then subtracting the step from the height
        If L.Height - N > 0 Then
            L.Height = L.Height - N
            ' Otherwise,
            ' changing the sign of the step to the opposite
        Else
            N = -N
            Label1.ForeColor = Color.Red
```

```
        Label2.Text = "Cats"
    End If

End Sub


Private Sub Timer1_Tick(ByVal sender As Object, ByVal e As System.EventArgs) _
Handles Timer1.Tick
    ' Passing the labels to the processing procedure
    Call LabelMove(Label1, A, LH)
    Call LabelMove(Label2, A, LH)

    ' Enabling the timer after the labels
    ' return to their initial size
    If Label1.Height > LH Then
        Timer1.Enabled = False
        ' changing the value of the step to the opposite
        A = A * -1
    End If
End Sub
```

Almost the entire code is copied from the old VB project. The only thing that had to be changed was the LabelMove procedure. The VB 6.0 version of the procedure looked like this:

```
Public Sub LabelMove(L As Label, N As Integer, H As Integer)
```

I believe the comments explain the processing quite clearly and make it unnecessary to provide additional explanations.

12.4.2. Shimmering Text

To create shimmering text, you will need to place another timer, Timer2, and a butSecond button labeled Second Effect on the form of the AniLabel project. The effect is created by gradually changing the intensity of the text or background color of the label. The source code for this effect is provided in Listing 12.10.

Listing 12.10. Creating Shimmering Text

```
Private Sub butSecond_Click(ByVal sender As System.Object, ByVal e As _
System.EventArgs) Handles butSecond.Click
    Timer2.Enabled = True
End Sub


Private Sub Timer2_Tick(ByVal sender As System.Object, ByVal e As System.EventArgs) _
Handles Timer2.Tick
```

```
     Static A As Integer
     A = A + 10 : If A > 510 Then A = 0

     ' You can change the "Abs (A - 255)" range
     ' You can change the timer interval
     Label1.BackColor = Color.FromArgb(Math.Abs(A - 255), 0, 0)
     Label2.ForeColor = Color.FromArgb(Math.Abs(A - 255), 200, 100)
  End Sub
```

In the example above, I used the old color-rendering capabilities of Visual Basic 6.0. VB 6.0 uses a simplified color model, in which colors are built from three main components: red, green, and blue. VB .NET color model uses an additional component, the alpha component, which allows you to control color transparency. Let's make use of this new component to create the effect of disappearing text. All we have to do is to call another overloaded version of the `Color` structure:

```
' To make the text on the form disappear
' Label2.ForeColor = Color.FromArgb(Math.Abs(A - 255), 200, 200, 100)
```

In this case, not a color component, but the alpha component will undergo changes and, when it reaches the maximum value, the text will dissolve into the form.

12.5. Menu Controls

VB .NET has two types of menu controls: `MainMenu` and `ContextMenu`. Working with these controls doesn't usually present problems for the user. I will show you how to leave the beaten path and create non-standard menus — with images, colored different colors, etc.

12.5.1. Creating Colored Menu Items

Any menu item has the `OwnerDraw` property. Setting it to `True`, we take all of the work to draw the menu on our own shoulders. In this case, event handlers need to be written for the `MeasureItem` and `DrawItem` events. Let's take a look at the process from the very beginning. Create a new, ColorMenu, project. Place a `MainMenu` control on the form. A box with the `Type Here` text will appear under the form title bar. Enter the following text:

```
Unusual Menu
```

This will be the text for the upper menu level. Clicking the mouse on this item will open two more `Type Here` items: to the right of and below the first. Select the bottom item and enter `Colored Item`. This will be `MenuItem2`. In the property editor, set the `OwnerDraw` property for this item to `True`. This concludes the visual part of the project, and now you can start writing the code. The source code is given in Listing 12.11.

Listing 12.11. Creating Colored Menu Items

```
'--------------------------------------
' ColorMenu  © 2004 Alexander Klimov
'--------------------------------------
    Private Const FONT_NAME As String = "Tahoma"
    Private Const FONT_SIZE As Single = 12
    Private Const FONT_STYLE As FontStyle = FontStyle.Bold

    Private Sub MenuItem2_MeasureItem(ByVal sender As Object, _
        ByVal e As System.Windows.Forms.MeasureItemEventArgs) Handles _
MenuItem2.MeasureItem
        ' Creating the font to output text
        Dim menu_font As New Font( _
            FONT_NAME, FONT_SIZE, FONT_STYLE)

        ' Text size
        Dim text_size As SizeF = _
            e.Graphics.MeasureString("Red Item", menu_font)

        ' Setting the necessary dimensions for the menu item
        e.ItemHeight = text_size.Height
        e.ItemWidth = text_size.Width
    End Sub

    Private Sub MenuItem2_DrawItem(ByVal sender As Object, ByVal e As _
System.Windows.Forms.DrawItemEventArgs) Handles MenuItem2.DrawItem
        ' Creating the font to output text
        Dim menu_font As New Font( _
            FONT_NAME, FONT_SIZE, FONT_STYLE)

        ' If the mouse pointer is over the menu item
        If e.State And DrawItemState.Selected Then
            ' Draw a shaded background.
            Dim clr As Double
            Dim dclr As Double
            Dim Y As Long

            e.Graphics.FillRectangle( _
                System.Drawing.Brushes.LightSkyBlue, _
                e.Bounds.X, e.Bounds.Y, _
                e.Bounds.Width, e.Bounds.Height)

            ' Displaying the text
```

```
            e.Graphics.DrawString("New Text", menu_font, _
                System.Drawing.Brushes.AliceBlue, _
                e.Bounds.X, e.Bounds.Y)
        Else
            ' The mouse pointer is beyond the item boundaries.
            ' Changing the background color
            e.Graphics.FillRectangle( _
                System.Drawing.Brushes.Red, _
                e.Bounds.X, e.Bounds.Y, _
                e.Bounds.Width, e.Bounds.Height)

            ' Displaying the text
            e.Graphics.DrawString("Colored Item", menu_font, _
                System.Drawing.Brushes.Blue, _
                e.Bounds.X, e.Bounds.Y)
        End If
    End Sub
```

Note that not only the menu item background color, but also the text color and the menu item's text itself can be changed. These properties can be configured differently for events when the mouse pointer is over the menu item or when it is not.

12.5.2. Adding Images to Menu

In addition to changing the font properties for menu items, you can also use images in them. In practice, images are not used in menus that often, but a little example demonstrating how to do it will only contribute to your overall programming knowledge. As in the previous project, this one, BitmapMenu, uses the MeasureItem and DrawItem events. Additionally, I placed a picture box on the form and loaded an image of a cat into it. This image will serve as a template for the menu item created. Then a short menu is created. Don't forget to set the OwnerDraw property of the menu items to True, because we will redraw them ourselves. The source code for the project is provided in Listing 12.12.

Listing 12.12. Adding Images to Menus

```
'----------------------------------------
' BitmapMenu  © 2004 Alexander Klimov
'----------------------------------------
    Private img As Bitmap

    Private Sub mnuBitmap_MeasureItem(ByVal sender As Object, ByVal e As _
System.Windows.Forms.MeasureItemEventArgs) Handles mnuBitmap.MeasureItem
        e.ItemWidth = img.Width
```

```
      e.ItemHeight = img.Height
   End Sub

   Private Sub mnuBitmap_DrawItem(ByVal sender As Object, ByVal e As    _
System.Windows.Forms.DrawItemEventArgs) Handles mnuBitmap.DrawItem
      Dim rect As Rectangle = e.Bounds
      rect.X = e.Bounds.Width - img.Width
      rect.Width = img.Width
      e.DrawBackground()
      e.Graphics.DrawImage(img, rect)

   End Sub

   Private Sub Form1_Load(ByVal sender As System.Object, ByVal e As System.EventArgs) _
Handles MyBase.Load
      img = PictureBox1.Image
   End Sub

   Private Sub mnuBitmap_Click(ByVal sender As System.Object, ByVal e As   _
System.EventArgs) Handles mnuBitmap.Click
      MsgBox("You have clicked on the cat!")
   End Sub
```

First, we need to set the dimensions for our menu items. I simply made the menu item size the same as the image size:

```
e.ItemWidth = img.Width
e.ItemHeight = img.Height
```

The DrawItem method draws the specified image in the menu item. Run the program, and click on the **Menu** item. This should open the submenu item with the image of a cat (Fig. 12.2). Clicking on the image will produce the corresponding message.

Fig. 12.2. Using images in menus

12.5.3. Back to Colored Menus

The previous example demonstrated how to change the colors of menu items. But it cannot be used to change the color of the menu background, that is, the color of the bar, on which the upper level menu items are located. There is, however, a way to solve this problem as well. As you have probably already guessed, we will have to resort to the Windows API functions again to do this. Create a new project, and name it ColorMainMenu. Place a MainMenu control on the form, and create a small submenu group yourself. The submenu items are not really necessary to demonstrate the example, so don't get carried away. The source code for the project is provided in Listing 12.13.

Listing 12.13. Coloring the Menu Bar

```
'--------------------------------------
' ColorMainMenu  © 2004 Alexander Klimov
'--------------------------------------
    ' The structure and Windows API functions
    Public Structure MENUINFO
        Public cbSize As Int32
        Public fMask As Int32
        Public dwStyle As Int32
        Public cyMax As Int32
        Public hbrBack As IntPtr
        Public dwContextHelpID As Int32
        Public dwMenuData As Int32
        Public Sub New(ByVal owner As Control)
            cbSize = _
              System.Runtime.InteropServices.Marshal.SizeOf(_
                                      GetType(MENUINFO))
        End Sub
    End Structure

    Declare Function DrawMenuBar Lib "user32.dll" _
            (ByVal hwnd As IntPtr) As Int32
    Declare Function SetMenuInfo Lib "user32.dll" _
            (ByVal hmenu As IntPtr, _
             ByRef mi As MENUINFO) As Int32
    Declare Function CreateSolidBrush Lib "gdi32.dll" _
            (ByVal crColor As Int32) As IntPtr
    Declare Function DeleteObject Lib "gdi32.dll" _
            Alias "DeleteObject" (ByVal hObject As IntPtr) _
            As Boolean

    ' Constants
```

```
    Private Const MIM_BACKGROUND As Int32 = &H2
    Private hMenuBrush As IntPtr

    Private Sub Form1_Load(ByVal sender As System.Object, ByVal e As System.EventArgs) _
Handles MyBase.Load
        ' Creating a color brush
        hMenuBrush = CreateSolidBrush(RGB(250, 125, 65))

' Another way to specify the color can be used:
' hMenuBrush = CreateSolidBrush(ColorTranslator.ToOle(Color.Red))

    End Sub

    Private Sub Form1_Closed(ByVal sender As Object, ByVal e As System.EventArgs) _
Handles MyBase.Closed
        ' Releasing the resources when closing the form
        DeleteObject(hMenuBrush)
    End Sub

    Private Sub Form1_Paint(ByVal sender As Object, ByVal e As _
System.Windows.Forms.PaintEventArgs) Handles MyBase.Paint
        Dim mi As MENUINFO = New MENUINFO(Me)
        mi.fMask = MIM_BACKGROUND
        mi.hbrBack = hMenuBrush
        SetMenuInfo(Menu.Handle, mi)
        DrawMenuBar(Handle)
    End Sub
```

The example works as follows. First, the `CreateSolidBrush` function is called to create a brush of the specified color. If you are more used to setting the color using the `Color` structure, then use the `ToOle` function of the `ColorTranslator` class.

```
    hMenuBrush = CreateSolidBrush(ColorTranslator.ToOle(Color.Red))
```

After the handle for the brush of the specified color is obtained, it is passed to the `SetMenuItem` function as a field of the `MENUINFO` structure. The `DrawMenuBar` function redraws the modified menu. Run the program and you will see that the menu bar is colored.

12.6. The *RadioButton* Control

The `RadioButton` control is named as such because it looks similar to actual radio controls. Only one radio button can be checked at a time (the `Checked` property set to `True`). The `RadioButtonSample` project (Listing 12.14) demonstrates how to determine, which of the radio buttons is checked.

Listing 12.14. Determining the Checked Radio Button

```
'---------------------------------------
' RadioButtonSample  © 2004 Alexander Klimov
'---------------------------------------
    Private Sub Button1_Click(ByVal sender As System.Object, ByVal e As _
System.EventArgs) Handles Button1.Click
        Select Case True
            Case RadioButton1.Checked
                ' Your code goes in here.
                MsgBox("You have selected RadioButton1")
            Case RadioButton2.Checked
                MsgBox("You have selected RadioButton2")
            Case RadioButton3.Checked
                MsgBox("You have selected RadioButton3")
        End Select
    End Sub
```

Naturally, before running the sample program, you have to place three `RadioButton` and one `Button` controls on the form. Also, do not forget to set the `Checked` property of one of the radio buttons to `True`.

12.7. The *Timer* Control

The `Timer` control is very simple and has not changed much from the VB 6.0 version. One change is that new methods, `Start` and `Stop`, have been added that are equivalent to the `True` and `False` values of the `Enabled` property, respectively. By the way, the default value of the `Enabled` property is now `False`, as opposed to `True` in the old version. This circumstance used to confuse me at first. I would run a program, and could not understand why, then, nothing would happen. It usually took me a bit to remember that the timer had to be enabled. The examples given in this book frequently use timers. So I will give another interesting example of the use of this control. The example will use the principle employed by some demo-version programs. The source code for the project, named AutoClose, is provided in Listing 12.15. The purpose of the example is to allow the user to examine the program's features for a certain period of time. When this period expires, the program closes automatically.

Listing 12.15. Automatic Program Closing

```
'---------------------------------------
' AutoClose  © 2004 Alexander Klimov
'---------------------------------------
```

```
    Private Sub Timer1_Tick(ByVal sender As System.Object, ByVal e As  _
System.EventArgs) Handles Timer1.Tick
        ' Stopping the timer
        Timer1.Stop()
        ' Closing the program
        Close()
    End Sub
```

You will only have to set the necessary interval for the timer.

12.8. The *StatusBar* Control

Our next guinea pig will be the StatusBar control. This control has no built-in property for changing its background color or the font of the text displayed. If you are overwhelmed with the desire to do this, you will have to take care of it yourself. The instructions are presented in the ColorStatusBar project. Find the StatusBar control on the **Toolbox** bar, and place it on the form. Name it sbColor. Select the Panels property for the status bar created in the property manager window, and click on the ellipsis button. This will open the **StatusBarPanel Collection Editor** dialog window. Click the **Add** button three times. This will create three panels named StatusBarPanel1, StatusBarPanel2, and StatusBarPanel3. Set the Style property of each panel to OwnerDraw, and click the **OK** button to close the dialog window. In the property editor, set the ShowPanels property of the sbColor status bar to True. This concludes the visual part of the project. Now, switch to the code editor panel and write the code necessary to redraw the status bar (Listing 12.16).

Listing 12.16. Creating a Colored Status Bar

```
'--------------------------------------
' ColorStatusBar   © 2004 Alexander Klimov
'--------------------------------------
    Dim p As Pen = New Pen(Color.White)
    Dim sbr = New SolidBrush(Color.YellowGreen)
    Dim color_br(2) As SolidBrush

Private Sub sbColor_DrawItem(ByVal sender As Object, _
    ByVal sbdevent As System.Windows.Forms.StatusBarDrawItemEventArgs) _
                                        Handles sbColor.DrawItem
        Dim g As Graphics = sbdevent.Graphics
        Dim sb As StatusBar = CType(sender, StatusBar)
        Dim rectf = New RectangleF(_
```

```
                    sbdevent.Bounds.X, sbdevent.Bounds.Y, _
                    sbdevent.Bounds.Width, sbdevent.Bounds.Height)

        g.DrawRectangle(p, sbdevent.Bounds)
        g.FillRectangle(color_br(sbdevent.Index), sbdevent.Bounds)
        g.DrawString("Bar" & sbdevent.Index, sb.Font, sbr, rectf)
    End Sub

    Private Sub Form1_Load(ByVal sender As System.Object, _
    ByVal e As System.EventArgs) Handles MyBase.Load
        color_br(0) = New SolidBrush(Color.Red)
        color_br(1) = New SolidBrush(Color.White)
        color_br(2) = New SolidBrush(Color.Blue)
    End Sub

    Protected Overloads Overrides Sub Dispose(ByVal disposing As Boolean)
        If disposing Then
            If Not (components Is Nothing) Then
                components.Dispose()
            End If

            p.Dispose()
            sbr.Dispose()
            Dim i As Integer
            For i = 0 To color_br.Length - 1
                color_br(i).Dispose()
            Next
        End If

        MyBase.Dispose(disposing)
    End Sub
```

Running the program, you will see three panels in the status bar colored red, white and blue, the colors of the U.S. flag. The task of drawing the stars and stripes is left to you.

12.9. The *ListView* Control

The ListView control is used to display lists of various items. The right pane of Windows Explorer is constructed using this control. You can learn how to use this control by studying the appropriate documentation yourself, but I will try to give you an idea here of what you will find there. One of the elements of the ListView control is the header. The header can contain not only text, but also pictures. Pictures, however, cannot be placed into the header by standard means. To accomplish this task, you have to resort to using unmanaged code. An example is provided in the BitmapListView project. Place a ListView, a Button, and an ImageList control on the project form. Leave the default values for each of these controls. Set the Images property of the ImageList control to any two images. Because these images will be placed into headers, they should be about the size of images placed on toolbar buttons. The code for placing images into ListView images headers is provided in Listing 12.17, and its result on Fig. 12.3.

Listing 12.17. Placing Images into ListView Headers

```
'-------------------------------------
' BitmapListView   © 2004 Alexander Klimov
'-------------------------------------
Imports System.Runtime.InteropServices
    Public Const LVM_GETHEADER = 4127
    Public Const HDM_SETIMAGELIST = 4616
    Public Const LVM_SETCOLUMN = 4122
    Public Const LVCF_FMT = 1
    Public Const LVCF_IMAGE = 16
    Public Const LVCFMT_IMAGE = 2048


    ' The LVCOLUMN structure
    <StructLayout(LayoutKind.Sequential, pack:=8, CharSet:=CharSet.Auto)> _
    Structure LVCOLUMN
        Dim mask As Integer
        Dim fmt As Integer
        Dim cx As Integer
        Dim pszText As IntPtr
        Dim cchTextMax As Integer
        Dim iSubItem As Integer
        Dim iImage As Integer
        Dim iOrder As Integer
    End Structure


    ' Two versions of the overloaded SendMessage function
    ' The difference is in the last parameter.
    <DllImport("User32.dll")> _
    Public Overloads Shared Function SendMessage _
        (ByVal hWnd As IntPtr, ByVal Msg As Integer, _
         ByVal wParam As Integer, ByVal lParam As Integer) As IntPtr
    End Function

    <DllImport("User32", CharSet:=CharSet.Auto)> _
```

```
Public Overloads Shared Function SendMessage _
     (ByVal hWnd As IntPtr, ByVal msg As Integer, _
      ByVal wParam As Integer, ByRef lParam As LVCOLUMN) As IntPtr
End Function


Private Sub Form1_Load(ByVal sender As System.Object, ByVal e As System.EventArgs) _
Handles MyBase.Load
     ListView1.View = View.Details
     ListView1.Columns.Add("Header 0", ListView1.Width / 2, _
                                      HorizontalAlignment.Left)
     ListView1.Columns.Add("Header 1", ListView1.Width / 2, _
                                      HorizontalAlignment.Left)
End Sub


Private Sub Button1_Click(ByVal sender As System.Object, ByVal e As _
System.EventArgs) Handles Button1.Click
     Dim hwnd As IntPtr
     Dim iRet As IntPtr
     Dim i As Integer

     ' Getting the header's handle
     hwnd = SendMessage(ListView1.Handle, LVM_GETHEADER, 0, 0)

     ' Linking ImageList to the header
     iRet = SendMessage(hwnd, HDM_SETIMAGELIST _
                     0, (ImageList1.Handle).ToInt32)

     For i = 0 To ListView1.Columns.Count - 1
         Dim col As LVCOLUMN
         col.mask = LVCF_FMT Or LVCF_IMAGE
         col.fmt = LVCFMT_IMAGE
         ' Obtaining an image from ImageList
         col.iImage = i
         col.cchTextMax = 0
         col.cx = 0
         col.iOrder = 0
         col.iSubItem = 0
         col.pszText = IntPtr.op_Explicit(0)

         ' Sending the LVM_SETCOLUMN message
         iRet = SendMessage(ListView1.Handle, LVM_SETCOLUMN, i, col)
     Next
End Sub
```

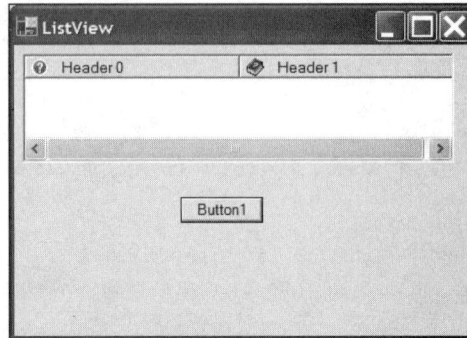

Fig. 12.3. A ListView header with images in it

12.10. A Blinking Icon in the System Tray

The question of how to place a program icon into the system tray used to be a frequent subject of forum discussions. Those who asked were advised by other forum participants, in chorus, to "read the FAQ section." Before a week had passed, of course, there would be another beginner online asking the same question. This led Microsoft to take some steps to make programmers' life easier. They finally offered an easy method in VB .NET for placing an icon in the system tray with the help of the special NotifyIcon control. The manner of working with this control is described in good detail in the package documentation. But simple examples are too boring. Therefore, I offer you my own example — a blinking icon. The first steps for creating the project are standard. Create a new project, named BlinkNotify (Listing 12.18), and place two controls on the form: Timer and NotifyIcon. Note that these controls are moved from the form to the special area below it. Set the Interval property of the timer to 1000. Set the Icon property of the NotifyIcon control to any icon in your collection. Enter any text for the Text property and set the Visible property to False. Also, place a button to start the timer on the form.

Listing 12.18. Blinking Icon in the System Tray

```
'-------------------------------------------
' BlinkNotify  © 2004 Alexander Klimov
'-------------------------------------------
Private Sub Button1_Click(ByVal sender As System.Object, ByVal e As System.EventArgs) _
Handles Button1.Click

Me.Timer1.Start()
End Sub
```

```
Private Sub NotifyIcon1_Click(ByVal sender As Object, ByVal e As System.EventArgs) _
Handles NotifyIcon1.Click

        Me.Timer1.Stop()
        Me.NotifyIcon1.Visible = False
        MsgBox("Blinking Suspended")
End Sub


Private Sub Timer1_Tick(ByVal sender As System.Object, ByVal e As System.EventArgs) _
Handles Timer1.Tick

        With Me.NotifyIcon1
            .Visible = (IIf(.Visible = True, False, True))
        End With
End Sub
```

The flashing icon technique is used quite often in programming. You can use it, for example, to get the user's attention when a new mail or ICQ message arrives.

12.11. Windows XP Visual Styles

Now that you are familiar with a number of techniques for working with the form and various controls, you can move on to learning how to work with Window XP visual styles. With the release of Windows XP, users saw a new graphical interface: controls with rounded corners, objects lighting up when the mouse pointer passes over them, an unusual progress bar, etc. Many users really liked the new Windows look. This engendered the question of how to use all this beauty in your own applications. The explanations that follow pertain only to Windows XP. For starters, let's compare the Windows XP and Windows classical styles (Figs. 12.4 and 12.5, respectively).

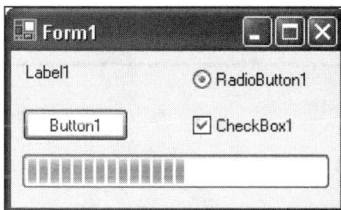

Fig. 12.4. The Windows XP style

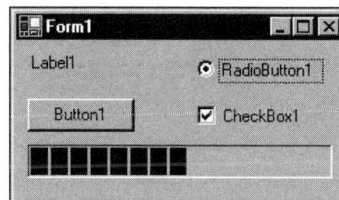

Fig. 12.5. The classical style

Fig. 12.4 shows the slick new appearance of Windows XP controls; Fig. 12.5 shows controls used in Visual Basic.

As you likely already know, the form consists of the client and non-client areas. The non-client area comprises the form title bar, its borders, and the scroll bars. These elements of the form will have the Windows XP style without you having to write a single line of code. We will work with the controls in the client area.

NOTE

The new look of the controls is supported by the version 6.0 Comctl32.dll file. The following is a list of controls supported by this file and that can, therefore, have the new style:

- TextBox
- ListView
- RichTextBox
- TreeView
- HscrollBar
- DateTimePicker
- VscrollBar

- MonthCalendar
- ProgressBar
- Splitter
- TabControl
- TrackBar
- MainMenu
- StatusBar

- ContextMenu
- ToolBar
- ComboBox
- TreeView
- DataGrid
- ListView
- ListBox

This group also includes the button-type controls (Button, RadioButton, GroupBox, and CheckBox), which, in addition to being defined in the Comctl32.dll file, must have their FlatStyle property set to the System value.

12.11.1. The EnableVisualStyle Method

There are several ways to make the controls enumerated above use Windows XP visual styles. The easiest way is to use the built-in EnableVisualStyles method of the Application class. This method must be called before a control is created (as a rule, in the Main procedure), while controls must have their FlatStyle property set to the System value. An example is demonstrated in the EnableStyles project (Listing 12.19). It is not necessary to have the special manifest file (which will be described in Section 12.11.2).

Listing 12.19. Using the EnableVisualStyles Method

```
'-------------------------------------
' EnableStyles  © 2004 Alexander Klimov
'-------------------------------------
    Public Shared Sub Main()
        System.Windows.Forms.Application.EnableVisualStyles()
        ' If there are problems, then add the following line:
        Application.DoEvents()
        System.Windows.Forms.Application.Run(New Form1)
    End Sub
```

12.11.2. Using the Manifest File

But there is more than one way to skin this cat. If you want to use Windows XP visual styles in your applications, you should add what is called the *manifest* to them. The manifest file tells the system that the application must use Comctl32.dll version 6 wherever possible. Windows XP itself uses both versions 5.0 and 6.0. By default, the system uses the standard version, 5.0. Consequently, in order to use the new styles, you have somehow to tell the system that this is your wish. How can you do this? This is where the manifest comes in. In essence, the manifest is a special XML file that is embedded into an application as a resource, or is placed in the same folder with the applications as a separate file.

Let's consider this concept in practice. Create a new, Manifest, project. Place one each of the following controls on the form: Button; RadioButton; ProgressBar; CheckBox; and Label. Set the FlatStyle property of all these controls to System. Add the following code to the button-click event-handler subroutine:

```
    Private Sub Button1_Click(ByVal sender As System.Object, ByVal e As _
System.EventArgs) Handles Button1.Click
        ProgressBar1.Value = 50
    End Sub
```

Save your work. We can now proceed with writing the manifest. In the Solution Explorer window, right-click on the project name, and select the **Add/Add New Item** command sequence. In the left panel (**Categories:**) of the dialog window that appears, select the **Local Project** item. In the right panel (**Templates:**), select the **Text File** item. In the **Name:** field, write the name of the file as follows: Project Name.exe.manifest. Thus, if your application name is WindowsApplication1, the XML file should be named WindowsApplication1.exe.manifest. In our example, the file name is Manifest.exe.manifest. Click the **Open** button to create the XML file, and close the window. A blank test file will be added to the text editor tab. Add to this file the code provided in Listing 12.20.

Listing 12.20. The Contents of the Manifest File

```
<?xml version="1.0" encoding="UTF-8" standalone="yes"?>
<assembly xmlns="urn:schemas-microsoft-com:asm.v1" manifestVersion="1.0">
<assemblyIdentity
    version="1.0.0.0"
    processorArchitecture="X86"
    name="Microsoft.Winweb.<Executable Name>"
    type="win32"
/>
<description>.NET control deployment tool</description>
<dependency>
    <dependentAssembly>
```

```
    <assemblyIdentity
      type="win32"
      name="Microsoft.Windows.Common-Controls"
      version="6.0.0.0"
      processorArchitecture="X86"
      publicKeyToken="6595b64144ccf1df"
      language="*"
    />
  </dependentAssembly>
</dependency>
</assembly>
```

Replace the `<Executable Name>` text with the name of your application. The resulting line should look like the following:

```
name="Microsoft.Winweb.Manifest"
```

In the **Build** menu, select the **Build/Manifest** command sequence, and then save all project files. A manifest file will be placed in the project folder. Now, it has to be linked to the application. Move the Manifest.exe.manifest file to the same folder as the executable file. Depending on your settings, this may be either the Debug or Release subfolder in the obj folder. When running the executable file, you will see that all of the controls you had placed on it are of the Windows XP visual style.

12.11.3. Manifest as a Resource

The manifest file can be embedded into the executable file as a resource. The example project is called `Resource`. Create a new project, repeating all the steps from the previous example, including the creation of a manifest file. Next, in the **File** menu select the **Open** item, and click on the **File** item. Navigate to the folder containing your project. Open the obj folder there, then the Debug or Release folder (depending on the configuration of your system). Find the project's executable file (e.g., WindowsApplication1.exe) and double-click on it. The file will open in the Visual Studio integrated development environment. Right-click on the executable file in the designer, and select the **Add Resource** command. The **Add Resource** dialog window will open. Click on the **Import** button. Find the manifest file you created earlier. Make sure that the **All Files (*.*)** option is selected in the dialog window. Otherwise, the file will not show on the list. Double-click on the manifest file. This will open the **Custom Resource Type** dialog window. Type `RT_MANIFEST` in the **Resource Type** field, and click the **OK** button. In the property editor, set the value of the `ID` property to 1. In the **File** menu, execute the **Save All** command. When running the program, you will see that all controls support the visual styles, even though the manifest file is embedded in the program's resources.

12.11.4. Checking for Windows XP
Visual Styles Support

Just because your program actively uses Windows XP visual styles does not mean that it will be able to run on any computer, as particular user systems may simply not support them. In such a case, you may want to make the program's logic and interface different. Presently, a check on the Windows XP visual styles support can be performed using the IsThemeActive Window API function. The function is very easy to use and requires no parameters. Moreover, the user can disable the Windows XP visual styles at any moment in the following way: Open **Control Panel** and run the **Display** applet. In the **Windows and buttons** dropdown list on the **Appearance** tab, a choice of two visual styles is given: **Windows XP style** and **Windows Classic style**. The styles can be switched at any time. Consequently, Windows messaging can be used to check on the style-change event. The example is implemented in the StyleXP project (Listing 12.21). You will have to place one button and one label on the form.

Listing 12.21. Checking for Windows XP Visual Styles Support

```
'-------------------------------------
' StyleXP © 2004 Alexander Klimov
'-------------------------------------

    Declare Function IsThemeActive Lib "uxtheme.dll" () As Boolean
    Private Const WM_THEMECHANGED As Int32 = &H31A


    Private Sub Button1_Click(ByVal sender As System.Object, ByVal e As _
System.EventArgs) Handles Button1.Click
        Label1.Text = IsThemeActive.ToString
    End Sub


    Protected Overrides Sub WndProc(ByRef m As System.Windows.Forms.Message)
        Select Case m.Msg
            Case WM_THEMECHANGED
                Label1.Text = "The style has changed"
        End Select
        MyBase.WndProc(m)
    End Sub
```

Run the program, and try to change the visual style as explained earlier. As soon as Windows receives the message that the theme has been changed, a corresponding message will be displayed in the program's label field. Clicking the button, you will be able to determine whether the Windows XP visual style is currently supported.

NOTE

In the future .NET Framework 2.0 version and Visual Basic .NET 2005, a new property is planned for checking whether the theme is active: the `IsEnabledByUser` property of the `System.Windows.Forms.VisualStyles.VisualStyleInformation` class.

12.12. Suggestions and Recommendations

❏ To reinforce the materials in Section 12.1, try to create a custom-shaped control other than a button — a label, for example.

❏ Apply the technique used in Section 12.2 to other controls.

❏ Note that the text box allows digits to be entered. But, if you need to enter a fractional number, entering the division character may give you problems. You may have to rewrite the example completely to solve this problem.

PART V: ADVANCED EXAMPLES

Chapter 13: Pranks and Practical Jokes

This chapter presents some programs of a rather prankish nature. Despite the fact that the examples aren't particularly serious, studying them will help you to understand more deeply the structure of the Windows operating system, the principles, by which objects interact, and the processes taking place during mouse and keyboard operations. The only thing that I ask is that you do not to abuse the knowledge you acquire or use it to harm others. Jokes should be light-hearted and cheerful and brighten people's mood. You shouldn't write mean and nasty programs that can seriously frighten inexperienced users.

13.1. Hiding and Showing the Mouse Pointer

Our first example of a prank program hides the mouse pointer for a while. You have to be near the victim in order to witness the panic this trick will sow. The victim generally starts moving the mouse frantically all over the mouse pad, thinking the pointer has moved beyond the screen limits and trying to bring it back. The effect can be enhanced by having the form gradually get darker, before finally displaying a warning message executed in the Windows style: **The program has executed an illegal operation. The mouse pad driver urgently needs to be updated!** This example is very easy to implement. The Cursor class has the Hide method, which is responsible for hiding the mouse pointer. Because this method functions only within the form limits, the form needs to be maximized. The example is implemented in the Mouse project (Listing 13.1).

Listing 13.1. Hiding and Showing the Mouse Pointer

```
'-------------------------------------
' Mouse  © 2004 Alexander Klimov
'-------------------------------------
    Private Sub Form1_Load(ByVal sender As System.Object, ByVal e As System.EventArgs) _
Handles MyBase.Load
        Cursor.Hide()
    End Sub

    Private Sub Button1_Click(ByVal sender As System.Object, ByVal e As _
System.EventArgs) Handles Button1.Click
        Cursor.Show()
    End Sub
```

The `Hide` method must be used with care, as it has a cumulative property. If you call the `Hide` method twice, you will also have to call the `Show` method two times to restore the mouse pointer.

13.2. Swapping the Mouse Buttons

Any mouse has at least two buttons. If you are right-handed, your working button is left. The right button is used only to call the context menu. But southpaws have their point of view on the buttons and their main button is on the right. Mouse buttons are configured from the **Control Panel** in the **Mouse** applet. But you can also change these settings programmatically. How this is done is shown in the `Mouse` project (Listing 13.2).

Listing 13.2. Swapping the Mouse Buttons

```
Declare Function SwapMouseButton Lib "user32.dll" _
    Alias "SwapMouseButton" (ByVal bSwap As Integer) As Integer

    Private Sub butSwap_Click(ByVal sender As System.Object, ByVal e _
As System.EventArgs) Handles butSwap.Click
        ' Swapping the mouse button fucntions
        SwapMouseButton(1)
    End Sub
```

The effect obtained is quite unusual. The force of habit is so strong that, even once aware that the button functions are swapped, you constantly click the wrong one. To restore the standard mouse button functions, the same function is called with a different parameter:

```
SwapMouseButton(0)
```

13.3. A Restless Mouse Pointer

The mouse pointer can not only be hidden, but also moved around the screen, using the `Cursor.Position` property. This example is implemented in the `MadMouse` project (Listing 13.3). Place a button and a timer on the project form. The code in the event handler of the timer's click event makes the mouse pointer move all over the screen, using random numbers.

Listing 13.3. Moving the Mouse Pointer over Random Coordinates

---

```
'----------------------------------------

' MadMouse  © 2004 Alexander Klimov

'----------------------------------------

    Private Sub Timer1_Tick(ByVal sender As System.Object, ByVal e As System.EventArgs) _
Handles Timer1.Tick
        ' Generating a random number from 1 to 799
        Dim m_Value As Integer
        m_Value = CInt(Int((799 * Rnd()) + 1))

        ' Generating a random number from 1 to 599
        Dim m_Value2 As Integer
        m_Value2 = CInt(Int((599 * Rnd()) + 1))

        Randomize()
        Cursor.Position = New Point(m_Value, m_Value2)
    End Sub


    Private Sub Button1_Click(ByVal sender As System.Object, ByVal e As _
System.EventArgs) Handles Button1.Click
        ' Stopping the timer
        Timer1.Stop()
    End Sub
```

In this example, every half a second the mouse pointer moves to a random position within a 800 × 600-pixel rectangle. Setting the timer interval to a value that is too small will make it difficult to close the program using the mouse. To handle this contingency, I placed a button on the form. Because this is the only control on the form, it receives the focus when the form loads. This makes it possible to stop the timer by pressing the space or <Enter> key.

13.4. A Mousetrap

Poor mouse — all the abuse it has taken. But it had better get used to it, for there is more coming its way. If you have mice in your place, but your cat refuses to catch them, you have to use a mousetrap. To create a mousetrap for the computer mouse, you will need just one button. The code for the `MouseTrap` project is provided in Listing 13.4.

Listing 13.4. Creating a Virtual Mousetrap

```
'-------------------------------------
' MouseTrap  © 2004 Alexander Klimov
'-------------------------------------

    Private Sub Button1_Click(ByVal sender As System.Object, ByVal e As _
System.EventArgs) Handles Button1.Click
        ' To release the mouse,
        ' use the Ctrl+Alt+Del combination.
        Cursor.Clip = RectangleToScreen(_
                    New Rectangle(Button1.Location, Button1.Size))
    End Sub
```

Run the program, and ask the user to click the button. He or she shouldn't have listened to you: The mouse has been caught in the trap! The mouse pointer can no longer leave the confines of the button. Moreover, the limiting rectangle continues to function, even if another program becomes active. The only way to release the mouse from the trap is to pres the three-key combinations: <Ctrl>+<Alt>+<Del>. I wonder if the user will think of this.

13.5. A Runaway Button

Another cool-looking joke is the escaping button. It works as follows. There is a button on the form with some challenging words written on it, "Catch me if you can," for example. When the user tries to place the mouse pointer over the button, it suddenly jumps to another place on the screen. I personally have not managed to click on it, but perhaps you will have more luck. The effect is implemented in the `RunawayButton` (Listing 13.5) project. All you have to do is place one button on the project form labeled **Click Me**. The code for the button's `MouseMove` event handler creates the effect.

Listing 13.5. The Escaping Button Effect

```
'-------------------------------------
' RunawayButton  © 2004 Alexander Klimov
'-------------------------------------
    Private Sub Button1_MouseMove(ByVal sender As Object, ByVal e As _
System.Windows.Forms.MouseEventArgs) Handles Button1.MouseMove
        Button1.Left = Rnd() * (ClientSize.Width - Button1.Width)
        Button1.Top = Rnd() * (ClientSize.Height - Button1.Height)
    End Sub
```

Run the program and try to catch the button. The example, however, has one bug. The problem is that buttons can be clicked not only with the mouse pointer but also using the keyboard. Run the example again and press the space bar. Holding the space bar down, try to get the mouse pointer close to the button on the form. This will make the button jump around the form chaotically. To eliminate this effect, place the following code at the beginning of the code:

```
        If (e.X < 0) Or (e.Y < 0) Or _
           (e.X > Button1.Width) Or _
           (e.Y > Button1.Height) Then _
        Exit Sub
```

The essence of the example is very simple. As soon as the mouse pointer approaches the button, a MouseMove event is generated, and the program immediately moves the button to another random location using the Rnd function. Thus, the user is never able to catch up with it. Note that the Rnd function is used in this example, which has been inherited from VB 6.0. VB .NET has the Random class that is common to the .NET Framework class, which is best to use when writing a program in, for instance, C#.

13.6. You've Got No Choice!

In the previous example, you could not click on the button because it ran away from the mouse pointer. But there is another way to prevent the user from clicking on a button. This method is based on the fact that the mouse pointer can be moved programmatically to any necessary screen location. Suppose there are two buttons on the screen; one is labeled **Yes,** and the other **No.** As soon as the user moves the mouse pointer to the **No** button, the pointer immediately moves to the middle of the **Yes** button, meaning that the user has no other choice but to click on a button that may be unwanted. The effect is created in the TwoButtons project as follows. Place a label on the form. Type some question into its Text property. For my example, I used the question: **Do you want to visit the www.microsoft.com site again?** Place two buttons under the label. Set the Text property of one of them to **Yes**, and that of the other one to **No**. The code for the event handler of the second button's MouseMove event is given in Listing 13.6.

Listing 13.6. Forced Cursor Move

```
'--------------------------------------
' TwoButtons   © 2004 Alexander Klimov
'--------------------------------------
    Private Sub Button2_MouseMove(ByVal sender As Object, ByVal e As   _
System.Windows.Forms.MouseEventArgs) Handles Button2.MouseMove
        Dim startPoint As Point = Button1.PointToScreen(New Point(0, 0))
        startPoint.X += (Button1.Width / 2)
        startPoint.Y += (Button1.Height / 2)
        Cursor.Position = startPoint
    End Sub
```

The processing of the MouseMove event starts as soon as the mouse pointer approaches the button's borders. In the present case, the location of the first button is calculated, and the mouse pointer is moved to this location. Note that the button's coordinates are calculated using the PointToScreen method, which converts the location of the specified client point into screen coordinates. This trick has to be resorted to frequently, because the Position property of the Cursor class works only with screen coordinates. This example can actually be used for more than just playing jokes. It is necessary sometimes for a program to be able to place the mouse pointer in a certain place. I think it will be useful to implement the example as a universal procedure. Place another control on the project form, a LinkLabel, for example. In the code editor, write the code for the universal procedure (Listing 13.7).

Listing 13.7. Universal Mouse Pointer Moving Procedure

```
Public Sub JumpToControl(ByVal ctrl As Control)
    ' Moving the mouse pointer to the middle of the lower part of the control
        Dim objPoint As Point = ctrl.PointToScreen(New Point(0, 0))
        objPoint.X += (ctrl.Width / 2)
        objPoint.Y += ((ctrl.Height / 4) * 3)
        Cursor.Position = objPoint
End Sub

Private Sub Button1_Click(ByVal sender As System.Object, ByVal e As System.EventArgs)   _
Handles Button1.Click
        JumpToControl(LinkLabel1)
End Sub
```

As you can see, the procedure code is practically identical to the code for the **Yes/No** button example. All you need to do to customize the procedure is specify the control, to which the mouse pointer has to move. Note that the procedure moves the mouse pointer not to the middle of the control, but to a point one-third of the control's height.

13.7. The Taskbar

Jokes involving common Windows interface elements are especially interesting. All of us are used to the fact that the **Start** button is located in the lower left corner of the desktop (with the taskbar in its default position at the bottom of the screen). In addition to the **Start** button, the taskbar also contains buttons showing running programs, the system tray, and the system clock. In essence, all of these items are regular windows. This means that having access to one of these windows, its regular behavior can be modified. This cannot, however, be achieved using only the built-in .Net Framework classes, so you have to resort to Windows API functions. For the purposes of our examples, we will need two of these functions: FindWindowEx and ShowWindow. In Visual Basic .NET, these functions are declared as follows:

```
Private Declare Auto Function FindWindowEx Lib "user32.dll" ( _
        ByVal hwnd As IntPtr, _
        ByVal hWndChild As IntPtr, _
        ByVal lpszClassName As String, _
        ByVal lpszWindow As String _
    ) As IntPtr


Private Declare Auto Function ShowWindow Lib "user32.dll" ( _
        ByVal hwnd As IntPtr, _
        ByVal nCmdShow As Int32 _
    ) As Int32
```

We will also need the following two constants, which are responsible for displaying and hiding the window:

```
Private Const SW_HIDE As Int32 = 0
Private Const SW_SHOW As Int32 = 5
```

Now, we can use the two Windows API functions mentioned earlier to find the handle of the window in question by the name of its class. The following is a short list of the class names for the items located on the taskbar:

❑   Shell_TrayWnd — The taskbar
❑   Button — The **Start** button
❑   TrayNotifyWnd — The system tray, with various program icons and the system clock
❑   TrayClockWClass — The clock
❑   SysTabControl32 — The buttons of running programs

13.7.1. Abusing the Start Button

So, we have established that the **Start** button is just a regular window with certain properties. Our task now is to gain access to this window and modify its behavior. Naturally, having access to the button, we can devise numerous pranks to play on unsuspecting users.

13.7.1.1. Hiding the Start Button

In this example, I will show you how to gain access to a button and to hide it from the user programmatically. The project is named StartButton (Listing 13.8). Place two buttons on the project form. One button will be responsible for hiding the **Start** button, and the other for bringing it back in view.

Listing 13.8. Hiding the Start Button

```
'-------------------------------------
'   StartButton  © 2004 Alexander Klimov
'-------------------------------------
    ' Windows API functions
    Private Declare Auto Function FindWindowEx Lib "user32.dll" ( _
            ByVal hwnd As IntPtr, _
            ByVal hWndChild As IntPtr, _
            ByVal lpszClassName As String, _
            ByVal lpszWindow As String _
        ) As IntPtr

    Private Declare Auto Function ShowWindow Lib "user32.dll" ( _
            ByVal hwnd As IntPtr, _
            ByVal nCmdShow As Int32 _
        ) As Int32

    Private Declare Function MoveWindow Lib "user32" Alias "MoveWindow" _
            (ByVal hwnd As IntPtr, ByVal x As Integer, _
            ByVal y As Integer, _
            ByVal nWidth As Integer, ByVal nHeight As Integer, _
            ByVal bRepaint As Integer) As Integer

    Private Declare Function GetWindowRect Lib "user32" _
            (ByVal hWnd As IntPtr, ByRef lpRect As RECT) As Integer

    Private Declare Function SendMessage Lib "user32" _
            Alias "SendMessageA" _
            (ByVal hwnd As IntPtr, _
```

```
        ByVal wMsg As Integer, ByVal wParam As Integer, _
        ByVal lParam As Integer) As Integer

    ' Structures
    Private Structure RECT
        Public Left As Integer
        Public Top As Integer
        Public Right As Integer
        Public Bottom As Integer
    End Structure

    ' Constants
    Private Const SW_HIDE As Int32 = 0
    Private Const SW_SHOW As Int32 = 5
    Private Const WM_SYSCOMMAND As Int32 = &H112
    Private Const SC_TASKLIST As Long = &HF130

' The Start button handle
    Private hWndStart As IntPtr
' The system tray handle
    Private tray As IntPtr

    Private Sub butHide_Click(ByVal sender As System.Object, ByVal e As _
System.EventArgs) Handles butHide.Click
        ' Looking for the Shell_TrayWnd class window
        Dim hW As IntPtr = FindWindowEx(IntPtr.Zero, _
            IntPtr.Zero, "Shell_TrayWnd", vbNullString)
        ' Getting the  Start button handle
        hWndStart = FindWindowEx(hW, IntPtr.Zero, "BUTTON", vbNullString)
        ' Hiding the button
        ShowWindow(hWndStart, SW_HIDE)
    End Sub
```

Let's examine the example code in more detail. First, the global variable hWndStart is declared to hold the handle of the **Start** button. When the button labeled **Hide Start Button** is clicked, the hW variable is assigned the value of the taskbar's handle, which is returned by the FindWindowEx function through the specified Shell_TrayWnd class.

The **Start** button belongs to the BUTTON class and is a child window of the taskbar window. Therefore, the following code line finds the button's handle by its class name:

```
hWndStart = FindWindowEx(hW, IntPtr.Zero, "BUTTON", vbNullString)
```

The ShowWindow function is used to perform various window operations: hiding, showing, restoring, minimizing, maximizing, etc. In the present case, we need to hide the button using the SW_HIDE constant. But we also need to have a means of restoring the **Start** button to the screen. Otherwise, it will remain invisible until Windows is rebooted. Therefore, we need another Button control, with the following click event handler:

```
      Private Sub butShow_Click(ByVal sender As Object,   _
ByVal e As System.EventArgs) Handles butShow.Click
            ' Show the Start button.
            ShowWindow(hWndStart, SW_SHOW)
      End Sub
```

Because we used the hwndStart global variable for the button's handle, we do not have to call the FindWindowEx function again to get the handle. We can immediately call the ShowWindow function with the SW_SHOW constant (as an alternative, the SW_RESTORE constant can be used). Naturally, having access to the **Start** button window, you can hide not only the button, but also perform other window operations on it.

13.7.1.2. Moving the *Start* Button

Having access to the window handle (the window of the **Start** button in the present case), we can move the window to another location on the screen. To do this, we will also need the MoveWindow and GetWindowRect Windows API functions again, as well as the RECT structure. The GetWindowRect function obtains the window dimensions and coordinates; the MoveWindow function moves the window to the specified location. You already know how to get the button's handle. All that remains is to obtain the button's dimensions and location, and then to move it to the new location. Add two new buttons — butMoveRight and butMoveLeft — to the project form. The first button will move the **Start** button 100 pixels to the right (Fig. 13.1); the other button will return the **Start** button to its usual location. The source code for moving the **Start** button is provided in Listing 13.9.

Listing 13.9. Moving the *Start* Button to the Right

```
    Private Sub butMoveRigth_Click(ByVal sender As System.Object, ByVal e As   _
System.EventArgs) Handles butMoveRigth.Click
      Dim r As RECT
      ' Getting the  dimensions of the Start button
      GetWindowRect(hWndStart, r)
      ' Moving the button to the right
      MoveWindow(hWndStart, r.Left + 100, 0, _
          r.Right - r.Left, r.Bottom - r.Top, True)
    End Sub
```

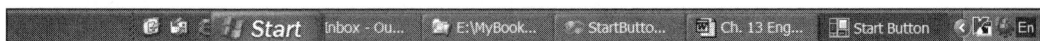

Fig. 13.1. Moving the *Start* button

In the code, the information about the position and dimensions of the **Start** button is obtained using the GetWindowRect function and is then stored in the RECT structure. Now we need only to put the information we have obtained to the right use. I do not recommend moving the button along the Y-axis or changing its height, as the results may not be particularly attractive. But try to make the button wider and the user will be shocked! To return the button to its regular place, restore the previous coordinates for the button (Listing 13.10).

Listing 13.10. Returning the *Start* Button to Its Regular Place

```
Private Sub butMoveLeft_Click(ByVal sender As System.Object, ByVal e As _
System.EventArgs) Handles butMoveLeft.Click
    Dim r As RECT
    GetWindowRect(hWndStart, r)
    MoveWindow(hWndStart, 0, 0, _
        r.Right - r.Left, r.Bottom - r.Top, True)
End Sub
```

These examples show how some interesting results can be achieved. I, for example, supply my friends with programs, in which the **Start** button periodically jumps up and then drops down, presses itself at the most inopportune moments (more about this later), changes its label to some specified text, etc. Try to write your own programs producing similar effects. And if you come up with some exquisite method to abuse the **Start** button, take a little of your time and send your prank to my email box: **rusproject@mail.ru**.

13.7.1.3. Pressing the *Start* Button Programmatically

Another method for giving the user a good scare is suddenly to press the **Start** button programmatically. This can be done using the Timer control. I will only provide a template for the example (Listing 13.11)

Listing 13.11. Pressing the *Start* Button Programmatically

```
Private Sub butPress_Click(ByVal sender As System.Object, ByVal e As  _
System.EventArgs) Handles butPress.Click
    ' Clicking the Start button
    SendMessage(Me.Handle, WM_SYSCOMMAND, SC_TASKLIST, 0)
End Sub
```

First, the SendMessage Windows API function and the WM_SYSCOMMAND message with the SC_TASKLIST constant have to be declared. Now this function can be called from anywhere in the code, opening the menu of the **Start** button.

13.7.2. The System Tray

I suggest that we expand the example to better grasp the material. Let's try to hide the system tray. The system tray is the part of taskbar where the system clock, the language indicator, and icons for some programs are located. The technology for doing this was presented in the previous example. Declare a global variable `tray` to hold the system tray handle. The rest of the code is practically identical to the code used to hide the **Start** button (Listing 13.12).

Listing 13.12. Hiding and Showing the System Tray

```
    Private Sub butHideTray_Click(ByVal sender As System.Object, ByVal e As  _
System.EventArgs) Handles butHideTray.Click
        Dim hW As IntPtr = FindWindowEx(IntPtr.Zero, _
            IntPtr.Zero, "Shell_TrayWnd", vbNullString)
        ' The system tray handle
        tray = FindWindowEx(hW, IntPtr.Zero, _
            "TrayNotifyWnd", vbNullString)
        ' Hiding the system tray
        ShowWindow(tray, SW_HIDE)
    End Sub


Private Sub butShowTray_Click(ByVal sender As System.Object, ByVal e As  _
System.EventArgs) Handles butShowTray.Click
        ShowWindow(tray, SW_SHOW)
End Sub
```

13.7.2.1. The System Clock

The example of hiding the system tray just considered may have induced you to try to hide the system clock on your own, especially since I already gave you the name of its class: `TrayClockWClass`. But haste makes waste, and you will likely have failed. This is because there is a bit of a trick to this. The thing is that the system clock is not, as you may have thought, a child window of the taskbar window. Its parent window is the system tray. Consequently, we will have to call the `FindWindowEx` function twice to obtain the system clock window's handle.

Listing 13.13. Hiding and Showing the System Clock

```
    Private Sub butClockHide_Click(ByVal sender As System.Object, ByVal e As  _
System.EventArgs) Handles butClockHide.Click
    ' The taskbar handle
        Dim hW As IntPtr = FindWindowEx(IntPtr.Zero, IntPtr.Zero, _
```

```
                                    "Shell_TrayWnd", vbNullString)
    ' The system tray handle
        tray = FindWindowEx(hW, IntPtr.Zero, "TrayNotifyWnd", _
                            vbNullString)
    ' The system clock handle
        Dim trayclock = FindWindowEx(tray, IntPtr.Zero, _
                        "TrayClockWClass", vbNullString)
    ' Hiding the system clock
        ShowWindow(trayclock, SW_HIDE)
    End Sub


    Private Sub butClockShow_Click(ByVal sender As System.Object, ByVal e As _
System.EventArgs) Handles butClockShow.Click
        Dim hW As IntPtr = FindWindowEx(IntPtr.Zero, _
                IntPtr.Zero, "Shell_TrayWnd", vbNullString)
        tray = FindWindowEx(hW, IntPtr.Zero, _
                "TrayNotifyWnd", vbNullString)
        Dim trayclock = FindWindowEx(tray, IntPtr.Zero, _
                "TrayClockWClass", vbNullString)
        ShowWindow(trayclock, SW_SHOW)
    End Sub
```

13.7.2.3. Replacing the System Clock with a Scrolling Line

Hiding the system clock is too simple as a task. It is much more challenging to replace this clock with your own creation. I will show you how to replace the system clock with a scrolling line (project TrayClockReplace). First, the FormBorderStyle property of the form has to be set to None. Now place a Label and a Timer controls on the form. Set the Enabled property of the timer to True and the Interval property to 10 milliseconds. All of the other control properties will be set at runtime (Listing 13.14).

Listing 13.14. Replacing the System Clock with a Scrolling Line

```
'-------------------------------------
' TrayClockReplace © 2004 Alexander Klimov
'-------------------------------------
    Structure RECT
        Public Left As Integer
        Public Top As Integer
        Public Right As Integer
        Public Bottom As Integer
    End Structure

    Declare Auto Function FindWindowEx Lib "user32.dll" ( _
```

```
            ByVal hwnd As IntPtr, _
            ByVal hWndChild As IntPtr, _
            ByVal lpszClassName As String, _
            ByVal lpszWindow As String _
        ) As IntPtr

    Declare Function GetWindowRect Lib "user32" _
            (ByVal hWnd As IntPtr, ByRef lpRect As RECT) _
            As Integer

    Declare Function SetParent Lib "user32" _
            (ByVal hWndChild As IntPtr, _
            ByVal hWndNewParent As IntPtr) As Integer

  Private Const sText As String = "Message    "

    Private Sub Form1_Load(ByVal sender As System.Object, ByVal e As System.EventArgs) _
Handles MyBase.Load

        Dim r As RECT

  ' The taskbar handle
        Dim hShell As IntPtr = FindWindowEx(IntPtr.Zero, IntPtr.Zero, _
                                    "Shell_TrayWnd", vbNullString)

  ' The system tray handle
        Dim tray As IntPtr = FindWindowEx(hShell, IntPtr.Zero, _
                                    "TrayNotifyWnd", vbNullString)

        ' The system clock handle
        Dim trayclock = FindWindowEx(tray, IntPtr.Zero, "TrayClockWClass", vbNullString)

        ' Clock's dimensions
        GetWindowRect(trayclock, r)

  ' Setting the form's dimensions
        With Me
            .Top = 1
            .Left = 1
            .Height = r.Bottom - r.Top - 1
            .Width = r.Right - r.Left - 1
        End With

  ' Placing the form into the clock area
```

```
        SetParent(Me.Handle, trayclock)
    End Sub


    Private Sub Timer1_Tick(ByVal sender As System.Object, ByVal e As System.EventArgs) _
Handles Timer1.Tick
        Label1.Text = sText
        If Label1.Left + Label1.Width < 0 Then Label1.Left = Me.Width
        Label1.Left = Label1.Left - 1
    End Sub


    Private Sub Label1_Click(ByVal sender As System.Object, ByVal e As _
System.EventArgs) Handles Label1.Click
        Close()
    End Sub


    Private Sub Form1_Resize(ByVal sender As Object, ByVal e As System.EventArgs) _
Handles MyBase.Resize
        Label1.Top = (Me.Height - Label1.Height) / 2
    End Sub


    Private Sub Form1_DoubleClick(ByVal sender As Object, ByVal e As System.EventArgs) _
Handles MyBase.DoubleClick
        Close()
    End Sub
```

Now, run the program. You should see, instead of the system clock, a scrolling line in the bottom right corner of the screen.

13.8. Opening and Closing the CD-ROM Tray

One of the most popular practical jokes programmers like to play is to periodically open and close the CD-ROM tray. A virus performing this operation is probably the only type of virus that damages computer hardware, as opposed to software, which is the case with other viruses. Imagine that in the middle of the night a virus triggers the opening and closing of the CD-ROM tray at one-second intervals. (There are users who leave their computers on even at night.) The service life of any mechanical device is limited, so you may find your CD-ROM dead by the morning. My example, of course, is not intended to damage any CD-ROM drives. But being familiar with this technique may come in handy when, for example, writing your own player. This task requires only one Windows API function — mciSendString — to implement. The project is named OpenCD and the source code for it is shown in Listing 13.15.

Listing 13.15. Opening the CD-ROM Tray

```
'-------------------------------------
' OpenCD © 2004 Alexander Klimov
'-------------------------------------
    Private Declare Function mciSendString Lib "winmm.dll _
                            Alias "mciSendStringA" _
                            (ByVal lpstrCommand As String, _
                            ByVal lpstrReturnString As String, _
                            ByVal uReturnLength As Long, _
                            ByVal hwndCallback As Long) As Long

    Private Sub butOpenCD_Click(ByVal sender As System.Object, ByVal e As _
System.EventArgs) Handles butOpenCD.Click
        ' Opening the CD-ROM tray
        mciSendString("set CDAudio door open", 0, 127, 0)
    End Sub

    Private Sub butCloseCD_Click(ByVal sender As System.Object, ByVal e As _
System.EventArgs) Handles butCloseCD.Click
    ' Closing the CD-ROM tray
        mciSendString("set CDAudio door closed", 0, 127, 0)
    End Sub
```

As you can see, two lines of code is all it takes to write quite and effective program.

13.9. Blocking the Keyboard and Mouse

But let's return to our mice. Instead of hiding the mouse pointer, you can temporarily block it. The keyboard can also be blocked for good measure. Imagine the scare the user will get when the mouse pointer freezes in the middle of some important work. To carry out this example, we will need only one Windows API function: BlockInput. But, as we are not sadists, let's block the mouse and the keyboard for three seconds only. The project is called BlockAll (Listing 13.16). Place a button on the form, and clicking it will produce the desired effect.

Listing 13.16. Blocking the Keyboard and Mouse

```
'-------------------------------------
' BlockAll  © 2004 Alexander Klimov
'-------------------------------------
    Declare Function BlockInput Lib "User32" _
```

```
      (ByVal fBlockIt As Boolean) As Boolean

   Private Sub butBlock_Click(ByVal sender As System.Object, ByVal e As _
System.EventArgs) Handles butBlock.Click
   ' Start blocking the keyboard and mouse
        BlockInput(True)
   ' Blocking for 3 seconds
        Me.Text = "Blocked for three seconds"
        System.Threading.Thread.Sleep(3000)
   ' Removing the block
        BlockInput(False)
   Me.Text = "Blocking removed"
   End Sub
```

Now, when this button is clicked, all of the mouse-button clicking and keyboard-key pressing will be a simple case of flogging a dead horse. The only way to unblock the two is to press the three-key combination <Ctrl>+<Alt>+<Del>. It is rare for a user to have his or her wits enough about them to think of doing this.

13.10. A Typewriter

Many science fiction movies show the horrors that occur when thinking machines rebel against human control. Imagine something like that happening not in a movie, but to you, with the keyboard that has served you faithfully for years suddenly becoming independent and starting to type all on its own! Would you like to know how to make this happen? Then let's get down to business. Create a new project, TypingComputer, and place one button and one timer on the form. Set the Text property of the button to Start and the Interval property of the timer to 400. Leave the default values for the rest of the properties. The code in the button's click-event handler only starts the timer and hides the form. The main processing takes place in the handler of the timer's Tick event (Listing 13.17).

Listing 13.17. A Typewriter

```
'------------------------------------
' TypingComputer © 2004 Alexander Klimov
'------------------------------------
   Private Sub Button1_Click(ByVal sender As System.Object, ByVal e As _
System.EventArgs) Handles Button1.Click
        Me.Hide()
        Timer1.Enabled = True
   End Sub

   Private Sub Timer1_Tick(ByVal sender As System.Object, ByVal e As _
System.EventArgs) Handles Timer1.Tick
```

```
        Dim a As Integer
        Randomize()
        a = Rnd() * 100 + 1
        'If a < 45 Then SendKeys.SendWait(Chr(Rnd() * 26))
        If a > 45 And a < 70 Then SendKeys.SendWait("Who said meow? {Left 16} Bow-bow!")
        If a > 70 And a < 80 Then SendKeys.SendWait("{enter 2} Meow-meow{enter}")
        If a = 72 Then Timer1.Enabled = False
        'If a > 80 And a < 93 Then SendKeys.SendWait("{BS}")
        'If a > 93 And a < 99 Then SendKeys.SendWait("^{BS}")
        'If a > 99 Then SendKeys.SendWait("+{HOME}{BS}")
End Sub
```

I decided to go easy on your mental health and chose the sparing mode of operation for the program. First launch Notepad (notepad.exe), and then the program. When you click on the **Start** button, the program's window will minimize and the focus will move to Notepad. Because the timer is still running and sending commands to the keyboard, various words will be typed in Notepad. But the SendKeys class is very rich in capabilities. It can emulate pressing not only the character keys, but also keys like <Del>, <BackSpace>, <Alt>, <Ctrl>, etc. I commented out a number of lines of this type in the code. To enhance the effect, launch a few applications that can accept keyboard input. Remove all of the comments from the code, and run the program. You will witness outright pandemonium. Within a few seconds of my starting the program, it managed to delete the contents of several files, rename them, and even delete some of them.

Exercise great care when running this program! Close all important documents and programs. Provide the program with some means to terminate forcibly should this become necessary. Use the program at your own risk!

IMPORTANT

13.11. A Mind Reader

I first saw this trick on the site **www.arbuz.uz**. I advise all math aficionados with a sense of humor to visit this site, where they will find many informative articles written in very easy-to-understand language. Many articles contain source code listings in Visual Basic, Pascal, and Java. But let's get back to our mind reader. The publication of this little prank made the site very popular. Visitors to this page numbered in the thousands per day, with all of them trying to figure out how the program could manage to read human thoughts. But there is no great mystery there. I simply developed a special algorithm, which can also be demonstrated on paper. Think of any two-digit number — 54, for example. Subtract the sum of the digits making up the number from the number. In our example, this will be $54 - (5 + 4) = 45$. Find the resulting number and the corresponding symbol in the table (Fig. 13.2).

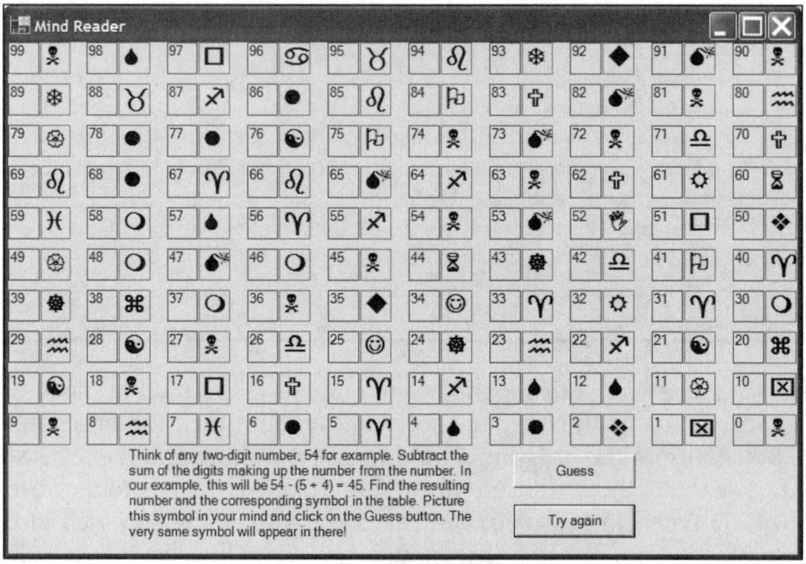

Fig. 13.2. Mind reader

Fig. 13.3. The symbol guessed by the program

Imagine this symbol in your mind. Now, look at Fig. 13.3 and you will see the very same symbol there!

Here is how this is implemented in Visual Basic .NET (the `Mind` project). Place two labels and two buttons on the project form. The first label will display the information needed to use the program. The second label will hold the selected image (Listing 13.18). It must be made invisible by setting the `Visible` property to `False`.

Listing 13.18. The Mind-Reading Program

```
'--------------------------------------
' Mind  © 2004 Alexander Klimov
'--------------------------------------
    ' A string array
    Dim alphaArray() As String = {"a", "b", "d", "f", "h", "{", "i", "l", "v", "x",
"z", "I", "J", "M", "N", "o", "O", "R", "S", "T", "U", "m", "6", "^", "u", "_", "[", "]"}
    ' A random number
    Dim MyValue As Integer

    Private Sub Button1_Click(ByVal sender As System.Object, ByVal e As  _
System.EventArgs) Handles Button1.Click
```

```
    Label1.Visible = True

    Dim g As Graphics = CreateGraphics()
    g.Clear(Me.BackColor)
End Sub


Private Sub Form1_Paint(ByVal sender As Object, ByVal e As _
System.Windows.Forms.PaintEventArgs) Handles MyBase.Paint
    Button2.PerformClick()
End Sub


Private Sub Button2_Click(ByVal sender As System.Object, ByVal e As _
System.EventArgs) Handles Button2.Click
    Dim i, y As Integer
    Dim g As Graphics = CreateGraphics()
    g.Clear(BackColor)
    Label1.Visible = False
    Dim MyValue As Integer
    MyValue = CInt(Int(20 * Rnd()))

    For i = 0 To 9
        For y = 0 To 9
            Dim to9 As Integer
            to9 = 99 - ((i) + (y * 10))

            g.DrawRectangle(Pens.Red, i * 80, y * 40, 30, 30)

            g.DrawString(Convert.ToString(to9) _
                Me.Font, New SolidBrush(Color.Black), i * 80, y * 40)

            g.DrawRectangle(Pens.Gray, i * 80 + 32, y * 40, 30, 30)

            Dim randnum As Random
            randnum = New Random

            Dim f As Font = New Font("wingdings", 24, _
                        FontStyle.Bold, GraphicsUnit.Pixel)

            If to9 Mod 9 = 0 Then
                g.DrawString(alphaArray(MyValue), f, _
                    New SolidBrush(Color.Black), i * 80 + 32, y * 40)
                Label1.Text = alphaArray(MyValue)
            ElseIf to9 Mod 9 = 1 Then
                g.DrawString(alphaArray(randnum.Next(28)), f, _
```

```
                New SolidBrush(Color.Black), i * 80 + 32, y * 40)
        Else
            g.DrawString(alphaArray(Int((28 * Rnd()))), f _
                New SolidBrush(Color.Black), i * 80 + 32, y * 40)
        End If

    Next
  Next
  g.Dispose()

End Sub
```

As you have probably already guessed, the program does not even try to guess your thoughts. Those who like solving various mathematical puzzles will have no problems figuring out how the program guesses the selected symbol. I will not divulge the secret in this book, leaving you to figure it out. If you examine the program code, you should have no problems doing this. The program starts by declaring an array `alphaArray` and a variable `MyValue`. In order to save resources, the program uses not images, but the Wingdings font symbols. There are many interesting images in this font. We will use some of these symbols for guessing by placing them into the `alphaArray` array. The `MyValue` variable will hold one of these randomly-selected symbols. When the form is loaded, the code for `Button2` is executed (the `PerformClick` method). The program's main code is located in the click event handler of `Button2`. It draws 99 pairs of rectangles, using nested loops. The first rectangle of each pair holds its sequence number from 0 to 99. The other rectangle holds a randomly selected Wingding symbol. Because this is where the secret of the program lies, I will not explain anything else.

13.12. Artificial Intelligence

I recently had a very interesting conversation with my computer. I was asking it different questions on important subjects and it was answering them. Here is a short excerpt from our dialog:

— Who are you?
— I'm your daddy.
— Are you sure?
— Probably.
— What's your name?
— Bad question.
— When will I be rich?
— You'll be too old when this happens to enjoy it.
— And who will be the president then?

— Don't you think it will be Elvis Presley?
— You aren't lying, are you?
— Everyone knows that I am.
— Why are you lying?
— I'm just a machine…

How about your computer? Can it hold its own in a conversation like this? If it can't, I will help you to teach it to talk, with the AI project. Place a button, a label, a text box, and a list box on the form. The source code for the program is provided in Listing 13.19.

Listing 13.19. Creating Artificial Intelligence

```
'---------------------------------------
' AI  © 2004 Alexander Klimov
'---------------------------------------
    Function OldQuestion(ByRef UseText As String) As Boolean
        Dim i As Integer
        For i = 0 To lstUsed.Items.Count - 1
            If UCase(lstUsed.Items(i)) = UCase(UseText) Then
                OldQuestion = True
                Exit Function
            Else
                OldQuestion = False
            End If
        Next
    End Function


    Function OkQuestion(ByRef TheText As String) As String
        Dim TempText As String
        Dim Extra As String
        Dim Text(9) As String
        Dim Number As Short

        If InStr(1, TheText, "elvis", CompareMethod.Text) Then GoTo Theking

        TempText = Replace(TheText, " ", "")
        If TheText = TempText Then
            Extra = ""
        Else
            Extra = " "
        End If
Start:
        If InStr(1, TheText, "What" & Extra, CompareMethod.Text) Then GoTo WhichWhatHow
        If InStr(1, TheText, "How" & Extra, CompareMethod.Text) Then GoTo WhichWhatHow
```

```
        If InStr(1, TheText, "Where" & Extra, CompareMethod.Text) Then GoTo Where
        If InStr(1, TheText, "Why" & Extra, CompareMethod.Text) Then GoTo Why
        If InStr(1, TheText, "Which" & Extra, CompareMethod.Text) Then GoTo WhichWhatHow
        If InStr(1, TheText, "Who" & Extra, CompareMethod.Text) Then GoTo Who
        If InStr(1, TheText, "When" & Extra, CompareMethod.Text) Then GoTo When_Renamed

        Text(0) = "I think so."
        Text(1) = "And what do you think?"
        Text(2) = "Yes."
        Text(3) = "No."
        Text(4) = "No, as everyone knows"
        Text(5) = "Probably."
        Text(6) = "I'm not sure."
        Text(7) = "Yes, definitely."
        Text(8) = "No."
        Text(9) = "Yes, as everyone knows."
        Number = Int((Rnd() * 10) + 1) - 1
        Return Text(Number)
        Exit Function
WhichWhatHow:
        Text(0) = "How should I know?"
        Text(1) = "I'm tired. Let's talk about it tomorrow."
        Text(2) = "I wish I had your problems."
        Text(3) = "Well, how can I put it to you."
        Text(4) = "An interesting question. Someone has already asked it."
        Text(5) = "Bad question."
        Text(6) = "Would you like to know what I think about it all?"
        Text(7) = "I don't want to talk about it."
        Text(8) = "Sorry, I've forgotten."
        Text(9) = "I can't stand nosy people."
        Number = Int((Rnd() * 10) + 1) - 1
        Return Text(Number)
        Exit Function
Where:
        Text(0) = "Perhaps in Florida?"
        Text(1) = "I think somewhere in California."
        Text(2) = "Give me a sec, I'll look it up in the atlas."
        Text(3) = "In Germany."
        Text(4) = "Right in the heavens."
        Text(5) = "In the farm-yard."
        Text(6) = "Figure it out yourself."
        Text(7) = "In the White House."
        Text(8) = "The last time I saw him he was wearing only his underwear."
        Text(9) = "Perhaps in the washing machine?"
```

```
        Number = Int((Rnd() * 10) + 1) - 1
        Return Text(Number)
        Exit Function
Why:

        Text(0) = "Because, silly!"
        Text(1) = "Look it up in the encyclopedia!"
        Text(2) = "This is the fate."
        Text(3) = "H'm, I don't know."
        Text(4) = "And I want it this way!"
        Text(5) = "Ask Monica Lewinsky."
        Text(6) = "Look, you here, ask something easier."
        Text(7) = "I don't remember."
        Text(8) = "Could you make your question more specific?"
        Text(9) = "Why don't you ask your mom about this?"
        Number = Int((Rnd() * 10) + 1) - 1
        Return Text(Number)
        Exit Function
Who:

        Text(0) = "Don't you think this is Elvis Presley?"
        Text(1) = "Bond. James Bond."
        Text(2) = "Jim Carrey."
        Text(3) = "The Alien."
        Text(4) = "Uncle Sam."
        Text(5) = "A brain surgeon."
        Text(6) = "Your worst nightmare."
        Text(7) = "Your daddy."
        Text(8) = "Bill Clinton."
        Text(9) = "Pamela Anderson."
        Number - Int((Rnd() * 10) + 1) - 1
        Return Text(Number)
        Exit Function
When_Renamed:

        Text(0) = "Tomorrow."
        Text(1) = "Yesterday."
        Text(2) = "It was in 1900."
        Text (3) = "You will be too old when this happens."
        Text(4) = "It was such a long time ago."
        Text(5) = "During the Civil War."
        Text(6) = "When you were born."
        Text(7) = "When you shaved for the first time."
        Text(8) = "Well, it was when Bill Clinton and Monica Lewinsky..."
        Text(9) = "Now."
        Number = Int((Rnd() * 10) + 1) - 1
```

```
        Return Text(Number)

        Exit Function
Theking:

        If InStr(1, TheText, "alive", CompareMethod.Text) Or InStr(1, TheText, _
"living", CompareMethod.Text) Or InStr(1, TheText, "dead", CompareMethod.Text) Then

            Return "And what did you think? Of course he's alive. He's the king now;)"
        Else
            GoTo Start
        End If
    End Function


    Function NoQuestion() As Object
        Dim Text(9) As String
        Dim Number As Short
        Text(0) = "Well, try to think."
        Text(1) = "I'd rather be answering questions."
        Text(2) = "Perhaps it would be better to ask me a little question."
        Text(3) = "I like questions."
        Text(4) = "Ask me a question, please."
        Text(5) = "I'm just a machine... Ask me, please."
        Text(6) = "Try to ask me again."
        Text(7) = "Alright, but now ask me a question."
        Text(8) = "Try to ask me a question."
        Text(9) = "I only answer questions."
        Randomize()
        Number = Int((Rnd() * 10) + 1) - 1
        NoQuestion = Text(Number)
    End Function


    Function AI(ByRef Text As String) As String

        Dim TempText As String
        Dim Extra As String
        TempText = Replace(Text, " ", "")
        If OldQuestion(TempText) = False Then
            lstUsed.Items.Add(TempText)

            If Text = TempText Then
                Extra = ""
            Else
                Extra = " "
```

```
        End If
        If InStr(1, Text, "What" & Extra, CompareMethod.Text) Then GoTo Question
        If InStr(1, Text, "How" & Extra, CompareMethod.Text) Then GoTo Question
        If InStr(1, Text, "Where" & Extra, CompareMethod.Text) Then GoTo Question
        If InStr(1, Text, "Why" & Extra, CompareMethod.Text) Then GoTo Question
        If InStr(1, Text, "Which" & Extra, CompareMethod.Text) Then GoTo Question
        If InStr(1, Text, "Who" & Extra, CompareMethod.Text) Then GoTo Question
        If InStr(1, Text, "When" & Extra, CompareMethod.Text) Then GoTo Question
        If Microsoft.VisualBasic.Right(TempText, 1) = "?" Then GoTo Question
        Return NoQuestion()
        Exit Function
Question:
        Return OkQuestion(Text)
    Else
        Return "I have already answered this."
    End If
End Function
    Private Sub Button1_Click(ByVal sender As System.Object, ByVal e As _
System.EventArgs) Handles Button1.Click
        Label1.Text = AI(TextBox1.Text)
    End Sub
```

The backbone of the program is an old code written in Visual Basic 5.0. I tried to keep the changes to the old program to the minimum, so you will see many obsolete constructions. The essence of the program lies in the processing of the first word of the question. For example, if the question starts with the word "Why," the program picks an answer randomly from the small collection of sentences in the Why section of the OkQuestions function. The above code is only a template for creating an artificial intelligence program. But, with a creative approach, the program can provide you with many minutes, if not exactly hours, of fun.

13.13. I Can See Everything!

Now, I want to submit for your judgment another funny program. This program draws cat's eyes that constantly track the mouse movements on the screen. Regardless of where the mouse pointer is on the screen, the eyes will look at that spot. The project is called Spycat and the code for it is provided in Listing 13.20.

Listing 13.20. Tracking the Mouse's Movements

```
'-------------------------------------
' Spycat  © 2004 Alexander Klimov
'-------------------------------------
```

```vbnet
' The position of the mouse pointer
Private CursorPos As Point

' The screen coordinates of the left and right eyes
Private LeftEye As Point
Private RightEye As Point

' The distance between the eye and the cursor
Private LeftDistance As Double
Private RightDistance As Double

' Sines and cosines of the angles from the eyes to the mouse pointer
Private LeftSin As Single
Private LeftCos As Single
Private RightSin As Double
Private RightCos As Double

' The form coordinates of the eyes
Private Const LX As Long = 60          ' The X-axis coordinate
Private Const RX As Long = LX + 24     ' The X-axis coordinate
Private Const BY As Long = 60          ' The Y-axis coordinate

' The diameter of the pupil of the eye
Private Const PupilRad As Single = 6
' The diameter of the pupil movement
Private Const MoveRad As Single = 3
' The eye diameter
Private Const EyeRad As Single = 12


Private Sub Timer1_Tick(ByVal sender As System.Object, ByVal e As System.EventArgs) _
Handles Timer1.Tick

    ' Calculating the position of the eyes in the screen coordinates
    LeftEye = PointToScreen(New Point(LX, BY))
    RightEye = PointToScreen(New Point(RX, BY))

    ' Obtaining the position of the mouse pointer
    CursorPos = Cursor.Position

    ' Calculating the distances
    LeftDistance = _
      Math.Sqrt((LeftEye.X - CursorPos.X) ^ 2 + _
      (LeftEye.Y - CursorPos.Y) ^ 2)

    RightDistance =   _
```

```
    Math.Sqrt((RightEye.X - CursorPos.X) ^ 2 + _
    (RightEye.Y - CursorPos.Y) ^ 2)

If LeftDistance = 0 Then ' Division by 0 is not allowed
    LeftDistance = 1
End If

If RightDistance = 0 Then ' Division by 0 is not allowed
    RightDistance = 1
End If

' Calculating the sine and the cosine of the angle
LeftSin = (LeftEye.Y - CursorPos.Y) / LeftDistance
LeftCos = (LeftEye.X - CursorPos.X) / LeftDistance

RightSin = (RightEye.Y - CursorPos.Y) / RightDistance
RightCos = (RightEye.X - CursorPos.X) / RightDistance

Dim g As Graphics = CreateGraphics()
g.Clear(BackColor)

' Drawing the cat's face
g.FillEllipse(Brushes.Gold, LX - 15, BY - 15, 60, 60)

' The ears
Dim aptLEar() As Point = _
  {New Point(50, 60), New Point(40, 25), New Point(64, 49)}
g.FillPolygon(Brushes.Gold, aptLEar)

Dim aptREar() As Point = _
  {New Point(86, 47), New Point(105, 29), New Point(97, 56)}
g.FillPolygon(Brushes.Gold, aptREar)

' The nose and the mouth
g.FillEllipse(Brushes.Black, 72, 72, 8, 8)
g.DrawArc(Pens.Black, 66, 71, 20, 20, 30, 120)

' The whiskers
g.DrawLine(Pens.White, 77, 83, 135, 71)
g.DrawLine(Pens.White, 77, 83, 133, 80)
g.DrawLine(Pens.White, 77, 83, 133, 90)

g.DrawLine(Pens.White, 77, 83, 10, 70)
g.DrawLine(Pens.White, 77, 83, 13, 80)
```

```
g.DrawLine(Pens.White, 77, 83, 13, 90)

' The eyes
g.FillEllipse(Brushes.White, LX - 3, BY - 3, EyeRad, EyeRad)
g.FillEllipse(Brushes.White, RX - 3, BY - 3, EyeRad, EyeRad)

' The pupils
Dim LPupil As Point
LPupil.X = CInt(LX - MoveRad * LeftCos)
LPupil.Y = CInt(BY - MoveRad * LeftSin)
g.FillEllipse(Brushes.Green, _
    LPupil.X, LPupil.Y, PupilRad, PupilRad)

Dim RPupil As Point
RPupil.X = CInt(RX - MoveRad * RightCos)
RPupil.Y = CInt(BY - MoveRad * RightSin)
g.FillEllipse(Brushes.Green, _
    RPupil.X, RPupil.Y, PupilRad, PupilRad)

g.Dispose()
End Sub
```

Fig. 13.4. Cat eyes following the mouse pointer

The program's activity is based on trigonometric functions. First, the distance between the pupils and the mouse pointer is calculated using the familiar Pythagorean Theorem. Next, using the sides of the imaginary right triangle, the sine and cosine of the angle between the mouse pointer and its projection on the coordinate axes are found. Because these calculations are performed dynamically at the timer click event, the pupils know where the mouse pointer is located at any given moment and turn according to the specified angle (Fig. 13.4).

13.14. The Falling Snow of Yesteryear

I will conclude this chapter with what I think is a very interesting example, one that delights many users. You can use this program as a template for creating an interactive greeting card or a screensaver. When running the program, you will see snow falling and accumulating on various objects (Fig. 13.5). I first saw this program on the site **www.emu8086.com/vb**. At that time, it was written in Visual Basic 6.0. But the program's author did not abandon his creation and rewrote the program for VB .NET 2003 and Java. In the comments, the author admits that he does not know how to make the program more flexible. The problem is that the program uses a certain existing image. I have modified the program in such a way as to make it possible to use not only the existing image, but to add your own graphic objects (strings, rectangles, ellipses). This was very easy to do. The object Graphics had to be obtained using not the CreateGraphics method but, instead, the FromImage function. You can download the original program from the site and compare its results with those produced by my modification (The WhiteChristmas project, Listing 13.21).

Listing 13.21. Falling Snow

```
'Copyright (C) 2004 Free Code
'http://www.emu8086.com/vb/
' Modified by A. Klimov on January 1, 2005


'-------------------------------------
' WhiteChristmas© 2004 Alexander Klimov
'-------------------------------------
Public Class Form1
    Inherits System.Windows.Forms.Form



    Structure xParticle
        Dim X As Integer
        Dim Y As Integer
        Dim oldX As Integer
        Dim oldY As Integer
        Dim iStopped As Integer
    End Structure

    Public Const MAXP As Integer = 400
```

```vbnet
Public Snow(MAXP + 1) As xParticle


Dim fMouseDown_X As Single
Dim fMouseDown_Y As Single
Dim bMOUSE_DOWN As Boolean

Dim img As Image = _
    Image.FromFile(Application.StartupPath & "..\..\source.bmp")


Dim g As Graphics
Dim gr As Graphics = Graphics.FromImage(img)
Dim b As Bitmap
Dim TheBlackPixel As Color
Dim mWidth As Integer
Dim mHeight As Integer

Private Sub Form1_Load(ByVal eventSender As System.Object, ByVal eventArgs As _
System.EventArgs) Handles MyBase.Load
    InitSnow()
End Sub

Sub InitSnow()
    Randomize()
    g = Me.CreateGraphics
    Dim i As Integer

    b = New Bitmap(Me.ClientRectangle.Width + 1, _
        Me.ClientRectangle.Height + 1)
    b = b.FromFile(Application.StartupPath & "..\..\source.bmp")

    Dim gr As Graphics = Graphics.FromImage(b)

    ' Adding a custom string
    gr.DrawString("Visual Basic .NET", New Font("tahoma", 24), Brushes.HotPink, 100, 50)

    ' For some reason "Color.Black" cannot be used, so this is used:
    TheBlackPixel = b.GetPixel(0, 0)

    mWidth = b.Width - 1
    mHeight = b.Height - 1

    ' Drawing the first layer of snow for a better look and
```

```
    ' snow falling algorithm calculations:
    For i = 0 To mWidth
        b.SetPixel(i, mHeight, Color.White)
    Next i

    ' The RND formula!
    ' Int((upperbound - lowerbound + 1) * Rnd + lowerbound)
    For i = 0 To MAXP
        newParticle(i)
        Snow(i).X = Int(mWidth * Rnd())
        Snow(i).Y = Int(mHeight * Rnd())
    Next i

    ' Setting the form's dimensions
    Dim hDif As Integer
    hDif = Me.Width - Me.ClientRectangle.Width
    Me.Width = mWidth + hDif + 1
    hDif = Me.Height - Me.ClientRectangle.Height
    Me.Height = mHeight + hDif + 1

    ' Enabling the timer
    Timer1.Enabled = True

End Sub

Sub DrawSnow()
    Dim i As Integer

    Dim newX As Integer
    Dim newY As Integer

    For i = 0 To MAXP
        b.SetPixel(Snow(i).oldX, Snow(i).oldY, TheBlackPixel)
        b.SetPixel(Snow(i).X, Snow(i).Y, System.Drawing.Color.White)
    Next i

    g.DrawImage(b, 0, 0)

    For i = 0 To MAXP
        Snow(i).oldX = Snow(i).X
        Snow(i).oldY = Snow(i).Y

        ' A trick to get both positive and negative random values:
```

```
newX = Snow(i).X + Int(2 * Rnd())
newX = newX - Int(2 * Rnd())

' Don't allow our snow to run away:
If newX < 0 Then newX = 0
If newX >= mWidth Then newX = mWidth - 1

If Snow(i).Y >= mHeight Then

    newParticle(i)

Else

    newY = Snow(i).Y + 1

    If b.GetPixel(newX, newY).Equals(TheBlackPixel) Then
        Snow(i).X = newX
        Snow(i).Y = newY
    Else
        '----------------------------
        If Snow(i).iStopped = 10 Then ' If stopped 10 times, make new!

            If Snow(i).X >= mWidth Then
                newParticle(i)
            ElseIf Snow(i).Y >= mHeight Then
                newParticle(i)
            Else
                ' Move according to basic SNOW RULE:
                If b.GetPixel(Snow(i).X + 1, _
                    Snow(i).Y + 1).Equals(TheBlackPixel) Then
                    Snow(i).X = Snow(i).X + 1
                    Snow(i).Y = Snow(i).Y + 1
                    Snow(i).iStopped = 0
                ElseIf Snow(i).X > 0 Then
                    If b.GetPixel(Snow(i).X - 1, _
                        Snow(i).Y + 1).Equals(TheBlackPixel) Then
                        Snow(i).X = Snow(i).X - 1
                        Snow(i).Y = Snow(i).Y + 1
                        Snow(i).iStopped = 0
                    Else
                        newParticle(i)
                    End If
                Else
```

```
                            newParticle(i)
                      End If

                End If

            Else
                Snow(i).iStopped = Snow(i).iStopped + 1
            End If

          End If

        End If

    Next i

  End Sub

  Sub newParticle(ByRef i As Integer)
      Snow(i).X = Int(mWidth * Rnd())
      Snow(i).Y = 0
      Snow(i).oldX = 0
      Snow(i).oldY = 0
      Snow(i).iStopped = 0
  End Sub

  Private Sub Form1_Closing(ByVal eventSender As System.Object, ByVal eventArgs As _
System.ComponentModel.CancelEventArgs) Handles MyBase.Closing
      Dim Cancel As Integer = eventArgs.Cancel
      Timer1.Enabled = False
      g.Dispose()
      eventArgs.Cancel = Cancel
  End Sub

  Private Sub Timer1_Tick(ByVal eventSender As System.Object, ByVal eventArgs As _
System.EventArgs) Handles Timer1.Tick
      DrawSnow()
  End Sub

  Private Sub Form1_Click(ByVal sender As Object, ByVal e As System.EventArgs)   _
Handles MyBase.Click
      InitSnow()   ' Starting over again
  End Sub
End Class
```

Fig.13.5. Falling snow

13.15. Suggestions and Recommendations

❑ In Section 13.3, the mouse pointer randomly moves in a rigidly set area that is 800 × 600 pixels in size. Write a universal example, taking into account the actual size of the monitor.

❑ Optimize the Runaway Button program. Modify the example to use the Random class instead of the Rnd() function.

❑ Write an example, in which a button chases the mouse pointer, begging the user to click on it.

❑ Write a program to hide the taskbar. You already know how to obtain the handle of the taskbar window.

Chapter 14: Illusions

An illusion is a deception that is based on human weaknesses. The most typical of these weakness is the tendency to stereotype. Illusions trigger stereotypes, evoking laughter or enjoyment on the part of the illusion's creator. But illusions are also widely used in many industries and activities, including programming.

The most illustrative example of this is buttons and other controls that appear to be three-dimensional. Even though monitors are flat, the buttons on them can appear to our eyes to protrude above the surface or sink deeper into it when clicked on by a mouse.

14.1. Orbison's Illusion

If a square is drawn over concentric circles, its appearance will be distorted. My personal observation is that the effect is enhanced if the square is placed in such a way that its center does not coincide with the center of the concentric circles, but is offset somewhat to one side. The source code for creating this effect — the Illusions project — is provided in Listing 14.1.

Listing 14.1. Orbison's Illusion

```
'-------------------------------------
' Illusions © 2004 Alexander Klimov
'-------------------------------------
    Private Sub mnuOrbison_Click(ByVal sender As System.Object, ByVal e As _
System.EventArgs) Handles mnuOrbison.Click
        Dim g As Graphics = CreateGraphics()
        g.Clear(BackColor)
        Dim redpen As Pen = Pens.Red
        g.DrawEllipse(redpen, 70, 70, 160, 160)
        g.DrawEllipse(redpen, 80, 80, 140, 140)
        g.DrawEllipse(redpen, 90, 90, 120, 120)
        g.DrawEllipse(redpen, 100, 100, 100, 100)
        g.DrawEllipse(redpen, 110, 110, 80, 80)
        g.DrawEllipse(redpen, 120, 120, 60, 60)
        g.DrawEllipse(redpen, 130, 130, 40, 40)
        g.DrawEllipse(redpen, 140, 140, 20, 20)
        g.DrawRectangle(redpen, 100, 100, 60, 60)
        g.Dispose()
    End Sub
```

If your eyes don't believe what they see in Fig. 14.1 and are leading you to believe that your monitor is in need of an adjustment, redo the program yourself. First, display a square on the screen. Make sure that it is indeed square, and then draw a series of concentric circles. You will see that everything is in order with your monitor settings and that you are simply experiencing an optical illusion.

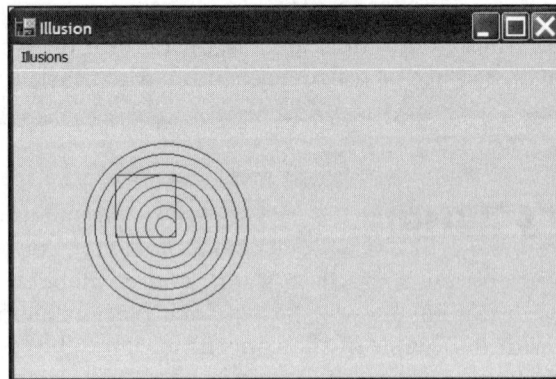

Fig. 14.1. Orbison's illusion

14.2. Café Wall

This illusion is named after a café in 19th-century Bristol, England. One of its walls was tiled in a specific way, with alternating white and black tiles (Fig. 14.2). The code for reproducing this effect is given in Listing 14.2.

Listing 14.2. The Café Wall Illusion

```
    Private Sub mnuCafeWall_Click(ByVal sender As System.Object, ByVal e As _
System.EventArgs) Handles mnuCafeWall.Click
        Dim g As Graphics = CreateGraphics()
        g.Clear(BackColor)
        Dim blbr As SolidBrush = New SolidBrush(Color.Black)

        Dim counter As Integer
        For counter = 0 To 8
            g.FillRectangle(blbr, counter * 60, 10, 30, 30)
            g.DrawLine(New Pen(Color.Gray), 0, 40, 540, 40)
            g.FillRectangle(blbr, counter * 60 + 10, 40, 30, 30)
            g.DrawLine(New Pen(Color.Gray), 0, 70, 540, 70)
            g.FillRectangle(blbr, counter * 60 + 20, 70, 30, 30)
            g.DrawLine(New Pen(Color.Gray), 0, 100, 540, 100)
            g.FillRectangle(blbr, counter * 60 + 10, 100, 30, 30)
            g.DrawLine(New Pen(Color.Gray), 0, 130, 540, 130)
            g.FillRectangle(blbr, counter * 60, 130, 30, 30)
        Next
        g.Dispose()
    End Sub
```

To enhance the illusion, the seams between the tiles are light-colored, which separates the black and white tiles more distinctly, making the effect more pronounced. As you can see from the source code, all of the rectangles are of the same size. But how do they appear? Let's examine why this happens. The fact is that our brain perceives light objects against a dark background to be larger than they really are, while dark object appear to be smaller. In this case, we are judging the size of the tiles relative to the line between the horizontal rows of tiles. Therefore, when black and white tiles alternate in the lower row while there is a white tile in the upper row, the line between the rows will seem to rise towards the right. If the conditions are reversed, it will seem to fall. So, if you have decided to renovate your bathroom and instructed the workers to lay the tiles this way, don't be so quick to decide that the job has been botched. The tiler is not to blame. Once you get used to it, you will have a bathroom with a wall tiled in an original manner that will be a subject of much talk among your friends and visitors.

Fig. 14.2. The Café Wall illusion

14.3. Are These Lines Really Parallel?

We were taught in school that one of the basic characteristics of parallel lines is that they do not converge. But is this really true? Draw a pair of parallel lines and cross them with short evenly spaced lines angled at opposite angles on each line. The code for doing this is provided in Listing 14.3.

Listing 14.3. Parallel Lines

```
Dim g As Graphics = CreateGraphics()
g.Clear(Color.Black)

' The first effect
g.DrawLine(New Pen(Color.White), 50, 50, 500, 50)
g.DrawLine(New Pen(Color.White), 50, 70, 500, 70)

Dim i As Integer
For i = 50 To 480 Step 10
    g.DrawLine(New Pen(Color.White), i, 45, i + 10, 55)
    g.DrawLine(New Pen(Color.White), i, 75, i + 10, 65)
Next
g.Dispose()
```

When running the program, you will see that the lines are not really parallel, but diverge to the right (Fig. 14.3, top). It looks like math teachers have been fooling us all these years and math textbooks should be revised. Here is another program to prove that parallel lines are not really parallel (Listing 14.4).

Listing 14.4. Another Parallel-Line Illusion

```
' Another parallel lines illusion
Dim g As Graphics = CreateGraphics()
g.Clear(Color.Black)

g.DrawLine(New Pen(Color.White), 10, 100, 450, 100)
g.DrawLine(New Pen(Color.White), 10, 180, 450, 180)

Dim i As Integer
For i = -30 To 430 Step 30
    g.DrawLine(New Pen(Color.White), 230, 150, i + 30, 80)
    g.DrawLine(New Pen(Color.White), 230, 150, i + 30, 190)
Next
g.Dispose()
```

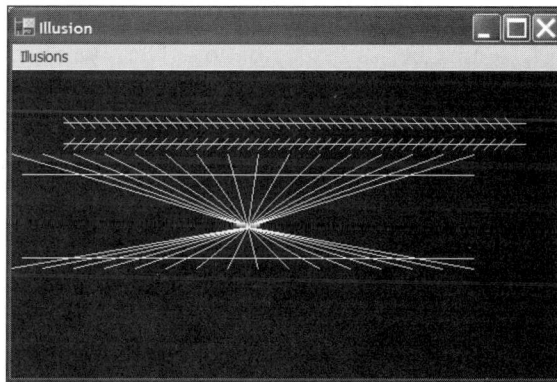

Fig. 14.3. Don't you think these lines will cross?

Now, you can see that parallel lines converge at both ends (Fig. 14.3, bottom). If you extend these lines in your mind, they will undoubtedly cross. If you are still attending school, show this example to your math teacher as proof that he or she is feeding you with the wrong information. I, however, assume no responsibility for the possible consequences, especially if you wait until the final exam to prove your point! Do this at your own risk.

14.4. 3D Shapes

In addition to being entertaining, illusions also have a practical value. In *Chapter 2*, we covered how to create 3D text. The illusion of objects having volume is widely used in graphical operating systems. When Windows 95 with its graphical interface was released, millions of people who were still using DOS were stunned. Everyone was captivated by the appearance of applications with 3D controls.

We will try to follow the developers' footsteps and give our shapes volume. Our first example will be a simple rectangle. When you understand the main idea for creating the 3D effect, you will have no difficulty creating your own 3D buttons, texts, etc. Taking a closer look at a shape that appears to be 3D, you will notice that this effect is achieved by using thin lines of various colors at the sides of the shape. First, let's place a label on the form to be used as a sample for imitation. Set its BorderStyle property to Fixed3D and the Text property to blank. The label's dimensions and location are of no particular importance. I set them to the following values:

- Location = 10;10
- Size = 50;40

Run the program, and examine the label carefully. As you can see, the left and right sides of the label are framed with dark-gray lines, while the bottom and right sides are framed with white lines. Remember this information. The source code for the procedure creating an analogous effect is provided in Listing 14.5.

Listing 14.5. Creating a 3D Relief Illusion

```
'-------------------------------------
' 3D Shapes © 2004 Alexander Klimov
'-------------------------------------
    Private Sub Draw3DBorder(ByVal g As Graphics, ByVal rect As Rectangle, _
Optional ByVal sunken As Boolean = True)
        ' The procedure for creating the 3D effect

        Dim colors() As Color

        If sunken Then
            colors = New Color() { _
                SystemColors.ControlDark, _
                SystemColors.ControlLightLight _
            }
        Else
            colors = New Color() { _
```

```
            SystemColors.ControlLightLight, _
            SystemColors.ControlDark _
    }
End If

Dim p As Pen
p = New Pen(colors(0))
g.DrawLine(p, rect.X, rect.Y + rect.Height - 1, rect.X, rect.Y)
g.DrawLine(p, rect.X, rect.Y, rect.X + rect.Width - 1, rect.Y)

p = New Pen(colors(1))
g.DrawLine(p, rect.X, rect.Y + rect.Height - 1, _
    rect.X + rect.Width - 1, rect.Y + rect.Height - 1)
g.DrawLine(p, rect.X + rect.Width - 1, _
    rect.Y + rect.Height - 1, rect.X + rect.Width - 1, rect.Y)

End Sub
```

Let's examine in detail what this procedure does. First, an array is declared that will hold the colors of the lines creating the 3D effect. It is followed by an If … Else condition. For the time being, we will consider only the If branch, which executes when the sunken condition is met. This piece of code implements the sinking effect. For this, we will need to call the two colors developed by Microsoft especially for this mode: ControlDark and ControlLightLight. You can obtain more detailed information about these colors in the VB .NET documentation. The rectangle will be drawn using four calls of the DrawLine method, instead of the DrawRectangle method. Moreover, the first two calls use the ControlDark color and the last two use the ControlLightLight color. If you recall, I asked you to note the appearance of the label. Now you can compare the sample label with your own creation. For this, add the following code to the Form1_Paint event handler:

```
Draw3DBorder(e.Graphics, _
    New Rectangle(70, 10, _
        50, 40), _
    True)
```

Because I placed the reference label at the coordinates (10, 10) and its width is 50 pixels, the created shape is placed 10 pixels to the right of the sample label. I believe that you will agree that the appearance of the shape created programmatically is absolutely the same as the sample label. You have probably already guessed that the Else branch draws a raised shape.

```
Else
    colors = New Color() { _
        SystemColors.ControlLightLight, _
```

```
          SystemColors.ControlDark _
    }
End If
```

All you have to do to achieve this effect is change the places of the colors used to draw the sunken shape. To see what a raised shape looks like on the screen, add the following code to the `Form1_Paint` event handler:

```
Draw3DBorder(e.Graphics, _
          New Rectangle(70, 60, _
               50, 40), _
          False)
```

This will produce a shape resembling a button right under the sample label. But there is more to come. Microsoft has two more colors in its stores arsenal to make shapes look 3D: `ControlDarkDark` and `ControlLight`. Using these two colors along with the two described earlier produces a more sunken or raised effect. To demonstrate this, I used all four colors in a new procedure: `Draw3Border2` (Listing 14.6). See also Fig. 14.4.

Listing 14.6. The Second Procedure for Creating 3D Shapes

```
    Private Sub Draw3DBorder2(ByVal g As Graphics, ByVal rect As Rectangle, Optional _
ByVal sunken As Boolean = True)
        ' The procedure for creating a more pronounced 3D effect

        Dim colors() As Color

        If sunken Then
            colors = New Color() { _
                SystemColors.ControlDark, _
                SystemColors.ControlDarkDark, _
                SystemColors.ControlLightLight, _
                SystemColors.ControlLight _
            }
        Else
            colors = New Color() { _
                SystemColors.ControlLightLight, _
                SystemColors.ControlLight, _
                SystemColors.ControlDark, _
                SystemColors.ControlDarkDark _
            }
        End If

        Dim p As Pen
        p = New Pen(colors(0))
```

```
        g.DrawLine(p, rect.X, rect.Y + rect.Height - 1, rect.X, rect.Y)
        g.DrawLine(p, rect.X, rect.Y, rect.X + rect.Width - 1, rect.Y)
        p = New Pen(colors(1))
        g.DrawLine(p, rect.X + 1, rect.Y + rect.Height - 2, rect.X + 1, rect.Y + 1)
        g.DrawLine(p, rect.X + 1, rect.Y + 1, rect.X + rect.Width - 2, rect.Y + 1)
        p = New Pen(colors(2))
        g.DrawLine(p, rect.X, rect.Y + rect.Height - 1, rect.X + rect.Width - 1, _
rect.Y + rect.Height - 1)
        g.DrawLine(p, rect.X + rect.Width - 1, rect.Y + rect.Height - 1, rect.X + _
rect.Width - 1, rect.Y)
        p = New Pen(colors(3))
        g.DrawLine(p, rect.X + 1, rect.Y + rect.Height - 2, rect.X + rect.Width - 2, _
rect.Y + rect.Height - 2)
        g.DrawLine(p, rect.X + rect.Width - 2, rect.Y + rect.Height - 2, rect.X + _
rect.Width - 2, rect.Y + 1)

    End Sub
```

This procedure contains nothing new in the way of ideas, so there is no need to explain the code. Examine the code and figure out how it works on your own. The code for calling the two procedures we created in the `Form1_Paint` event handler is given in Listing 14.7.

Listing 14.7. Calling the 3D-Effect Procedures

```
    Private Sub Form1_Paint(ByVal sender As Object, ByVal e As _
System.Windows.Forms.PaintEventArgs) Handles MyBase.Paint

        Draw3DBorder(e.Graphics, _
            New Rectangle(70, 10, _
                50, 40), _
            True)

        Draw3DBorder(e.Graphics, _
                New Rectangle(10, 60, _
                        50, 40), _
                False)

        Draw3DBorder2(e.Graphics, _
                New Rectangle(10, 110, _
                        50, 40), _
                True)

        Draw3DBorder2(e.Graphics, _
                New Rectangle(70, 110, _
```

```
                            50, 40), _
          False)


     End Sub
```

Now, you have at your disposal a powerful template that you can use in your projects. What can be done with this is, again, only limited by your imagination. Now that you can create the same standard controls as the Microsoft programmers, you can try to convince your less knowledgeable friends that you have gotten hold of the Windows source codes.

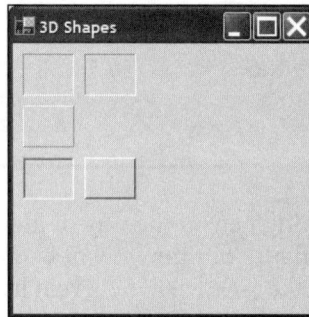

Fig. 14.4. Creating 3D shapes

14.5. Suggestions and Recommendations

I have given examples of only a few of the most simple illusions. In fact, there are many more. Examples of visual illusions can often be found in books and magazines devoted to the subject. Try to recreate similar illusions on your computer. You might find that you can use some of them in your own applications.

Chapter 15: The Sounds of Music

This chapter is devoted to sound reproduction. It is impossible to imagine the modern computer without the multimedia devices that are used to listen to music, play card games, make your own music, etc.

15.1. Playing Back Audio Files

Let's consider the simplest example: playing a WAV audio file. At present, .NET Framework offers no built-in means for playing audio files. Therefore, we will have to resort to Windows API functions. Launch a new project: PlaySound. Declare a function by the same name — PlaySound — and a few attendant constants. All you need to do to play the audio file is to call the declared function with the file's name as one of the parameters (Listing 15.1).

Listing 15.1. Playing Back an Audio File

```
'--------------------------------------
' PlaySound © 2004 Alexander Klimov
'--------------------------------------
    Public Const SND_SYNC = &H0
    Public Const SND_ASYNC = &H1
```

```
Public Const SND_FILENAME = &H20000
Public Const SND_RESOURCE = &H40004
Private Declare Auto Function PlaySound Lib "winmm.dll" _
        (ByVal name As String, _
         ByVal hmod As Integer, ByVal flags As Integer) As Integer


  Private Sub butPlay_Click(ByVal sender As System.Object, ByVal e As _
System.EventArgs) Handles butPlay.Click
       PlaySound(Application.StartupPath & "../../meow.wav", _
                         Nothing, SND_FILENAME Or SND_ASYNC)
   End Sub
```

In this example, the program searches for the specified audio file and plays it. Note that the function plays only WAV files. Unfortunately, the `PlaySound` function does not support other popular formats, such as MP3.

> The developers are promising to add a new class — `SoundPlayer` — in VB .NET 2005, which will allow WAV files to be played back without having to resort to unmanaged Windows API code.
>
> NOTE

15.2. Checking for the Audio Card

When considering the above example, that of playing an audio file, we left out one very important point: Is the computer physically capable of reproducing audio files? It is common for an office computers not being able to do this. So it would be a good idea to check that the computer is equipped with sound reproducing devices before attempting actual playback. This check is carried out as follows with the help of the `waveOutGetNumDev` Windows API function:

```
Private Declare Function waveOutGetNumDevs Lib "winmm" () As Integer
```

A successful call returns the number of audio processing devices in the system. Consequently, any number returned other than zero means that the computer is equipped with an audio card. The call of this function can be implemented as a user-defined function from some place in the code (Listing 15.2).

Listing 15.2. Checking for the Audio Card

```
Function IsSoundCardPresent() As Boolean
    Return waveOutGetNumDevs() >= 1
End Function
```

```
    Private Sub butSoundCard_Click(ByVal sender As System.Object, ByVal e  _
As System.EventArgs) Handles butSoundCard.Click
        MsgBox(IsSoundCardPresent)
    End Sub
```

A little laugh

An exhausted programmer whose computer is plagued by bugs calls a radio station to make a request:

— Could you please play "*Driving me crazy*," by Phil Collins?

15.3. Sound-Recording Devices

In addition to playing audio files, computers can also record sound from a microphone. To determine whether a particular computer has this capability, you can make use of the waveInGetNumDevs function, which is similar to the function from the previous example.

```
    Private Declare Function waveInGetNumDevs Lib "winmm.dll" () As Integer
```

Calling this function returns the number of devices capable of recording sound (Listing 15.3).

Listing 15.3. Determining the Presence and Number of Sound Recording Devices

```
    Private Sub butIn_Click(ByVal sender As System.Object, ByVal e As System.EventArgs)  _
Handles butIn.Click
        lblInfo.Text = waveInGetNumDevs() & " sound recording device(s) available"
    End Sub
```

There turned out to be two such devices on my computer!

15.4. Playing Back MIDI Files

As has already been pointed out, the PlaySound function can only play WAV audio files. But there is another very common musical format — MIDI. How can these files be reproduced? Here, we need to resort to another Windows API function: mciSendString. We have already used this function to open and close CD-ROM tray (see *Chapter 13*). But this function has much greater capabilities, which we will take advantage of in playing MIDI files. I have picked one of the several MIDI files contained in the Windows system files (Listing 15.4).

Listing 15.4. Playing Back MIDI Files

```
' The function to play back MIDI
Private Declare Function mciSendString Lib "winmm.dll" _
                              Alias "mciSendStringA" _
                              (ByVal lpstrCommand As String, _
                              ByVal lpstrReturnString As String, _
                              ByVal uReturnLength As Long, _
                              ByVal hwndCallback As Long) As Long

Public Sub butMidi_Click(ByVal sender As System.Object, ByVal e As _
System.EventArgs) Handles butMidi.Click
      Dim lRet As Long

      Dim testmidi As String = "C:\Windows\Media\town.mid"

      ' Opening the device to play back the MIDI file
      lRet = mciSendString( _
        "open " & testmidi & " type sequencer alias mplayer", _
          0&, 0, 0)

      ' Beginning the playback
      lRet = mciSendString("play mplayer", 0&, 0, 0)

End Sub

   Private Sub butCloseMidi_Click(ByVal sender As System.Object, ByVal e As _
System.EventArgs) Handles butCloseMidi.Click
      ' Closing the file and the device
      mciSendString("close mplayer", 0&, 0, 0)
   End Sub
```

You have to be careful when playing back MIDI files in your programs. This should be done in the following sequence: Open the file and the device; start the playback; stop the device; and, finally, close the device and the file. Ignoring these rules may cause your program to hang in some cases. More detailed information concerning working with MIDI files can be found at the following site: **http://msdn.microsoft.com**.

15.5. The Virtual Piano

The fact that it is possible to play a music file programmatically means that it is possible to create a virtual musical instrument, a piano, for example. The piano, like your computer keyboard, has keys, a circumstance we will take advantage of. The idea is as follows. A row of keys is drawn on the form corresponding to actual piano keys. Each key is assigned a particular note. The program is then equipped with a keyboard interface. After all of these steps are carried out, you can run the program and, by pressing corresponding keyboard keys, produce the desired melody, or at least as close to the melody as your musical talents allow. I can't promise that this will get you an appearance in the TV Star Search, but you can certainly please (hopefully) those close to you with some happy tunes.

The program I created is just a skeleton version. Your task is to finish it off to suit your specific needs. The VBPiano project begins with obtaining audio files to play individual notes. You will find several files of this type in my collection, provided on the accompanying CD-ROM. The next step is to make the keys drawn on the form resemble actual piano keys. By the way, you can avoid the tedious job of placing each button on the form by creating an indexed array of buttons with the specified properties. I went about it the old way, and placed all twenty buttons on the form manually. Twelve buttons should be white, while the rest are black. For a better visualization, I also placed twelve labels on the form to be used as colored indicators (Listing 15.5).

Listing 15.5. Creating a Virtual Piano

```
'---------------------------------------
' VBPiano © 2004 Alexander Klimov
'---------------------------------------
    Public Const SND_ASYNC = &H1
    Public Const SND_NODEFAULT = &H2
    Public Const SND_FILENAME = &H20000

    Private Declare Auto Function PlaySound Lib "winmm.dll" _
            (ByVal name As String, ByVal hmod As Integer, _
            ByVal flags As Integer) As Integer

    Private Sub Form1_KeyDown(ByVal sender As Object, ByVal e As _
System.Windows.Forms.KeyEventArgs) Handles MyBase.KeyDown

        Select Case e.KeyCode
            Case Keys.D1
                Button1.PerformClick()
            Case Keys.D2
                Button2.PerformClick()
            Case Keys.D3
                Button3.PerformClick()
            Case Keys.D4
                Button4.PerformClick()
            Case Keys.D5
                Button5.PerformClick()
            Case Keys.D6
```

```
                    Button6.PerformClick()
            Case Keys.D7
                    Button7.PerformClick()
            Case Keys.D8
                    Button8.PerformClick()
            Case Keys.D9
                    Button9.PerformClick()
            Case Keys.D0
                    Button10.PerformClick()
            Case Keys.OemMinus
                    Button11.PerformClick()
            Case Keys.Oemplus
                    Button4.PerformClick()
            Case Keys.F1
                    Button13.PerformClick()
            Case Keys.F2
                    Button14.PerformClick()
            Case Keys.F3
                    Button15.PerformClick()
            Case Keys.F4
                    Button16.PerformClick()
            Case Keys.F5
                    Button17.PerformClick()
            Case Keys.F6
                    Button18.PerformClick()
            Case Keys.F7
                    Button19.PerformClick()
            Case Keys.F8
                    Button20.PerformClick()
        End Select
    End Sub


    Private Sub Button1_Click(ByVal sender As System.Object, ByVal e As  _
System.EventArgs) Handles Button1.Click
        Dim filename As String
        Const wavefile As String = "..\..\1.wav"
        filename = Application.StartupPath & wavefile
        PlaySound(filename, Nothing, SND_FILENAME Or SND_ASYNC)
    End Sub


    Private Sub Button1_MouseUp(ByVal sender As Object, ByVal e As  _
System.Windows.Forms.MouseEventArgs) Handles Button1.MouseUp
        Label1.BackColor = Color.Chartreuse
```

```
    End Sub

    Private Sub Button1_MouseDown(ByVal sender As Object, ByVal e As    _
System.Windows.Forms.MouseEventArgs) Handles Button1.MouseDown
        Label1.BackColor = Color.Green
    End Sub
```

The code itself is clear. Pressing a keyboard key produces a sound from the speakers, and the corresponding label/color indicator lights up at the same time (Fig. 15.1). Because the code for the rest of the buttons is the same as the code for the first button, I don't see the point of listing it in the book. The Form_KeyDown event, however, deserves separate consideration. The form's KeyPreview property needs to be set to True. This will make it possible to process not only mouse clicks on the buttons/piano keys but also keyboard keystrokes. In the example, I used the keys from the two upper keyboard rows: the eight function keys (<F1> through <F8>) and 12 number keys (<1> through <=>). Run the program, and begin your piano-bar show. But please turn down the volume!

A little laugh

A programmer comes to visit a musician. The musician is bragging about his new piano. The programmer gives it a good lookover, and finally says: — The keyboard is nothing to write home about, as there are only 89 keys. But pressing the <Shift> key with your feet, now that's cool!

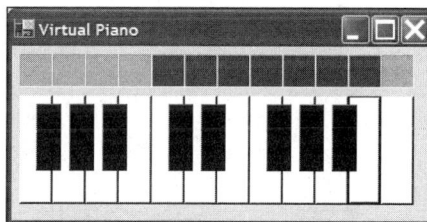

Fig. 15.1. The virtual piano

15.6. The WinAmp Player

One of the most popular software players is WinAmp (**www.winamp.com**). In the following example, I want to show how your program can obtain the name of the song currently being played in WinAmp. To do this, we will need the help of the FindWindow and GetWindowText Windows API functions. The former is used to find the WinAmp program window, while the latter obtains the text in its title bar. The player's class name can be obtained on the player author's site: it is Winamp v1.x. Moreover, the player always adds the Winamp word to the title of the song being played. Knowing the name of the class, we can easily get the window's handle, and then its title. I implemented the source code of the program for doing this as an independent function: GetWinampTitle (Listing 15.6).

Listing 15.6. Obtaining the Name of the WinAmp Song

```
'-------------------------------------
' WinAmp © 2004 Alexander Klimov
'-------------------------------------
    Private Declare Auto Function FindWindow Lib "user32" ( _
      ByVal lpClassName As String, _
      ByVal lpWindowName As String) As IntPtr
    Private Declare Auto Function GetWindowText Lib "user32" ( _
       ByVal hwnd As IntPtr, _
       ByVal lpString As String, _
       ByVal cch As Integer) As Integer
    Private Const lpClassName = "Winamp v1.x"
    Private Const strTtlEnd = " - Winamp"

    Private Function GetWinampTitle() As String
        ' The Winamp window handle
        Dim hwnd As IntPtr
        hwnd = FindWindow(lpClassName, vbNullString)

        ' The window title
        Dim lpText As String

        If hwnd.Equals(IntPtr.Zero) Then Return "WinAmp is not started!"

        lpText = New String(Chr(0), 100)
        Dim intLength As Integer = GetWindowText(hwnd, lpText, _
          lpText.Length)

        If (intLength <= 0) OrElse (intLength > lpText.Length) _
                Then Return "Not identified"

        Dim strTitle As String = lpText.Substring(0, intLength)
        Dim intName As Integer = strTitle.IndexOf(strTtlEnd)

        If (strTitle.EndsWith(strTtlEnd)) AndAlso _
            (strTitle.Length > strTtlEnd.Length) Then _
            strTitle = strTitle.Substring(0, _
```

```
            strTitle.Length - strTtlEnd.Length)

        Dim intDot As Integer = strTitle.IndexOf(".")
        If (intDot > 0) AndAlso (IsNumeric( _
                strTitle.Substring(0, intDot))) Then _
            strTitle = strTitle.Remove(0, intDot + 1)

        Return strTitle.Trim
    End Function

    Private Sub butGetSong_Click(ByVal sender As System.Object, ByVal e As _
System.EventArgs) Handles butGetSong.Click
        TextBox1.Text = GetWinampTitle()
    End Sub
```

The `GetWinampTitle` function turned out to be a bit long, but this approach is justified. The fact is that just calling the `GetWindowText` function returns superfluous information. First of all, the located string will contain the song's number in the playlist, followed by a period and a space. These are followed by the song title, in which we are interested in and concludes with a string " - `Winamp`". Consequently, the information we need must be extracted from this string, which is what our function does. Now, to obtain the name of the current song, all you do is call the `GetWinampTitle` function without any parameters. Don't forget to place a button and a text box on the form to display the song's name.

> **NOTE**
>
> When the song is paused or stopped, additional words — **[Paused]** or **[Stopped]**, respectively — are displayed in the WinAmp window's title. Consequently, you also have to make provisions for this situation.

15.7. MP3 File Tags

The example just considered assumes that the user has WinAmp installed. But what if the user isn't particularly fond of this program? Then you can offer the user your own MP3 player! Here, a detailed description of the MP3 file structure is in order. You have probably noticed that during playback of MP3 files the player sometimes shows additional information about the song: its title, the artist, the year, the album name, etc. Have you ever wondered where the player gets this information? As turns out, MP3 files have several bytes reserved, in which this information is written in a special format. Knowing the format, in which the data are stored in the file, allows players to extract the necessary information from it.

I will explain to you how this is done, and then you will be able to read the hidden data yourself. So pay attention carefully. MP3 files can store metadata such as the performer, song title, album name, etc. This information is stored in the so-called ID3 *tag*. This tag is stored in the last 128 bytes of an MP3 file (but it is not mandatory for a file to have this tag). Consequently, to extract the necessary information you need to read the last 128 bytes of the file, check for the presence of the special signature (the first three characters must be TAG), and, if it is present, consider these 128 bytes to be the ID3 tag. The tag, in turn, is broken into several fields, each of several bytes, holding the information. The information about the structure of the 1.0 ID3 v1.0 tag is shown in Table 15.1.

Table 15.1. Contents of the ID3 v1.0 Tag

Byte	No. of characters	Name	Contents
0	Char[3]	Signature	"TAG" (if there is no signature, then it is not an ID3 tag)
3	Char[30]	Title	The song's title
33	Char[30]	Artist	The song's performer
63	Char[30]	Album	The album's title
93	Char[4]	Year	Year produced
97	Char[30]	Comment	Comment
127	byte	Genre	Genre

As you can see, the song's title, album title, the performer's name, and the comment each fit into no more than 30 characters. If there are fewer than 30 characters in a string, it is padded with characters whose code is 0 (the first character coded as 0 is considered the end of a string). There is also a minor expansion of the format — the ID3 v1.1 — which is used to store the track number of the CD, from which the file was ripped. The last byte of the comment field is allocated for this. To make sure that this is actually the track number and not a character from a very long comment, it is necessary to check whether the penultimate byte equals zero. In our example, we will use the 1.1 version, as it is more widely used at present. Moreover, there is already the ID3 v2.0 specification, which provides additional information. You can easily find more detailed information about the MP3 tag specification on the Internet. But let's get back to Table 15.1. The last byte of the tag stores the genre code. Table 15.2 lists the genres and their corresponding codes.

Table 15.2. Last Byte ID3 v2.0 Tag Genre Codes

Genre	Byte Value	Genre	Byte Value
Blues	0	Country	2
ClassicRock	1	Dance	3

continues

Table 15.2 Continued

Genre	Byte Value	Genre	Byte Value
Disco	4	Classical	32
Funk	5	Instrumental	33
Grunge	6	Acid	34
HipHop	7	House	35
Jazz	8	Game	36
Metal	9	SoundClip	37
NewAge	10	Gospel	38
Oldies	11	Noise	39
Other	12	AlternRock	40
Pop	13	Bass	41
RnB	14	Soul	42
Rap	15	Punk	43
Reggae	16	Space	44
Rock	17	Meditative	45
Techno	18	InstrumentalPop	46
Industrial	19	InstrumentalRock	47
Alternative	20	Ethnic	48
Ska	21	Gothic	49
DeathMetal	22	Darkwave	50
Pranks	23	TechnoIndustrial	51
Soundtrack	24	Electronic	52
EuroTechno	25	PopFolk	53
Ambient	26	Eurodance	54
TripHop	27	Dream	55
Vocal	28	SouthernRock	56
JazzFunk	29	Comedy	57
Fusion	30	Cult	58
Trance	31	Gangsta	59

continues

Table 15.2 Continued

Genre	Byte Value	Genre	Byte Value
Top40	60	LoFi	71
ChristianRap	61	Tribal	72
PopFunk	62	AcidPunk	73
Jungle	63	AcidJazz	74
NativeAmerican	64	Polka	75
Cabaret	65	Retro	76
NewWave	66	Musical	77
Psychadelic	67	RocknRoll	78
Rave	68	HardRock	79
Showtunes	69	None	255
Trailer	70		

It is entirely likely that the list of genre names will be expanded in the future. You can also search for the relevant information on the Internet.

After this short introduction to theory, we are ready to move on to the practice. I found a very good example once on the site **www.codeproject.com**. This example was the starting point for my project. Start Visual Basic .NET 2003, and create a new project: MP3. To extract information from MP3 files, we will create a separate class: MP3TAG. In the **Solution Explorer** window, right-click on the project name, and select the **Add/Add Class** command sequence. This will open the **Add New Item** dialog window. Select **Class** as the item to add. Change the Class.vb default name of the class to be created to MP3TAG.vb, and click the **Open** button to create the class. The class created is just a skeleton, so it needs some fleshing out. Start by importing the System.IO namespace, which is used for reading and writing files (Listing 15.7).

Listing 15.7. Extracting Information from MP3 Files

```
'-------------------------------------
' MP3 File Tags© 2004 Alexander Klimov
'-------------------------------------
' The class for working with MP3 tags
Imports System.IO
Public Class MP3TAG
    ' The constructor
    Public Sub New(Optional ByVal Filename As String = "")
```

```
    MyBase.New()
    If (Filename <> "") Then Me.Filename = Filename
End Sub

' Genres
Public Enum Genres As Byte
    Blues = 0
    ClassicRock = 1
    Country = 2
    Dance = 3
    Disco = 4
    Funk = 5
    Grunge = 6
    HipHop = 7
    Jazz = 8
    Metal = 9
    NewAge = 10
    Oldies = 11
    Other = 12
    Pop = 13
    RnB = 14
    Rap = 15
    Reggae = 16
    Rock = 17
    Techno = 18
    Industrial = 19
    Alternative = 20
    Ska = 21
    DeathMetal = 22
    Pranks = 23
    Soundtrack = 24
    EuroTechno = 25
    Ambient = 26
    TripHop = 27
    Vocal = 28
    JazzFunk = 29
    Fusion = 30
    Trance = 31
    Classical = 32
    Instrumental = 33
    Acid = 34
    House = 35
    Game = 36
    SoundClip = 37
```

```
Gospel = 38
Noise = 39
AlternRock = 40
Bass = 41
Soul = 42
Punk = 43
Space = 44
Meditative = 45
InstrumentalPop = 46
InstrumentalRock = 47
Ethnic = 48
Gothic = 49
Darkwave = 50
TechnoIndustrial = 51
Electronic = 52
PopFolk = 53
Eurodance = 54
Dream = 55
SouthernRock = 56
Comedy = 57
Cult = 58
Gangsta = 59
Top40 = 60
ChristianRap = 61
PopFunk = 62
Jungle = 63
NativeAmerican = 64
Cabaret = 65
NewWave = 66
Psychadelic = 67
Rave = 68
Showtunes = 69
Trailer = 70
LoFi = 71
Tribal = 72
AcidPunk = 73
AcidJazz = 74
Polka = 75
Retro = 76
Musical = 77
RocknRoll = 78
HardRock = 79
None = 255
```

```
End Enum

' Information about the song
Public Enum Tag_Info As Byte
    Title = 0   ' The song's title
    Artist = 1  ' The song's performer
    Album = 2   ' The album's title
    Year = 3    ' Year produced
    Track = 4   ' Track number
    Comment = 5 ' Comments
    Genre = 6   ' Genre
End Enum

' The file name
Private strFileName As String
Public Property Filename() As String
    Get
        Return strFileName
    End Get
    Set(ByVal Value As String)
        Dim checkFile As File
        If (checkFile.Exists(Value)) Then
            strFileName = Value
            Refresh()
        Else
            Throw New System.IO.FileLoadException( _
                "There is no such file", Value)
        End If
    End Set
End Property

' Is there a tag in the file?
Private bTagExists As Boolean
Public ReadOnly Property TagExists() As Boolean
    Get
        Return bTagExists
    End Get
End Property

' Information blocks
Private mobjFrame(7) As Object
Public Property Frame(ByVal FrameType As Tag_Info)
    Get
        Return mobjFrame(FrameType)
```

```
    End Get
    Set(ByVal Value)
        mobjFrame(FrameType) = Value
    End Set
End Property

' Extracting information from the specified file
Public Sub Refresh()

    ' The look-up table
    Dim strTag As New String(" ", 3)
    Dim strTitle As New String(" ", 30)
    Dim strArtist As New String(" ", 30)
    Dim strAlbum As New String(" ", 30)
    Dim strYear As New String(" ", 4)
    Dim strComment As New String(" ", 28)
    Dim bytDummy As Byte
    Dim bytTrack As Byte
    Dim bytGenre As Byte

    ' Opening the file
    Dim intFile As Integer = FreeFile()
    FileOpen(intFile, strFileName, OpenMode.Binary, _
        OpenAccess.Read, OpenShare.LockWrite)

    ' Calculating the file's length
    Dim lngLOF As Long = LOF(intFile)
    If (lngLOF > 128) Then

        ' Looking for the ID3v1 tag
        FileGet(intFile, strTag, lngLOF - 127, True)
        If (strTag.ToUpper <> "TAG") Then

            ' The ID3v1 tag not found.
            bTagExists = False
            mobjFrame(0) = ""
            mobjFrame(1) = ""
            mobjFrame(2) = ""
            mobjFrame(3) = ""
            mobjFrame(4) = ""
            mobjFrame(5) = ""
            mobjFrame(6) = ""

        Else
```

```
        ' The ID3v1 tag found.
        bTagExists = True

        ' Reading the information blocks from the file
        FileGet(intFile, strTitle)
        FileGet(intFile, strArtist)
        FileGet(intFile, strAlbum)
        FileGet(intFile, strYear)
        FileGet(intFile, strComment)
        FileGet(intFile, bytDummy)
        FileGet(intFile, bytTrack)
        FileGet(intFile, bytGenre)

        ' Correlating the contents of the blocks with the properties
        mobjFrame(0) = strTitle
        mobjFrame(1) = strArtist
        mobjFrame(2) = strAlbum
        mobjFrame(3) = strYear
        mobjFrame(4) = bytTrack
        mobjFrame(5) = strComment
        mobjFrame(6) = bytGenre

    End If
  End If

  ' Closing the file
  FileClose(intFile)

End Sub

' Updating the information
Public Sub Update()

  ' The look-up table
  Dim strTag As New String(" ", 3)
  Dim strTitle As New String(" ", 30)
  Dim strArtist As New String(" ", 30)
  Dim strAlbum As New String(" ", 30)
  Dim strYear As New String(" ", 4)
  Dim strComment As New String(" ", 28)
  Dim bytDummy As Byte
  Dim bytTrack As Byte
  Dim bytGenre As Byte

  ' Opening the file
  Dim intFile As Integer = FreeFile()
```

```
FileOpen(intFile, strFileName, OpenMode.Binary, _
    OpenAccess.ReadWrite, OpenShare.LockWrite)

' Obtaining the file's length
Dim lngLOF As Long = LOF(intFile)
If (lngLOF > 0) Then
    If (lngLOF > 128) Then

        ' Checking for the ID3v1 tag presence
        FileGet(intFile, strTag, lngLOF - 127)
        If (strTag.ToUpper <> "TAG") Then

            ' If there is no tag, then adding it
            Seek(intFile, lngLOF)
            strTag = "TAG"
            FilePut(intFile, strTag)

        End If

        ' Allocating blocks for writing
        strTitle = LSet(mobjFrame(0), Len(strTitle))
        strArtist = LSet(mobjFrame(1), Len(strArtist))
        strAlbum = LSet(mobjFrame(2), Len(strAlbum))
        strYear = LSet(mobjFrame(3), Len(strYear))
        bytTrack = mobjFrame(4)
        strComment = LSet(mobjFrame(5), Len(strComment))
        bytGenre = mobjFrame(6)

        ' Writing the data to the file
        FilePut(intFile, strTitle)
        FilePut(intFile, strArtist)
        FilePut(intFile, strAlbum)
        FilePut(intFile, strYear)
        FilePut(intFile, strComment)
        FilePut(intFile, bytDummy)
        FilePut(intFile, bytTrack)
        FilePut(intFile, bytGenre)

    End If
End If

' Closing the file
FileClose(intFile)

End Sub
End Class
```

A short explanation of what the class just created does is in order. First of all, it processes the file's name. If there is no such file, a corresponding message is issued. Next, the file itself is processed. The last 128 bytes of the file are read and a search for the special signature is conducted. If the signature is found, further processing of the file begins. Various song data are determined by comparing the bytes to the information in the tag look-up table. This concludes the file processing.

Now, we can either extract information contained in MP3 files or replace it with new information. This is what is carried out in the main form of the project. Add seven labels on the form named lblTitle, lblArtist, lblAlbum, lblYear, lblTrack, lblComment, and lblGenre. Set their Text properties to the following values: Album name, Artist, Album, Year, Track, Comment, and Genre, respectively. Now, the first six labels need to be correlated with six text boxes named as follows: txtTitle, txtArtist, txtAlbum, txtYear, txtTrack, and txtComment. The Genre label is correlated with a list box named cboGenre: txtTitle, txtArtist, txtAlbum, txtYear, txtTrack, txtComment, cboGenre. Set the Text properties of the newly-added controls to blank. Now, add two buttons, which will be used to read and write information. Name them butGetTag and butUpdate, respectively. Set the Text properties of these buttons to Extract Information and Update. This concludes the visual programming stage of the project. Now, we are ready to start writing code. First we need to fill the list box with genre names. This will be done when the form is loaded (Listing 15.8).

Listing 15.8. Extracting Information from File Tags

```
    Private Sub Form1_Load(ByVal sender As System.Object, ByVal e As System.EventArgs) _
Handles MyBase.Load
        ' A sample of genre names
        cboGenre.Items.Add("Blues")
        cboGenre.Items.Add("ClassicRock")
        cboGenre.Items.Add("Country")
        cboGenre.Items.Add("Dance")
        cboGenre.Items.Add("Disco")
        cboGenre.Items.Add("Funk")
        cboGenre.Items.Add("Grunge")
        cboGenre.Items.Add("Hip-Hop")
        cboGenre.Items.Add("Jazz")
        cboGenre.Items.Add("Metal")
        cboGenre.Items.Add("NewAge")
        cboGenre.Items.Add("Oldies")
        cboGenre.Items.Add("Other")
        cboGenre.Items.Add("Pop")
        ' Finish the list yourself ☺
```

```
End Sub

Private Sub Button1_Click(ByVal sender As System.Object, ByVal e As  _
System.EventArgs) Handles butGetTag.Click
        Dim mp3 As New MP3TAG(Application.StartupPath & "..\..\cat.mp3")
        If (mp3.TagExists) Then
            txtTitle.Text = mp3.Frame(MP3TAG.Tag_Info.Title)
            txtArtist.Text = mp3.Frame(MP3TAG.Tag_Info.Artist)
            txtAlbum.Text = mp3.Frame(MP3TAG.Tag_Info.Album)
            txtYear.Text = mp3.Frame(MP3TAG.Tag_Info.Year)
            txtTrack.Text = MP3TAG.Tag_Info.Track
            txtComment.Text = mp3.Frame(MP3TAG.Tag_Info.Comment)
            cboGenre.SelectedIndex = mp3.Frame(MP3TAG.Tag_Info.Genre)
        End If
End Sub

Private Sub butUpdate_Click(ByVal sender As System.Object, ByVal e As  _
System.EventArgs) Handles butUpdate.Click
        Dim mp3 As New MP3TAG("e:\down\18.mp3")
        mp3.Frame(MP3TAG.Tag_Info.Title) = txtTitle.Text
        mp3.Frame(MP3TAG.Tag_Info.Album) = txtAlbum.Text
        ' I leave the task of implementing the genre number writing mechanism to you for
        ' self-development.
        mp3.Update()
End Sub
```

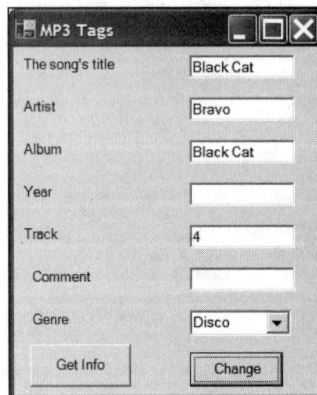

Fig. 15.2. MP3 tag editor

Frankly, I am tired of entering genre names into the list. I think you should also do your share of the work. I already listed all of the genres earlier. The information is extracted by simply clicking on the **Extract Information** button (Fig. 15.2). First, the name of the music file is specified. (For the experiment, I used "*Double Vision*," by Foreigner. You can use any MP3 song that you have on your computer). Next, the file is checked to see if it has the signature. If there is such a signature in the file, the necessary information is extracted and pigeonholed. The reverse process is also possible. If it is necessary to modify or add information, the file is opened for writing, and the data are written to the necessary place. The source code for this procedure is shown in the `butUpdate_Click` event. The code for this event does not include the operation for writing the genre number. I leave this task to you as homework.

Well, there you are! You have learned how to extract and add information to MP3 files. Now, you can create you own music player tag-editor plug-in.

15.8. Suggestions and Recommendations

There is a virtual piano sample written in VB 6.0 on the Microsoft site (the Midismpl.exe file). This example is very similar to the project described in *Section 15.5*, with the only difference being that, instead of WAV files, the program generates MIDI tones. Try to write this program in VB .NET.

Chapter 16: Programs That Talk

This chapter discusses the creation of speech applications using the SAPI (Speech Application Programming Interface) speech synthesis and recognition technology. At present, there are SAPI versions 4.0 and 5.0, which can be installed side by side. SAPI 4.0 is used extensively in the Microsoft Agent 2.0 technology, while SAPI 5.0 is included in operating systems of Windows releases XP and higher. Using speech engines in applications has become very fashionable of late. Many applications have acquired the ability to read out text, creating the effect of the program being alive.

16.1. The MS Agent 2.0 Technology

Speech engines comprise an integral part of the Microsoft Agent 2.0 technology. This technology is a complex of various advanced technologies designed to synthesize and recognize speech. The apotheosis of this technology is the use of animated characters, as these characters become distinctive by way of their being interactive and their ability to understand oral commands, and reproduce a specified text. The aspect of this technology that we will consider here is the use of MS Agent characters in VB .NET programs. Create a new project, and name it MSAgent. Now, you have to add a reference to the Microsoft Agent Control 2.0 to your project. This is done as follows. In the **Project** menu, select the **Add Reference** command. In the **Add Reference** dialog window that opens, select the **COM** tab, and then find **Microsoft Agent Control 2.0** line in the list. Select this line, and click on the **Select** button (Fig. 16.1).

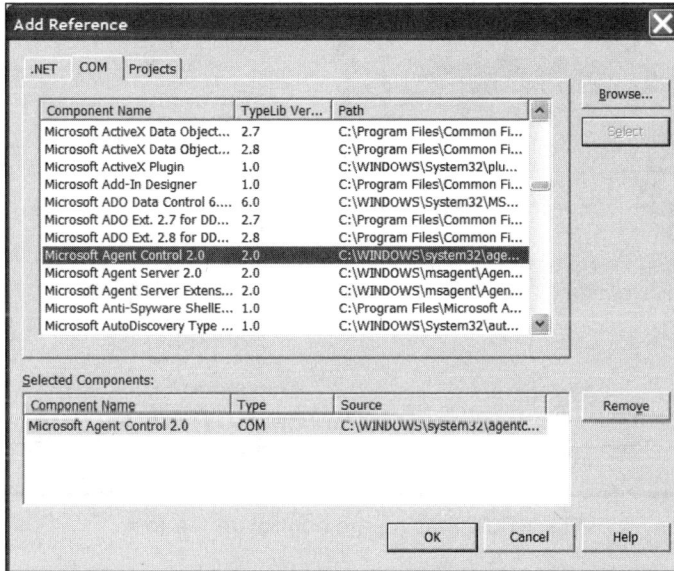

Fig. 16.1. Adding a reference to MS Agent to the project

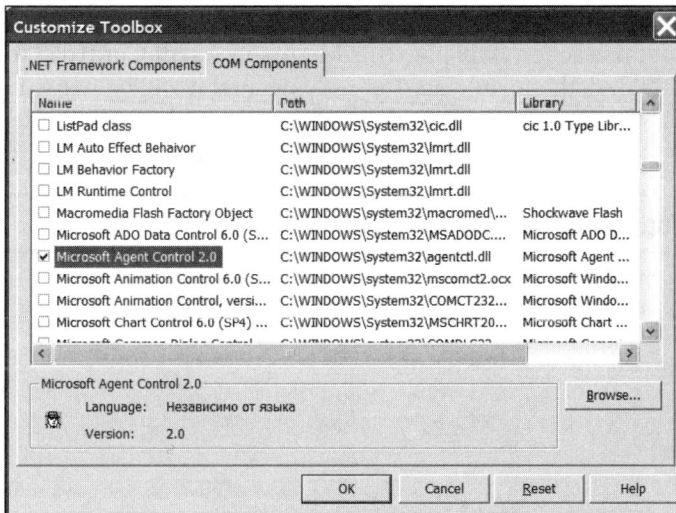

Fig. 16.2. Adding the control on the **Toolbox** bar

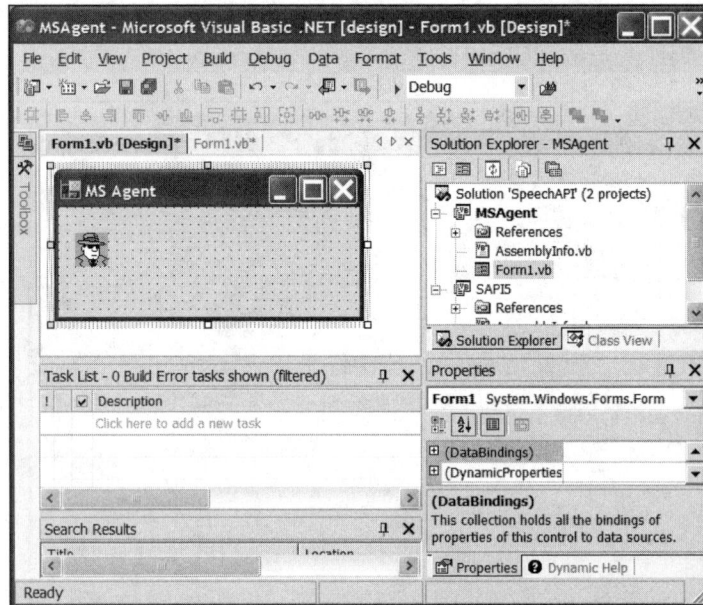

Fig. 16.3. Placing the control on the form

Then the control referenced has to be placed on the **Toolbox** bar. Select the **Add/ Remove Tools Item** in the **Tools** menu, and open the **COM Components** tab in the **Customize Toolbox** dialog window that opens. Put a check mark in the box for the **Microsoft Agent Control 2.0** (Fig. 16.2), and click the **OK** button.

Executing all of these actions will place the **Microsoft Agent Control 2.0** on the **Toolbox** bar. Place this control on the form (Fig. 16.3). By default, it will be named AxAgent1.

This concludes the visual programming part of the project. Now, open the code editor, and add the following code to the project (Listing 16.1).

Listing 16.1. Using MS Agent in Programs

```
'----------------------------------------
' MSAgent © 2004 Alexander Klimov
'----------------------------------------
Dim MyChar As AgentObjects.IAgentCtlCharacterEx

    Private Sub Form1_Load(ByVal sender As System.Object, ByVal e As System.EventArgs) _
Handles MyBase.Load
        ' Loading the character
        AxAgent1.Characters.Load("CharacterID")
        MyChar = AxAgent1.Characters("CharacterID")
```

```
' Displaying the character
MyChar.Show()
' Setting English language
MyChar.LanguageID = &H409
' Selecting a woman's voice
MyChar.TTSModeID = "{CA141FD0-AC7F-11D1-97A3-006008273008}"
' Speaking
MyChar.Speak("I thought I saw a pussycat!")
End Sub
```

Fig. 16.4. The animated character

Compile the project and launch the program. You will see an animated character saying the specified phrase (Fig. 16.4).

I should warn you right off the bat that your character may appear different than the character shown in Fig. 16.4. I have been using this technology for a long time and have more than 100 various characters in my collection. You can also replenish your collection of agents by visiting the site **http://www.msagentring.org/chars.htm**. By default, you most likely have only one character installed on your machine (for Windows Me/2000/XP and higher).

In addition to displaying the specified text in a balloon, characters can also speak it. But you need to install a few additional files for this to be the case. Owners of machines running under Windows XP also have to install SAPI 4.0 support, despite the fact that Windows XP already provides built-in SAPI 5.1 support. The confusion with the SAPI versions created a surge of bewilderment on forums devoted to MS Agent. Without fail, each new member asks the same old question: Why don't the characters on my computer running under WinXP talk? The two SAPI versions can be installed side-by-side on one system. More detailed information about installing the necessary files can be obtained on the following site: **www.microsoft.com/msagent/downloads/user.asp**.

16.2. Using Two Characters

Having been introduced to the MS Agent, we can now move on to a more sophisticated example. In the TwoAgents project, we will consider working with more than one character, adding commands to their context menu, and controlling an agent's actions with spoken commands.

In my example, I used two feline characters named Oscar and Felini, which I downloaded from the **http://www.msagentring.org/chars.htm** site and placed in the /Windows/ msagent/chars folder. This folder is the standard storage spot for characters. When a character is stored in the standard character-storage folder, it is no longer necessary to specify the full path to the character file, as simply providing the file's name is sufficient. If you prefer to use characters other than mine, you will have to change the names of the characters in the source code of the example. Unlike the first example, here we are not using the default character (which relieved us of the necessity to specify the path to the character file) but, instead, are instructing the program to use specific characters, with which to work. The source code for the program is provided in Listing 16.2.

Before getting down to coding, don't forget to reference the Microsoft Agent Control 2.0 to the project and to place an AxAgent1 control on the form.

Listing 16.2. Using MS Agent Characters

```
'-------------------------------------
' TwoAgents © 2004 Alexander Klimov
'-------------------------------------
    Dim Char1 As AgentObjects.IAgentCtlCharacterEx
    Dim Char2 As AgentObjects.IAgentCtlCharacterEx
    Dim Request As AgentObjects.IAgentCtlRequest

    Private Sub Form1_Load(ByVal sender As System.Object, ByVal e As System.EventArgs) _
Handles MyBase.Load
        ' Loading the characters
        AxAgent1.Characters.Load("felini", "felini.acs")
        Char1 = AxAgent1.Characters("felini")
        AxAgent1.Characters.Load("oscar", "oscar.acs")
        Char2 = AxAgent1.Characters("oscar")

        ' Displaying the characters on the screen in the specified locations
        Char1.Show()
        Char1.MoveTo(100, 200)
        Char2.Show()
        Char2.MoveTo(500, 200)

        ' Setting English language
        Char1.LanguageID = &H409
```

```
        Char2.LanguageID = &H409

        ' Add the Greeting command.
        Char2.Commands.Add("Hi", "Greeting", "hello", True, True)

        ' Setting a woman's and a man's voices
        Char1.TTSModeID = "{CA141FD0-AC7F-11D1-97A3-006008273008}"
        Char2.TTSModeID = "{CA141FD0-AC7F-11D1-97A3-006008273000}"

        ' Speaking
        Char2.Speak("Hello, pussycat! Who is your favorite movie actor?")
        Request = Char2.Play("GestureRight")

        ' Waiting till Oscar gestures right
        Char1.Wait(Request)

        ' Answering
        Char1.Play("Surprised")
        Request = Char1.Speak(txtSpeak.Text)

        Char2.Wait(Request)
        Request = Char2.Speak("I think he is the greatest, too!\Mrk=1\")
    End Sub

    Private Sub butSpeak_Click(ByVal sender As System.Object, ByVal e As _
System.EventArgs) Handles butSpeak.Click
        ' Enter your text into the text box.
        Char1.Speak(txtSpeak.Text)

    End Sub

    Private Sub AxAgent1_Command(ByVal sender As Object, ByVal e As _
AxAgentObjects._AgentEvents_CommandEvent) Handles AxAgent1.Command

        If e.userInput.name = "Hi" Then
            ' If the user says "Hello,"
            ' wave a paw in response.
            Char2.Play("Greet")
            Char2.Speak("Hi, buddy? Can you spare some milk?")
        End If
    End Sub

    Private Sub AxAgent1_Bookmark(ByVal sender As Object, ByVal e As _
AxAgentObjects._AgentEvents_BookmarkEvent) Handles AxAgent1.Bookmark
        If e.bookmarkID = 1 Then
            Char1.MoveTo(300,300)
        End If
    End Sub
```

Let's examine what the code you just wrote does. At the very beginning, we declare a few variables. The `Char1` and `Char2` variables are objects holding the properties and methods of the characters. The `Request` object is used to synchronize the code's execution. The problem is that the characters operate in asynchronous mode. Imagine the following situation: You need to reproduce a certain dialog between two characters and have patiently, word-by-word, written out all of the lines for the characters but, when you run the program, you do not hear them talking the way they should be. Instead, all of your characters talk at the same time, without waiting for their turn.

```
' Displaying the characters on the screen in the specified locations
Char1.Show()
Char1.MoveTo(100, 200)
Char2.Show()
Char2.MoveTo(500, 200)
```

So the characters are first displayed on the screen. The `MoveTo` method is used to specify a specific location to place an agent. By the way, if you want your character to appear at the specified location right away, call the `MoveTo` method before calling the `Show` method. In our example, the characters first appear in the upper left-hand corner of the screen, and then move to the specified locations.

```
' Setting English language
Char1.LanguageID = &H409
Char2.LanguageID = &H409
```

In the above code, we make sure that the appropriate language ID is set to reproduce English speech. Languages other than English can also be used, but you will have to learn how to do this on your own from the appropriate documentation.

```
' Add the Greeting command.
Char2.Commands.Add("Hi", "Greeting", "hello", True, True)
```

The `Add` operator is used to add your own commands to the characters' context menus. I added the `Greeting` command. When this command is selected, the character plays back the specified animation. This command is an alternative to the spoken command `Hello`, in case you have no microphone connected. If you do have a microphone connected, you can give spoken commands. We will consider this aspect a little later.

So, now that the language has been selected, we have to choice a voice: male or female.

```
' Selecting a man's and a woman's voices
Char1.TTSModeID = "{CA141FD0-AC7F-11D1-97A3-006008273008}"
Char2.TTSModeID = "{CA141FD0-AC7F-11D1-97A3-006008273000}"
```

You will have to find the values for different voices in the VB .NET documentation on your own. Next, the first phrase is displayed on the screen and the `GestureRight` animation is played (the character points to the left of the screen). This is where we will need the `Request` object.

```
Request = Char2.Play("GestureRight")
```

The second character will not do anything until the event we had predefined takes place. As soon as this happens, the character starts performing its actions. Note that we use the `Request` object again here to synchronize the actions.

```
Request = Char1.Speak(txtSpeak.Text)
Char2.Wait(Request)
Request = Char2.Speak("I think he is the greatest, too!\Mrk=1\")
```

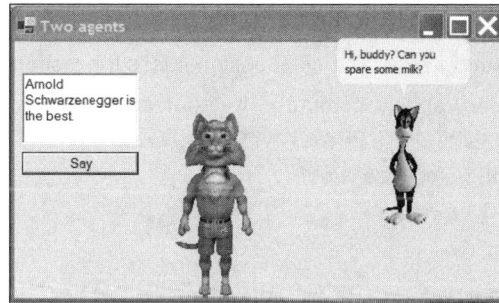

Fig. 16.5. Two characters talking

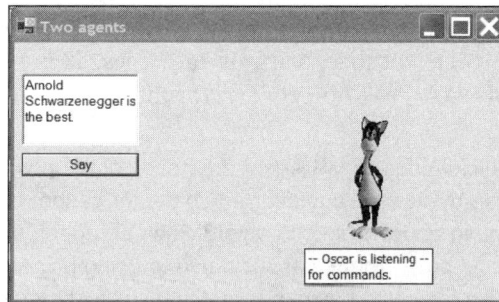

Fig. 16.6. The character is trying to understand a microphone command

There is another way to synchronize characters' actions, using `Mrk` tags, which define a bookmark in the spoken text. As soon as the character speaks the phrase containing the bookmark, the command defined in this bookmark by the `AxAgent.Bookmark` procedure is executed. This code makes the Felini character move to another location on the screen. The reaction to voice commands is specified in the `AxAgent1.Command` procedure.

And now, the final touches. Place a text box and a timer on the project form. I entered "Arnold Schwarzenegger is the best." in the text box for the ensuing dialog to make sense. Afterwards, the character will speak any text entered in the text box upon a click of the button. You can now run the program. When you do this, you will be treated to a short two-actor play (Fig. 16.5). After the characters are done talking to each other, say "Hello" into the microphone while holding the <Scroll Lock> key down (Fig. 16.6). If you pronounce this word properly, the character will recognize it and carry out the specified action.

Any phrase can be entered in the text field. Pressing the button will read this text with a synthesized voice.

I have described just a minute fraction here of what can be done using the MS Agent technology. Using the two examples described above as a base, you can create remarkable programs that will amaze users by way of their unusual interface.

A little laugh

A new-generation computer is being presented at a computer show somewhere in the not-so-distant future. The chief designer tells the visitors:

— This is a very unique computer. It understands spoken commands. Now any of you can try to control this prodigy machine.

A voice from the crowd calls out:

— Format C:. Enter!

16.3. Using SAPI 5.1

Using animated assistants in a program is not always justified. Sometimes, you only need text to be read out, without any visual agents. Windows XP contains a very interesting utility, called Narrator, which vocalizes various messages. It is started by executing the **Start/Programs/Accessories/Accessibility/Narrator** menu sequence.

By the way, aficionados of MS Agent 2.0 have come up with a very interesting trick. The fact is that, by design, a minimized character cannot talk. But what is to prevent you from creating an invisible character? Such an agent, or rather, an empty space, was created and programmers accustomed to using MS Agent use the new agent in their programs. Users don't even suspect that it is a character that talks to them!

NOTE

Thus, if you only need to read text, without any characters prancing around, you can take advantage of the SAPI 5.1 speech synthesis technology.

The technology is demonstrated in the SAPI5 project. First, you will have to reference the necessary components to the project. Select the **Add Reference** command in the **Project** menu item, open the **COM** tab in the dialog window that opens, and find the **Microsoft Voice Text** item. Select this line, and click on the **Select** button. After selecting the necessary object, click the **OK** button to close the dialog window. Next, right-click on the **Toolbox** bar, and select the **Add/Remove Items** command in the context menu. Open the **COM Components** tab in the dialog window that opens, and put a mark in the check box next to the **TextToSpeech Class**. Click on the **OK** button to close the dialog window. This will place a new component of the same name on the **Components** tab of the **Toolbox** bar, with an icon looking like a half-open mouth.

Place this control on the form. The result will be somewhat unexpected: There will be a large half-open mouth on the form! If you do not want this mouth to show during program execution, you can set its Visible property to False. We will not hide the mouth in our example, and will be treated to an interesting show: The lips will move in sync with the spoken text, creating the illusion of a human talking. All of the code is contained in the click event handler of the button (Listing 16.3).

Listing 16.3. A Talking Mouth

```
'------------------------------------
' SAPI5 © 2005 Alexander Klimov
'------------------------------------

    Private Sub Button1_Click(ByVal sender As System.Object, ByVal e As _
System.EventArgs) Handles Button1.Click
        AxTextToSpeech1.Speak("I love cats!")
    End Sub
```

Run the program, make sure that the computer speakers are on, and click on the button. You should hear my declaration of love (Fig. 16.7).

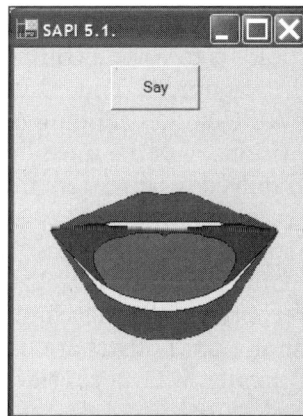

Fig. 16.7. The talking mouth program in action

16.4. Suggestions and Recommendations

Speech synthesis is used extensively for creating audio books, reference documentation, educational games for children, etc. You can obtain more information on the subject in the documentation on the site **http://msdn.microsoft.com**.

Chapter 17: The Laws of Nature

Everything that surrounds us obeys the laws of nature: an apple falling on someone's head, a balloon rising into the sky, a ball bouncing up and down, etc. Once, when I was still in school, my physics teacher told us to write a composition on the subject "One Day without Friction" as a homework assignment. This assignment had the students' make their imaginations go wild: There were clothes slipping off, cars wrecking, etc. The class, during which we read our compositions, was the most entertaining physics class we ever had. But, all jokes aside, if friction indeed disappeared, the actual consequences would be difficult to imagine.

However paradoxical it may sound, it is much easier to write a computer program modeling one or another law of nature. You must realize that studying these laws is not idle curiosity, but a necessary precondition for developing dynamic games. Games like ping-pong, flight simulators, arcanoids, and others are based on the laws of gravity, elasticity, free fall, and others. In this chapter, we will consider several typical examples of the use of the laws of nature.

17.1. Bouncing

Bouncing shapes off surfaces is a very popular technique employed when creating games. This is most often encountered in arcade games. The most striking examples of shapes bouncing off surfaces are games like ping-pong and billiards. So our task, then, is to learn to write programs, in which a shape (usually a ball) bounces off a surface and moves in the opposite direction according to certain laws of physics.

As a rule, books describe bouncing algorithms that are entirely ready for use. But this approach has a significant, in the fact that programmers do not obtain the necessary programming skills. Consequently, when a programmer encounters a similar problem, not possessing the gcneral knowledge of solving complex problems, he or she becomes disoriented. I suggest that you take a different approach. When defining a complex task, first try to make it as simple as possible. Then start adding new conditions to it, gradually arriving at the desired goal. Let's break down the bouncing problem into constituent parts, starting with the simplest.

Create a new project and name it Bounce. Place a label on the form and name it lblBall. This is our first simplification. Programs usually draw a circle to imitate the ball. But this approach creates pitfalls that can prevent us from concentrating on comprehending the bouncing technique. Using a ready object will make our life easier. To make the label look at least somewhat like a ball, set its Text property to 0, and also increase the font size and set its background color to red.

- ❏ Name = lblBall
- ❏ AutoSize = True
- ❏ BackColor = Red
- ❏ Font.Size = 20
- ❏ Text = 0

Also, place a timer and a button to start our improvised ball moving on the form. Set their properties to the following values:

- ❏ Name = butStart
- ❏ Text = Start
- ❏ Name = tmrBounce
- ❏ Interval = 50

The visual part of the programming is done, so you can now start writing the code. The simplest thing that can be done with the ball is to make it move in some direction. Let's make it move to the left. Note that we are throwing the ball strictly horizontally (remember our rule: Set yourself as simple a task as possible). This task can be solved by the code provided in Listing 17.1.

Listing 17.1. Making an Object Move to the Left

```
'-------------------------------------------
' Bounce © 2004 Alexander Klimov
'-------------------------------------------
    Private Sub butStart_Click(ByVal sender As System.Object, ByVal e As _
System.EventArgs) Handles butStart.Click
```

```
        tmrBounce.Enabled = True
    End Sub


    Private Sub tmrBounce_Tick(ByVal sender As System.Object, ByVal e As        _
System.EventArgs) Handles tmrBounce.Tick
        lblBall.Left = lblBall.Left - 1
    End Sub
```

The code is quite primitive. Clicking on the button starts the timer, which, in turn, moves the object one pixel left with every tick. As an exercise, try to modify the code to move the improvised ball to the right, up, and down. I hope that you have been able to handle this task successfully. Now, let's make things a bit more difficult. In the program as it is now, the ball keeps on moving in the specified direction when it reaches the form's edge, ultimately disappearing from the form. Let's make it stop when it reaches the form's left edge (Listing 17.2).

Listing 17.2. Stopping the Moving Ball

```
    Private Sub tmrBounce_Tick(ByVal sender As System.Object, ByVal e As        _
System.EventArgs) Handles tmrBounce.Tick
        If lblBall.Left <= 0 Then
            tmrBounce.Enabled = False
        End If
        lblBall.Left = lblBall.Left - 1

    End Sub
```

Here, we have introduced a check to see if the ball has reached the left edge of the form. When this event occurs, the timer is stopped. Now pay close attention! We are going to learn how to have the ball bounce off of the form's edge. As you can see, during the rebound movement, the object's coordinates increase instead of decreasing. In mathematical terms, this means that the sign of the movement vector has changed to the opposite. For this, we will need a new, class-level variable, gDirection, which will be responsible for the direction of the ball's movement. This flag will take on two values: +1 and −1. We will use the value of this flag to determine, in which direction the object must be moved. But, first, the flag must be initialized:

```
Dim gDirection As Integer = 1
```

And one line is modified in the tmrBounce_Tick event handler code:

```
lblBall.Left = lblBall.Left - 1 * gDirection
```

As soon as the object reaches the edge of the form (If lblBall.left <=0), the value of the gDirection flag is changed to the opposite, thereby making the object's coordinates start increasing. Run the program (Listing 17.3) to make sure that this is actually the case. As you have likely already guessed, a similar technique is used to bounce the ball off the right side of the form (don't forget to account for the width of the ball itself).

Listing 17.3. Bouncing an Object off Walls

```
    Private Sub tmrBounce_Tick(ByVal sender As System.Object, ByVal e As _
System.EventArgs) Handles tmrBounce.Tick
        lblBall.Left = lblBall.Left - 1 * gDirection

        ' Bouncing off the form's left edge
        If lblBall.Left <= 0 Then
            gDirection = -1
        End If

        ' Bouncing off the form's right edge. The ball's width is taken into account.
        If lblBall.Left >= ClientSize.Width - lblBall.Width Then
            gDirection = 1
        End If
    End Sub
```

17.2. Angled Bouncing

We have learned to bounce objects off sides, provided that they move strictly perpendicular to them. But, in the real life, objects move at an angle to surfaces. Consequently, we need to learn to bounce objects moving at an angle. Create a new project, Bounce2, and copy into it all of the code from the previous example, which will serve as a template. When the ball is bounced strictly horizontally (or vertically), the ball's coordinates change along only one coordinate axis. Angled bouncing involves changes in both coordinate axes. Consequently, we need to change two object properties simultaneously: Top and Left.

Let's consider this process in more detail. As usual, we will take the simplest case. When the ball bounces off the vertical sides of the form, a careful examination of the ball's trajectory reveals that the value of the X (Left) coordinate changes to the opposite: After bouncing off the left side it starts increasing, and after bouncing off the right side it starts decreasing. Analogously, when the ball bounces off of the horizontal sides of the form, the value of the Y (Top) coordinate changes to the opposite. Summing up these observations, we arrive at the conclusion that, for bouncing off at an angle, one global variable to indicate the ball's direction is not sufficient. Consequently, the gDirection variable is removed, and two global variables are created in its place: gDirX and gDirY. Accordingly, the code for the timer's tick event is modified to process all four of the possible versions of the ball bouncing off the form's sides (Listing 17.4).

Listing 17.4. Angled Bouncing

```
'-------------------------------------
' Bounce2 © 2004 Alexander Klimov
'-------------------------------------
    Dim gDirX As Integer = 1
    Dim gDirY As Integer = 1


    Private Sub tmrBounce_Tick(ByVal sender As System.Object, ByVal e As _
System.EventArgs) Handles tmrBounce.Tick
        lblBall.Left = lblBall.Left - 5 * gDirX
        lblBall.Top = lblBall.Top - 5 * gDirY


        ' Bouncing off the form's left edge
        If lblBall.Left <= 0 Then
            gDirX = -1
        End If


        ' Bouncing off the form's right edge. The ball's width is taken into account.
        If lblBall.Left >= ClientSize.Width - lblBall.Width Then
            gDirX = 1
        End If


        ' Bouncing off the form's top edge
        If lblBall.Top <= 0 Then
            gDirY = -1
        End If


        ' Bouncing off the form's bottom edge. The ball's width is taken into account.
        If lblBall.Top >= ClientSize.Height - lblBall.Height Then
            gDirY = 1
        End If
    End Sub


    Private Sub butStart_Click(ByVal sender As System.Object, ByVal e As _
System.EventArgs) Handles butStart.Click
        tmrBounce.Enabled = True
    End Sub
```

17.3. Bouncing a Real Ball

In practice, no one bounces buttons, labels, lists, or other controls. These are intended for entirely different purposes. In reality, when writing games, programmers use shapes provided by the Graphics class, as is demonstrated in the RealBall project (Listing 17.5).

Listing 17.5. Bouncing Graphics Objects

```
'-------------------------------------
' RealBall © 2004 Alexander Klimov
'-------------------------------------
    ' The ball's current coordinates
    Private xCenter, yCenter As Integer

    ' The ball's size
    Private xBallSize As Integer = 40
    Private yBallSize As Integer = 40

    ' The direction of the ball's movement
    Dim gDirX, gDirY As Integer

    Dim cxTotal, cyTotal As Integer
    Private bm As Bitmap

    Private Sub Form1_Resize(ByVal sender As Object, ByVal e As System.EventArgs) _
Handles MyBase.Resize
        Dim g As Graphics = CreateGraphics()

        gDirX = 3
        gDirY = 3
        cxTotal = (xBallSize + 2 * gDirX)
        cyTotal = (yBallSize + 2 * gDirY)

        bm = New Bitmap(cxTotal, cyTotal)
        g = Graphics.FromImage(bm)
        g.Clear(BackColor)
        DrawBall(g, New Rectangle(gDirX, gDirY, _
                                  xBallSize, yBallSize))
        g.Dispose()

        ' Placing the ball in the center of the form
        xCenter = ClientSize.Width \ 2
```

```
        yCenter = ClientSize.Height \ 2
    End Sub


    Protected Overridable Sub DrawBall(ByVal g As Graphics, _
                                    ByVal rect As Rectangle)
        ' Drawing the ball
        g.FillEllipse(Brushes.Plum, rect)
    End Sub


    Private Sub Timer1_Tick(ByVal sender As System.Object, ByVal e As System.EventArgs) _
Handles Timer1.Tick
        Dim g As Graphics = CreateGraphics()
        g.DrawImage(bm, xCenter - cxTotal \ 2, _
                        yCenter - cyTotal \ 2, cxTotal, cyTotal)
        g.Dispose()


        xCenter += gDirX
        yCenter += gDirY


        ' Changing the direction of the movement on reaching any edge
        If (xCenter + xBallSize / 2 >= ClientSize.Width) OrElse _
           (xCenter - xBallSize / 2 <= 0) Then
            gDirX = -gDirX
        End If


        If (yCenter + yBallSize / 2 >= ClientSize.Height) OrElse _
           (yCenter - yBallSize / 2 <= 0) Then
            gDirY = -gDirY
        End If
    End Sub
End Sub
```

Now, our example looks more like a real program and can be used as a foundation for creating games, in which objects are bounced off surfaces.

17.4. The Diminishing Bounce

Diminishing bounce is a special case of bounce. If you raise a ball over your head and then drop it, the ball will obey the law of gravity and fall to the ground, bounce up (acted on by the force of elasticity), and then start falling again. Every time the ball bounces, it will return to a point lower then on the previous bounce. As usual, we will simplify our task and take the ball always dropping onto the same spot as a given. We will also use another simplification, making a regular button to represent the ball.

> Without question, a rectangular button bears only a remote resemblance to a ball. Actually, it does not look like a ball at all. But it will do to help us understand the important part: the principle of the diminishing bounce.
>
> *NOTE*

In real life, a bouncing object loses some energy with each bounce and, consequently, each consecutive bounce is lower than the previous one. This means that we will need an additional variable to control the diminishment of the bounce. The project to demonstrate the diminishing bounce is called `FallBall`. Place two buttons and one timer on the project form. The code controlling the ball button's bounces is located in the handler of the timer's `Tick` event.

Listing 17.6. A Diminishing Bounce

```
'--------------------------------------
' FallBall © 2004 Alexander Klimov
'--------------------------------------
        ' The current position of the object
        Dim cy As Integer
        ' The lower edge of the form
        Dim floorY As Integer = ClientSize.Height
        ' The falling speed
        Dim ymov As Integer
        ' The force of gravity
        Dim gravity As Integer = 1
        ' The fade coefficient
        Dim decay As Single = 0.9

        Private Sub Button1_Click(ByVal sender As System.Object, ByVal e As _
System.EventArgs) Handles Button1.Click
            ' Returning the button to the upper part of the form
            Button2.Top = 10
            ' Enabling the timer
            Timer1.Enabled = True
        End Sub

        Private Sub Timer1_Tick(ByVal sender As System.Object, ByVal e As  _
System.EventArgs) Handles Timer1.Tick

            ymov += gravity
            cy = Button2.Top + ymov ' Dropping
            Button2.Top = cy
```

```
        If Button2.Height + Button2.Top >= floorY Then
            ' If the lower edge of the form is reached,
            ' bouncing up, reversing the direction of the movement
            ' and with fading speed
            ymov *= -1 * decay
            Button2.Top = floorY - Button2.Height
        End If
    End Sub
```

Let's examine the example. At the beginning of the program, I declared several class-level variables responsible for the direction and speed of the movement, as well as the rate, at which the bounce will be diminished. Everything else is simple. Pressing the first button starts the timer, and the object starts falling under the force of its own weight (imitating the force of gravity).

```
    ymov += gravity
    cy = Button2.Top + ymov ' Dropping
    Button2.Top = cy
```

When the object reaches the lower edge of the form, the direction of the movement is reversed, and the force of the bounce is reduced, with the help of the decay variable. The force of the bounce can be controlled by changing the value of this variable. When the value of the variable approaches 0, the ball will drop dead, without the slightest of a bounce. I tried to simplify the above example to the minimum. You may have to modify the example to fit your own requirements.

17.5. Suggestions and Recommendations

In this short chapter, I considered only the simplest examples based on various laws of nature. Try to remember other laws of nature and model them on your computer. Try, for example, to model the trajectory of a cannon ball, which, as is known, is parabolic. You can provide for changing the angle of the shot, thereby changing how far the cannon ball flies and where it falls. As you can see, to be able to write an example of this type requires that you have knowledge of mathematics and physics. And if you plan on concentrating on writing games in the future, you simply have to come to love the pure sciences.

Chapter 18: Games

He who programs his own computer games enjoys them twice.

Jacques Arsak

Any programmer has probably tried to write a computer game. Programming computer games is one of the most popular subjects and is of interest to both beginning and experienced programmers. Creating computer games presents a good opportunity for professional development. Programming games requires good knowledge not only of programming languages but also of mathematics, physics, graphics, etc. In this chapter, I will show you how to write a few games. Note that the subject of computer games programming is so extensive that even a whole book on it would just nick its surface. The scope of this book simply will not allow me to consider all aspects related to programming games. Therefore, I will only consider the simplest implementations of some of the most interesting games. My goal is to awaken your interests to programming games and to show that such programming is not difficult.

18.1. Crack the Safe: Version 1

There was a popular quest-like game once, named *"The Pilot Brothers: Following the Striped Elephant."* Once while playing this game I got stuck on one level on a task in which a safe had to be opened. The locking system was the following: There were 16 handles on the door, arranged in four rows and four columns. Some handles were oriented horizontally, others vertically. When a handle was turned, the orientation of all handles in the same row and column was changed to the opposite. This was where I got stuck for a long time. The same fate befell many other users, who were flooding game forums with questions about how to open the safe. By some miracle I managed to hit on the right combination and to move on. But there was that lingering feeling of dissatisfaction with how I did it. So I decided to write a program to recreate this problem. At that time, I was only beginning my career in programming and was somewhat apprehensive to set about this task. Fortuitously, on the vast expanses of the Internet, I came across a site that had this game written in VBScript, which is a simplified version of Visual Basic. So it was easy for me to migrate the code to VB 5.0. The code, being so simple, also made it possible to migrate the game to VB 6.0 and VB .NET 2003. Unfortunately, I have lost the name of the author who wrote the game script. Still, I am thankful to him for setting me in the right direction. Before we start writing our first game in VB .NET 2003, look at its HTML version (Listing 18.1).

Listing 18.1. The Crack the Safe Game in VBScript

```
<HTML><HEAD><TITLE>THE PILOT BROTHERS</TITLE>
<META http-equiv=Content-Type content="text/html;

charset=windows-1252">
<STYLE type=text/css>
.button {
       BORDER-TOP-WIDTH: 5px; FONT-WEIGHT: bold;

BORDER-LEFT-WIDTH: 5px; FONT-SIZE: 30px; BORDER-LEFT-COLOR:

steelblue; BACKGROUND: darkslategray; BORDER-BOTTOM-WIDTH: 5px;

BORDER-BOTTOM-COLOR: steelblue; WIDTH: 50px; COLOR: #ffffff;

BORDER-TOP-COLOR: steelblue; HEIGHT: 50px; BORDER-RIGHT-WIDTH:

5px; BORDER-RIGHT-COLOR: steelblue
}
.button1 {
       BORDER-TOP-WIDTH: 7px; FONT-WEIGHT: bold;

BORDER-LEFT-WIDTH: 7px; FONT-SIZE: 13px; BORDER-LEFT-COLOR:

steelblue; BACKGROUND: steelblue; BORDER-BOTTOM-WIDTH: 7px;

BORDER-BOTTOM-COLOR: steelblue; WIDTH: 100px; COLOR: #ffffff;

BORDER-TOP-COLOR: steelblue; HEIGHT: 35px; BORDER-RIGHT-WIDTH:
```

```
7px; BORDER-RIGHT-COLOR: steelblue
}
</STYLE>
</HEAD>
<BODY>
<H2>THE PILOT BROTHERS</H2>
  <FORM name=game>
<div id="start">
  <P>A game based on THE PILOT BROTHERS quest.
  Click the cells until all of them have dots or O's in them.
  Click the Start button to play.</P></DIV>

  <DL>
    <DD align="center">
    <TABLE cellSpacing=0 cellPadding=0 width=200 border=0>
      <TBODY>
      <TR>
        <TD width=100><TT><INPUT class=button1 type=button value=START name=start></TT>
        </TD>
        <TD width=100><TT><INPUT class=button1 type=button name=points></TT>
        </TD></TR></TBODY></TABLE>
    <TABLE id=pole height=200 cellSpacing=0 cellPadding=0 width=200 border=0>
      <TBODY>
      <TR>
        <TD width=50><INPUT class=button type=button name=but1></TD>
        <TD width=50><INPUT class=button type=button name=but2></TD>
        <TD width=50><INPUT class=button type=button name=but3></TD>
        <TD width=50><INPUT class=button type=button name=but4></TD></TR>
      <TR>
        <TD width=50><INPUT class=button type=button name=but5></TD>
        <TD width=50><INPUT class=button type=button name=but6></TD>
        <TD width=50><INPUT class=button type=button name=but7></TD>
        <TD width=50><INPUT class=button type=button name=but8></TD></TR>
      <TR>
        <TD width=50><INPUT class=button type=button name=but9></TD>
        <TD width=50><INPUT class=button type=button name=but10></TD>
        <TD width=50><INPUT class=button type=button name=but11></TD>
        <TD width=50><INPUT class=button type=button name=but12></TD></TR>
      <TR>
        <TD width=50><INPUT class=button type=button name=but13></TD>
        <TD width=50><INPUT class=button type=button name=but14></TD>
        <TD width=50><INPUT class=button type=button name=but15></TD>
        <TD width=50><INPUT class=button type=button name=but16></TD>
      </TR></TBODY></TABLE></FORM>
```

```vbscript
    <SCRIPT language=VBScript>
<!--
' An inversion game, based on one of the tasks in THE PILOT BROTHERS game
dim c(16)
dim a(16)
dim s
dim nn
 Randomize
pole.style.visibility = "hidden"
start.style.visibility = ""
sub start_onclick
s=0
        for i=1 to 16
        c(i)=int(rnd(1)+0.5)
         if c(i)=0 then a(i)="0" else a(i)="."
        next
pole.style.visibility = ""
start.style.visibility = "hidden"
 call move
end sub
sub points_onclick
        nn = nn + 1
        if nn >= 10 then
                alert "Not tired of clicking yet? Better get down to business!"
                nn = 0
        end if
end sub
sub move
document.game.but1.value=a(1)
document.game.but2.value=a(2)
document.game.but3.value=a(3)
document.game.but4.value=a(4)
document.game.but5.value=a(5)
document.game.but6.value=a(6)
document.game.but7.value=a(7)
document.game.but8.value=a(8)
document.game.but9.value=a(9)
document.game.but10.value=a(10)
document.game.but11.value=a(11)
document.game.but12.value=a(12)
document.game.but13.value=a(13)
document.game.but14.value=a(14)
document.game.but15.value=a(15)
document.game.but16.value=a(16)
```

```
f=0
for i=1 to 16
if a(i)="." then f=f+1
next
if f=16 then call winner
s=s+1
document.game.points.value=s-1 & "move(s)"
end sub
sub winner
document.game.but1.value="Y"
document.game.but2.value="O"
document.game.but3.value="U"
document.game.but4.value=""
document.game.but5.value="H"
document.game.but6.value="A"
document.game.but7.value="V"
document.game.but8.value="E"
document.game.but9.value=""
document.game.but10.value="W"
document.game.but11.value="O"
document.game.but12.value="N"
document.game.but13.value="!"
document.game.but14.value="!"
document.game.but15.value="!"
document.game.but16.value="!"

end sub

sub but1_onclick
 for i=1 to 4
 if a(i)="0" then a(i)="." else a(i)="0"
 next
  for i=5 to 13 step 4
  if a(i)="0" then a(i)="." else a(i)="0"
  next
 call move
end sub

sub but2_onclick
 for i=1 to 4
 if a(i)="0" then a(i)="." else a(i)="0"
 next
  for i=6 to 14 step 4
  if a(i)="0" then a(i)="." else a(i)="0"
```

```
 next
 call move
end sub

sub but3_onclick
 for i=1 to 4
 if a(i)="0" then a(i)="." else a(i)="0"
 next
  for i=7 to 15 step 4
  if a(i)="0" then a(i)="." else a(i)="0"
  next
 call move
end sub

sub but4_onclick
 for i=1 to 4
 if a(i)="0" then a(i)="." else a(i)="0"
 next
  for i=8 to 16 step 4
  if a(i)="0" then a(i)="." else a(i)="0"
  next
 call move
end sub

sub but5_onclick
 for i=5 to 8
 if a(i)="0" then a(i)="." else a(i)="0"
 next
  if a(1)="0" then a(1)="." else a(1)="0"
  if a(9)="0" then a(9)="." else a(9)="0"
  if a(13)="0" then a(13)="." else a(13)="0"
 call move
end sub

sub but6_onclick
 for i=5 to 8
 if a(i)="0" then a(i)="." else a(i)="0"
 next
  if a(2)="0" then a(2)="." else a(2)="0"
  if a(10)="0" then a(10)="." else a(10)="0"
  if a(14)="0" then a(14)="." else a(14)="0"
 call move
end sub
```

```
sub but7_onclick
 for i=5 to 8
 if a(i)="0" then a(i)="." else a(i)="0"
 next
  if a(3)="0" then a(3)="." else a(3)="0"
  if a(11)="0" then a(11)="." else a(11)="0"
  if a(15)="0" then a(15)="." else a(15)="0"
 call move
end sub

sub but8_onclick
 for i=5 to 8
 if a(i)="0" then a(i)="." else a(i)="0"
 next
  if a(4)="0" then a(4)="." else a(4)="0"
  if a(12)="0" then a(12)="." else a(12)="0"
  if a(16)="0" then a(16)="." else a(16)="0"
 call move
end sub

sub but9_onclick
 for i=9 to 12
 if a(i)="0" then a(i)="." else a(i)="0"
 next
  if a(1)="0" then a(1)="." else a(1)="0"
  if a(5)="0" then a(5)="." else a(5)="0"
  if a(13)="0" then a(13)="." else a(13)="0"
 call move
end sub

sub but10_onclick
 for i=9 to 12
 if a(i)="0" then a(i)="." else a(i)="0"
 next
  if a(2)="0" then a(2)="." else a(2)="0"
  if a(6)="0" then a(6)="." else a(6)="0"
  if a(14)="0" then a(14)="." else a(14)="0"
 call move
end sub

sub but11_onclick
 for i=9 to 12
 if a(i)="0" then a(i)="." else a(i)="0"
 next
```

```
 if a(3)="0" then a(3)="." else a(3)="0"
 if a(7)="0" then a(7)="." else a(7)="0"
 if a(15)="0" then a(15)="." else a(15)="0"
 call move
end sub

sub but12_onclick
 for i=9 to 12
 if a(i)="0" then a(i)="." else a(i)="0"
 next
  if a(4)="0" then a(4)="." else a(4)="0"
  if a(8)="0" then a(8)="." else a(8)="0"
  if a(16)="0" then a(16)="." else a(16)="0"
 call move
end sub

sub but13_onclick
 for i=13 to 16
 if a(i)="0" then a(i)="." else a(i)="0"
 next
  for i=1 to 9 step 4
  if a(i)="0" then a(i)="." else a(i)="0"
  next
 call move
end sub

sub but14_onclick
 for i=13 to 16
 if a(i)="0" then a(i)="." else a(i)="0"
 next
  for i=2 to 10 step 4
  if a(i)="0" then a(i)="." else a(i)="0"
  next
 call move
end sub

sub but15_onclick
 for i=13 to 16
 if a(i)="0" then a(i)="." else a(i)="0"
 next
  for i=3 to 11 step 4
  if a(i)="0" then a(i)="." else a(i)="0"
  next
 call move
```

```
end sub

sub but16_onclick
 for i=13 to 16
 if a(i)="0" then a(i)="." else a(i)="0"
 next
  for i=4 to 12 step 4
  if a(i)="0" then a(i)="." else a(i)="0"
  next
 call move
end sub
-->
</SCRIPT>
</dl>
</BODY></HTML>
```

If you want to, you can easily run this game. Create a text file, copy the code in the listing to it, and rename the file as safe.htm (this file is also provided on the accompanying CD-ROM). You can play the game by simply opening the file in the Internet Explorer browser (Fig. 18.1).

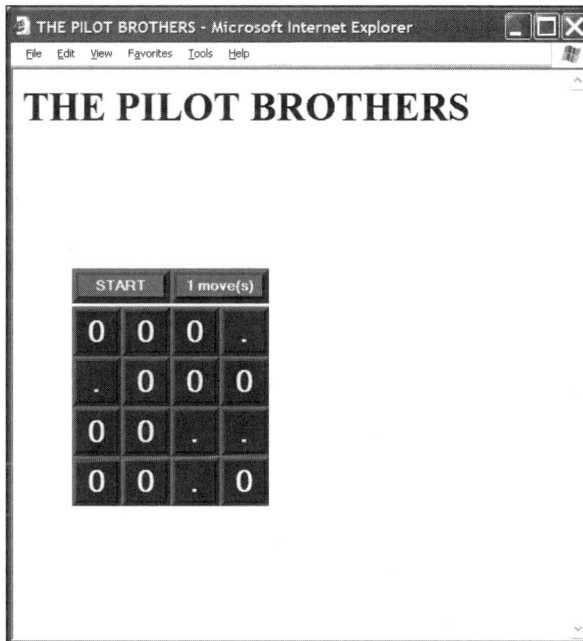

Fig. 18.1. The Crack the Safe game in VBScript

The task here, however, is to migrate this game from VBScript to VB .NET 2003. I intentionally did not optimize the program too much for the first example. The object of the exercise is to show that even beginning programmers, who are still having problems getting their bearings in many of the language's constructions, can program the game. Launch VB .NET and create a new project, `Safe`. First, simply place 16 buttons on the form. Be careful in this task and place buttons one after another with four buttons to a row. Then, place another button labeled **Start** and a label with the `Text` property set to 0. Now, simply rewrite the VBScript code. As you can see, the changes are minimal (Listing 18.2).

Listing 18.2. The VB .NET Version of the Crack the Safe Game

```
'----------------------------------------
' Safe © 2005 Alexander Klimov
'----------------------------------------
    Dim c(16) As Integer
    Dim a(16) As String
    Dim s As Integer
    Dim i As Integer
    Dim f As Integer

    Private Sub Moves()
        Button1.Text = a(1)
        Button2.Text = a(2)
        Button3.Text = a(3)
        Button4.Text = a(4)
        Button5.Text = a(5)
        Button6.Text = a(6)
        Button7.Text = a(7)
        Button8.Text = a(8)
        Button9.Text = a(9)
        Button10.Text = a(10)
        Button11.Text = a(11)
        Button12.Text = a(12)
        Button13.Text = a(13)
        Button14.Text = a(14)
        Button15.Text = a(15)
        Button16.Text = a(16)
        s = s + 1
        Label1.Text = Str(s - 1)
        f = 0
        For i = 1 To 16
            If a(i) = "." Then
                f = f + 1
```

```
            End If
        Next
        If f = 16 Then
            Call Winner()
        End If
    End Sub


    ' The Winner() procedure simply writes "YOU HAVE WON" on the buttons.
    Private Sub Winner()
        Button1.Text = "Y"
        Button2.Text = "O"
        Button3.Text = "U"
        Button4.Text = ""
        Button5.Text = "H"
        Button6.Text = "A"
        Button7.Text = "V"
        Button8.Text = "E"
        Button9.Text = ""
        Button10.Text = "W"
        Button11.Text = "O"
        Button12.Text = "N"
        Button13.Text = "!"
        Button14.Text = "!"
        Button15.Text = "!"
        Button16.Text = "!"
End Sub

Private Sub butStart_Click(ByVal sender As System.Object, ByVal e As System.EventArgs) _
Handles butStart.Click
        s = 0
        For i = 1 To 16
            c(i) = Int(Rnd(1) + 0.5)
            Randomize()
            If c(i) = 0 Then
                a(i) = "0"
            Else : a(i) = "."
            End If
        Next


        Call Moves()
End Sub

Private Sub Button1_Click(ByVal sender As System.Object, ByVal e As System.EventArgs) _
Handles Button1.Click
```

```
    For i = 1 To 4
        If a(i) = "0" Then
            a(i) = "."
        Else
            a(i) = "0"
        End If
    Next
    For i = 5 To 13 Step 4
        If a(i) = "0" Then
            a(i) = "."
        Else
            a(i) = "0"
        End If
    Next
    Call Moves()
End Sub
```

I provided code only for the first button, because the code for the remaining buttons is virtually identical to the code in the VBScript example. First, a loop is launched and the array is initialized to random values from 0 to 1. If the value of the array cell is 0, then the value of the corresponding button is set to 0. Otherwise, the value of the button is set to "." (the dot character). All that remains is to write the code for each button that simply changes the values of the buttons in its row and column to the opposite. That's it! The game is ready. You can run and play it (Fig. 18.2). What is the merit of this example? Its simplicity. Using this approach, you can easily migrate this game to, say, Java or C#. But I must admit that the example is far from ideal. The code is too cumbersome and awkward. So let's rewrite it, taking advantage of the features offered by VB .NET 2003.

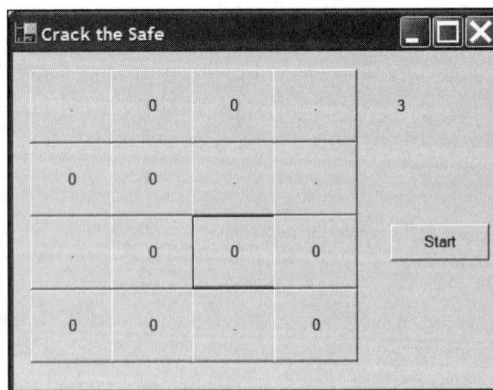

Fig. 18.2. The Crack the Safe game, version 1

18.2. Crack the Safe: Version 2

This time, we will try to write a more advanced code from a technical standpoint. First, we will dispense with manually creating and placing 16 buttons on the form. This is too tedious. Remember the Windows Miner game? Its game field can be made up of hundreds of buttons. Can you imagine how much time it would take to simply arrange these buttons on the form? We will delegate this task to the computer and create an array of buttons programmatically. Moreover, we will make some cosmetic changes to the program to make it more aesthetically appealing. Create a new project and name it Safe2. This time, other than placing a MainMenu control on the form, skip the visual programming part and move straight to the code editor, creating the code in Listing 18.3.

Listing 18.3. The Crack the Safe Game, Version 2

```
'-------------------------------------
' Safe2 © 2005 Alexander Klimov
'-------------------------------------
Private Const BUTTONS16 As Integer = 16
Private SQUARE_ROOT As Integer = _
    Convert.ToInt32(Math.Sqrt(BUTTONS16))
Private btn(BUTTONS16 - 1) As Button

    Private Sub Form1_Load(ByVal sender As System.Object, ByVal e As System.EventArgs) _
Handles MyBase.Load
        ' Setting the form's properties
        MyBase.MaximizeBox = False
        MyBase.FormBorderStyle = FormBorderStyle.Fixed3D
        MyBase.Text = "Safe-2"

        Dim i As Integer
        Dim w As Integer = MyBase.ClientSize.Width / SQUARE_ROOT
        Dim h As Integer = MyBase.ClientSize.Height / SQUARE_ROOT
        For i = 0 To BUTTONS16 - 1
            btn(i) = New Button
            btn(i).Width = w
            btn(i).Height = MyBase.ClientSize.Height / SQUARE_ROOT
            btn(i).Left = (i Mod SQUARE_ROOT) * w
            btn(i).Top = (i \ SQUARE_ROOT) * h
            btn(i).BackColor = Color.SkyBlue
            AddHandler btn(i).Click, AddressOf btn_Click
            btn(i).Tag = 0
            MyBase.Controls.Add(btn(i))
```

```
    Next

End Sub
Private Sub ChangeButtonState(ByVal i As Integer)
    If (Convert.ToInt32(btn(i).Tag) = 0) Then
        btn(i).Tag = 1
        btn(i).BackColor = Color.Red
    Else
        btn(i).Tag = 0
        btn(i).BackColor = Color.SkyBlue
    End If
End Sub
Public Sub btn_Click(ByVal sender As Object, ByVal e As EventArgs)

    If Equals(sender, btn(0)) Then
        ChangeButtonState(0)
        ChangeButtonState(1)
        ChangeButtonState(2)
        ChangeButtonState(3)
        ChangeButtonState(4)
        ChangeButtonState(8)
        ChangeButtonState(12)
    End If
    ' For the 2nd button
    If Equals(sender, btn(1)) Then
        ChangeButtonState(0)
        ChangeButtonState(1)
        ChangeButtonState(2)
        ChangeButtonState(3)
        ChangeButtonState(5)
        ChangeButtonState(9)
        ChangeButtonState(13)
    End If
    ' For the 3rd button
    If Equals(sender, btn(2)) Then
        ChangeButtonState(0)
        ChangeButtonState(1)
        ChangeButtonState(2)
        ChangeButtonState(3)
        ChangeButtonState(6)
        ChangeButtonState(10)
        ChangeButtonState(14)
    End If
    ' For the 4th button
```

```
If Equals(sender, btn(3)) Then
    ChangeButtonState(0)
    ChangeButtonState(1)
    ChangeButtonState(2)
    ChangeButtonState(3)
    ChangeButtonState(7)
    ChangeButtonState(11)
    ChangeButtonState(15)
End If
' For the 5th button
If Equals(sender, btn(4)) Then
    ChangeButtonState(0)
    ChangeButtonState(4)
    ChangeButtonState(5)
    ChangeButtonState(6)
    ChangeButtonState(7)
    ChangeButtonState(8)
    ChangeButtonState(12)
End If
' For the 6th button
If Equals(sender, btn(5)) Then
    ChangeButtonState(1)
    ChangeButtonState(4)
    ChangeButtonState(5)
    ChangeButtonState(6)
    ChangeButtonState(7)
    ChangeButtonState(9)
    ChangeButtonState(13)
End If
' For the 7th button
If Equals(sender, btn(6)) Then
    ChangeButtonState(2)
    ChangeButtonState(4)
    ChangeButtonState(5)
    ChangeButtonState(6)
    ChangeButtonState(7)
    ChangeButtonState(10)
    ChangeButtonState(14)
End If
If Equals(sender, btn(7)) Then
    ChangeButtonState(3)
    ChangeButtonState(4)
    ChangeButtonState(5)
    ChangeButtonState(6)
```

```
        ChangeButtonState(7)
        ChangeButtonState(11)
        ChangeButtonState(15)
    End If
    If Equals(sender, btn(8)) Then
        ChangeButtonState(0)
        ChangeButtonState(4)
        ChangeButtonState(8)
        ChangeButtonState(9)
        ChangeButtonState(10)
        ChangeButtonState(11)
        ChangeButtonState(12)
    End If
    If Equals(sender, btn(9)) Then
        ChangeButtonState(1)
        ChangeButtonState(5)
        ChangeButtonState(8)
        ChangeButtonState(9)
        ChangeButtonState(10)
        ChangeButtonState(11)
        ChangeButtonState(13)
    End If
    If Equals(sender, btn(10)) Then
        ChangeButtonState(2)
        ChangeButtonState(6)
        ChangeButtonState(8)
        ChangeButtonState(9)
        ChangeButtonState(10)
        ChangeButtonState(11)
        ChangeButtonState(14)
    End If
    If Equals(sender, btn(11)) Then
        ChangeButtonState(3)
        ChangeButtonState(7)
        ChangeButtonState(8)
        ChangeButtonState(9)
        ChangeButtonState(10)
        ChangeButtonState(11)
        ChangeButtonState(15)
    End If
    If Equals(sender, btn(12)) Then
        ChangeButtonState(0)
        ChangeButtonState(4)
        ChangeButtonState(8)
```

```
        ChangeButtonState(12)
        ChangeButtonState(13)
        ChangeButtonState(14)
        ChangeButtonState(15)
    End If
    If Equals(sender, btn(13)) Then
        ChangeButtonState(1)
        ChangeButtonState(5)
        ChangeButtonState(9)
        ChangeButtonState(12)
        ChangeButtonState(13)
        ChangeButtonState(14)
        ChangeButtonState(15)
    End If
    If Equals(sender, btn(14)) Then
        ChangeButtonState(2)
        ChangeButtonState(6)
        ChangeButtonState(10)
        ChangeButtonState(12)
        ChangeButtonState(13)
        ChangeButtonState(14)
        ChangeButtonState(15)
    End If
    If Equals(sender, btn(15)) Then
        ChangeButtonState(3)
        ChangeButtonState(7)
        ChangeButtonState(11)
        ChangeButtonState(12)
        ChangeButtonState(13)
        ChangeButtonState(14)
        ChangeButtonState(15)
    End If

    If CheckForWin() Then Congratulation()
End Sub
Private Function CheckForWin() As Boolean
    Dim i As Integer
    For i = 0 To BUTTONS16 - 1
        If (Convert.ToInt32(btn(i).Tag) = 0) Then Return False
    Next
    Return True
End Function
Private Sub Congratulation()
    MessageBox.Show("Congratulations!!!")
```

```
        Dim i As Integer
        For i = 0 To BUTTONS16 - 1
            btn(i).BackColor = Color.SkyBlue
            btn(i).Tag = 0
        Next
    End Sub

    Private Sub mnuStart_Click(ByVal sender As System.Object, ByVal e As  _
System.EventArgs) Handles mnuStart.Click
        Dim i As Integer
        Dim c(15)
        For i = 0 To 15
            c(i) = Int(Rnd(1) + 0.5)
            Randomize()
            If c(i) = 0 Then
                btn(i).BackColor = Color.SkyBlue
                btn(i).Tag = 0
            Else
                btn(i).BackColor = Color.Red
                btn(i).Tag = 1
            End If
        Next
    End Sub
```

The BUTTONS16 constant was declared to hold the number of buttons used in the game. The SQUARE_ROOT variable can be considered the space occupied by one button. The btn array will hold objects of the Button type, which will allow us to easily access various properties of any button and to write event handlers for it. The properties of the form and the buttons are set when the form is loaded (during the Load event). As you can see, the dimensions for one button are calculated in the loop and a simple algorithm is used to place all buttons of this size in a 4 × 4 grid on the form. At the same time, all buttons are colored the same color and their Tag properties are set to 0. Instead of putting dull labels on the buttons, we will be changing the color of the buttons. This approach is more fitting to games. This conception is implemented using the ChangeButtonState procedure. All that remains is to write the event handler for the Click event for all 16 buttons. This task is handled by the btn_Click event handler, added in the program using the AddHandler statement. Its code changes the color of the buttons according to the game's rules. I chose the path of the least resistance and wrote code for each individual button. Perhaps you will be able to find a more compact solution and optimize the example. The last two procedures — CheckForWin() and Congratulation() — are used to determine a winning combination and to display the congratulatory message. The game is practically ready (Fig. 18.3). Its only shortcoming is the lack of an initialization procedure: When the game is started, all squares are of the same color. So we need to add some code to randomly color the squares in one of the two game colors. This can be done either in the `Form_Load` event or in the `Click` event of an additional button or menu item. As you should have noticed, I dispensed with counting the number of moves in the example. I believe you will be able to handle this task on your own. In addition, you will find a few recommendations about how to improve the game at the end of the chapter. Good luck!

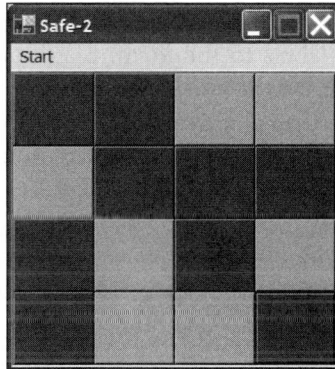

Fig. 18.3. The Crack the Safe game, version 2

18.3. Beach Tic-Tac-Toe

Everyone probably knows this game. Nevertheless, it is good practice to define the tasks to be solved before starting the actual programming of the game. In this, case, we will be considering the so-called beach version of the game. By this, I mean that the game process should resemble a real-life match as closely as possible. That is, the game board is two vertical and two horizontal lines drawn with a stick in the sand. The players pass the stick to each other and draw **X**s or **O**s on this makeshift game board. In other words, we are talking about the player-vs.-player version of the game. The player-vs.-computer version is considered in the next example.

18.3.1. The Theory behind the Game

The two players take turns drawing moves in a square, 3×3 game board. One player draws an **X** in a free square; the other draws an **O**. Before the game starts, the players must agree on who will make the first move and what symbol each player will use. The game is won by the first player to place three of his marks in a row vertically, horizontally, or diagonally. If there are no more vacant squares left on the board and no player has managed to place three marks in a row, the game is a draw.

18.3.2. Building the Game Board

Start VB .NET 2003 and create a new project: XO. Set the Text property value of the form to Tic-Tac-Toe. Because we are implementing the beach version, we will need four lines. But VB .NET 2003 has no such control as Line. All lines are drawn on the form programmatically. However, if you are a veteran of VB programming and the habit of drawing lines the visual way is deeply ingrained, you can use the Label control. To draw a 3 × 3 grid, add four labels to the form. Blank out their Text property and set the BackColor property to any color that strikes your fancy. In my example, I set the color of the labels to ActiveCaption from the **System** tab. Note that you can make the labels that are lines only so thin using the mouse. Set the line to the minimal possible width using the mouse, then switch to the property editor. Find the **Size** item and click the plus symbol to expand the item. Now, set the necessary line width manually. This will be the Height property for the horizontal lines and the Width property for the vertical lines. I set their values to four. We will also need something, on which to draw the players' **X**s and **O**s. The grid we created using labels as lines has nine empty squares. Place buttons in them. I chose buttons for this purpose because this will allow us to concentrate on the programming aspects and leave the chore of performing many maintenance tasks to the programming environment. A game is started with all squares empty; consequently, the Text property of all buttons is blanked out. In principle, it is not important, which player makes the first move. We will not be loading the game with extra controls to keep the score and other nonsense; we are concentrating on the game itself. The only other control that probably needs to be added is a **Start** button to start a new game.

18.3.3. Writing the Code

Now, we can start writing the code. The operations that all buttons will perform are identical: When a button is clicked, either an **X** or an **O** is displayed on it and the button is disabled. This makes it impossible to click the button again. Consequently, it makes no sense to write individual code for each button. Later, I will show you how to distribute the same code to all buttons. For the time being, write the code for the first button (Listing 18.4).

Listing 18.4. The Code for the First Button

```
'---------------------------------------
' XO © 2005 Alexander Klimov
'---------------------------------------
Private Sub Button1_Click(ByVal sender As Object, ByVal e As System.EventArgs) _
Handles Button1.Click

        If flag Then
            sender.Text = "O"
```

```
        flag = False
    Else
        sender.Text = "X"
        flag = True
    End If
    sender.Enabled = False
End Sub
```

The `flag` variable is a global variable that can take on two values: `True` or `False`. It must be declared after the `Inherits System.Windows.Form.Form` line as follows:

```
Dim flag As Boolean
```

Depending on the value of `flag`, either an **X** or an **O** is displayed on the button. In essence, the flag simply toggles the players' turns: First the **X** player makes his move, then the **O** player does.

Run the program and click the first button. If you did not make any errors when writing the code, you will see an **O** displayed on the button, and the button will become disabled. Close the program and return to the code editor. Because all buttons perform the same operations as the first button, there is no need to write the same code for each button. Pay close attention! VB .NET has a handy feature that allows the remaining buttons to share the event handler of the first button — simply list all buttons' names separated by commas in the `Handles` parameter, as follows:

```
Private Sub Button1_Click(ByVal sender As Object, ByVal e As System.EventArgs) _
Handles Button1.Click, Button2.Click, Button3.Click, Button4.Click, Button5.Click, _
Button6.Click, Button7.Click, Button8.Click, Button9.Click
```

Recompile the project and launch the program again to make sure that there are no errors and everything is working as intended. The program's only shortcoming is that it does not determine the winner; the players must decide who has won a game and to start a new game. Fortunately, I providently added a **Start** button to start the game anew. Its click event handler clears the text from all buttons and enables them (Listing 18.5).

Listing 18.5. The Code for Starting the Game

```
    Private Sub btnStart_Click(ByVal sender As System.Object, ByVal e As _
System.EventArgs) Handles btnStart.Click
        Button1.Enabled = True
        Button1.Text = ""
        Button2.Enabled = True
        Button2.Text = ""
        Button3.Enabled = True
        Button3.Text = ""
        Button4.Enabled = True
```

```
    Button4.Text = ""
    Button5.Enabled = True
    Button5.Text = ""
    Button6.Enabled = True
    Button6.Text = ""
    Button7.Enabled = True
    Button7.Text = ""
    Button8.Enabled = True
    Button8.Text = ""
    Button9.Enabled = True
    Button9.Text = ""
End Sub
```

Run the program again and check the work of the **Start** button. As you can see, now you can start a new game at any time. But the program still cannot determine the winner. Why is the computer so stupid? Perhaps you once aided some not-too-computer-literate acquaintances to buy a computer. Such people are convinced that any computer fresh out of the shop is such a smart machine that it can answer any questions; they do not have the slightest idea about operating systems and various application software packages, not to mention about having to install them. They have acquired this belief on the strength of the Hollywood blockbusters they have watched, in which computers answer the trickiest questions without hesitation. But I digress. If you take your time to count the total number of winning combinations, you will be surprised to find only eight: three horizontally, three vertically, and two diagonally. This is not that many for a smart machine. So return to the drawing board and write the procedure to detect a winning combination by checking the text on the buttons (Listing 18.6). The procedure must check all possible combinations and display an appropriate message if there is a winner.

Listing 18.6. The Code for Detecting a Winning Combination

```
Private Sub CheckWin()
    If (Button1.Text = Button2.Text And Button1.Text = Button3.Text And Button1.Text <> "") _
    Or (Button4.Text = Button5.Text And Button4.Text = Button6.Text And Button4.Text <> "") _
    Or (Button7.Text = Button8.Text And Button7.Text = Button9.Text And Button7.Text <> "") _
    Or (Button1.Text = Button4.Text And Button1.Text = Button7.Text And Button1.Text <> "") _
    Or (Button2.Text = Button5.Text And Button2.Text = Button8.Text And Button2.Text <> "") _
    Or (Button3.Text = Button6.Text And Button3.Text = Button9.Text And Button3.Text <> "") _
    Or (Button1.Text = Button5.Text And Button1.Text = Button9.Text And Button1.Text <> "") _
    Or (Button3.Text = Button5.Text And Button3.Text = Button7.Text And _
    Button3.Text <> "") Then
        Dim Str As String
        If flag Then
            Str = "X"
```

```
    Else
        Str = "O"
    End If
    MsgBox(UCase(Str) & "is the winner.", MsgBoxStyle.OKOnly)

    End If
    If counter = 9 Then
        MsgBox("This is a draw.")
    End If
End Sub
```

Add a call to the procedure at the end of the `Button1.Click` event handler:

...

```
Call CheckWin()
```

The game is 99 percent finished. Run it and enjoy (Fig. 18.4).

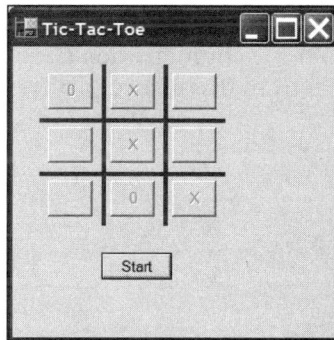

Fig. 18.4. Beach Tic-Tac-Toe

Unless you have carefully thought out all possible outcomes of the game, you will not understand why the program is not finished. Not paying enough attention to seemingly trifling details is a trap that many game developers fall into. Sometimes, they do not take into account some minute detail and release the game. Then dissatisfied customers start flooding the developer with letters (in the best case), begging for help. I remember this case in my own experience. Once, when Pokémon mania was in full swing, I downloaded a game starring Pikachu, a favorite Pokémon character with kids. In this game, he had to dodge a ball thrown at him. I played the game for several days, following the rules diligently and inevitable losing, because the ball was flying at inconceivable trajectories and was always hitting my poor Pikachu. Then I installed the game for one little girl and she passed all the levels in half an hour! As it turned out, when Pikachu was placed close to his enemy, all balls would miss him. This made the game seem pointless to play.

But return to our tic-tac-toe game. In addition to one of the players winning, there can be a draw! This problem is a cinch to take care of. It does not take a rocket scientist to realize that a draw is produced in only one situation: All the squares of the game board must be filled (in our case, there are nine). Consequently, it will suffice to add a counter variable and increment it by one with each move. When the counter reaches nine, the game is a draw and a corresponding message is displayed. The global counter variable counter is declared after the flag variable as follows:

```
Dim counter As Integer = 0
```

To keep the track of the number of moves, the following line of code is added to the Button1.Click event handler:

```
counter += 1
```

The code simply increments the counter value by one. Finally, the following condition is added to the CheckWin() procedure:

```
If counter = 9 Then
        MsgBox("This is a draw.")
  End If
```

Also, do not forget to zero out the counter when starting a new game; otherwise, you will get your share of angry letters from dissatisfied players:

```
Private Sub btnStart_Click...
...
 counter = 0
End Sub
```

This seems to be it.

18.3.4. Smart Tic-Tac-Toe

There is not always, however, a human partner available to play the game. In this case, the role of the opponent is assigned to the computer. However, for the machine to play on equal terms, it has to be endowed with a sufficient degree of intelligence. The subject of artificial intelligence in games is a complicated one and requires separate discussion. What I will do in this book is write another tic-tac-toe game, this time endowing the computer with the rudiments of intellect: the TicTacToe project. For various reasons I will not go into here, I will use another technique to create the game. The process of creating the program can be broken into three parts: creating the model of the game, designing the graphical interface, and directing the behavior of the opponent (the artificial intelligence).

18.3.4.1. The Game's Interface and Model

I will start with the simple stuff first: creating the game's interface. This time, use nine labels instead of buttons to make the game board. Place them on the form in a 3 × 3 grid and blank out their texts. Because the labels are the same color as the form, change their color to one contrasting with the form. The labels are named in a special way. They must reflect their game field coordinates in their names. The coordinates for all nine labels can be represented as the following table:

```
0,0  0,1  0,2
1,0  1,1  1,2
2,0  2,1  2,2
```

According to this table, name the labels as follows: lbl00, lbl01, lbl02, lbl10, and lbl11.... We can leave our form for now and move on to writing the code of the game's model. For this, use a new class: GameModel.vb. Right-click on the project's name in **Solution Explorer** and select the **Add/Add Class** command. In the **Add New Item** dialog window that opens, replace the default Class.vb class name with GameModel.vb and click the **Open** button. This will open the code editor for the class just created. This class will contain the game's model: the properties, enumeration, and events (Listing 18.7).

Listing 18.7. The Class for the Smart Tic-Tac-Toe Model

```
'--------------------------------------
' TicTacToe © 2004 Alexander Klimov
'--------------------------------------
Public Class GameModel
    Private m_Square(2, 2) As SquareStatus
    Private m_Winner As SquareStatus

    ' The victory flag
    Private bVictory As Boolean

    ' The winning combination event
    Public Event Win(ByVal Winner As SquareStatus)
    ' The draw event
    Public Event Draw()

    ' The three possible states of a square
    Public Enum SquareStatus
        Empty = 0
        PlayerX = 1
        PlayerO = 2
    End Enum

    Public Sub New()
        Me.Clear()
```

```
End Sub

' Clearing the game board
Public Sub Clear()
    Dim iRow As Integer, iCol As Integer
    For iRow = 0 To 2
        For iCol = 0 To 2
            m_Square(iRow, iCol) = SquareStatus.Empty
        Next
    Next
    bVictory = False
    m_Winner = SquareStatus.Empty
End Sub

Public Property Square(ByVal iRow As Integer, ByVal iCol As Integer) As SquareStatus
    Get
        Return m_Square(iRow, iCol)
    End Get
    Set(ByVal Value As SquareStatus)
        If m_Square(iRow, iCol) = SquareStatus.Empty And _
           bVictory = False Then
            m_Square(iRow, iCol) = Value
            m_Winner = CheckWin()
            If m_Winner = SquareStatus.Empty Then
                If CheckDraw() = True Then
                    RaiseEvent Draw()
                End If
            Else
                bVictory = True
                RaiseEvent Win(m_Winner)
            End If
        End If
    End Set
End Property

Public Property Square(ByVal SC As SquareCoordinate) As SquareStatus
    Get
        Return m_Square(SC.Row, SC.Column)
    End Get
    Set(ByVal Value As SquareStatus)
        Me.Square(SC.Row, SC.Column) = Value
    End Set
End Property

Private Function CheckWin() As SquareStatus
```

```
    Dim iTemp As SquareStatus

    iTemp = CheckForHorizontalWin()
    If iTemp <> SquareStatus.Empty Then Return iTemp

    iTemp = CheckForVerticalWin()
    If iTemp <> SquareStatus.Empty Then Return iTemp

    Return CheckForDiagonalWin()
End Function

Private Function CheckForHorizontalWin() As SquareStatus
    Dim iRow As Integer

    Dim iFirstSquarePlayer As SquareStatus

    For iRow = 0 To 2
        iFirstSquarePlayer = m_Square(iRow, 0)
        If iFirstSquarePlayer = m_Square(iRow, 1) And _
           iFirstSquarePlayer = m_Square(iRow, 2) Then
            Return iFirstSquarePlayer
        End If
    Next

    Return SquareStatus.Empty
End Function

Private Function CheckForVerticalWin() As SquareStatus
    Dim iCol As Integer
    Dim iFirstSquarePlayer As SquareStatus

    For iCol = 0 To 2
        iFirstSquarePlayer = m_Square(0, iCol)
        If iFirstSquarePlayer = m_Square(1, iCol) And _
           iFirstSquarePlayer = m_Square(2, iCol) Then
            Return iFirstSquarePlayer
        End If
    Next

    Return SquareStatus.Empty
End Function

Private Function CheckForDiagonalWin() As SquareStatus
    Dim iCol As Integer
```

```
        Dim iRow As Integer
        Dim iFirstSquarePlayer As SquareStatus

        iFirstSquarePlayer = m_Square(1, 1)

        If iFirstSquarePlayer = m_Square(0, 0) And _
           iFirstSquarePlayer = m_Square(2, 2) Then
            Return iFirstSquarePlayer
        End If

        If iFirstSquarePlayer = m_Square(0, 2) And _
           iFirstSquarePlayer = m_Square(2, 0) Then
            Return iFirstSquarePlayer
        End If
    End Function

    Private Function CheckDraw() As Boolean
        Dim iRow As Integer, iCol As Integer
        For iRow = 0 To 2
            For iCol = 0 To 2
                If m_Square(iRow, iCol) = SquareStatus.Empty Then Return False
            Next
        Next

        Return True
    End Function

End Class
Public Class SquareCoordinate
    Private m_Row As Integer
    Private m_Col As Integer

    Public Sub New()
        m_Row = 0 : m_Col = 0
    End Sub

    Public Sub New(ByVal iRow As Integer, ByVal iCol As Integer)
        m_Row = iRow : m_Col = iCol
    End Sub

    Public Property Row()
        Get
            Return m_Row
        End Get
```

```
        Set(ByVal Value)
            m_Row = Value
        End Set
    End Property

    Public Property Column()
        Get
            Return m_Col
        End Get
        Set(ByVal Value)
            m_Col = Value
        End Set
    End Property

    Public Overrides Function ToString() As String
        Return " [" & m_Row & ", " & m_Col & "] "
    End Function
End Class
```

So each square of the game can be in one of three states: empty, **X**, or **O**. We will place these states into a SquareStatus enumeration. The game board, thus, is a 3 × 3 grid of squares, with each m_Square square assigned one of the SquareStatus values. The next step is to create a property Square that will obtain or set the status of the square's SquareStatus. A player can set it to either **X** or **O**. If a square is already set, an attempt to change its state will be ignored. This property also checks for a winning combination or a draw, with subsequent processing of these events. Note that two overloaded versions of the property are implemented in the code. The second version of the property makes it possible to specify one parameter instead of two: iRow and iCol. The check for a win or draw is performed by examining the status of the rows horizontally, vertically, and diagonally. If three squares in a row have the same status, the associated player wins. A draw is detected using the CheckDraw function as follows: The status of all squares is checked in a loop, and if at least one of them is Empty, False is returned; if all squares are filled, it is a draw.

18.3.4.2. Artificial Intelligence

The logic of the artificial intelligence of the game is contained in the GameAI class (Listing 18.8) (the gameai.vb file). The artificial intelligence applies the following four rules:

❏ Win (if possible)
❏ Prevent the opponent from winning
❏ Determine the best move for a future win
❏ Make the next legal move

Listing 18.8. The Class for the Game's Artificial Intelligence

```
'---------------------------------------
' TicTacToe © 2004 Alexander Klimov
'---------------------------------------
Public Class GameAI
    Private m_iAIPlayer As GameModel.SquareStatus
    Private m_iHumanPlayer As GameModel.SquareStatus
    Private m_CurrentBoard As GameModel

    Public Sub New(ByVal iAIPlayer As GameModel.SquareStatus)
        m_iAIPlayer = iAIPlayer

        If iAIPlayer = GameModel.SquareStatus.PlayerX Then
            m_iHumanPlayer = GameModel.SquareStatus.PlayerO
        Else
            m_iHumanPlayer = GameModel.SquareStatus.PlayerX
        End If
    End Sub

    Public Function GetAIMove(ByVal aTTT As GameModel) As SquareCoordinate
        Dim MoveList As New ArrayList
        m_CurrentBoard = aTTT

        Dim iRow As Integer
        For iRow = 0 To 2
            Dim possibleMoves() As SquareCoordinate
            Try
                possibleMoves = GetPossibleRowMoves(iRow)
            Catch ex As NullReferenceException
                Stop
            Catch ex As Exception
                Stop
            End Try

            If Not possibleMoves Is Nothing Then
                Dim x As Integer
                For x = 0 To possibleMoves.Length - 1
                    MoveList.Add(DetermineMoveEntry(possibleMoves(x)))
                Next
            End If
        Next

        ' Returning a blocking move or the next regular move
```

```
        Dim NormalMoveList As New ArrayList
        Dim aMoveEntry As MoveEntry

        ' Checking for a wining move
        For Each aMoveEntry In MoveList
            Select Case aMoveEntry.MoveType
                Case MoveType.Winning
                    Console.Write(ControlChars.CrLf & aMoveEntry.ToString)
                    Return aMoveEntry.SquareCoordinate
            End Select
        Next

        ' If no winning move, making a blocking move
        For Each aMoveEntry In MoveList
            Select Case aMoveEntry.MoveType
                Case MoveType.Blocking
                    Console.Write(ControlChars.CrLf & aMoveEntry.ToString)
                    Return aMoveEntry.SquareCoordinate
                Case Else
                    NormalMoveList.Add(aMoveEntry)
            End Select
        Next

        ' Searching for the next best move
        Try
            Dim bnME As SquareCoordinate = _
            DetermineBestNormalMove(NormalMoveList)
            Console.Write(ControlChars.CrLf & "Best -->" & bnME.ToString)
            Return bnME
        Catch ex As Exception

        End Try

        ' A random move
        Dim iRandomItem As Integer = _
            CInt(Int(((NormalMoveList.Count - 1) - 0 + 1) * Rnd() + 0))
        Dim nME As MoveEntry = NormalMoveList(iRandomItem)
        Console.Write(ControlChars.CrLf & nME.ToString)
        Return nME.SquareCoordinate
End Function

Private Function GetPossibleRowMoves(ByVal iRow As Integer) As SquareCoordinate()
    Dim PossibleMoves As New ArrayList
    Dim iCol As Integer
```

```
        For iCol = 0 To 2
            If m_CurrentBoard.Square(iRow, iCol) = GameModel.SquareStatus.Empty Then
                PossibleMoves.Add(New SquareCoordinate(iRow, iCol))
            End If
        Next

        If PossibleMoves.Count > 0 Then
            Dim returnSC(PossibleMoves.Count - 1) As SquareCoordinate
            Dim x As Integer
            For x = 0 To PossibleMoves.Count - 1
                returnSC(x) = CType(PossibleMoves(x), SquareCoordinate)
            Next
            Return returnSC
        Else
            Dim returnSC() As SquareCoordinate
            Return returnSC
        End If
End Function

Private Function DetermineMoveEntry(ByVal aSC As SquareCoordinate) As MoveEntry
        Dim iRow As Integer = aSC.Row
        Dim iCol As Integer = aSC.Column

        ' Horizontally
        Dim iGE1 As GameModel.SquareStatus
        Dim iGE2 As GameModel.SquareStatus

        Select Case iCol
            Case 0
                iGE1 = m_CurrentBoard.Square(iRow, 1)
                iGE2 = m_CurrentBoard.Square(iRow, 2)
            Case 1
                iGE1 = m_CurrentBoard.Square(iRow, 0)
                iGE2 = m_CurrentBoard.Square(iRow, 2)
            Case 2
                iGE1 = m_CurrentBoard.Square(iRow, 0)
                iGE2 = m_CurrentBoard.Square(iRow, 1)
        End Select

        If CheckPossibleWin(iGE1, iGE2, m_iAIPlayer) = True Then
            Return New MoveEntry(aSC, MoveType.Winning)
        End If

        If CheckPossibleWin(iGE1, iGE2, m_iHumanPlayer) = True Then
```

```
            Return New MoveEntry(aSC, MoveType.Blocking)
End If


' Vertically
Select Case iRow
    Case 0
        iGE1 = m_CurrentBoard.Square(1, iCol)
        iGE2 = m_CurrentBoard.Square(2, iCol)
    Case 1
        iGE1 = m_CurrentBoard.Square(0, iCol)
        iGE2 = m_CurrentBoard.Square(2, iCol)
    Case 2
        iGE1 = m_CurrentBoard.Square(0, iCol)
        iGE2 = m_CurrentBoard.Square(1, iCol)
End Select

If CheckPossibleWin(iGE1, iGE2, m_iAIPlayer) = True Then
    Return New MoveEntry(aSC, MoveType.Winning)
End If


If CheckPossibleWin(iGE1, iGE2, m_iHumanPlayer) = True Then
    Return New MoveEntry(aSC, MoveType.Blocking)
End If

' Diagonally
Select Case GetSquareType(aSC)
    Case SquareType.UpperLeft
        iGE1 = m_CurrentBoard.Square(1, 1)
        iGE2 = m_CurrentBoard.Square(2, 2)

        If CheckPossibleWin(iGE1, iGE2, m_iAIPlayer) = True Then
            Return New MoveEntry(aSC, MoveType.Winning)
        End If

        If CheckPossibleWin(iGE1, iGE2, m_iHumanPlayer) = True Then
            Return New MoveEntry(aSC, MoveType.Blocking)
        End If
    Case SquareType.UpperRight
        iGE1 = m_CurrentBoard.Square(1, 1)
        iGE2 = m_CurrentBoard.Square(2, 0)

        If CheckPossibleWin(iGE1, iGE2, m_iAIPlayer) = True Then
            Return New MoveEntry(aSC, MoveType.Winning)
```

```
        End If

        If CheckPossibleWin(iGE1, iGE2, m_iHumanPlayer) = True Then
            Return New MoveEntry(aSC, MoveType.Blocking)
        End If

Case SquareType.Center
    iGE1 = m_CurrentBoard.Square(0, 2)
    iGE2 = m_CurrentBoard.Square(2, 0)

    If CheckPossibleWin(iGE1, iGE2, m_iAIPlayer) = True Then
        Return New MoveEntry(aSC, MoveType.Winning)
    End If

    If CheckPossibleWin(iGE1, iGE2, m_iHumanPlayer) = True Then
        Return New MoveEntry(aSC, MoveType.Blocking)
    End If

    iGE1 = m_CurrentBoard.Square(0, 0)
    iGE2 = m_CurrentBoard.Square(2, 2)

    If CheckPossibleWin(iGE1, iGE2, m_iAIPlayer) = True Then
        Return New MoveEntry(aSC, MoveType.Winning)
    End If

    If CheckPossibleWin(iGE1, iGE2, m_iHumanPlayer) = True Then
        Return New MoveEntry(aSC, MoveType.Blocking)
    End If
Case SquareType.BottomLeft
    iGE1 = m_CurrentBoard.Square(1, 1)
    iGE2 = m_CurrentBoard.Square(0, 2)

    If CheckPossibleWin(iGE1, iGE2, m_iAIPlayer) = True Then
        Return New MoveEntry(aSC, MoveType.Winning)

    End If
    If CheckPossibleWin(iGE1, iGE2, m_iHumanPlayer) = True Then
        Return New MoveEntry(aSC, MoveType.Blocking)
    End If
Case SquareType.BottomRight
    iGE1 = m_CurrentBoard.Square(1, 1)
    iGE2 = m_CurrentBoard.Square(0, 0)

    If CheckPossibleWin(iGE1, iGE2, m_iAIPlayer) = True Then
```

```
                Return New MoveEntry(aSC, MoveType.Winning)
            End If

            If CheckPossibleWin(iGE1, iGE2, m_iHumanPlayer) = True Then
                Return New MoveEntry(aSC, MoveType.Blocking)
            End If
    End Select

    Return New MoveEntry(aSC, MoveType.Normal)
End Function

Private Function DetermineBestNormalMove(ByVal aNormalMoveList As ArrayList) As _
SquareCoordinate
    Dim aSC As SquareCoordinate
    Dim aME As MoveEntry
    Dim aGE1 As GameModel.SquareStatus
    Dim aGE2 As GameModel.SquareStatus

    For Each aME In aNormalMoveList
        aSC = aME.SquareCoordinate
        ' Horizontally
        If CheckBestHorizontal(aSC) Then
            Return aSC
        End If

        If CheckBestVertical(aSC) Then
            Return aSC
        End If

        If GetSquareType(aSC) <> SquareType.Other Then
            If CheckBestDiagonal(aSC) Then
                Return aSC
            End If
        End If
    Next
End Function

Private Function CheckBestHorizontal(ByVal aSC As SquareCoordinate) As Boolean
    Dim iCol As Integer = aSC.Column
    Dim iRow As Integer = aSC.Row
    Dim iGE1 As GameModel.SquareStatus
    Dim iGE2 As GameModel.SquareStatus

    Select Case iCol
```

```
        Case 0
            iGE1 = m_CurrentBoard.Square(iRow, 1)
            iGE2 = m_CurrentBoard.Square(iRow, 2)
        Case 1
            iGE1 = m_CurrentBoard.Square(iRow, 0)
            iGE2 = m_CurrentBoard.Square(iRow, 2)
        Case 2
            iGE1 = m_CurrentBoard.Square(iRow, 0)
            iGE2 = m_CurrentBoard.Square(iRow, 1)
    End Select

    If iGE1 = m_iHumanPlayer Or iGE2 = m_iHumanPlayer Then
        Return False
    End If

    If iGE1 = m_iAIPlayer Or iGE2 = m_iAIPlayer Then
        Return True
    End If

    Return False
End Function

Private Function CheckBestVertical(ByVal aSC As SquareCoordinate) As Boolean
    Dim iCol As Integer = aSC.Column
    Dim iRow As Integer = aSC.Row
    Dim iGE1 As GameModel.SquareStatus
    Dim iGE2 As GameModel.SquareStatus

    Select Case iRow
        Case 0
            iGE1 = m_CurrentBoard.Square(1, iCol)
            iGE2 = m_CurrentBoard.Square(2, iCol)
        Case 1
            iGE1 = m_CurrentBoard.Square(0, iCol)
            iGE2 = m_CurrentBoard.Square(2, iCol)
        Case 2
            iGE1 = m_CurrentBoard.Square(0, iCol)
            iGE2 = m_CurrentBoard.Square(1, iCol)
    End Select

    If iGE1 = m_iHumanPlayer Or iGE2 = m_iHumanPlayer Then
        Return False
```

```
        End If

        If iGE1 = m_iAIPlayer Or iGE2 = m_iAIPlayer Then
            Return True
        End If

        Return False
End Function


Private Function CheckBestDiagonal(ByVal aSC As SquareCoordinate) As Boolean
        Return False
End Function


Private Enum SquareType
        UpperLeft = 1
        UpperRight = 2
        Center = 3
        BottomLeft = 4
        BottomRight = 5
        Other = 6
End Enum


Private Function CheckPossibleWin(ByVal iGE1 As GameModel.SquareStatus, _
                                  ByVal iGE2 As GameModel.SquareStatus, _
                                  ByVal iPlayer As GameModel.SquareStatus) As Boolean

        If (iGE1 = iPlayer) And (iGE2 = iPlayer) Then
            Return True
        Else
            Return False
        End If
End Function


Private Function GetSquareType(ByVal aSC As SquareCoordinate) As SquareType
        If aSC.Row = 0 And aSC.Column = 0 Then Return SquareType.UpperLeft
        If aSC.Row = 0 And aSC.Column = 2 Then Return SquareType.UpperRight
        If aSC.Row = 1 And aSC.Column = 1 Then Return SquareType.Center
        If aSC.Row = 2 And aSC.Column = 0 Then Return SquareType.BottomLeft
        If aSC.Row = 2 And aSC.Column = 2 Then Return SquareType.BottomRight
        Return SquareType.Other
End Function


Enum MoveType
        Normal = 0
```

```
            Blocking = 1
            Winning = 2
        End Enum

    Private Class MoveEntry
        Private m_iMoveType As MoveType
        Private m_SquareCoordinate As SquareCoordinate

        Public Sub New(ByVal aSC As SquareCoordinate, ByVal iMoveType As MoveType)
            m_iMoveType = iMoveType
            m_SquareCoordinate = aSC
        End Sub

        Public ReadOnly Property [MoveType]() As MoveType
            Get
                Return m_iMoveType
            End Get
        End Property

        Public ReadOnly Property [SquareCoordinate]() As SquareCoordinate
            Get
                Return m_SquareCoordinate
            End Get
        End Property

        Public Overrides Function ToString() As String
            Dim sOutput As String
            sOutput = Me.MoveType.ToString & " : " & _
                      "[" & Me.m_SquareCoordinate.Row & ", " & _
                      Me.m_SquareCoordinate.Column & "]"
            Return sOutput
        End Function
    End Class
End Class
```

Well, the game's model and the artificial intelligence are ready. Now, we can write the code for the game itself (Listing 18.9).

Listing 18.9. The Code for the Smart Tic-Tac-Toe Game

```
'-------------------------------------
' TicTacToe © 2005 Alexander Klimov
'-------------------------------------
```

```
Private m_TicTacToeGame As New GameModel
Private m_CurPlayer As GameModel.SquareStatus = GameModel.SquareStatus.PlayerX
Private m_TicTacToeAI As New GameAI(GameModel.SquareStatus.PlayerO)
Private m_bIsAIEnabled As Boolean = True
Private m_bGameEnded As Boolean = False

Private Sub lbl00_Click(ByVal sender As System.Object, ByVal e As System.EventArgs) _
Handles lbl00.Click, lbl01.Click, lbl02.Click, lbl10.Click, lbl11.Click, lbl12.Click, _
lbl20.Click, lbl21.Click, lbl22.Click
    Try
        Dim aLabelControl As Label = CType(sender, Label)
        Dim sName As String = aLabelControl.Name
        Dim iRow As Integer = sName.Substring(sName.Length - 2, 1)
        Dim iCol As Integer = sName.Substring(sName.Length - 1, 1)
        If m_TicTacToeGame.Square(iRow, iCol) = GameModel.SquareStatus.Empty Then
            m_TicTacToeGame.Square(iRow, iCol) = m_CurPlayer
            ToggleCurrentPlayer()
            DrawBoard()
        End If
    Catch ex As Exception
        Stop
    End Try

End Sub
Private Sub ToggleCurrentPlayer()
    If m_CurPlayer = GameModel.SquareStatus.PlayerX Then
        m_CurPlayer = GameModel.SquareStatus.PlayerO
        If m_bGameEnded = False Then
            PerformAIMove()
        End If
    Else
        m_CurPlayer = GameModel.SquareStatus.PlayerX
    End If
End Sub
Private Sub DrawBoard()
    Dim iRow As Integer
    Dim iCol As Integer
    Dim aLabelControl As Label

    For iRow = 0 To 2
        For iCol = 0 To 2
            Try
                aLabelControl = GetLabelControl(iRow, iCol)
                Select Case m_TicTacToeGame.Square(iRow, iCol)
```

```
                    Case GameModel.SquareStatus.Empty
                        aLabelControl.Text = ""
                    Case GameModel.SquareStatus.PlayerX
                        aLabelControl.Text = "X"
                    Case GameModel.SquareStatus.PlayerO
                        aLabelControl.Text = "O"
                End Select
            Catch ex As Exception


            End Try
        Next
    Next

End Sub

Private Sub PerformAIMove()
    Try
        Dim aSC As SquareCoordinate
        Try
            aSC = _
            m_TicTacToeAI.GetAIMove(m_TicTacToeGame)

        Catch ex As NullReferenceException
            Stop
        Catch ex As Exception
            Stop
        End Try
        m_TicTacToeGame.Square(aSC) = GameModel.SquareStatus.PlayerO
        DrawBoard()
        ToggleCurrentPlayer()
    Catch ex As Exception
        Stop
    End Try

End Sub

Private Function GetLabelControl(ByVal iRow As Integer, ByVal iCol As Integer) As Label
    Dim x As Integer
    Dim aControl As Control
    For x = 0 To Me.Controls.Count - 1
        aControl = Me.Controls(x)
        If aControl.Name = "lbl" & iRow & iCol Then Return aControl
```

```
        Next
    End Function


    Private Sub DrawState()
        DrawBoard()
        MessageBox.Show("It's a draw.")
        m_bGameEnded = True
        NewGame()
    End Sub


    Private Sub NewGame()
        Dim rtnDlgResult As DialogResult
        rtnDlgResult = MessageBox.Show("Do you want to play again?", "A new game", _
MessageBoxButtons.YesNo)
        If rtnDlgResult = DialogResult.Yes Then
            m_TicTacToeGame.Clear()
            m_bGameEnded = False
        Else
            Me.Close()
        End If
    End Sub
    Private Sub WeHaveAWinner(ByVal iWinner As GameModel.SquareStatus)
        DrawBoard()
        Dim sMessage As String = "Player"
        Select Case iWinner
            Case GameModel.SquareStatus.PlayerX
                sMessage = sMessage & "X has won."
            Case GameModel.SquareStatus.PlayerO
                sMessage = sMessage & "O has won."
        End Select
        MessageBox.Show(sMessage)
        m_bGameEnded = True
        NewGame()
    End Sub


    Private Sub Reset()
        m_TicTacToeGame.Clear()
        DrawBoard()
    End Sub
```

The code used in the example has been taken virtually without changes from **http://www.codeproject.com**. Versions of the game implemented in different languages can also be found on this site.

18.4. Card Games

I am sure that there is no computer user who has not played the standard Windows card games: Solitaire, Hearts, Free Cell, or Spider Solitaire. These are rather simple games, and after awhile, players tire of them and would like to play something more sophisticated. In this case, you can write a game yourself! This task is easier than you may think because Windows XP includes the cards.dll library, which is used by the games mentioned earlier. Using this library, you can create a card game in VB .NET 2003 to suit any tastes.

> *NOTE*
>
> The cards.dll library is included with practically any Windows version. But different Windows versions use different versions of the library, both the 16-bit and the 32-bit varieties. Moreover, the files of the library can be named differently, cards32.dll, for example. In our example, we are considering only the library included with Windows XP.

The library provides the following three main functions needed to create card games.

```
Declare Function cdtInit Lib "cards.dll" (ByRef width As Integer, _
   ByRef height As Integer) As Boolean
Declare Function cdtDrawExt Lib "cards.dll" (ByVal hdc As IntPtr, _
   ByVal x As Integer, ByVal y As Integer, ByVal dx As Integer, _
   ByVal dy As Integer, ByVal card As Integer, _
   ByVal suit As Integer, ByVal color As Long) As Boolean
Declare Sub cdtTerm Lib "cards.dll" ()
```

The cdtInit function is used to initialize the cards.dll library. The width and height variables hold the dimensions of the cards needed to display them on the screen. The cdtTerm variable is used to complete work with the cards.dll library and to release the memory resources. The cdtDrawExt function is the main function used to create a game: It displays cards on the screen. It uses the following parameters:

❑ hdc — The device context of the form or PictureBox
❑ x — The X coordinate of the left edge of the card in pixels
❑ yx — The Y coordinate of the top edge of the card in pixels
❑ dx — The card width
❑ dy — The card height
❑ card — A number from 0 to 55 describing the type of card being output
❑ suit — A value describing the card's output method
❑ color — An invertible color

Now that you know the main functions, you can start creating a game. First, we will consider the simplest example of displaying one card on the form. I hope that you have already created a new project and are ready to write the code (Listing 18.10). First, declare two global variables, w and h, to hold the cards' dimensions.

Listing 18.10. Creating a Card Game

```
'------------------------------------
' Creating a card game © 2004 Alexander Klimov
'------------------------------------
    Private w As Integer = 0
    Private h As Integer = 0


    ' Initializing the card library
    Private Sub Form1_Load(ByVal sender As System.Object, _
      ByVal e As System.EventArgs) Handles MyBase.Load
        cdtInit(w, h)
    End Sub


    Private Sub Form1_Paint(ByVal sender As Object, _
      ByVal e As System.Windows.Forms.PaintEventArgs) Handles MyBase.Paint
        DrawOneCard(e.Graphics, 10, 10, w, h)
    End Sub


    Declare Function cdtInit Lib "cards.dll" (ByRef width As Integer, _
      ByRef height As Integer) As Boolean
    Declare Function cdtDrawExt Lib "cards.dll" (ByVal hdc As IntPtr, _
      ByVal x As Integer, ByVal y As Integer, ByVal dx As Integer, _
      ByVal dy As Integer, ByVal card As Integer, _
      ByVal suit As Integer, ByVal color As Long) As Boolean
    Declare Sub cdtTerm Lib "cards.dll" ()


    Public Sub DrawOneCard(ByVal g As Graphics, ByVal x As Integer, _
        ByVal y As Integer, ByVal dx As Integer, ByVal dy As Integer)
        Dim FCardFace As Integer = 1
        Dim FSuit As Integer = 2
        Dim card As Integer
        Dim hdc As IntPtr = g.GetHdc()
        Try
            card = CType(FCardFace, Integer) * 4 + FSuit
            cdtDrawExt(hdc, x, y, dx, dy, 0, 0, 0)
        Finally
            g.ReleaseHdc(hdc)
        End Try
```

```
End Sub

Private Sub Form1_Closing(ByVal sender As Object, _
   ByVal e As System.ComponentModel.CancelEventArgs) Handles MyBase.Closing
      cdtTerm()
End Sub
```

After the initialization, the w and h variables hold the actual dimensions of the cards. You can check them out by adding the following two lines after the initialization code:

```
' Checking out the cards' dimensions
Debug.WriteLine(w)
Debug.WriteLine(h)
```

It is not mandatory to use these values; you can set your own card dimensions. After the initialization, the code displays cards on the screen. For familiarization, I set the process of outputting a single predetermined card into a separate procedure named DrawOneCard. This is a simple procedure. First, we obtain the handle to the device context, on which the card is to be drawn. Then, we call the cdtDrawExt function, passing it the necessary parameters.

This function must be explained in more detail. As you know, there are 52 cards in the standard card deck. There are four card suits with 13 different cards each. The card parameter corresponds to the number that determines the card denomination. Numbers in the range from 0 to 51 correspond to one of the 52 standard cards. Thus, value 0 corresponds to the ace of clubs (♣), value 1 corresponds to the ace of diamonds (♦), value 2 corresponds to the ace of hearts (♥), value 3 corresponds to the ace of spades (♠), etc., with value 51 corresponding to the king of spades. Numbers from 52 to 55 correspond to different card backs and to some special images (a red **X** or a green **O**). A card crossed with a red **X** means that the game is over, and one with a green **O** means that the deck can be reshuffled and the game can be continued. The suit parameter is used to display cards in different views. For example, the card parameter has been set to a value from 0 to 51 (the normal view). In this case, with the suit parameter set to 0, the standard view of the card is displayed. With the same value of the card parameter, but with the suit parameter set to 2, the card is displayed in the negative view, thereby indicating that that card has been selected. To show the back of a card, set the suit parameter to 1 and the card parameter to one of the values in the range from 53 to 68. The function does not use the last parameter, color, so set it to 0. Finally, place the call to the DrawOneCard procedure described earlier into the Form1_Paint event handler, and run the program:

```
Private Sub Form1_Paint(ByVal sender As Object, _
   ByVal e As System.Windows.Forms.PaintEventArgs) Handles MyBase.Paint
      DrawOneCard(e.Graphics, 10, 10, w, h)
End Sub
```

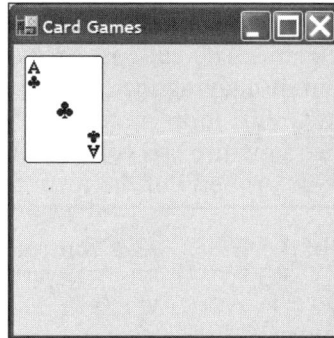

Fig. 18.5. Displaying a card on the screen

A picture of the ace of clubs should be displayed in the upper left corner of the form (Fig. 18.5). The cdtTerm procedure is called when terminating the program to release the resources:

```
Private Sub Form1_Closing(ByVal sender As Object, _
   ByVal e As System.ComponentModel.CancelEventArgs) Handles MyBase.Closing
      cdtTerm()
End Sub
```

This information is enough for you to start creating your own card games. But if you think that I will do it for you, you are in for a big disappointment.

18.5. Snake

Snake is one of the most widespread computer games. It was even played on the first computers because it did not require graphical capabilities to implement. Gamers know this game under different names: Snake, Anaconda, Viper, etc. The game looks as follows: A small snake moves on the game field. Its movements are controlled by the keyboard keys. The goal of the game is to direct the snake to and eat the food (a stylized rabbit), which appears on the field in random places. With each devoured rabbit, the snake grows longer. The game has one restriction: the snake cannot eat itself. The game ends if the snake's head touches its body, meaning it has dined on itself. In some versions of the game, the field borders also cannot be touched. The game seems easy at first. But as the snake grows longer (and moves faster), the task becomes increasingly difficult.

By lucky chance, when I had just started writing my own version of the game I stumbled onto an interesting site devoted to this game. To top it off, there were versions of the game for different programming languages. The VB .NET code for the program is located at **http://neuron.csie.ntust.edu.tw/homework/91/PL/A9015047/VB.NETSnakeGame.htm.** I made some cosmetic modifications to the program, but it is so well-written that I had to abstain from doing anything more than that to it. I suggest that you examine this game in detail yourself. I added comments to some portions of the code, which will help you understand the principle of the game. The code is extensive and complex, consisting of several classes. To save space, I am not giving the entire code in the book; you can find it on the accompanying CD-ROM. Only a short piece of the code is given in the book. Create a new project, Snake, and place a picture box control on the form to use as the field for the snake to move on. Set the Size property of the form to 472, 405 and the Text property to Snake.

Set the following properties of the PictureBox1 control:

☐ Anchor = Top, Bottom, Left, Right
☐ BackColor = DarkOrange
☐ BorderStyle = Fixed3D
☐ Size = 450, 350

You will also need to place a few labels and a timer on the form. The labels can be placed in any convenient spot on the form. They will contain information about how to control the game. I tried to place labels near the center of the form. The background and text colors are left to your discretion. Fig. 18.6 shows my version of the starting screen of the game.

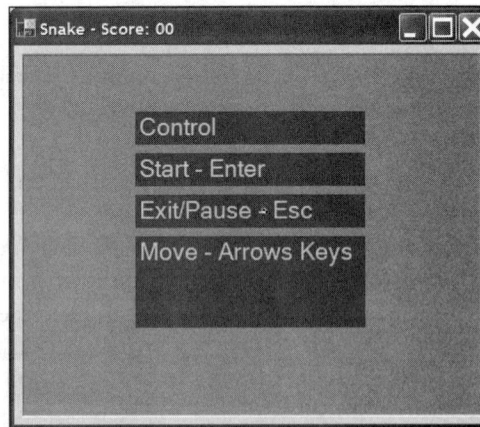

Fig. 18.6. The starting screen of the game

The visual part of programming the game is over. Now, you can start writing the code (Listing 18.11).

Listing 18.11. Snake

```
'---------------------------------------
' Snake © 2004 Alexander Klimov
'---------------------------------------
```

```vb
' Form1.vb
    ' The number of segments to add to the snake
    Private Const GROWTH_FACTOR As Integer = 3

    ' The width of a segment in pixels
    Private Const SNAKE_WIDTH As Integer = 8

    ' The snake object
    Private m_snake As snake

    ' Controlling the snake's moves
    Private m_control As SnakeControl

    ' Checking whether the game is running
    Private m_running As Boolean = False

    ' Checking whether the snake is growing longer
    Private m_growing As Boolean = False

    ' A rectangle used for the food (the dimensions and location)
    Private m_foodrec As Rectangle

    ' The score
    Private m_score As Integer

    Private Sub Form1_Load(ByVal sender As System.Object, ByVal e As System.EventArgs) _
Handles MyBase.Load
        ' Starting the game
        StartGame()
    End Sub

    Private Sub PictureBox1_Paint(ByVal sender As Object, ByVal e As _
System.Windows.Forms.PaintEventArgs) Handles PictureBox1.Paint
        ' If the game is running
        If Not m_running Then

            e.Graphics.Clear(PictureBox1.BackColor)

            Exit Sub

        End If

        ' Drawing food
        e.Graphics.FillEllipse(Brushes.Cornsilk, m_foodrec)

        ' A temporary variable to work with
        ' the snake's segments in the loop
```

```vb
    Dim thisseg As SnakeSegment

    ' Looping through all of the segments and drawing them
    For Each thisseg In m_snake.Segments

        ' Each segment is a small, colored rectangle.
        e.Graphics.FillRectangle(_
      Brushes.LimeGreen, thisseg.Rectangle)
    Next

End Sub

Private Sub Timer1_Tick(ByVal sender As System.Object, ByVal e As System.EventArgs) _
Handles Timer1.Tick
        ' Updating the game
        UpdateGame()

        ' Redrawing the game field
        PictureBox1.Invalidate()

End Sub

Private Sub GameOver()

    ShowMsg()
    MsgBox("Game is over!", vbOKOnly, "Snake")
    Label1.Visible = True
    Label2.Visible = True
    Label3.Visible = True
    Label4.Visible = True

    ' Starting a new game
    StartGame()

End Sub

Public Sub PlaceFood()
    ' Randomly selecting a place for
    ' the food for the snake on the field

    Dim foodpt As Point

    ' Making sure the food is not
    ' on the snake's body
```

```
        Do
            foodpt = GetRandomPoint()

            ' If there is a snake
            If Not (m_snake Is Nothing) Then

                ' Checking whether the food is on the snake
                If Not m_snake.PointOnSnake(foodpt) Then Exit Do
            Else
                Exit Do
            End If

        Loop
        ' Finding a position for the food
        m_foodrec.Location = foodpt

    End Sub

    Private Sub frmMain_KeyUp(ByVal sender As Object, ByVal e As  _
System.Windows.Forms.KeyEventArgs) Handles MyBase.KeyUp
        Select Case e.KeyCode

            Case Keys.Enter ' Game's start
                HideMsg()
                Cursor.Hide()
            Case Keys.Escape ' Pause/Exit
                If m_running Then
                    ShowMsg()
                Else
                    Me.Close()
                    Cursor.Show()
                End If
        End Select

    End Sub

    Private Sub frmMain_KeyDown(ByVal sender As Object, ByVal e As  _
System.Windows.Forms.KeyEventArgs) Handles MyBase.KeyDown
        Select Case e.KeyCode

            Case Keys.Right, Keys.NumPad6 ' Moving right

                m_control.Direction = SnakeControl.SnakeDirection.Right
```

```
        Case Keys.Down, Keys.NumPad2 ' Moving down

            m_control.Direction = SnakeControl.SnakeDirection.Down

        Case Keys.Left, Keys.NumPad4 ' Moving left

            m_control.Direction = SnakeControl.SnakeDirection.Left

        Case Keys.Up, Keys.NumPad8 ' Moving up

            m_control.Direction = SnakeControl.SnakeDirection.Up

        End Select

End Sub

Private Sub StartGame()
    ' Starting the game

    ' Zeroing out the score
    m_score = 0

    ' Initializing a food rectangle
    m_foodrec = New Rectangle(0, 0, SNAKE_WIDTH, SNAKE_WIDTH)

    ' Placing the food on the field
    PlaceFood()

    ' The starting location of the snake (center of the picture box)
    Dim startpt As New Point( _
    CInt(PictureBox1.ClientSize.Width / 2 / SNAKE_WIDTH + 0.5) * SNAKE_WIDTH, _
    CInt(PictureBox1.ClientSize.Height / 2 / SNAKE_WIDTH + 0.5) * SNAKE_WIDTH)

    ' Initializing a one-segment snake
    m_snake = New snake(startpt, SNAKE_WIDTH, 1)

    ' Initializing the snake control
    m_control = New SnakeControl(SNAKE_WIDTH, m_snake.Head.Location, _
SnakeControl.SnakeDirection.Right)

    ' The snake grows longer in small increments
    ' in the beginning of the game
    m_growing = True
```

```
End Sub

Private Sub UpdateGame()

    ' The number of segments by which to increase the snake's length
    Static targetgrowth As Integer = GROWTH_FACTOR

    ' The number of segments already added
    Static segmentsadded As Integer

    ' Exiting if the game is over
    If Not m_running Then Exit Sub

    ' Enabling the snake control
    m_control.Move(PictureBox1.ClientRectangle)

    ' If the snake has bitten itself
    If m_snake.PointOnSnake(m_control.Location) Then
        ' Zeroing out the variables
        targetgrowth = 0
        segmentsadded = 0
        ' The game is over
        GameOver()
        Return

        ' If the snake has eaten the food,
    ElseIf m_foodrec.Contains(m_control.Location) Then

        ' it grows longer.
        targetgrowth += GROWTH_FACTOR
        m_growing = True

        ' Placing a new portion of food
        PlaceFood()

        ' and incrementing the score
        m_score += 10
        Text = "Snake - Score:" + m_score.ToString
    End If

    ' Checking whether the snake can grow
    If m_growing Then

        ' Clearing the value if yes
```

```
            If targetgrowth < GROWTH_FACTOR Then targetgrowth = GROWTH_FACTOR

            ' If the snake is long enough,
            If segmentsadded >= targetgrowth Then

                m_growing = False
                segmentsadded = 0
                targetgrowth = 0

                ' The snake no longer grows
                ' but simply moves.
                m_snake.Slither(m_control.Location)

            Else

                ' Adding a new segment in the direction of the
                ' snake's move
                m_snake.Add(m_control.Location)

                ' Increasing the number of the segments already added
                segmentsadded += 1

            End If

        Else
            ' Moving the snake to a new point
            m_snake.Slither(m_control.Location)
        End If

End Sub

Private Sub ShowMsg()
    ' The procedure to pause the game
    ' and to display a message
    m_running = False
    Timer1.Enabled = False
    Label1.Visible = True
    Label2.Visible = True
    Label3.Visible = True
    Label4.Visible = True
End Sub


Private Sub HideMsg()
```

```
' Hiding the previous message
' and continuing the game

Label1.Visible = False
Label2.Visible = False
Label3.Visible = False
Label4.Visible = False

m_running = True

Timer1.Enabled = True

End Sub
```

And so on. Start the game, press the <Enter> key, and start controlling the snake using the arrow keys (Fig. 18.7).

Fig. 18.7. The Snake game

18.6. Suggestions and Recommendations

See if you can improve version two of the Crack the Safe game (*Section 18.2*). For example, instead of coloring buttons different colors, you can load a piece of an image into each button. Then the player will have the additional incentive to play of seeing the entire picture.

Using numerical data when creating a card game is inconvenient. Devise a way to correlate the value of a card with its description. For example, the card with value 0 can be correlated with the variable ClubsAce.

Chapter 19: Tricks

This chapter presents some tricks frequently used by programmers. The same tricks are used in most diverse programming languages. Most of these tricks are based on using the Windows API system functions. It is impossible to describe in one book all of these functions, which number is the tens of thousands.

19.1. Placing the Program Window in a Specified Location on the Screen

Sometimes, the program window has to be placed in a certain location on the screen, with the screen size and the taskbar taken into account. This task is easily solved using the `WorkingArea` property of the `SystemInformation` class. Don't forget that the taskbar can be parked not only at the bottom of the screen but also at one of the sides or at the top. A professionally designed program must take into account all of these circumstances and adjust itself to the user's preferences. The `RightCorner` project demonstrates how to place the form in the bottom right corner of the screen. The code to do this is placed into the handler of the form's `Load` event (Listing 19.1).

Listing 19.1. Placing the Form in the Specified Location on the Screen

```
'-------------------------------------
' RightCorner © 2004 Alexander Klimov
'-------------------------------------
    Private Sub Form1_Load(ByVal sender As System.Object, ByVal e As System.EventArgs) _
Handles MyBase.Load
        Dim wa As Rectangle = SystemInformation.WorkingArea
        Dim x As Integer = wa.Left + wa.Width - Me.Width
        Dim y As Integer = wa.Top + wa.Height - Me.Height
        Me.Location = New Point(x, y)
    End Sub
```

During the form-loading process, the work area of the screen is calculated and the co-ordinates of the upper left corner of the form are determined using simple mathematical calculations. Running the program, you will see that the program's window is displayed exactly above the taskbar (if the latter is parked at the bottom of the screen) in the lower right corner of the screen. Exit the program and place the taskbar in another location. Run the program again; you will see that its window is still displayed in the lower right corner of the screen.

19.2. Easter Eggs

Sometimes, to protect their intellectual property or for other reasons, programmers hide secret elements in their programs, things such as lists of the program developers, images, coded messages, or secret commands. These things are called *Easter eggs*. What a particular Easter egg does depends on the imagination of its developer. Sometimes, to find the Easter egg you have to perform a series of complex manipulations with the keyboard and the mouse, following a strict sequence. There are entire sites containing collections of various famous Easter eggs. Easter eggs have been found in such popular products as Internet Explorer, Windows 95, Adobe Photoshop, and Microsoft Excel. A simple Easter egg example can be seen in the popular WinRAR archiver (**http://www.rarlab.com**). Launch WinRAR and select the **About WinRAR** command. This will open a dialog window containing the version number and the names of the developers. To the left of the credentials, you will see the program's logo: a stack of bound books. Left-click on this stack and voilá! The stack of books starts to fall slowly, hits the bottom, bounces a few times, and finally comes to rest on the bottom.

We will now consider how to create a simple Easter egg. Create a new project and name it `EasterEgg`. The code to track keyboard strokes is shown in Listing 19.2.

Listing 19.2. Creating an Easter Egg

```
'---------------------------------------
' EasterEgg © 2004 Alexander Klimov
'---------------------------------------
    Private Sub Form1_KeyDown(ByVal sender As Object, ByVal e As _
System.Windows.Forms.KeyEventArgs) Handles MyBase.KeyDown
        Const EASTER_EGG As String = "CAT"
        Static COMPARE_STRING As String

        COMPARE_STRING = COMPARE_STRING & e.KeyCode.ToString
        If Microsoft.VisualBasic.Left(EASTER_EGG, Len(COMPARE_STRING)) <> COMPARE_STRING
Then
            ' If there is not a match, starting over
            COMPARE_STRING = ""
        Else
            ' If there is a match, meowing
            If EASTER_EGG = COMPARE_STRING Then
                MsgBox("Meow")
                COMPARE_STRING = ""
            End If
        End If
    End Sub
```

Set the form's `KeyPreview` property to `True` and run the program. Now type the word "cat," and you will see the corresponding message displayed on the screen. Playing a cat's meow audio file at the same time would be the icing on the cake. See whether you can handle this task yourself.

19.3. Launching Applications

If you need to launch another application from a program, you can take advantage of the `Start` method of the `Process` class. The `RunApp` project (Listing 19.3) demonstrates how to use this method to launch the standard Windows calculator.

Listing 19.3. Launching Applications

```
'---------------------------------------
' RunApp © 2004 Alexander Klimov
'---------------------------------------
    Private Sub butCalc_Click(ByVal sender As System.Object, ByVal e As _
System.EventArgs) Handles butCalc.Click
        ' Launching the calculator
        Process.Start("calc.exe")
    End Sub
```

This is the simplest case. A more complex example is launching an application with arguments. Suppose you need to launch Internet Explorer and automatically go to a certain site. The code for doing this is shown in Listing 19.4.

Listing 19.4. Running Internet Explorer and Opening a Specified Site

```
    Private Sub butIE_Click(ByVal sender As System.Object, ByVal e As System.EventArgs) _
Handles butIE.Click
        ' Running the browser and opening the specified site
        Process.Start("IExplore.exe", "E:\mysite\vb\index.htm")
    End Sub
```

If in addition to opening an application you want to specify the dimensions and location of its window, you can use the MoveWindow Widows API function:

```
Private Declare Function MoveWindow Lib "user32" Alias "MoveWindow" _
        (ByVal hwnd As IntPtr, ByVal x As Integer, _
        ByVal y As Integer, ByVal nWidth As Integer, _
        ByVal nHeight As Integer, _
        ByVal bRepaint As Integer) As Integer
```

After the application is launched, this function is passed the necessary parameters. Listing 19.5 shows the code to launch the standard Notepad with specified window dimensions and location.

Listing 19.5. Running Notepad in a Specified Size of Window and Location on the Screen

```
    Private Sub butNotepad_Click(ByVal sender As System.Object, ByVal e As _
System.EventArgs) Handles butNotepad.Click
        ' Launching Notepad
        Dim p As System.Diagnostics.Process = _
            System.Diagnostics.Process.Start("notepad.exe")
        p.WaitForInputIdle()
        ' Moving the window and setting its new dimensions
        MoveWindow(p.MainWindowHandle, 0, 10, 700, 200, 1)
    End Sub
```

19.4. One Application at a Time, Please

Some applications will not let the user to launch more than one instance of them. One of the simplest examples of such an application is Outlook Express. You cannot run more than one instance of this program, which is fully justified. Allowing more than one instance of this application to run would create confusion with receiving and sending mail. There are several techniques that can be used to achieve this limitation. I want to offer for your perusal one such technique, implemented in the OneInstance project (Listing 19.6).

Listing 19.6. Disallowing Another Instance of the Application to Run

```
'---------------------------------------
' OneInstance © 2004 Alexander Klimov
'---------------------------------------
    Public Enum ShowWindowConstants
        SW_HIDE = 0
        SW_SHOWNORMAL = 1
        SW_SHOWMINIMIZED = 2
        SW_SHOWMAXIMIZED = 3
        SW_MAXIMIZE = 3
        SW_SHOWNOACTIVATE = 4
        SW_SHOW = 5
        SW_MINIMIZE = 6
        SW_SHOWMINNOACTIVE = 7
        SW_SHOWNA = 8
        SW_RESTORE = 9
        SW_SHOWDEFAULT = 10
        SW_FORCEMINIMIZE = 11
    End Enum

    Declare Auto Function ShowWindowAsync Lib "user32.dll" ( _
        ByVal hwnd As IntPtr, _
        ByVal nCmdShow As Int32 _
      ) As Int32
    Public Shared Sub Main()

        ' Changing the application name if necessary
        Dim RunningProcesses As Process() = _
            Process.GetProcessesByName("OneInstance")

        If (RunningProcesses.Length = 1) Then
            Application.Run(New Form1)
        Else
            ShowWindowAsync( _
                    RunningProcesses(0).MainWindowHandle, _
                    ShowWindowConstants.SW_SHOWMINIMIZED)
            ShowWindowAsync( _
```

```
                RunningProcesses(0).MainWindowHandle, _
                ShowWindowConstants.SW_RESTORE)
        End If
    End Sub
```

In this example, the name of the process is obtained using the `Process` class and the situation is processed. If the application instance being launched is the first one, the length of the `RunningProcesses` array equals 1 and the application is launched in the normal mode. Otherwise, the previously-launched program is simply activated. Note the interesting use of the Windows API constants. Instead of declaring constants manually as usual, the example uses the `ShowWindowConstants` enumeration. If you enter the code into the preceding listing manually, you will see a pop-up box with a list of the available constants. Using this technique makes it easier to write code for complex applications.

19.5. Changing the Desktop Wallpaper

There is an entire class of programs that change the desktop wallpaper at scheduled intervals. There are scores of sites on the Internet with collections of thousands of beautiful (and some not so beautiful) desktop wallpapers. I will show you how to programmatically install a picture of you favorite cat as desktop wallpaper. Create a new project and name it `Wallpaper`. Place a button on the form and leave all of its default properties values. Now, switch into the code editor. First, we need to declare the `SystemParametersInfo` Windows API function and a few constants used by the function (Listing 19.7).

Listing 19.7. Changing the Desktop Wallpaper

```
'-------------------------------------
' Wallpaper © 2004 Alexander Klimov
'-------------------------------------
    Private Const SPI_SETDESKWALLPAPER As Integer = &H14
    Private Const SPIF_UPDATEINIFILE As Integer = &H1
    Private Const SPIF_SENDWININICHANGE As Integer = &H2
    Private Declare Auto Function SystemParametersInfo Lib "user32.dll" _
        (ByVal uAction As Integer, ByVal uParam As Integer, _
          ByVal lpvParam As String, ByVal fuWinIni As Integer) As Integer

  Dim imageLocation As String = Application.StartupPath & "..\..\mycat.bmp"

    Private Sub Button1_Click(ByVal sender As System.Object, ByVal e As _
System.EventArgs) Handles Button1.Click
        Try
            SystemParametersInfo(SPI_SETDESKWALLPAPER, 0, imageLocation, _
```

```
                 SPIF_UPDATEINIFILE Or SPIF_SENDWININICHANGE)
        Catch Ex As Exception
            MsgBox("Error installing wallpaper: " & Ex.Message)
        End Try
    End Sub
```

If necessary, you can change the path to the image file for your version of the project. Note that only BMP images can be used as wallpaper. It is also desirable to adjust the image dimensions to the dimensions of your monitor. In the example, I set up a check for a possible error when installing the wallpaper. Installing the image as wallpaper consists of calling the SystemParametersInfo function. The SPIF_UPDATEINIFILE and SPIF_SENDWININICHANGE parameters are used to inform Windows about the wallpaper change and to tell it to refresh the desktop image. As you can see, there is nothing complicated about it. Run the program. Close or minimize any other running programs, leaving only your program's form so that you could see the desktop. Click the button and you will see the fruits of your labors.

19.6. Animated Cursors

Most likely, you have seen the type of cursors Microsoft calls animated. Unfortunately, the Cursor class does not support either animated or colored cursors. But this problem is easily solved by calling the LoadCursorFromFile Windows API function, as demonstrated in the AniCursors project (Listing 19.8). The project code starts with declaring the function.

Listing 19.8. Using Animated Cursors

```
'-------------------------------------
' AniCursors © 2004 Alexander Klimov
'-------------------------------------
Imports System.IO

Private Declare Unicode Function LoadCursorFromFile _
    Lib "user32.dll" _
    Alias "LoadCursorFromFileW" (ByVal filename As String) As IntPtr

Private Const animatcursor As String = "cat.ani"

    Private Sub Button1_Click(ByVal sender As System.Object, ByVal e As _
System.EventArgs) Handles Button1.Click
        Dim filename As String
        Dim hCursor As IntPtr
        filename = Path.Combine(Application.StartupPath, animatcursor)
        hCursor = LoadCursorFromFile(filename)
```

```
        Me.Cursor = New Cursor(hCursor)
    End Sub


    Private Sub Form1_Click(ByVal sender As Object, ByVal e As System.EventArgs)    _
Handles MyBase.Click
        Me.Cursor = Cursors.Default
    End Sub
```

Build the project and run the program. When the button is clicked, the mouse pointer will change into an image of a running kitten. This cursor will be effective only within the limits of the client area of the form. To return the cursor to its usual appearance, its default property needs to be set. In this example, this is done by clicking anywhere on the form (the Form1_Click event).

19.7. An Unusual Caret

When the mouse pointer is placed over text, it takes on a special shape known to programmers as a *caret*. In programming, a caret is often drawn as a thin, vertical line. The caret is the default cursor for text fields, but its height and thickness can be changed; even the shape can be exchanged for an icon! Using an icon as the caret is demonstrated in the Caret project (Listing 19.9).

Listing 19.9. Using an Icon as the Caret

```
'-------------------------------
' Caret © 2005 Alexander Klimov
'-------------------------------
    Declare Function CreateCaret Lib "user32" _
        (ByVal hwnd As IntPtr, ByVal hBitmap As IntPtr, _
        ByVal nWidth As Integer, ByVal nHeight As Integer) As Integer
    Declare Function DestroyCaret Lib "user32.dll" () As Integer
    Declare Function SetCaretPos Lib "user32.dll" _
                (ByVal x As Integer, ByVal y As Integer) As Integer
    Declare Function HideCaret Lib "user32.dll" _
                (ByVal hwnd As IntPtr) As Integer
    Declare Function ShowCaret Lib "user32" _
        (ByVal hwnd As IntPtr) As Integer

    Dim bm As Bitmap = New Bitmap(Application.StartupPath & "..\..\sound.ico")
    Dim hBitmap As System.IntPtr = bm.GetHbitmap()

    Private Sub TextBox1_GotFocus(ByVal sender As Object, ByVal e As System.EventArgs)  _
Handles TextBox1.GotFocus
```

```
        CreateCaret(TextBox1.Handle, hBitmap, 16, 16)
        ShowCaret(TextBox1.Handle)
End Sub
```

First, you have to place a text box on the form to use as the proving grounds for the caret experiments. In the code editor, declare a few Windows API functions used to work with the caret. In essence, only two of these functions are used in the example, but I added the rest in case you decide to expand the project's capabilities. Because we are going to use an icon as the caret, the program needs to be shown the path to it. For aesthetic reasons, I selected an icon 16 × 16 pixels in size, but this is not mandatory. It must be said that Windows insistently tries to restore the conventional shape of the caret, so the functions have to be called continuously. The most convenient place for calling the functions is the GotFocus event. I must warn you that text boxes do not support full-fledged icons but distort them somewhat; consequently, if you decide to use icons as carets in your program, take care to have them look presentable.

19.8. A Colorful Console

In some cases, it is more convenient to use console applications instead of windows with a graphical interface. But the standard console with the black-and-white screen and white text is soooo boring. What about using other colors? Have you ever thought about this? You should have! I will show you how to make the console multicolored. Currently, the .NET framework has no direct means for changing the console colors and we have to resort to Windows API functions again to solve this task. Launch the Visual Basic .NET visual studio and create a console project. Name it ColorConsole. Add a new class to the project. By default, its name is class1.vb. We will place the calls to the functions we will need in this class (Listing 19.10).

Listing 19.10. The Class Used To Hold Function Calls

```
'---------------------------------------------
' ColorConsole © 2004 Alexander Klimov
'---------------------------------------------
Imports System.Runtime.InteropServices

  Public Class Class1

    Private hConsoleHandle As IntPtr
    Private ConsoleOutputLocation As COORD
    Private ConsoleInfo As CONSOLE_SCREEN_BUFFER_INFO
    Private OriginalColors As Integer
```

```
Private Const STD_OUTPUT_HANDLE As Integer = &HFFFFFFF5

Private Declare Auto Function GetStdHandle Lib "kernel32.dll" _
                    (ByVal nStdHandle As Integer) As IntPtr

Private Declare Auto Function GetConsoleScreenBufferInfo _
    Lib "kernel32.dll" (ByVal hConsoleOutput As IntPtr, _
                    ByRef lpConsoleScreenBufferInfo As _
                    CONSOLE_SCREEN_BUFFER_INFO) As Integer

Private Declare Auto Function SetConsoleTextAttribute _
    Lib "kernel32" (ByVal hConsoleOutput As IntPtr, _
                    ByVal wAttributes As Integer) As Long

Public Enum Foreground
    Blue = &H1
    Green = &H2
    Red = &H4
    Intensity = &H8
End Enum

Public Enum Background
    Blue = &H10
    Green = &H20
    Red = &H40
    Intensity = &H80
End Enum

<StructLayout(LayoutKind.Sequential)> _
Private Structure COORD
    Dim X As Short
    Dim Y As Short
End Structure

<StructLayout(LayoutKind.Sequential)> _
Private Structure SMALL_RECT
    Dim Left As Short
    Dim Top As Short
    Dim Right As Short
    Dim Bottom As Short
End Structure

<StructLayout(LayoutKind.Sequential)> _
```

```
Private Structure CONSOLE_SCREEN_BUFFER_INFO
    Dim dwSize As COORD
    Dim dwCursorPosition As COORD
    Dim wAttributes As Integer
    Dim srWindow As SMALL_RECT
    Dim dwMaximumWindowSize As COORD
End Structure

Sub New()
    hConsoleHandle = GetStdHandle(STD_OUTPUT_HANDLE)
    GetConsoleScreenBufferInfo(hConsoleHandle, ConsoleInfo)
    OriginalColors = ConsoleInfo.wAttributes
End Sub

Public Sub TextColor(ByVal Colors As Integer)
    ' Setting the text color
    SetConsoleTextAttribute(hConsoleHandle, Colors)
End Sub

Public Sub ResetColor()
    ' Restoring the original colors
    SetConsoleTextAttribute(hConsoleHandle, OriginalColors)
End Sub
End Class
```

Now, switch to the main module, module1.vb, and write the main code in there (Listing 19.11).

Listing 19.11. Using the Color Console

```
'-------------------------------------------
' ColorConsole © 2004 Alexander Klimov
'-------------------------------------------
Imports System.Console
Module Module1

    Sub Main()
        Dim TextChange As New Class1
        WriteLine("The original colors")
        WriteLine("Press ENTER to start the demonstration")
        ReadLine()

        TextChange.TextColor(_
            Class1.Foreground.Green + Class1.Foreground.Intensity)
```

```
      WriteLine("Text is displayed in green")
      WriteLine("Press ENTER to change the text color")
      ReadLine()
      TextChange.TextColor(_
        Class1.Foreground.Red + Class1.Foreground.Intensity)
      WriteLine("Now the text is red")
      WriteLine("Press ENTER to change the text color again")
      ReadLine()
      TextChange.TextColor(_
        Class1.Foreground.Blue + _
        Class1.Foreground.Intensity + _
        Class1.Background.Green + _
        Class1.Background.Intensity)
      WriteLine("Now the text is blue and the background is green")
      WriteLine("Press ENTER to restore the original colors")
      ReadLine()
      TextChange.ResetColor()
      WriteLine("Color settings are restored")
      WriteLine("Press ENTER to exit")
      ReadLine()

    End Sub
End Module
```

The example is simple and does not require additional explanation.

> **NOTE**
> The developers have promised to add new classes in VB .NET 2005 to work with console applications that will implement the capabilities demonstrated in the example.

19.9. Obtaining the Program Version Information

As a rule, in the **About the program** dialog window, the author places his or her name, the company name, the trademark, the copyright information, and the program version. Such data can be written manually in the program's code. But nobody usually does it manually because there is a way to automate this routine job. When a new project is created in VB .NET 2003, a special file, assemblyinfo.vb, is created for storing this type of data along with the other files. Open this file in the code editor; you will see approximately the following code:

```
Imports System
Imports System.Reflection
```

```
Imports System.Runtime.InteropServices

' General information about an assembly is controlled through
' the following set of attributes. Change these attribute values
' to modify the information associated with an assembly.

' Review the values of the assembly attributes.

<Assembly: AssemblyTitle("")>
<Assembly: AssemblyDescription("")>
<Assembly: AssemblyCompany("")>
<Assembly: AssemblyProduct("")>
<Assembly: AssemblyCopyright("")>
<Assembly: AssemblyTrademark("")>
<Assembly: CLSCompliant(True)>

' The following GUID is for the ID of typelib if this project
' is exposed to COM.
<Assembly: Guid("AD5CF26B-20A8-44E7-83EB-C08C8BB74528")>

' Version information for an assembly consists of four values:
'
'       Major Version
'       Minor Version
'       Build Number
'       Revision
'
' You can specify all the values, or you can apply the default for
' the build and revision numbers by using the '*' as follows:

<Assembly: AssemblyVersion("1.0.*")>
```

Some values in this code can be modified. The default values are used for parameters that are not modified. Here is how I modified some code lines in our example:

```
<Assembly: AssemblyTitle("Information about the program assembly")>
<Assembly: AssemblyDescription("An example of obtaining the program version information")>
<Assembly: AssemblyCompany("Alexander Klimov")>
<Assembly: AssemblyVersion("2.0.*")>
```

With the new values set for project assembly, you can obtain these data programmatically. The project version example (Listing 19.12) demonstrates how to do this. Before writing the code, place three labels on the form to display the necessary values.

Listing 19.12. Obtaining the Program Version Information

```
'-------------------------------------
' Version © 2004 Alexander Klimov
'-------------------------------------
Imports System.Reflection

    Private Sub Form1_Load(ByVal sender As System.Object, ByVal e As System.EventArgs) _
Handles MyBase.Load
        MyAssembly = [Assembly].GetExecutingAssembly()

        lblGetDescr.Text = GetAssemblyDescription()
        lblGetVersion.Text = GetAssemblyVersion()
        lblGetCompany.Text = GetAssemblyCompany()
    End Sub

    ' Returning the value of the Description attribute
    Private Function GetAssemblyDescription() As String
        If MyAssembly.IsDefined(GetType(AssemblyDescriptionAttribute), True) Then
            Dim attr As Attribute = _
                Attribute.GetCustomAttribute(MyAssembly, _
                    GetType(AssemblyDescriptionAttribute))
            Dim description_attr As AssemblyDescriptionAttribute = _
                DirectCast(attr, AssemblyDescriptionAttribute)
            Return description_attr.Description
        Else
            Return ""
        End If
    End Function

    ' Returning the value of the Company attribute
    Private Function GetAssemblyCompany() As String
        If MyAssembly.IsDefined(GetType(AssemblyCompanyAttribute), True) Then
            Dim attr As Attribute = _
                Attribute.GetCustomAttribute(MyAssembly, _
                    GetType(AssemblyCompanyAttribute))
            Dim company_attr As AssemblyCompanyAttribute = _
                DirectCast(attr, AssemblyCompanyAttribute)
            Return company_attr.Company
        Else
            Return ""
        End If
    End Function

    ' Returning the value of the Version attribute
```

```
Private Function GetAssemblyVersion() As String
    Dim myVersion As AssemblyName = MyAssembly.GetName()

    Return myVersion.Version.Major.ToString & "." & _
        myVersion.Version.Minor.ToString & "." & _
        myVersion.Version.Build.ToString & "." & _
        myVersion.Version.Revision.ToString
End Function
```

19.10. Converting Roman Numerals

In everyday life, we often use Roman numerals: on clock and watch faces, for numbering book pages, for dates on monuments, etc. But can we all determine without prolonged thought what number is, for example, MCMXCV? Most of us would have problems telling what number this is, and some people cannot even use the Roman numeral system. It is too cumbersome and too inconvenient to use. But an educated person, or someone who claims to be so, must have at least some knowledge of this system. There is the following rule about the Roman numeral system: If the greater digit is in front of the smaller, they are added. If the smaller digit is in front of the larger, it is subtracted from the greater digit. Here are some examples:

```
VI = 5 + 1 = 6
IXX = 20 - 1 = 19
```

An American scientist, Stephen Schwartzman, suggested a special standard, International Standard Roman Numerals (ISRN), that describes rules to depict Roman numerals. For example, one of the rules states that there cannot be more than three identical digits in a row. But don't be surprised if you see numbers that do not fit this standard on some antique clocks: the standard was introduced relatively recently. In particular, the number 4 is often written as IIII instead of IV. Table 19.1 lists Roman numerals and their corresponding Arabic equivalents.

Table 19.1. Roman Numerals and Their Arabic Equivalents

Units		Tens		Hundreds		Thousands	
1	I	10	X	100	C	1000	M
2	II	20	XX	200	CC	2000	MM
3	III	30	XXX	300	CCC	3000	MMM
4	IV	40	XL	400	CD		
5	V	50	L	500	D		

continues

Table 19.1 Continued

Units		Tens		Hundreds		Thousands
6	VI	60	LX	600	DC	
7	VII	70	LXX	700	DCC	
8	VIII	80	LXXX	800	DCCC	
9	IX	90	XC	900	CM	

But there is no need for you to memorize this table. In the Roman2Arab project, I will show you how to write a program to convert Roman numerals into the familiar Arabic ones. You will need to place two text box controls and one button on the form. Set the following properties of the first text box, into which Roman numbers will be entered:

❑ Name = txtRoman   ❑ CharacterCasing = Upper   ❑ Text = X

Set the following properties of the second text box, in which the corresponding Arabic numbers will be output:

❑ Name = txtArab   ❑ ReadOnly = True   ❑ Text = 10

Set the following properties of the button:

❑ Name = butConvert   ❑ Text = Convert

Because Roman numerals are customarily written in uppercase letters, I set the value of the CharacterCasing property to Upper, which automatically converts symbols to uppercase. The code for the function to convert Roman numerals into Arabic is given in Listing 19.13.

Listing 19.13. A Roman-to-Arabic Numeral Converter

```
'---------------------------------------
' Roman2Arab © 2004 Alexander Klimov
'---------------------------------------
    ' Returning the number in Arabic numerals
    Private Function RomanToArabic(ByVal roman As String) As Long
        Dim i As Integer
        Dim ch As String
        Dim result As Long
        Dim new_value As Long
```

```
Dim old_value As Long

old_value = 1000

For i = 1 To Len(roman)
    ch = Mid$(roman, i, 1)
    Select Case ch
        Case "I"
            new_value = 1
        Case "V"
            new_value = 5
        Case "X"
            new_value = 10
        Case "L"
            new_value = 50
        Case "C"
            new_value = 100
        Case "D"
            new_value = 500
        Case "M"
            new_value = 1000
    End Select

    If new_value > old_value Then
        ' If the new value is greater than the preceding
        ' character, then add this value to the result
        ' and subtract the preceding character twice.
        result = result + new_value - 2 * old_value
    Else
        ' If the new value is smaller than or equal to the
        ' preceding character, then add this value to the result.
        result = result + new_value
    End If

    old_value = new_value
Next i
Return result
End Function

Private Sub butConvert_Click(ByVal sender As System.Object, ByVal e As _
System.EventArgs) Handles butConvert.Click
    txtArab.Text = RomanToArabic(txtRoman.Text)
End Sub
```

Now, you can check whether you correctly deciphered the Roman number mentioned at the beginning of the section.

19.11. File Properties

Right-clicking on a file icon opens the context menu for the file. One of its items is **Properties**; selecting this opens the same-name dialog window listing various file properties. You can write a program to open a file properties window. The FileProperties project shows you how to do this. All necessary file properties are contained in the FileVersionInfo class. Place seven text boxes on the form. These will receive the descriptions of the obtained properties and the properties themselves. To identify, which text box holds which property, mark them with labels. Place another text box at the top of the form and use it to enter the path to the necessary file. The code for obtaining file properties is placed in the button's click event handler (Listing 19.14).

Listing 19.14. Obtaining File Properties

```
'---------------------------------------
' FileProperties © 2004 Alexander Klimov
'---------------------------------------

    Private Sub Button1_Click(ByVal sender As System.Object, ByVal e As _
System.EventArgs) Handles Button1.Click
        ' Obtaining file properties from the specified file
        Dim FileProperties As FileVersionInfo = _
FileVersionInfo.GetVersionInfo(txtFilePath.Text)

        ' The file description
        TextBox1.Text = FileProperties.FileDescription
        ' The file version
        TextBox2.Text = FileProperties.FileVersion
        ' The internal file name
        TextBox3.Text = FileProperties.InternalName
        ' The initial file name
        TextBox4.Text = FileProperties.OriginalFilename
        ' The product name
        TextBox5.Text = FileProperties.ProductName
        ' The product version
        TextBox6.Text = FileProperties.ProductVersion
        ' The language
        TextBox7.Text = FileProperties.Language
    End Sub
```

Now, you can determine the necessary file properties programmatically.

19.12. Screenshots

In Section 9.4, we considered taking a screenshot of either the entire screen or the active window only by programmatically pressing the <Print Scrn> key (the PrintScreen project). But that method is not flexible enough. So let's return to this subject and consider other methods for taking screenshots. In case you have forgotten, screenshots are snapshots of the monitor screen. Their use is most widespread in gaming magazines to give gamers an idea what a new game is like. Screenshots are also widely used to give potential buyers an idea about the appearance and features of programs offered for sale on the Internet. Screenshots can be taken in several ways: of the entire screen, of a program form, or of an individual control. I want to give you a basic idea about how to take such screenshots programmatically. The example is implemented in the GetScreenShot project (Listing 19.15). Place one picture box and three buttons on the form. You can leave the default names of the controls, but it would be a good idea to change the texts of the buttons to avoid confusion about what each button does.

Listing 19.15. Obtaining Screenshots

```
'------------------------------------
' GetScreenShot © 2004 Alexander Klimov
'------------------------------------
    ' Windows API structures
    Private Structure POINTAPI
        Public x As Int32
        Public y As Int32
    End Structure

    Private Structure RECT
        Public Left As Int32
        Public Top As Int32
        Public Right As Int32
        Public Bottom As Int32
    End Structure

    ' Windows API functions
    Private Declare Function GetDesktopWindow Lib "user32.dll" _
        () As IntPtr

    Private Declare Function GetWindowRect Lib "user32.dll" _
        (ByVal hWnd As IntPtr, ByRef lpRect As RECT) As Int32

    Private Declare Function ScreenToClient Lib "user32.dll" _
```

```
            (ByVal hWnd As IntPtr, ByRef lpPoint As POINTAPI) As Int32

    Private Declare Function GetDC Lib "user32.dll" _
            (ByVal hWnd As IntPtr) As IntPtr

    Private Declare Function BitBlt Lib "gdi32" Alias "BitBlt" _
            (ByVal hDestDC As Integer, ByVal x As Integer, _
             ByVal y As Integer, ByVal nWidth As Integer, _
             ByVal nHeight As Integer, ByVal hSrcDC As Integer, _
             ByVal xSrc As Integer, ByVal ySrc As Integer, _
             ByVal dwRop As Integer) As Integer

    Private Declare Function GetWindowDC Lib "user32" Alias "GetWindowDC" _
            (ByVal hwnd As Integer) As IntPtr

    Private Declare Function ReleaseDC Lib "user32.dll" _
            (ByVal hWnd As IntPtr, ByVal hdc As IntPtr) As Int32

    Private Declare Function StretchBlt Lib "gdi32.dll" _
            (ByVal hdc As IntPtr, ByVal x As Int32, _
             ByVal y As Int32, ByVal nWidth As Int32, _
             ByVal nHeight As Int32, ByVal hSrcDC As IntPtr, _
             ByVal xSrc As Int32, ByVal ySrc As Int32, _
             ByVal nSrcWidth As Int32, ByVal nSrcHeight As Int32, _
             ByVal dwRop As Int32) As Int32

    ' The constant
    Private Const SRCCOPY As Int32 = &HCC0020

    Private Sub Button1_Click(ByVal sender As System.Object, ByVal e As _
System.EventArgs) Handles Button1.Click
        ' Taking a screenshot of the entire screen
        Dim hWndDesktop As IntPtr

        ' Obtaining the desktop handle
        hWndDesktop = GetDesktopWindow()

        ' Obtaining the window size
        Dim rct As RECT
        GetWindowRect(hWndDesktop, rct)
        Dim Width As Int32 = rct.Right - rct.Left
        Dim Height As Int32 = rct.Bottom - rct.Top

        ' Coordinates in the client coordinate system
```

```
    Dim pt As New POINTAPI
    pt.y = rct.Top
    pt.x = rct.Left
    ScreenToClient(hWndDesktop, pt)
    rct.Left = pt.x
    rct.Top = pt.y

    ' The bitmap object, in which the screenshot will be held
    Dim b As New Bitmap(Width, Height)

    ' Creating a graphics object
    Dim g As Graphics = Graphics.FromImage(b)

    ' Obtaining the screen device context
    Dim hdcWindow As IntPtr = GetDC(hWndDesktop)

    ' Obtaining the graphics object device context
    Dim hdc As IntPtr = g.GetHdc()

    BitBlt(hdc.ToInt32, 0, 0, _
        Width, Height, hdcWindow.ToInt32, _
        rct.Left, rct.Top, SRCCOPY)

    ' Releasing resources
    ReleaseDC(hWndDesktop, hdcWindow)
    g.ReleaseHdc(hdc)

    ' Placing the screenshot in the graphics object
    PictureBox1.Image = b
End Sub

Private Sub Button2_Click(ByVal sender As System.Object, ByVal e As  _
System.EventArgs) Handles Button2.Click
    ' A screenshot of a button
    ' Obtaining the button device context through its handle
    Dim hdcWindow As IntPtr = GetDC(Button1.Handle)
    Dim rct As RECT
    Dim pt As New POINTAPI
    pt.y = rct.Top
    pt.x = rct.Left
    ScreenToClient(hdcWindow, pt)
    rct.Left = pt.x
    rct.Top = pt.y

    Dim b As New Bitmap(PictureBox1.Width, PictureBox1.Height)

    Dim g As Graphics = Graphics.FromImage(b)
```

```vb
    Dim hdc As IntPtr = g.GetHdc()
    BitBlt(hdc.ToInt32, 0, 0 _
       Button1.Width, Button1.Height, hdcWindow.ToInt32, _
       rct.Left, rct.Top, SRCCOPY)

    PictureBox1.Image = b
    ReleaseDC(Button1.Handle, hdcWindow)
    g.ReleaseHdc(hdc)
    g.Dispose()

End Sub

Private Sub Button3_Click(ByVal sender As System.Object, _
      ByVal e As System.EventArgs) Handles Button3.Click

    Dim hdcForm As IntPtr = GetWindowDC(Me.Handle.ToInt32)
    Dim rct As RECT
    Dim pt As New POINTAPI
    pt.y = rct.Top
    pt.x = rct.Left
    ScreenToClient(hdcForm, pt)
    rct.Left = pt.x
    rct.Top = pt.y

    Dim b As New Bitmap(PictureBox1.Width, PictureBox1.Height)

    Dim g As Graphics = Graphics.FromImage(b)
    Dim hdc As IntPtr = g.GetHdc()

    StretchBlt(hdc, 0, 0, _
    PictureBox1.Width, PictureBox1.Height, _
    hdcForm, rct.Left, rct.Top, Width, Height, SRCCOPY)

    PictureBox1.Image = b
    ReleaseDC(Button1.Handle, hdcForm)
    g.ReleaseHdc(hdc)
    g.Dispose()

End Sub

Private Sub Button4_Click(ByVal sender As System.Object, ByVal e As _
System.EventArgs) Handles Button4.Click
      ' Taking a timed screenshot

      ' Changing the mouse pointer
```

```
      Me.Cursor = Cursors.WaitCursor

      ' Setting the interval to 3 seconds
      Timer1.Interval = 3000
      Timer1.Enabled = True
  End Sub

  Private Sub Timer1_Tick(ByVal sender As System.Object, ByVal e As  _
  System.EventArgs) Handles Timer1.Tick
      Timer1.Enabled = False
      Dim hWndDesktop As IntPtr

      hWndDesktop = GetDesktopWindow()
      ' Obtaining the screen device context
      Dim hdcWindow As IntPtr = GetDC(hWndDesktop)

      Dim desk_bounds As Rectangle
      desk_bounds = Screen.GetBounds(New Point(1, 1))
      Dim desk_w As Int32 = desk_bounds.Width
      Dim desk_h As Int32 = desk_bounds.Height

      ' The bitmap object, in which the screenshot will be held
      Dim b As New Bitmap(desk_w, desk_h)

      ' Creating a graphics object
      Dim g As Graphics = Graphics.FromImage(b)

      ' Obtaining the device context of the graphics object
      Dim hdc As IntPtr = g.GetHdc()

      ' Obtaining the image
      StretchBlt( _
          hdc, 0, 0, desk_w, desk_h, _
          hdcWindow, 0, 0, desk_w, desk_h, _
          SRCCOPY)

      ' Releasing resources
      ReleaseDC(hWndDesktop, hdcWindow)
      g.ReleaseHdc(hdc)

      ' Placing the screenshot in the graphics object
      PictureBox1.Image = b
      ' Restoring the standard mouse pointer
      Me.Cursor = Cursors.Default
  End Sub
```

Let's examine the example. First, we need to declare a few Windows API structures and functions, because the standard VB .NET means are not sufficient for the job at hand. Then, we can start implementing the task. The first objective is to take a screenshot of the entire screen. For this, we obtain the screen handle by calling the `GetDesktopWindow` function. Once this handle is available, we obtain the screen dimensions using the `GetWindowRect` function. We must perform a few simple mathematical calculations in the process:

```
' Obtaining the window size
Dim Width As Int32 = rct.Right - rct.Left
Dim Height As Int32 = rct.Bottom - rct.Top
```

Having obtained the necessary dimensions, we convert them into the client coordinate system with the help of the `ScreenToClient` function. Next, we create `Bitmap` and `Graphics` objects for working with graphics. Once the window handle and graphics objects are available, we call the `BitBlt` function to create the device context that works directly with graphics. This function allows a rectangular area to be copied from one device context into another device context. The obtained screenshot is placed in the `PictureBox` control. Having completed all work, don't forget to release the resources:

```
ReleaseDC(hWndDesktop, hdcWindow)
g.ReleaseHdc(hdc)
```

19.12.1. Taking a Screenshot of an Individual Control

The analogous technology can be used to take a screenshot of an individual control. For example, the second button on the form can be used to obtain a screenshot of the first button. In this case, there is no need to use the Windows API function to obtain the handle, because the button already has the necessary property: `Button1.Handle`. The rest of the code is practically the same as the code for obtaining a screenshot of the entire screen. Run the program and click the second button to get a screenshot of the first button.

19.12.2. Taking a Screenshot of a Form

There is one final detail involved when obtaining a screenshot of a form: Calling only the `GetDC` function allows only a screenshot of the client area of the form to be obtained. To work around this limitation and obtain a screenshot of the entire form, including the title bar, menu, and scrolling bars, the `GetWindowsDC` function needs to be called. The rest of the procedure is the same as in the previous two cases. For variety, instead of the `BitBlt` function I used a similar function, `StretchBlt`, which stretches or compresses the image.

19.12.3. Taking a Screenshot After a Specified Interval

The code in the click event of the fourth button allows screenshots to be taken after a specified time interval. This may be necessary when taking a screenshot of such program windows as the task-switching window, which opens by pressing the <Alt>+<Tab> key combination. In this situation, the window disappears when the keys are released, and a screenshot cannot be made. This problem can be solved with the help of a timer. Click the corresponding button and press and hold the necessary key combination. After the specified time interval elapses, the screenshot of the screen with the task-switching window will appear in the picture box.

19.13. The International Friday

Do you know how to write "Friday" in Arabic? How about German? Spanish? It is not necessary for you to hit foreign language dictionaries to be able to write this word in at least seven different languages. You can do this with the help of the VB .NET CultureInfo class. The example is implemented in the Friday project (Listing 19.16). You will have to place seven text boxes and one button on the form.

Listing 19.16. Writing "Friday" in Different Languages

```
'-------------------------------------
' Friday © 2004 Alexander Klimov
'-------------------------------------
Imports System.Globalization

    Private Sub butFriday_Click(ByVal sender As System.Object, ByVal e As _
System.EventArgs) Handles butFriday.Click
        ' In Russian
        Dim ci As New CultureInfo("ru-RU")
        ' Obtaining the DateTimeFormatInfo object
        Dim dtfi As DateTimeFormatInfo = ci.DateTimeFormat
        TextBox1.Text = (dtfi.GetDayName(DayOfWeek.Friday))

        ' In Egyptian Arabic
        ci = New CultureInfo("ar-EG")
        dtfi = ci.DateTimeFormat
        TextBox2.Text = (dtfi.GetDayName(DayOfWeek.Friday))

        ' In Belarusian
        ci = New CultureInfo("be-BY")
        dtfi = ci.DateTimeFormat
```

```
    TextBox3.Text = (dtfi.GetDayName(DayOfWeek.Friday))

    ' In Bulgarian
    ci = New CultureInfo("bg-BG")
    dtfi = ci.DateTimeFormat
    TextBox4.Text = (dtfi.GetDayName(DayOfWeek.Friday))

    ' In Finnish
    ci = New CultureInfo("fi-FI")
    dtfi = ci.DateTimeFormat
    TextBox5.Text = (dtfi.GetDayName(DayOfWeek.Friday))

    ' In French
    ci = New CultureInfo("fr-FR")
    dtfi = ci.DateTimeFormat
    TextBox6.Text = (dtfi.GetDayName(DayOfWeek.Friday))

    ' In Ukrainian
    ci = New CultureInfo("uk-UA")
    dtfi = ci.DateTimeFormat
    TextBox7.Text = (dtfi.GetDayName(DayOfWeek.Friday))
End Sub
```

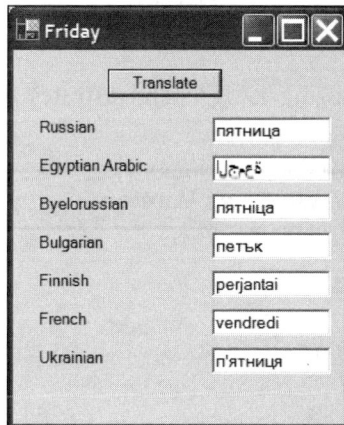

Fig. 19.1. Translating "Friday" into different languages

The necessary language is set using the CultureInfo class; then the DayOfWeek.Friday constant, which corresponds to Friday, is translated into the specified language (Fig. 19.1). The same method can be used to translate constants defining month and weekday names into other languages.

19.14. Determining the Windows Version

Every time a new Windows version is introduced, programmers face new problems maintaining the compatibility of their programs because new functions are added to the operating system and old functions are removed. To make your program run properly under all Windows versions, you have to know the Windows version installed on a specific user's machine. This task is solved using the OperatingSystem class of the System namespace. In its properties, the class contains all necessary information for determining the operating system installed. Table 19.2 lists the properties of the OperatingSystem class that can be used to identify the operating system version.

Table 19.2. The Properties of the OperatingSystem Class Used for Identifying the Computer Platform

OS	Platform	Major	Minor
Win95	1	4	0
Win98	1	4	10
WinME	1	4	90
NT 3.51	2	3	51
NT 4.0	2	4	0
Win2000	2	5	0

The WinVersion project (Listing 19.17) demonstrates a technique for identifying the operating system version.

Listing 19.17. Determining the Windows Version

```
'---------------------------------------
' WinVersion © 2005 Alexander Klimov
'---------------------------------------
Imports System.Environment

    Private osInfo As OperatingSystem

    Private Sub Button1_Click(ByVal sender As System.Object, ByVal e As _
System.EventArgs) Handles Button1.Click
        MsgBox(GetWinVersion)
    End Sub

    Public Function GetWinVersion() As String
```

```
' The function used to determine the Windows version
osInfo = OSVersion
With osInfo
    Select Case .Platform

        Case .Platform.Win32Windows
            Select Case (.Version.Minor)
                Case 0
                    Return "Windows 95"
                Case 10
                    If .Version.Revision.ToString() = "2222A" Then
                        Return "Windows 98 Second Edition"
                    Else
                        Return "Windows 98"
                    End If
                Case 90
                    Return "Windows ME"
            End Select

        Case .Platform.Win32NT
            Select Case (.Version.Major)
                Case 3
                    Return "Windows NT 3.51"
                Case 4
                    Return "Windows NT 4.0"
                Case 5
                    If .Version.Minor = 0 Then
                        Return "Windows 2000"
                    Else
                        Return "Windows XP " & .Version.Major.ToString & _
                                       "." & .Version.Minor.ToString & _
                                       "." & .Version.Build & _
                                       "." & .Version.Revision

                    End If
            End Select

        Case Else
            GetWinVersion = "Error"
    End Select
End With
End Function
```

19.15. Mailing Letters

If you need to send a letter from an application, you can take advantage of the System.Web.Mail namespace. Create a new project and name it WebSendMail. The System.Web.Mail namespace is not referenced by projects by default; a reference to it has to be added manually. This is done as follows: In the **Project** menu, select the **Add Reference** command. In the **Add Reference** dialog window that opens, select the **.NET** tab. Select the **system.web.dll** item in the list and click the **Select** button. Click the **OK** button to close the dialog window. Place a button on the form. Its click event handler will contain the code responsible for sending letters (Listing 19.18).

Listing 19.18. Sending Letters from a Program

```
'------------------------------------
' WebSendMail © 2004 Alexander Klimov
'------------------------------------
Imports System.Web.Mail

    Private Sub butSendMail_Click(ByVal sender As System.Object, _
            ByVal e As System.EventArgs) Handles butSendMail.Click
        Dim oMsg As MailMessage = New MailMessage

        ' The sender's email address
        oMsg.From = "from_cat@sender_address.com"

        ' The recipient's email address
        oMsg.To = "to_kitty@dest_address.com"

        ' The letter subject
        oMsg.Subject = "In search of true love"

        ' The letter body
        oMsg.Body = "Single cat looking for a kitty" & _
                    "Myself: ginger tabby, whiskered, like to caterwaul"

        ' Here should be your SMTP server.
        SmtpMail.SmtpServer = "smtp.your.server.com"
        SmtpMail.Send(oMsg)

        oMsg = Nothing
    End Sub
```

When working with the example, change the email address in the oMsg.From = "from_cat@sender_address.com" line to your email address. You will also have to specify the real recipient's email address and the real SMTP mail server.

19.16. Open Sesame!

Now, we will write a hacker program to read text hidden under asterisks. Create a new project, OpenPass, and place a timer, a label, and a text box on the form. Set the PasswordChar property of the text box to * and the Enabled property of the timer to True. Leave the default values for the other properties of the controls. To obtain the text hidden under asterisks, the handle of the window containing the text has to be obtained. In this case, this will be the text box handle. With the necessary handle at your disposal, you can obtain the window's text using the GetWindowText function. Because we are going to write a universal program that can obtain handles of other windows, we will have to use a few other Windows API functions. The WindowFromPoint function returns the handle to the window that contains the specified point (the point under the mouse pointer); the GetCursorPos function returns the current coordinates of the mouse pointer in screen coordinates. Consequently, our task comes down to the following: The position of the mouse pointer is tracked and the handle to the window under it is obtained. Then we simply extract the window's text and place it where it can be observed. The code for doing this is given in Listing 19.19.

Listing 19.19. Extracting Passwords

```
'------------------------------------
' OpenPass © 2004 Alexander Klimov
'------------------------------------
    Structure POINTAPI
        Public x As Int32
        Public y As Int32
    End Structure

    Declare Function WindowFromPoint Lib "user32" _
        (ByVal xPoint As Integer, _
        ByVal yPoint As Integer) As Integer

    Declare Function GetCursorPos Lib "user32" _
        (ByRef lpPoint As POINTAPI) As Integer

    Public Declare Auto Function GetWindowText Lib "user32" _
        (ByVal hWnd As Integer, _
        ByVal lpString As System.Text.StringBuilder, _
```

```
        ByVal cch As Integer) As Integer

   Dim pt As POINTAPI

   Private Sub Timer1_Tick(ByVal sender As System.Object, ByVal e As    _
   System.EventArgs) Handles Timer1.Tick
        ' Obtaining the current position of the cursor
        GetCursorPos(pt)

        ' The handle to the window under the cursor
        Dim iret As Integer
        iret = WindowFromPoint(pt.x, pt.y)

        ' A string buffer
        Dim Caption As New System.Text.StringBuilder(256)

        ' The text being returned
        Dim t As String
        t = GetWindowText(iret, Caption, Caption.Capacity)

        ' Now, the buffer contains the window's text.
        Label1.Text = Caption.ToString
   End Sub
```

Build the project, run the program, and place the mouse pointer over the text hidden by asterisks. You will see this text in open in the label (Fig. 19.2)! I often used this technique in Windows 95/98/ME to extract forgotten passwords to my email or Internet connections. Then Microsoft developers redesigned the mechanism for hiding secret data, so this trick no longer works in Windows XP. But if you still use one of the older systems, the program will extract texts hidden by asterisks with no problems.

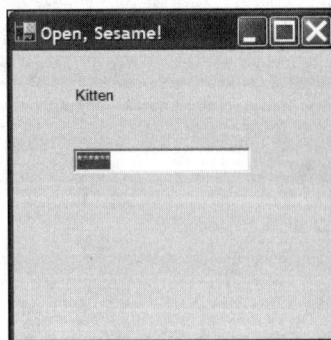

Fig. 19.2. Extracting text from other programs

You are not limited to using the program only as a tool for recovering forgotten passwords. Try placing the mouse pointer over various desktop objects, and you will see lots of interesting information. Place the mouse pointer, for example, over the **Start** button, the quick launch bar, or the clock in the system tray. The program's capabilities can be extended by providing it with additional functionalities. For example, not only the window's text but also other information about it can be extracted (e.g., the window's class and its dimensions).

A little laugh

One programmer to another: — I was told that using my cat's name as a password is a security risk. But I'm not gonna change the password! I'm so used to qZw813drgg1!

19.17. Extracting Icons from Files

This is one of the more advanced examples. It demonstrates extracting icons from resources embedded in EXE, DLL, CPL, and other files. Currently, GDI has no functionalities for extracting icons using managed code; therefore, we have to resort to using Windows API functions again. The example is implemented in the ExtractIcons project (Listing 19.20). First, declare the ExtractIcon function. For the guinea pig, I used the standard Paint program. Its executable file is mspaint.exe. You can use any other file instead. For convenience, I created two separate procedures: GetNumberOfIcons and ExtractIconsFromFile. The first procedure is a function and returns the number of icons contained in the specified file. The function is easy to use: Just specify the file path for its only parameter and the function will return the number of icons contained in it.

Listing 19.20. Extracting Icons from Files

```
'-------------------------------------
' ExtractIcons © 2004 Alexander Klimov
'-------------------------------------
    Declare Function ExtractIcon Lib "shell32.dll" Alias "ExtractIconA" _
        (ByVal hInst As Integer, _
        ByVal lpszExeFileName As String, _
        ByVal nIconIndex As Integer) As Integer

    ' The name of the file being examined
    Dim testfile As String = "c:\windows\system32\mspaint.exe"

    Private Function GetNumberOfIcons(ByVal str As String) As Integer
        Return ExtractIcon(Me.Handle.ToInt32, str, -1)
    End Function

    Private Sub butExtract_Click(ByVal sender As System.Object, ByVal e As _
System.EventArgs) Handles butExtract.Click
```

```
        ' Determining the number of icons in the file C:\Windows\System\mspaint.exe
        lblNumberOfIcons.Text = "There are " & GetNumberOfIcons(testfile) & " in the file."
    ' Extracting the icons
        ExtractIconsFromFile(testfile)
End Sub


    ' The procedure for extracting all icons from the specified file
    ' and outputting them to the form
    Private Sub ExtractIconsFromFile(ByVal str As String)
        ' The number of icons in the file
        Dim numicons As Integer
        ' Returning the value
        Dim retval As Integer
        ' Obtaining the number of icons
        numicons = GetNumberOfIcons(str)
        ' Extracting the first icon
        retval = ExtractIcon(Me.Handle.ToInt32, str, 0)
        ' Setting the Icon property of the form to the icon extracted
        Me.Icon = Icon.FromHandle(New IntPtr(retval))
        ' Looping through all icons
        For i As Integer = 0 To numicons - 1
            retval = ExtractIcon(Me.Handle.ToInt32, str, i)
            Dim g As Graphics = CreateGraphics()
            ' Outputting them to the form
            g.DrawIcon(Icon.FromHandle(_
                    New IntPtr(retval)), 15, i * 35 + 10)
            g.Dispose()
        Next
    End Sub
```

The `ExtractIcon` function can be used not only to count the number of the icons in the file but also to extract the icons from the file. Because the function extracts only one icon per function call, a `For ... Next` loop is employed to extract all icons. By the way, I set the `Icon` property of our program to the first icon extracted. There are six icons altogether in the Windows XP mspaint.exe file. But files exist that contain more than 200 icons! So now you have a tool to look inside such files and view the icons they hold. You're a real hacker now!

19.18. Suggestions and Recommendations

See whether you can write a program to convert Arabic numerals to Roman.

Chapter 20: Coding the Smart Way

Throughout this book, I have been showing and explaining to you various interesting and entertaining program examples. Now I want to draw your attention to the other side of programming: the code-writing process. I have always found it interesting to examine the programming styles of different programmers. What I have discovered is that some of them do not even suspect that there are various programming techniques that could make the code writing easier and the program development time shorter. This is especially true of Visual Basic 6.0 veterans. Having moved to the new development environment, they habitually continue using old techniques, missing out on the new, powerful features of VB .NET 2003. In this chapter, I present a collection of some useful programming techniques that will undoubtedly benefit your work.

20.1. My Profile

The Visual Studio .NET 2003 Integrated Development Environment (IDE) is flexible and can be easily configured to suit the most diverse needs. If over the years you have got too used to the appearance and features of the previous VB versions, then you, perhaps, should continue using the same arrangement in VB .NET 2003. Here is how you can do this: On the **Start Page** of **Visual Studio**, open the **My Profile** tab and select **Visual Basic Developer** in the **Profile** list. On the same tab, you can configure the keyboard, window location, help parameters, etc. You can change your profile at any time. Simply select the **Show Start Page** in the **Help** item of the menu.

20.2. Configuring IDE

Since VB 6.0, IDE has undergone considerable modifications. I recommend that you devote one day to studying the configuration settings of the package. Here, I will mention only a few interesting innovations. One of them is the heavily reworked source code text editor settings. Open the **Options** item in the **Tool** menu and select the **Basic** subfolder in the **Text Editor** folder in the list in the panel on the left. By putting a check mark in the **Line Numbers** check box in the **Display** section, you can enable the automatic code line numbering. This is a handy setting, especially when writing a book. In earlier text editor versions, this feature was available only by installing third-party plug-ins.

The text editor can also be configured to automatically indent text, as is the custom with experienced programmers. When a loop body is created, the loop termination keywords will be inserted automatically (I constantly forget about doing this) and each new line of the loop will be displayed with the necessary length of indent.

20.3. Collapsing Code Fragments

Using the code editor is a pure pleasure now. In addition to the intelligent hint feature, inherited from the previous versions, a feature to collapse code fragments has been introduced. This is a handy innovation, especially for long projects. Fig. 20.1 and 20.2 show code collapsing. When a new function or procedure is created, a minus sign (–) appears to the left of the first line of the subroutine. When clicked on, the minus sign changes into the plus sign (+) and the subroutine code collapses to the subroutine definition line that terminates with an ellipsis. When the mouse pointer is placed over the ellipsis, the rest of the collapsed code is displayed in a pop-up window (Fig. 20.2). The other way of doing this is too subtle for most programmers, and they seldom use it. In projects created using templates, you have most likely seen the following line:

```
Windows Form Designer generated code
```

Clicking on the plus sign to the left of this line will expand the code generated by the **Form Designer**. You can use the same syntax to define a section of your own code that you want to be collapsible. This is done by marking the start of the collapsible code region with the #Region keyword followed by the region's name in quotation marks:

```
#Region "My collapsible code region"
```

The end of the collapsible code region is marked by entering the #End Region keyword after the last code line of the region.

In this case, the minus sign also appears to the left of the region's name and the marked region can be collapsed into one line. This feature is handy when you are certain of a section of the code and want to hide it temporarily to make the entire code more manageable and easier to read.

```
#Region "My collapsible code region"
    ' Your code here
    Dim strCatName As String = "My name is Ginger"
#End Region
```

Fig. 20.1. Expanded code

```
My collapsible code region
    #Region "My collapsible code region"
    ' Your code here                          s ListView, ByVal item_t
    Dim strCatName As String = "My name is Ginger"
    #End Region
            Dim new_item As ListViewItem = lvw.Items.Add(item
```

Fig. 20.2. Collapsed code with the collapsed section displayed in a pop-up window

20.4. The Clipboard

The clipboard functionality has expanded significantly in VB .NET. Now, it can store several copied or cut text fragments (this feature should already be familiar to Microsoft Office XP users). They are accessed by selecting the **Clipboard Ring** tab of the **Toolbox** in the code-editing mode (Fig. 20.3). I use this feature often.

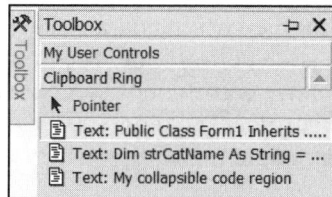

```
Toolbox                          ⊟ ✕
My User Controls
Clipboard Ring                      ▲
  ↖ Pointer
  📄 Text: Public Class Form1 Inherits .....
  📄 Text: Dim strCatName As String = ...
  📄 Text: My collapsible code region
```

Fig. 20.3. Using the **Clipboard Ring**

20.5. The Frequently-Used Code

Another feature that I started using frequently is creating storage for frequently-used sections of code. Here is how I do this. With the code editor open, right-click on the toolbox bar and select the **Add Tab** command in the context menu that appears. (The existing **General** tab can also be used, but this is not as convenient and can create confusion.) Give the new tab a name, **Frequently Used Code**, for example (Fig. 20.4). Now you can drag preselected sections of code onto this tab. For example, if you often use loops, you can place the counter declaration on this tab:

```
Dim counter as Integer
```

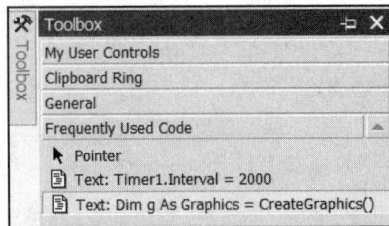

Fig. 20.4. The tab for frequently-used code sections

Double-clicking on the saved code section inserts it into the program at the current caret position. Examine your programs carefully and you will find repeating sections of code in them. Save the time you waste retyping or searching for repeating sections of code by using the technique just described.

20.6. Managing the Task List

Recently, I learned that VB .NET 2003 supports the **Task List,** a feature once implemented in the **Visual InterDev** package. This is a convenient feature when working with large projects. The essence of the **Task List** function is the following: You can create a comment token in the program body that describes the task that must be performed in the given portion of the code. The list of the outstanding tasks can be displayed in the **Task List** window at any time. Double-clicking on a task will place the pertinent section of the code in the view area of the code editor pane. See how it works in practice: Open an existing project. In a new line, enter a comment symbol (a single quotation mark) and one of the following predefined comment tokens: TODO, HACK, or UNDONE. The actual comment is added after the comment token:

```
' TODO Check out other timer intervals
Timer1.Interval = 2000
```

Insert comment tokens in different portions of the code in different project modules. All inserted bookmarks can be seen in the **Task List** window, which opens by executing the **View/Other Windows/Task List** command sequence or by pressing the <Ctrl>+<Alt>+<K> key sequence.

In addition to the predefined comment tokens, you can create your own custom comment tokens. When working on this book, I used a task bookmarked with a custom comment token named For_Book. To create a custom comment token, open the **Option** window (**Tools/Options** command sequence). Select the **Task List** subnode in the **Environment** node. Enter the name of the new comment token into the **Name** field (For_Book in my case), set its priority (high priority tokens are pointed out with an exclamation mark), and click the **Add** button to add the new token to the token list. To see to a particular bookmarked task, all you need to do is double-click on the corresponding task bookmark in the **Task Window** task list. My conclusion about this feature: a must use!

20.7. Templates

Another VB .NET innovation is the feature to change the source code used in the VB .NET templates. Now, the references used by default in each project can be changed. Moreover, custom templates can be created. The standard VB .NET templates are stored in the Program Files\Microsoft Visual Studio .NET 2003\Vb7\VBWizards folder. You can see many subfolders bearing familiar names in this folder, such as the WindowsApplication folder. The Templates\1033 folder is inside this folder; it contains the template for Windows applications. You can modify the files in this folder (assemblyinfo.vb, from.vb, and windowsapplication.vbproj) as you like.

20.8. The Tab Order

The mechanism for changing the order, in which the focus is moved from one control to another by pressing the <Tab> key (the tab order), has been simplified significantly. In the previous VB version, this was a cumbersome process, especially when dealing with many controls. Everything is much simpler with VB .NET. It has a new command — **View/Tab Order** — that makes the task easy to carry out. Executing this command assigns each control a sequence number, which can be changed by clicking the left or the right mouse button. The mode is toggled off by executing the **Tab Order** command again.

20.9. Declaring Variables

All VB 6.0 instruction books warned programmers not to declare variables in the following way:

```
Dim a, b, c as Integer
```

This was because, according to the syntax rules, only the last variable, c, was assigned the Integer type; the a and b variables were assigned the Variant type. This has resolved, and the variables in the preceding string are assigned the type common sense dictates, that is, all three variables are assigned the Integer type. The following construction can also be used:

```
Dim a, b as Integer, myVar, yourVar as Single
```

Here, the a and b variables are assigned the Integer type and the myVar and yourVar variables are assigned the Single type.

Also, a variable can be initialized (i.e., given a value) when declared. This is the type of feature that programmers have been impatiently waiting for. Finally, Microsoft has heeded the voice of the people and given them what they want. I am sure you will often use this feature in your projects. Previously, the code had to be written as follows:

```
Dim c as Integer
c=10
```

Now, it can be reduced to one line:

```
Dim c as Integer=10
```

Accordingly, several variables can be declared and initialized in the following way:

```
Dim myVar as Integer = 10, yourVar as Double = 0.27
```

20.10. The Shorthand Operation Notation

In VB 6.0, the operation of incrementing a variable by one was written as follows:

```
counter = counter + 1
```

Now, the same operation can be written in the following shortened notation:

```
counter += 1
```

This notation has been used by C++ and Java programmers for a long time. Naturally, this notation is not limited to the addition operation but can also be used with other operations, which are listed in Table 20.1.

Table 20.1.The Shorthand and Full Operation Notations

Shorthand Notation	Full Notation
A += B	A = A + B
A /= B	A = A / B
A *= B	A = A * B
A -= B	A = A - B
A ^= B	A = A ^ B
A &= B	A = A & B

I recommend that you study the documentation concerning this subject and become accustomed to this notation. This will make it easier for you to read code written in other programming languages.

20.11. The Short-Circuiting Check

VB .NET has acquired two new operators: `AndAlso` and `OrElse`. These operators are used to short-circuit logical conjunctions on two expressions. Consider how they work on an example. Suppose we need to evaluate the following compound conditions:

```
12 > 45 And MyFunction()
45 > 12 Or MyFunction()
```

In both cases, VB .NET 2003 evaluates both conditions, the second condition being the result returned by `MyFunction()` function. But a closer look reveals that the first expression, 12 > 45, is already false; therefore, there is no sense in evaluating the second condition. The same happens with the second line if the first condition, 45 > 12, is already being true, thus obviating the need for evaluating the second expression. Change the evaluation process as follows:

```
12 > 45 AndAlso MyFunction()
45 > 12 OrElse MyFunction()
```

Now, having evaluated the first part of the expression, the program terminates evaluation of the entire expression without evaluating the second part of it and moves on to executing other operations, thereby saving computer resources. This is the essence of the short-circuiting check: bypassing the evaluation of one expression depending on the result of the previous expression's evaluation.

20.12. Creating New Functions and Procedures

The VB .NET 2003 developers have offered an alternative to the standard technique for building functions. The new technique is more familiar to C++ programmers. The essence of the innovation lies in using the `Return` keyword. This command terminates the function call and returns the value specified after the command. Here is a small example: Imagine yourself at a job interview inquiring about the size of your potential paycheck. The following is a collection of your answers prepared in advance:

```
Public Function GetPaycheck(ByVal Dollar As Integer) As String
    If Dollar > 5000 Then Return "Great!"
    If Dollar > 3000 Then Return "It'll do."
    If Dollar > 2000 Then Return "This is terrible!"
    If Dollar > 1000 Then Return "I'm not a monkey who will work for bananas!"
    Return "If this is a joke, I don't get it."
End Function
```

As you can see, if the personnel officer offers me $6,000 per month, I automatically agree to take the job.

20.13. A Random Number Generator

In the examples demonstrated in this book, I sometimes used the Rnd() function inherited from VB 6.0. However, using it is not justified because this primitive function has been succeeded by the powerful Random class. The functionality of this class is more extensive than that of the old Rnd() function. The following code can be used to imitate a die throw:

```
Dim myRnD As New Random
Dim dice As Integer
dice = myRnD.Next(1, 7)
TextBox1.Text = CStr(dice)
```

Note that the upper boundary of the specified range (1, 7) is not included within the set of the random numbers generated. Consequently, only numbers from 1 to 6 are generated for dice throws.

20.14. Supplying Solutions with Documentation

Sometimes, it is necessary to supply the project code with short explanations. Theoretically, the documentation can be inserted directly into the code as comments. But superfluous information will litter the project. It is preferable to create the documentation as a separate file using, for example, hypertext pages. This is especially attractive because the VB .NET 2003 environment makes this an easy task. To add an HTML page to the solution, right-click on the solution's name and select the **Add/Add New Item** in the context menu. Select the **HTML Page** template in the dialog window that opens, and click the **Open** button. These actions will add an empty HTML page to the solution. You can enter text directly on the page or, if you know HTML, you can switch to the source code view mode and enter your information using HTML tags. In either mode, you can right-click on the page, select the **View in Browser** command in the context menu, and check what your page looks like in the browser. The documentation file added in this way is easy to distribute with the project.

20.15. Reflection

In conclusion, I want to tell you about *reflection*. Reflection is an important new feature of the .NET framework. The reason I find this feature important is the following: Consider, for example, the SystemInformation class with its numerous properties. Suppose that you have been given the task of writing a program that displays all properties of the class to the screen. You delve into the documentation, digging for information about the class's properties. Then you implement the solution by listing the properties using a loop or some other technique. Everything is working great and your boss is happy. But some time later, Microsoft developers add new properties to the class. The boss demands that the program be rewritten to take into account the newly-added properties. At first, it looks like there is no other way of doing this. But not when we have reflection at our disposal: This feature makes it possible to write universal code! Even with the new properties added to the class, your old program will work perfectly and display all properties. To learn more about this feature, you will have to hit the books and read the documentation dealing with this subject. Here, I will just show a few practical examples of using reflection in projects. Create a new project, name it `Reflection`, and place a `ListView` control on the form. Set the following properties:

❑ `Name = lvwInfo`   ❑ `Dock = Fill`   ❑ `View = Details`

This control will display all necessary information. Also, place a `MainMenu` control on the form. Set the `Text` property of the upper menu item to `Reflection` and of the first submenu item to `SystemInformation`. The code to output all available properties of the `SystemInformation` class is provided in Listing 20.1.

Listing 20.1. Displaying Class Properties

```
'--------------------------------------
' Reflection © 2004 Alexander Klimov
'--------------------------------------
Imports System.Reflection

    Private Sub LVWRow(ByVal lvw As ListView, ByVal item_title As String, ByVal _
ParamArray subitem_titles() As String)
        ' ListView columns
        Dim new_item As ListViewItem = lvw.Items.Add(item_title)

        For i As Integer = subitem_titles.GetLowerBound(0) To _
subitem_titles.GetUpperBound(0)
            new_item.SubItems.Add(subitem_titles(i))
        Next i
    End Sub

    Private Sub mnuSysInfo_Click(ByVal sender As System.Object, ByVal e As _
System.EventArgs) Handles mnuSysInfo.Click
        ' Column headers
        lvwInfo.Columns.Clear()
        lvwInfo.Columns.Add("Property", 10, HorizontalAlignment.Left)
        lvwInfo.Columns.Add("Value", 10, HorizontalAlignment.Left)

        ' A list of all properties of the SystemInformation class
        Dim propval As Object
        Dim myType As Type = GetType(SystemInformation)
        Dim propinfo As PropertyInfo() = myType.GetProperties()

        lvwInfo.Items.Clear()
```

```
    For i As Integer = 0 To propinfo.Length - 1
        With propinfo(i)
            If .GetIndexParameters().Length = 0 Then
                propval = .GetValue(Me, Nothing)
                If propval Is Nothing Then
                    LVWRow (lvwInfo, _
                        .Name, _
                        "<Nothing>")
                Else
                    LVWRow (lvwInfo, _
                        .Name, _
                        propval.ToString)
                End If
            Else
                LVWRow (lvwInfo, _
                    .Name, _
                    "<array>")
            End If
        End With
    Next i

    ' Setting the dimensions
    Dim new_wid As Integer = 30
    For i As Integer = 0 To lvwInfo.Columns.Count - 1
        lvwInfo.Columns(i).Width = -2
        new_wid += lvwInfo.Columns(i).Width
    Next i
    Me.Size = New Size(new_wid, Me.Size.Height)
End Sub
```

All properties of the `SystemInformation` class are returned by calling the `GetProperties` method. The obtained array of all properties is displayed to the screen using the `GetIndexParameters` method. As you can see, we do not use the names of the class properties explicitly. Consequently, regardless of the properties the `SystemInformation` class may acquire in the future, the program will display all of its properties correctly.

The capabilities of reflection extend way beyond those just demonstrated. Consider another example. The code provided in Listing 20.2 demonstrates how to obtain all events of the `CheckBox` control.

Listing 20.2. Displaying `CheckBox` Events

```
    Private Sub mnuEvents_Click(ByVal sender As System.Object, ByVal e As _
System.EventArgs) Handles mnuEvents.Click
        lvwInfo.Columns.Clear()
        lvwInfo.Columns.Add("Event", 10, HorizontalAlignment.Left)
```

```
        lvwInfo.Columns.Add("Description", 10, HorizontalAlignment.Left)

        ' The list of events
        Dim events_info As EventInfo() = _
            GetType(CheckBox).GetEvents()

        lvwInfo.Items.Clear()
        For i As Integer = 0 To events_info.Length - 1
            With events_info(i)
                LVWRow(lvwInfo, _
                    .Name, .ToString)
            End With
        Next i

        lvwInfo.Columns(0).Width = -2
        lvwInfo.Columns(1).Width = -2

        Dim new_wid As Integer = _
            lvwInfo.Columns(0).Width + _
            lvwInfo.Columns(1).Width + _
            30
        Me.Size = New Size(new_wid, Me.Size.Height)
    End Sub
```

The preceding code is placed into the click event of the mnuEvents menu subitem added to the menu. The way events are obtained is practically identical to the way properties are obtained in the previous example. This time, however, the GetEvents method is called instead of the GetProperties method. Consider the following code:

```
Dim events_info As EventInfo() = _
            GetType(CheckBox).GetEvents()
```

In it, you can replace the CheckBox class name with any other class name to obtain a list of its properties. Try, for example, to use the Form1 or MainMenu names. In concluding this subject, let's try to obtain all methods of a specified class. As you have probably already guessed, we will need to call the GetMethods method (Listing 20.3).

Listing 20.3. Obtaining All Methods of the Form1 Class

```
    Private Sub mnuMethods_Click(ByVal sender As System.Object, ByVal e As _
System.EventArgs) Handles mnuMethods.Click
        lvwInfo.Columns.Clear()
        lvwInfo.Columns.Add("Method", 10, _
```

```
        HorizontalAlignment.Left)
    lvwInfo.Columns.Add("Description", 10, _
        HorizontalAlignment.Left)

    ' The list of methods
    Dim methods_info As MethodInfo() = _
        GetType(Form1).GetMethods()
    lvwInfo.Items.Clear()
    For i As Integer = 0 To methods_info.Length - 1
        With methods_info(i)
            LVWRow(lvwInfo, _
                .Name, .ToString)
        End With
    Next i

    lvwInfo.Columns(0).Width = -2
    lvwInfo.Columns(1).Width = -2

    Dim new_wid As Integer = _
        lvwInfo.Columns(0).Width + _
        lvwInfo.Columns(1).Width + _
        30
    Me.Size = New Size(new_wid, Me.Size.Height)

End Sub
```

In addition to the features just considered, the Reflection namespace has other interesting and useful capabilities that you will undoubtedly encounter.

20.16. Suggestions and Recommendations

Most likely, you have developed your personal programming style over the years. A personal style is affected by exposure to other programming languages, workplace requirements, personal preferences and partialities, and many other factors. Nevertheless, you should listen to recommendations offered by experienced programmers in books, magazine articles, and elsewhere. Striving toward at least some standardization and unification not only will enable you to organize your program writing process better but also will allow you to understand code written by other programmers.

This concludes my coverage of VB .NET through practical examples. In *Conclusion*, I provide references to a few of my favorite books and to web sites that supplied me with examples for the book. I believe you will find those sources of information useful.

Conclusion

Learning such a powerful language as Visual Basic .NET 2003 is impossible without constant self-education through reading trade literature or consulting the web pages of recognized experts in the field. Here, I list the book and web resources I find particularly useful in this respect:

❐ *Programming Microsoft Windows with Microsoft Visual Basic .NET*, by Charles Petzold. This book is identical to his book on C# programming. All of the code listings have been, naturally, fully remade for the VB .NET syntax. The book is written in a clear and easy-to-understand language; but then, all books by this author are. The mass of interesting examples will leave no programmer indifferent. I could not resist using a few ideas from the book in my examples.

❐ **http://msdn.microsoft.com/vbasic** — This is VB's homeland. Visiting this site is simply a must for any programmer wishing to stay on top of the latest developments in the field. Examples, updates, interesting references, documentation — this is just a short list of the information available on the site.

❐ **http://www.bobpowell.net** — The site offers advice and examples involving the GDI+ technology. Unfortunately, some examples are offered only in C#, which presents certain difficulties for programmers practicing only VB.

❐ **http://www.vb-helper.com** — This is a regularly updated site of Robert Stephens, the author of many VB and Delphi books. A big plus of the examples available on the site is that they are offered in both VB 6.0 and VB .NET, which makes it handy for those who program in the both languages.

❐ **http://www.planet-sourcecode.com** — This site warehouses hundreds of thousands of source code lines sent by programmers from various countries for public review.

❐ **http://www.codeproject.com** — This is also a code warehouse site, but here authors usually accompany the source code with an article describing in detail what the code does. This approach makes understanding the code workings much easier than pouring over hundreds of source code lines on your own.

❐ **http://www.gotdotnet.com** — This is the homepage of an excellent forum for asking and answering questions and for discussing different issues.

CD-ROM Description

You can find the source codes for all examples used in the book on the accompanying CD-ROM. Each example is stored in a separate folder numbered the same as the corresponding chapter. All examples from a single chapter are combined into one solution. To launch an individual example, run the solution file (the SLN extension file) and select the **Set As StartUp** command in the context menu of the necessary project. The table below lists the contents of the CD-ROM folders.

Folder	Projects Contained	Chapter
/1	FlashText, Matrix, RunTitle, TypingText	1
/2	3DText, CatFont, Credits, ElectricFX, Outline, RotatedText, RunText, ScrollText, StarWars, UsingBrushes	2
/3	Beziers, CreatePolygon, DrawLineSample, Figures, HatchBrushStyles, SolidBrushSample, TextureBrush2, TextureBrushSample	3
/4	Curves, Curves2, DrawCurves, Hypocycloid, Spiderweb, Spiral	4
/5	Balls, Honeycomb, LinearGradientBrushSample, PathGradientBrushSample, Photoshop	5
/6	AnalogClock, Matrix, RotatedLine, Shear, WorldTransform	6
/7	Fractals, LSystem, Mandelbrot, Serpinski, Stars, Yin-Yang	7
/8	Animator, Animator2, Antialias, ColorMatrix, ColorMatrixFX, Drag, DrawCube, MakeTransparent, MakeTransparent2, Pixel, RotateAngle, SaveImage, Spin, Warp, Watermark	8
/9	KeyboardLayout, KeyState, LockKeys, PrintScreen, SendToCalculator	9
/10	LinesAPI, LinesControlPaint, LinesGDIPlus, MovingMouse, Overlay, SimplePaint, Web	10

continues

Continued

Folder	Projects Contained	Chapter
/11	ActiveForm, DisableX, DragForm, FlashWindow, RodStephens_Ssaver, Simple_Ssaver, SystemMenu, TextForm, TitleBarClick, TransparentForm	11
/12	AniLabel, AutoClose, BitmapListView, BitmapMenu, BlinkNotify, ColorMainMenu, ColorMenu, ColorStatusBar, DigitTextbox, EnablesStyles, Manifest, NumberLines, RadiobuttonSamples, RedCheckbox, Resource, RoundControls, StyleXP, TextBoxSamples, TextContextMenu	12
/13	AI, BlockAll, WhiteChristmas, MadMouse, Mind, Mouse, MouseTrap, OpenCD, StartButton, RunawayButton, SpyCat, TrayClockReplace, TwoButtons, TypingComputer	13
/14	3DShapes, Orbison	14
/15	MP3, PlaySound, VBPiano, Winamp	15
/16	MSAgent, SAPI5, TwoAgents	16
/17	Bounce, Bounce2, FallBall, RealBall	17
/18	Cards, Safe, Safe2, Snake, TicTacToe, XO	18
/19	AniCursors, Caret, ColorConsole, EasterEgg, ExtractIcons, FileProperties, Friday, GetScreenShot, OneInstance, OpenPass, RightCorner, Roman2Arab, RunApp, Version, Wallpaper, WebSendMail, WinVersion	19
/20	Reflection	20

The DivX511Bundle.exe file shows a video about A-List Publishing books. To watch this file, install Standard DivX Codec(FREE), available for free download from **http://www.divx.com/divx/**.

Index